PAUL AND SCRIPTURE

Society of Biblical Literature

Early Christianity and Its Literature

General Editor
Gail R. O'Day

Editorial Board
Warren Carter
Beverly Roberts Gaventa
Judith M. Lieu
Joseph Verheyden
Sze-kar Wan

Number 9

PAUL AND SCRIPTURE
Extending the Conversation

PAUL AND SCRIPTURE

EXTENDING THE CONVERSATION

Edited by
Christopher D. Stanley

Society of Biblical Literature
Atlanta

PAUL AND SCRIPTURE
Extending the Conversation

Copyright © 2012 by the Society of Biblical Literature

All rights reserved. No part of this work may be reproduced or transmitted in any form or by any means, electronic or mechanical, including photocopying and recording, or by means of any information storage or retrieval system, except as may be expressly permitted by the 1976 Copyright Act or in writing from the publisher. Requests for permission should be addressed in writing to the Rights and Permissions Office, Society of Biblical Literature, 825 Houston Mill Road, Atlanta, GA 30329 USA.

Library of Congress Cataloging-in-Publication Data

Paul and scripture : extending the conversation / edited by Christopher D. Stanley.
  p. cm. — (Early Christianity and its literature ; number 9)
 "This book marks the final chapter in the work of the Paul and Scripture Seminar, which operated for six years under the aegis of the Annual Meeting of the Society of Biblical Literature (2005–2010)"—Chapter 1.
 ISBN 978-1-58983-694-5 (paper binding : alk. paper) — ISBN 978-1-58983-695-2 (electronic format)
 1. Paul, the Apostle, Saint—Theology—Congresses. 2. Bible. N.T. Epistles of Paul—Criticism, interpretation, etc.—Congresses. I. Stanley, Christopher D. II. Series: Early Christianity and its literature ; no. 9.
 BS2651.P295 2012b
 270'.06—dc23   2012027355

Printed on acid-free, recycled paper conforming to
ANSI/NISO Z39.48-1992 (R1997) and ISO 9706:1994
standards for paper permanence.

Contents

Abbreviations vii

Introduction
   Christopher D. Stanley 1

Part 1: The Historical Context

By the Letter? Word for Word? Scriptural Citation in Paul
   Leonard Greenspoon 9

Identity, Memory, and Scriptural Warrant: Arguing Paul's Case
   Jeremy Punt 25

Paul among the Storytellers: Reading Romans 11 in the Context
of Rewritten Bible
   Bruce N. Fisk 55

Part 2: Text and Context

Does Paul Respect the Context of His Quotations?
   Steve Moyise 97

Respect for Context and Authorial Intention: Setting the
Epistemological Bar
   Mitchell Kim 115

Latency and Respect for Context: A Response to Mitchell Kim
   Steve Moyise 131

Part 3: Beyond the *Hauptbriefe*

Paul's Reliance on Scripture in 1 Thessalonians
E. Elizabeth Johnson 143

The Use of Scripture in Philippians
Stephen Fowl 163

Writing "in the Image" of Scripture: The Form and Function of References to Scripture in Colossians
Jerry L. Sumney 185

Part 4: Scripture in Paul's Theology

Scripture and Other Voices in Paul's Theology
Linda L. Belleville 233

Beyond Hays's *Echoes of Scripture in the Letters of Paul*: A Proposed Diachronic Intertextuality with Romans 10:16 as a Test Case
Matthew W. Bates 263

Approaching Paul's Use of Scripture in Light of Translation Studies
Roy E. Ciampa 293

Part 5: Conclusions

What We Learned—and What We Didn't
Christopher D. Stanley 321

Contributors 331

Index of Ancient Sources 335

Index of Modern Authors 353

Abbreviations

Primary Sources

Adv. Jud.	Tertullian, *Adversus Judaeos*
Ant.	Josephus, *Jewish Antiquities*
Apoc. Ab.	Apocalypse of Abraham
1 Apol.	Justin Martyr, *Apologia i*
C. Ap.	Josephus, *Contra Apionem*
CD	Damascus Document
Comm. Rom.	Origen, *Commentarii in Romanos*
Conf.	Philo, *De confusione linguarum*
Dial.	Justin Martyr, *Dialogus cum Tryphone*
1 En.	1 Enoch (Ethiopic Apocalypse)
2 En.	2 Enoch (Slavonic Apocalypse)
3 En.	3 Enoch (Hebrew Apocalypse)
Epid.	Irenaeus, *Epideixis tou apostolikou kērgymatos*
Fug.	Philo, *De fuga et inventione*
Haer.	Irenaeus, *Adversus haereses*
Jub.	Jubilees
J.W.	Josephus, *Jewish War*
L.A.B.	Pseudo-Philo, *Liber antiquitatum biblicarum*
Leg.	Philo, *Legum allegoriae*
Let. Aris.	Letter of Aristeas
Prax.	Tertullian, *Adversus Praxean*
Pss. Sol.	Psalms of Solomon
Somn.	Philo, *De somniis*
Spec.	Philo, *De specialibus legibus*
Spec. Laws	Philo, *On the Special Laws*
T. Dan	Testament of Dan
T. Levi	Testament of Levi
t. Sukkah	Tosefta Sukkah

Test.	Cyprian, *Ad Quirinum testimonia adversus Judaeos*; Pseudo-Gregory of Nyssa, *Testimonies against the Jews*
Tg. Onq.	Targum Onqelos

SECONDARY SOURCES

AB	Anchor Bible
ANF	*The Ante-Nicene Fathers*. Edited by Alexander Roberts and James Donaldson. 10 vols. 1885–1887. Repr., Peabody, Mass.: Hendrickson, 1994.
ANTC	Abingdon New Testament Commentaries
BBR	*Bulletin for Biblical Research*
BDF	F. Blass, A. Debrunner, and R. W. Funk, *A Greek Grammar of the New Testament and Other Early Christian Literature*. Chicago: University of Chicago Press, 1961.
BFCT	Beiträge zur Förderung christlicher Theologie
BHT	Beiträge zur historischen Theologie
BIS	Biblical Interpretation Series
BNTC	Black's New Testament Commentaries
BTB	*Biblical Theology Bulletin*
BZAW	Beihefte zur Zeitschrift für die alttestamentliche Wissenschaft
BZNW	Beihefte zur Zeitschrift für die neutestamentliche Wissenschaft
CBQ	*Catholic Biblical Quarterly*
CRINT	Compendia rerum iudaicarum ad Novum Testamentum
CTJ	*Calvin Theological Journal*
EKKNT	Evangelisch-katholischer Kommentar zum Neuen Testament
FC	Fathers of the Church
FRLANT	Forschungen zur Religion und Literatur des Alten und Neuen Testaments
HNT	Handbuch zum Neuen Testament
HUCA	*Hebrew Union College Annual*
IBS	*Irish Biblical Studies*
Int	*Interpretation*
JBL	*Journal of Biblical Literature*
JQR	*Jewish Quarterly Review*

JSJ	*Journal for the Study of Judaism in the Persian, Hellenistic, and Roman Periods*
JSNT	*Journal for the Study of the New Testament*
JSNTSup	Journal for the Study of the New Testament Supplement Series
JSOT	*Journal for the Study of the Old Testament*
JSP	*Journal for the Study of the Pseudepigrapha*
JSPSup	Journal for the Study of the Pseudepigrapha Supplement Series
JTS	*Journal of Theological Studies*
KNT	Kommentar zum Neuen Testament
LEC	Library of Early Christianity
LSJ	Liddell, H. G., R. Scott, and H. S. Jones, *A Greek–English Lexicon*. 9th ed. Oxford: Oxford University Press, 1996.
NA^{27}	*Novum Testamentum Graece*, Nestle-Aland, 27th ed.
Neot	*Neotestamentica*
NICNT	New International Commentary on the New Testament
NIDNTT	*New International Dictionary of New Testament Theology*
NIGTC	New International Greek Testament Commentary
NovT	*Novum Testamentum*
NovTSup	Supplements to Novum Testamentum
NTM	New Testament Monographs
NTS	*New Testament Studies*
OTL	Old Testament Library
PG	Patrologia graeca [= Patrologiae cursus completus: Series graeca]. Edited by J.-P. Migne. 162 vols. Paris: Migne, 1857–1886.
PRSt	*Perspectives in Religious Studies*
RB	*Revue biblique*
SBLDS	Society of Biblical Literature Dissertation Series
SBLMS	Society of Biblical Literature Monograph Series
SBLSCS	Society of Biblical Literature Septuagint and Cognate Studies
SBLSymS	Society of Biblical Literature Symposium Series
SBLWGRW	Society of Biblical Literature Writings from the Greco-Roman World

SC	Sources chrétiennes
SemeiaSt	Semeia Studies
SNTSMS	Society for New Testament Studies Monograph Series
SP	Sacra pagina
SUNT	Studien der Umwelt des Neuen Testaments
TDNT	*Theological Dictionary of the New Testament*. Edited by G. Kittel and G. Friedrich. Translated by G. W. Bromiley. 10 vols. Grand Rapids: Eerdmans, 1964–1976.
THKNT	Theologischer Handkommentar zum Neuen Testament
ThSt	Theologische Studiën
TLG	Thesaurus linguae graecae
TLZ	*Theologische Literaturzeitung*
TSAJ	Texts and Studies in Ancient Judaism
UBS[4]	*The Greek New Testament*, United Bible Societies, 4th ed.
WBC	World Biblical Commentary
WUNT	Wissenschaftliche Untersuchungen zum Neuen Testament
ZBK	Zürcher Bibelkommentare

Introduction

Christopher D. Stanley

This book marks the final chapter in the work of the Paul and Scripture Seminar, which operated for six years under the aegis of the annual meeting of the Society of Biblical Literature (2005–2010). A collection of essays from the first three years of the seminar, together with a few other articles that were commissioned to round out the discussion, was published in 2008 under the title *As It Is Written: Studying Paul's Use of Scripture*.[1] The present volume continues the conversation with essays from the last three years of the seminar and some additional articles that were written specifically for this collection. Taken together, the two volumes provide a thorough and well-rounded analysis of the key issues that have dominated scholarly debate in this area for the last two centuries while also opening up a number of new avenues for future scholarly investigation.

The Paul and Scripture Seminar was created to provide a venue for a select group of scholars to discuss (and attempt to resolve) a range of methodological problems that had arisen in the last few decades to complicate research into the apostle Paul's many and varied references to the Jewish Scriptures.[2] In previous generations, scholars shared many common ideas about which questions mattered and how one might go about resolving them, even when they disagreed in their conclusions. In recent years, however, scholarship on Paul's use of Scripture has grown increasingly fragmented. Scholars not only use different methods but ground their studies on different presuppositions. Some are convinced that Paul's explicit

---

1. Stanley E. Porter and Christopher D. Stanley, eds., *As It Is Written: Studying Paul's Use of Scripture* (SBLSymS 50; Atlanta: Society of Biblical Literature, 2008).

2. For an overview of the kinds of methodological problems that have frequently stymied progress in this area, see Christopher D. Stanley, "Paul and Scripture: Charting the Course," in Porter and Stanley, *As It Is Written*, 3–12.

quotations provide the best insights into his engagement with the ideas and language of Scripture, while others find it more beneficial to study his allusions and echoes or his use of biblical narratives. Some assert that Paul expected his audiences to know and supply the context of his quotations, allusions, and echoes, while others reject this presumption as unhistorical. Some insist that Paul's frequent references to Scripture reveal how profoundly his ideas were shaped by the biblical tradition, while others argue that Paul cited Scripture primarily for rhetorical effect.

Because of these and other fundamental differences over questions of method, dialogue among scholars working in this area has become increasingly difficult. Instead of examining the relative strengths and weaknesses of various modes of analysis, scholars more often simply talk past one another. Papers are presented and books and articles written with little or no effort to justify the methods and presumptions that are used. Scholars who approach the subject using different methods are either dismissed or ignored. Most of the discussion takes place among people who share common methodologies and presuppositions, with little conversation across methodological lines. Progress is made in particular areas, but little is done to integrate the findings into a coherent whole or to examine places where the use of different methods or presuppositions might lead to different conclusions.

The Paul and Scripture Seminar devoted six years to a methodical examination of the principle methodological questions that have divided scholars working in this area. The seminar began with approximately twenty members, but the membership changed over the years as some participants moved on to pursue other interests and new voices joined the discussion. Not all of the members prepared papers for the seminar; some were content to participate in the oral phase of the program, which involved discussing papers that were circulated in advance of each year's sessions. The discussions were consistently lively and engaging, and by the end of six years the members had addressed virtually all of the important problems that have plagued scholarship in this area. Not all of the sessions produced agreement—far from it—but the nature and reasons for the disagreements were clarified during the course of the sessions, and many of the broader methodological gaps were bridged to a greater or lesser extent.

As with any seminar, the published papers represent only a fraction of the dialogue and debate that occurred during the seminar sessions. The papers do, however, serve to identify the major issues that were discussed and lay out the nature and terms of the debate in this vital area of Pauline studies. The present volume, together with the previous one, was designed to provide a glimpse into the cutting-edge research that typified the work of the seminar so that those who were not present could share in the benefits that the seminar members (and the scores of people who attended the seminar sessions as audience members) received from these annual programs.

A brief review of the contents of the first volume will help to place the present volume into proper context. The first volume addressed four broad methodological questions. The first section (after the introduction) examined the *status quaestionis* concerning the various ways in which Paul engaged with the Jewish Scriptures in his letters: explicit quotations, allusions and echoes, the use of biblical language and ideas, and references to biblical narratives. The second section explored the immediate historical and cultural environment of Paul's appropriations of Scripture, looking at what can be known (or reasonably presumed) about Paul's own educational background and his audiences' familiarity with the Scriptures of Judaism. The third section dealt with the thorny question of how to determine when Paul is interacting with the language or ideas of Scripture and when he is engaging with other materials, such as Roman imperial propaganda (and what difference it makes). The final section investigated what might be learned by viewing Paul's appropriations of Scripture through the lenses of methods other than traditional historical-critical or literary scholarship, including essays that drew on insights from deconstruction, postcolonial studies, and feminist studies.

The present volume continues this focus on methodology by looking at four sets of issues that were not explicitly addressed in the first volume. The first section consists of three papers that examine the broader social context of Paul's engagement with his ancestral Scriptures. Leonard Greenspoon examines the historical evidence behind the oft-debated question of the role that memory played in Paul's references to the Jewish Scriptures vis-à-vis his reliance on written texts. In the end, he finds good reason to believe that Paul had committed substantial portions of Scripture to memory, from which he drew the bulk of his quotations while dictating his letters. Jeremy Punt draws on cultural memory theory to argue that Paul referred to the Jewish Scriptures not only to add rhetorical force to his arguments but also to indoctrinate his mostly non-Jewish audiences into the cultural memory (and thus the identity) of the people of Israel, which was profoundly rooted in the stories and applications of Scripture. He focuses especially on the way that Paul reinterpreted the story of Abraham as a resource for constructing the identity of non-Jewish Christ-followers in Galatia and Rome over against others who were using the same story to shape identity in a different direction. Finally, Bruce Fisk compares Paul's interpretations of biblical narratives with the techniques employed in the Jewish literary genre commonly known as "rewritten Bible" and finds enough similarities to suggest that this neglected body of texts should play a more prominent role in discussions of Paul's engagement with the Scriptures of Israel. Focusing on Rom 11:1–7, Fisk suggests that Paul may in fact have framed his interpretations of biblical narratives in a conscious dialogue with the kinds of Jewish interpretive traditions that we find in Pseudo-Philo and Josephus.

The second section comprises three papers that grapple with the methodological issues surrounding the long-running controversy over whether and how far Paul was influenced by (and sought to be loyal to) the original literary context of the biblical references that he includes in his letters. Steve Moyise begins the discussion by reviewing several possible meanings of the term "respect for context" and evaluating how Paul's handling of Scripture compares to each of these definitions. Whether Paul respects the context of his biblical references, Moyise concludes, depends on which of these meanings the interpreter has in mind. Mitchell Kim follows with an essay in which he insists that Moyise has set too high a standard for judging whether an author like Paul respects the context of his source text. Citing Michael Polanyi's concept of "latent knowledge," Kim argues that Paul often elicits a "latent sense" from the text that is consistent with the original context even when it diverges from the text's historical meaning. The final essay in this section contains Moyise's response to Kim's paper. Rejecting Kim's concept of latent sense, he argues that it makes better methodological sense to speak of Paul exploiting the "semantic potential" of the texts that he cites in his letters. According to Moyise, Kim's contention that texts can have a latent sense veils the role that the reader plays in creating meaning by linking texts with other intertexts, the interpreter's own situation, or both.

The third section seeks to extend the conversation regarding Paul's use of Scripture beyond the four *Hauptbriefe*, which have attracted the lion's share of scholarly attention due to their inclusion of explicit quotations, to other letters where Paul's engagement with Scripture is less obvious. Elizabeth Johnson examines the presence and function of biblical language in 1 Thessalonians, Stephen Fowl studies Philippians, and Jerry Sumney analyzes Colossians. These three letters were chosen for the diversity of situations that they represent: one was addressed to a congregation of newly converted "pagans" whose familiarity with the Jewish Bible would have been shallow at best, one to a well-established church that was close to Paul and could be expected to have a strong biblical foundation, and one to a community with which Paul (or someone writing in his name) has no personal experience and therefore cannot presuppose any prior biblical teaching. All three authors highlight Paul's indebtedness to the Jewish Scriptures for his language and ideas, and all three grapple seriously with the problem of how to judge whether Paul is in fact echoing or alluding to a particular passage of Scripture and whether his audiences might have recognized and understood such unmarked references. Finally, all three papers discuss the role of biblical references in the letter as a whole. When viewed together, these essays provide important data for developing an understanding of Paul's engagement with Scripture that does justice to all of his letters, not just the *Hauptbriefe*.

The fourth and final section looks at the place of Scripture in Paul's theology. It has become common in recent years to assert that the Jewish Scriptures played a formative role in Paul's thinking both before and after his becoming a Christ-follower, but less attention has been given to the question of how Scripture functioned alongside other influences in Paul's theology. The three papers in this section address different aspects of this problem. First, Linda Belleville asks how we can know when Paul is engaging directly with the text of Scripture and when he is interacting with Jewish interpretive traditions. Belleville cites a number of instances where the latter appears to be the case and argues that the influence of such extrabiblical sources must be taken into account when scholars are discussing the importance of Scripture in Paul's theology. Matthew Bates agrees that Jewish interpretive traditions prior to Paul are important for making sense of Paul's handling of Scripture, but he also proposes that later interpretations of the same texts by Jewish and Christian authors can shed light on the way Paul viewed and used Scripture. Bates criticizes Richard Hays for introducing an overly narrow understanding of intertextuality to the field of biblical studies and argues for a broader definition based on the theories of Julia Kristeva. Finally, Roy Ciampa examines the benefits that might accrue from applying the methods and insights of translation theory to the study of Paul's use of Scripture. Ciampa's approach underlines the importance of Paul's work as a "translator" of the biblically grounded early Christian message into linguistic and conceptual terms that his non-Jewish communities could understand. All three of these papers highlight methodological difficulties that must be taken into account in any effort to describe the role of Scripture in Paul's theological reflection.

The book concludes with an essay by Christopher Stanley that looks back over the six years of the seminar and evaluates how well the members succeeded in answering the questions that they set for themselves at their initial session and lays out a number of questions for further research. Stanley concludes that much was achieved by the seminar, but much also remains to be done. In the end, the value of the seminar will be judged by the degree to which it motivates other scholars to press forward toward the goal of understanding what Paul was doing when he read his ancestral Scriptures in the light of Christ and applied them to the lives of his churches.

Bibliography

Porter, Stanley E., and Christopher D. Stanley, eds. *As It Is Written: Studying Paul's Use of Scripture.* SBLSymS 50. Atlanta: Society of Biblical Literature, 2008.

Stanley, Christopher D. "Paul and Scripture: Charting the Course." Pages 3–12 in *As It Is Written: Studying Paul's Use of Scripture.* Edited by Stanley E. Porter and Christopher D. Stanley. SBLSymS 50 Atlanta: Society of Biblical Literature, 2008.

Part 1
The Historical Context

By the Letter? Word for Word? Scriptural Citation in Paul

Leonard Greenspoon

Introduction

My first entry into this topic—the degree to which Paul cited Scripture from memory (rather than from a written text) and the means by which we can detect this technique on his part—was serendipitous in precisely the way that much scholarship is. I was working on an article about the Jewish biblical scholar and Bible translator Harry M. Orlinsky when I ran across these comments (dated 29 November 1936) in a batch of correspondence between James Montgomery of the University of Pennsylvania and Orlinsky:

> And so in the N. T., a good scholar like Paul freely *memoriter* cites Scripture. I compare myself, a student of to-day. I was brought up on the Prayer Book translation of the Psalter (which precedes the King James Version), also the latter Version; then I have become acquainted with the subsequent Versions, to all of which I add my own knowledge of the originals. So when I quote, it is a pot pourri of a great variety of translations, and at times I must inquire whether I am quoting AV or RV or JV or my own *memoriter* translations.... As I have sometimes said to my students, a man like Paul, or for that matter any Rabbi, did not turn to a well stocked library for his citations, as we would to-day, but quoted from memory.[1]

When I first read this letter of Montgomery's, I did not know whether the ideas about Paul he was entertaining were novel, old hat, or somewhere in between. Many years, and many projects, have passed since my initial

---

1. This material is housed at the American Jewish Archives in Cincinnati, Ohio. Elsewhere, Montgomery refers to 2 Tim 4:13 as an example of Paul's citing Scripture with no manuscript at hand.

introduction to this topic via Montgomery. I am not surprised to learn that the sources and methods of Paul's scriptural citations remains a lively topic for discussion and analysis.

Answer and Questions

The answer is fairly straightforward: in his letters, Paul sometimes cited Scripture from memory rather than from a written source. Far less straightforward is the question to which this is the answer. Is it (simply), "Did Paul sometimes cite Scripture from memory?" Or, "Did Paul have the requisite training to have committed to memory large portions of Scripture?" Or, "Are there reasons to think that Paul lacked easy access to written Scripture when composing his letters?" Or, "Does Paul's citation of Scripture from memory help explain apparent inconsistencies or downright mistakes he made?" Or, "Does Paul's citation of Scripture from memory help explain the many unusual, but apt, connections he made between and among biblical passages?"

The number of questions being asked could be considerably expanded, although in general those positing such questions fall into two categories: those who think Paul cited from memory—and this was a considerable part of his artistry—and those who think Paul cited from memory—and this was a practice he should have avoided. Of course, I am leaving out, for the moment, a third category (to which we will return), namely, those who think that Paul never (or only very rarely) relied on his memory for scriptural citations and instead consistently made use of written sources.

Memorization as Part of Paul's Education

It is universally recognized and acknowledged that memorization played a substantial role in Greco-Roman pedagogy.[2] It represented an essential part of the upbringing of any child who could be described as educated, and it was considered indispensible for many of the more prominent professions.

---

2. This is amply demonstrated in a variety of sources, from the oft-cited Henri Marrou, *A History of Education in Antiquity* (New York: Sheed & Ward, 1956), to the recently published Mary Carruthers, "How to Make a Composition: Memory-Craft in Antiquity and in the Middle Ages," in *Memory: History, Theories, Debates* (ed. Susannah Radstone and Bill Schwarz; New York: Fordham University Press, 2010), 15–29, to which we will return below.

This largely held true throughout the periods of classical Greece, republican Rome, the Hellenistic era, and the early centuries of the monarchy.[3]

If, as some believe, the majority of Paul's education took place in the Diaspora, say in Tarsus, he would certainly have been exposed at an early age to the necessity of memorizing large sections of literary works.[4] It is not clear whether that would have included Homer, Athenian tragedies, works of philosophy, or a combination thereof. Given the fact that Paul shows himself to be thoroughly familiar with the "Old Testament" in Greek, we are relatively safe in picturing the LXX (here we use this term broadly to refer to any "scriptural" passage in Greek) as a central text in Paul's studies—and in imagining his growing confidence in the oral recitation of larger and larger portions of this sacred text.

The most compelling and (from my perspective) most congenial reconstruction of Paul's learning at Tarsus comes from Stanley Porter.[5] One of the factors that were unique to Tarsus (or at least unusual in antiquity) is that the young men stayed in their hometown for the initial stages of their studies, completing their studies abroad. After that, according to Strabo (as summarized by Porter), they tended to spend the remainder of their lives outside of Tarsus. Porter outlines the pattern of Paul's education in Tarsus as follows: Paul was "reared in a Jewish home in Tarsus and [learned] the Scriptures, while being educated in a Greek grammar school."[6]

As to the nature or format of his formal (school) education, Porter states: "The students learned to read, recite, and explain [major classical]

---

3. See more broadly the relevant chapters in the following collections: Jocelyn Penny Small, ed., *Wax Tablets of the Mind: Cognitive Studies of Memory and Literacy in Classical Antiquity* (London: Routledge, 1997); E. Anne Mackay, ed., *Orality, Literacy, Memory in the Ancient Greek and Roman World* (Leiden: Brill, 2007); and Stephen C. Barton, Loren T. Stuckenbruck, and Benjamin G. Wold, eds., *Memory in the Bible and Antiquity* (Tübingen: Mohr Siebeck, 2007).

4. On this, see most recently E. P. Sanders, "Paul between Judaism and Hellenism," in *St. Paul Among the Philosophers* (ed. John D. Caputo and Linda Martin Alcoff; Bloomington: Indiana University Press, 2009), 74–89, esp. 77–82.

5. Stanley E. Porter, "Paul and His Bible: His Education and Access to the Scriptures of Israel," in *As It Is Written: Studying Paul's Use of Scripture* (ed. Stanley E. Porter and Christopher D. Stanley; SBLSymS 50; Atlanta: Society of Biblical Literature, 2008), 97–124, especially the second section, "Paul and the Greco-Roman Educational System" (99–105).

6. Ibid., 102.

authors; in other words, there was a huge emphasis on the oral and mnemonic character of education."[7] While we do not know whether a similar emphasis on memory characterized Paul's Jewish education (whether at home or at some communal institution), it is certainly reasonable to assume that this was the case. Given Paul's growing competence in the Greek language, it can be speculated that the study, and memorization, of the Bible in Greek—that is, in (some form of) the Septuagint—occupied a role of some prominence in the pedagogical program set out for Paul.

Examples of prodigious feats of memory from antiquity abound: the sophist Hippias (late fifth century B.C.E.), who could repeat fifty names after hearing them only once; L. Scipio (early second-century B.C.E. consul of Rome), who had memorized the names of the entire Roman people (estimated to be almost a quarter million in number); and Charmadas (second half of the second century B.C.E.), who could recite by heart any book in the "libraries."[8] Some of these are more relevant to Paul's circumstances than others. However, the preponderance of evidence is clearly on the side of those who express confidence that memorizing a text of the length of the LXX was not outside of the realm of possibility for a Jew who received a classically conceived education.

But what if the context of Paul's education was primarily Judaean, specifically among the Pharisees? We must admit that, under such circumstances, it is less clear that Paul would have begun memorization in Greek at an early age, although it is probable that learning by memory was as much a feature of Pharisaic pedagogy as it was elsewhere. Here we can point, if only tentatively, to evidence of an admittedly later period in Judaism[9] and, for that matter, also in Christianity. According to Augustine, Antony memorized Scripture in spite of his being illiterate, Eusebius mentions a blind Egyptian who was said to have known whole books of Scripture by heart, and Jerome wrote to a correspondent that "he should make himself into a library for Christ."[10] Do these examples constitute

---

7. Ibid., 103.

8. For these examples, see William V. Harris, *Ancient Literacy* (Cambridge: Harvard University Press, 1989), 31–32.

9. See the important work of Martin S. Jaffee, *Torah in the Mouth: Writing and Oral Tradition in Palestinian Judaism 200 BCE–400 CE* (Oxford: Oxford University Press, 2001).

10. These examples are taken from Harris, *Ancient Literacy*, 301; and Carruthers, "How to Make a Composition," 16–17.

later developments, or are they part of a long, presumably evolving process that could easily date back a few centuries? I am comfortable with the latter notion while at the same time fully cognizant of the shortcomings that arise if we uncritically read rabbinic or early Christian phenomena back into a preceding age.

Catherine Hezser provides further support for the availability of Greek educators and Greek education in Palestine at this time.[11] Greek education for Jewish children was widely available, if not always partaken of, especially for those in upper-class families.[12] Although it is not possible to locate or even describe fully the precise institutional context in which Paul would have furthered his study of Greek in these circumstances, there is little doubt that opportunities for doing so existed.

The locale for Paul's education is often envisioned as being either Diaspora or Palestine. Porter wisely rejects such a bifurcation. Thus, after running through the basic elements of Paul's early education in Tarsus, Porter continues, "after his Bar Mitzvah (or the equivalent at the time), [Paul went] to Jerusalem to complete his education in Jewish law and related matters."[13] This reconstruction on the part of Porter accords well with my own understanding of Paul's educational process. In my view, it also accords well with the degree of familiarity that Paul demonstrates, in his letters, with Greek culture and Jewish erudition.

Availability and Accessibility of Written Materials

In almost every discussion of Paul's travels and writings, we are presented with a picture of how difficult it would have been for Paul to travel with scrolls containing Greek Scripture.[14] Some have calculated the weight and girth of such material, although there are undoubtedly many uncertainties in arriving at specifics in this regard. I prefer to think in terms of the dimensions of a modern Torah scroll, such as can be found in any synagogue today. And, of course, multiple scrolls would have been needed to transcribe or translate the entire Hebrew Bible.

---

11. Catherine Hezser, *Jewish Literacy in Roman Palestine* (TSAJ 81; Tübingen: Mohr Siebeck, 2001), esp. the subsection titled "Education" (39–109).
12. Ibid., 90–94.
13. Porter, "Paul and His Bible," 102.
14. See, among others, J. Ross Wagner, *Heralds of the Good News: Isaiah and Paul "in Concert" in the Letter to the Romans* (NovTSup 101; Brill: Leiden, 2002), 20.

The analogy of a contemporary Torah scroll also comes into play when we consider what it must have been like to look up a specific passage in any "biblical" scroll in antiquity. Just as is the case with today's Torah scroll, the text is essentially continuous without chapter and verse notations of the sort we rely on when citing Scripture. I don't know that we can fully appreciate the difficulties that someone like Paul would have had (although he may have had assistants to do some of the "dirty work"), but I have seen, and been involved in, what happens in a synagogue with only a single scroll when it is necessary to move from one passage to another that is in a different book or section: a lot of effort is expended in rolling and unrolling, squinting and straining eyes to find precisely the wording that is being sought.

But perhaps Paul and his contemporaries had the equivalent of bookmarks or section dividers. Maybe there were individuals trained to do just this sort of work. Or is it just possible that the seemingly tedious labor of looking up passages in scrolls was understood as part of the work entailed in writing letters such as Paul's, or preparing sermons on similar topics? Surely, much that was time consuming but necessary in research only a few years ago would be considered unthinkable by today's new generation of scholars.[15] Thus, while agreeing with much that Stanley Porter has contributed to this discussion, I am puzzled by his equation of "cumbersome" and "impossible" in the following statement: "Carrying around a large bag of scrolls for reference in letter composition would have been rather cumbersome (and thus impossible) in Paul's travels."[16]

It is possible, however, that Paul's (supposed) procedure of regularly consulting a written text does not depend on his actually carrying such a text with him. Instead, he may have availed himself of the opportunities that arose when he visited synagogues during his travels. For this to be a viable option, we would have to determine whether Greek "Bible" scrolls were an expected feature of ancient (Diaspora) synagogues and, in addition, whether Paul would have been granted access to such scrolls if synagogues did indeed house them.[17] So far as I know, neither of these propo-

---

15. This is to say nothing of the more than ten thousand handwritten file cards that Septuagint scholar Max L. Margolis prepared on variant readings in the Greek Joshua during the first decades of the twentieth century.

16. Porter, "Paul and His Bible," 121.

17. Porter speculates that "poor relations between Paul and many of his fellow Jews may have further limited Paul's and his colleagues' access to the Greek Scriptures."

sitions can be easily affirmed, although I suppose that, at some level, they also cannot be completely dismissed. Thus, Paul may have consulted written texts of Scriptures at synagogues (and also at other locations?) during his travel and, on the basis of such contacts, may have drawn the wording of passages that he would include in his letters.

This last sentence points in the direction of another "written" resource of which Paul may have availed himself, namely, lists of Scripture passages prepared by him or others. The existence of these lists, which characteristically bring together passages on similar themes or with similar wording, was often posited by scholars on the basis of later practice. With the discovery among the Dead Sea Scrolls of catena texts, this very practice can be brought into the chronological and perhaps theological context of Paul.[18] Paul's reliance on such lists, whether he or another produced them, would account for the many places where his letters contain a series of passages drawn from disparate sections of the Bible but linked thematically or linguistically. (As we will note below, this same phenomenon can also be accounted for by Paul's reliance on memory.)

There is, then, much to be said for the role of written lists in Paul's citation of Scripture. We are still left with trying to determine whether Paul made use of existing lists or compiled such lists himself when he happened to have access to the full, written text of Scripture. Christopher Stanley makes a strong case for the proposition that Paul himself was responsible for the preparation of such lists.[19] In his view, this proposal best resolves "features of Paul's citation technique that have often troubled modern investigators." Among these features are the diversity of text types in Paul's scriptural citations, the emphasis Paul placed on integrating these citations into their new context (often at the expense of explicit recognition of their earlier scriptural context), and the introduction of interpretive elements into the citations.[20] Alternately, Paul may have commissioned the making of lists as the occasion arose during his travels and letter writing. All of these options are possible, but they would seem to limit the sponta-

---

"Paul and His Bible," 121, referencing Christopher D. Stanley, "'Pearls before Swine': Did Paul's Audience Understand His Biblical Quotations?" *NovT* 41 (1999): 127.

18. On this, see Wagner, *Heralds of the Good News*, 21.

19. See Christopher D. Stanley, *Paul and the Language of Scripture: Citation Technique in the Pauline Epistles and Contemporary Literature* (Cambridge: Cambridge University Press, 1992), esp. 67–79.

20. Ibid., 78.

neity of Paul's written communications with his churches if he had to stop until he received a list or shift his arguments to take advantage of lists he had already prepared.

The "Problem" with Paul's Citations

To a certain extent, the "oral option" (as I will call it) arose to explain the fact that, while many of Paul's scriptural citations accord verbatim with known Greek versions (either "the LXX" or one of its revisions), not all of them do.[21] To help explain such discrepancies, it was useful, if also convenient, to assert that they were the result of Paul's reliance on his memory, which (like that of everyone else) is far from perfect.

There are many problems with structuring the "problem" in this way. For those of a certain religious sensibility, it would be theologically imprudent (or even impudent) to suggest that the letters of Paul, as part of Sacred Writ, contain errors. Surely, Paul was divinely inspired—and it is this inspiration, rather than the mechanics of citation, that must always be borne in mind.

I have respect for such a view, but it can hardly be allowed to limit the perspective from which we view this issue. In this regard, we can note that, with the discovery and publication of more and more Greek texts, the number of variations multiplies. Although some continue to picture an "accepted" Greek text in the first century (parallel to the MT, which would develop a generation or two later), there is little if any reason to assert that Paul or any of his contemporaries would have looked askance at a particular "LXX" text as being inferior or in error vis-à-vis some generally recognized exemplar. Thus, it is necessary for us to reckon with the probability that Paul had access to a wider variety of Greek "biblical" texts than is usually imagined and that some of the differences between Paul's Scripture and known LXX texts resulted from his use of written material that has not survived.

Brief excursus: At the end of the nineteenth and beginning of the twentieth centuries, contacts between LXX and New Testament scholars were close, especially in centers such as Oxford and Cambridge. Sometimes, one and the same scholar worked in both fields.[22] As a result of a number

---

21. For a summation of these issues from the mid-twentieth century, see E. Earle Ellis, *Paul's Use of the Old Testament* (Edinburgh: Oliver & Boyd, 1957).

22. As an example from this "golden period," see Henry Barclay Swete, *An Intro-*

of factors (including, I suppose, the continuous process of academic specialization), contact between specialists in the LXX and New Testament decreased in both quantity and intensity during the decades that followed.[23] If I am correct in my observations, the past two decades or so have seen the reestablishment of fruitful interaction, a process that we should, in my view, encourage in all ways possible.[24]

Moreover, where Paul and the "LXX" are seen to diverge and reliance on memory is given as the reason, no pattern can be easily, if at all, discerned. By this, I mean that we might expect that findings from "memory studies" could be brought to bear, so that, if we do suspect (unconscious) changes by Paul, we could identify what types of changes would be most likely. Instead, at least on the basis of my research, Paul's reliance on memory results in an exceedingly wide array of variations, none of which need strike an observer as distinctively dependent on memory. Here are a few examples: 1 Cor 9:9, with respect to the (nearly) synonymous terms θιμώσεις and κημώσεις;[25] 2 Cor 9:7 (with reference to Prov 22:8), where LXX has εὐλογεῖ ("blesses") and Paul uses ἀγαπᾷ ("loves");[26] and Rom

---

duction to the Old Testament in Greek (rev. Richard Rusden Ottley; Cambridge: Cambridge University Press, 1902; repr., New York: Ktav, 1968), esp. part 3, ch. 2, "Quotations from the Septuagint in the New Testament" (381–405).

23. In my view, this is immediately evident from the rather cursory discussion in Sidney Jellicoe, *The Septuagint in Modern Study* (Oxford: Oxford University Press, 1968; repr., Winona Lake, Ind.: Eisenbrauns, 1978), part 6 of ch. 11, "The Current Situation in Septuagint Studies" (353–58).

24. See, for example, the generous analysis in Natalio Fernández Marcos, *The Septuagint in Context: Introduction to the Greek Version of the Bible* (trans. W. G. E. Watson; Leiden: Brill, 2000).

25. Roy E. Ciampa and Brian S. Rosner, "1 Corinthians," in *Commentary on the New Testament Use of the Old Testament* (ed. G. K. Beale and D. A. Carson; Grand Rapids: Baker Academic, 2007), 720: "Assuming that Paul used the synonym [κημώσεις] rather than the word found in the LXX [θιμώσεις], we may conclude that probably he was quoting from memory (of either the Greek or the Hebrew text [Deut 25:4])."

26. Peter Balla, "2 Corinthians," in Beale and Carson, *Commentary*, 778: "It may be that he [Paul] is quoting from memory, or perhaps from a version of the Greek text different from that of the LXX" (quoting from M. E. Thrall, *A Critical and Exegetical Commentary on the Second Epistle to the Corinthians* [ICC; Edinburgh: T&T Clark, 1994–2000], 2:576). It is also worth noting that these two examples—one each from 1 and 2 Corinthians—are the only ones that I could locate in Beale and Carson's *Commentary* for which it is suggested that Paul may have relied on his memory.

11:2ff (in comparison with LXX 3 Kgdms 19:14ff).[27] In none of these cases, or in others I could cite, am I faulting the modern scholar's judgment about the possibility (or probability) of Paul's reliance on memory. Rather, I am noting that, at least so far as I can discern, there is no pattern or paradigm that seems to underlie or unify these individual observations.

"Creative" Paul and the "Memory" Solution

Increasingly, New Testament researchers have come to recognize that some of the differences between the language of known "LXX" passages and that found in Paul are the result of creative and conscious efforts made by Paul himself. No one has argued for this position more strenuously or effectively than Christopher Stanley. In fact, he identifies this as the major theme of his monograph *Paul and the Language of Scripture*:

> The present study aims to demonstrate two basic theses: (1) that Paul actively adapted the wording of his biblical quotations to communicate his own understanding of the passage in question and to obviate other possible readings of the same text, and (2) that, in offering such "interpretive renderings" of the biblical text, Paul was working consciously but unreflectively within the accepted literary conventions of his day.[28]

It is not the case, as was once argued, that Paul is unaware of the original scriptural (Old Testament) context of a passage; rather, for Paul it is the new, Christian context that matters. While researchers used to blame Paul's faulty memory for his failure to keep his citations properly contextualized, they are now able to recognize the role played by Paul's memory in his recontextualizing, and often re-wording, of passages.

It has been demonstrated many times that in antiquity individuals constructed mnemonic devices using images like palaces and flora, which consisted of rooms or appendages into which they could "place" passages with similar themes or other correspondences. Much valued was the ability of orators or writers—the intellectual elite of antiquity—to draw upon their memories, thus configured, to devise clever and apt collections of

---

27. Swete, *Introduction*, 401. He cites this as a case where "a wide departure from the LXX is probably to be explained by the supposition that the Apostle quotes from memory."

28. Stanley, *Paul and the Language of Scripture*, 29.

passages from the most disparate sources. The visualization of memorized material into appropriate rooms and the like was indispensible in this process of retrieval and reconstitution.[29] For me, it is fascinating to observe that "world-class memory athletes"—that is, the elite of modern elites—use these same techniques today.[30]

Paul could have achieved the same (or at least very similar) results by using written lists. However, as I suggested above, unless Paul had an almost unlimited number of such lists or had prepared beforehand for the details of the letters he would be writing to a particular community or on a particular set of travels, reliance on written lists would probably have limited the topics that he could cover and would certainly have constrained the spontaneity with which he could respond to fast-moving developments in the communities with which he corresponded.

It is also becoming clear that ancient audiences were equipped to receive both "exact" quotations and possibly periphrastic citations, and that they might be expected to distinguish between the two.[31] In the case of Paul, this naturally raises the question of the sophistication or background of his intended audience. To me, it is doubtless Paul's calculation that references to Scripture would be meaningful, perhaps even persuasive, to his audience. There has been recurrent scholarly debate over the validity of Paul's calculations in this regard. I find myself siding with, among others, Bruce Fisk, who argues that even a largely Gentile Christian community in Rome would have had considerable familiarity with Scripture.[32] He cites the strong possibility that synagogue worship regularly involved the public reading of Torah and also hypothesizes that Christian Gentiles who had even informal affiliation with a synagogue would probably have had higher than average rates of literacy. While not accepting all of the points he makes, I am convinced by the totality of his argumentation, as summed up in the concluding sentences of his article: "It does not appear unreasonable to think that many of those who first read or heard Paul's letters would have enjoyed considerable prior, and ongoing, exposure to

---

29. For this, see Carruthers, "How to Make a Composition," 20–22.

30. On this, see the amusingly revealing account by Joshua Foer, "Secrets of a Mind-Gamer: How I Trained My Brain and Became a World-Class Memory Athlete," *New York Times Magazine* (15 February 2011).

31. Carruthers, "How to Make a Composition," 20.

32. Bruce N. Fisk, "Influence and Scriptural Knowledge among the Christians of Rome," in Porter and Stanley, *As It Is Written*, 157–85.

a number of the scriptural passages Paul cites. Paul's best guess about his readers' competence may not be far off."[33]

Of course, Paul may have miscalculated the make-up of his audience and its members' attendant knowledge of Scripture. Christopher Stanley has proposed this as a possibility.[34] As he writes, "Paul's letters ... were written for a very different type of audience, one that was largely illiterate and possessed only a limited acquaintance with the text of Scripture."[35] In either case, over time his audience would have invariably changed, since it is difficult to imagine that his letters, once in a community, were quickly consigned to the dustbin. Rather, they would have become objects of discussion and debate, if not veneration.[36]

And with this renewed attention, it is likely that increased consideration was paid to Paul's use of Scripture. So far as I know, no objection is recorded from the ancient world along the lines that Paul "misquoted" Scripture.[37] Rather, his audience understood, or came to understand, the points he was making by use of Scripture.[38] It does not seem to have mattered whether it accorded precisely with the way in which such texts were read (chanted?) in a given church.

In fact, we can posit that Paul's creative use of Scripture increased the fluidity of the Greek text as it was transmitted in the early church. Although "textual fluidity" is most often associated with the status of the Hebrew text prior to the preeminence of the MT, I believe (as I noted above) that similar fluidity obtained for quite some time in Greek-speaking churches (and continues, if I understand correctly, in the Orthodox churches of today). A citation by Paul, whether derived from written sources or through the

---

33. Fisk, "Influence and Scriptural Knowledge," 184–85.

34. See, for example, his lively presentation in "Pearls before Swine"; idem, *Arguing with Scripture: The Rhetoric of Quotations in the Letters of Paul* (New York: T&T Clark, 2004), 38–61, esp. ch. 3, "Paul and His Audience[s]"); idem, "Paul's 'Use' of Scripture: Why the Audience Matters," in Stanley and Porter, *As It Is Written*, 125–55.

35. Stanley, "Paul's Use of Scripture," 145.

36. On this, see Wagner, *Heralds of the Good News*, 36–39.

37. Since, as we can discern from Paul's letters to the Corinthians, Galatians, and Romans (among others), he was often involved in heated correspondence with the recipients of his letters, it is not far-fetched to anticipate at least a few references to disagreements over "citation" of Scripture, if they had in fact arisen.

38. My reasoning here is in line with several of the (scholarly) assumptions Stanley seeks to counter; see especially *Arguing With Scripture*, ch. 3: "Paul and His Audience(s)," 38–61.

creative use of his memory, could easily have become *the* biblical text for a given community or in a given context.

Second brief excursus: I am among a group, probably a very small group, who believes that we can learn from the (more) modern world, where documentation is often quite full, about practices and procedures in antiquity, where documentation is often quite sparse or even nonexistent.[39] It is certainly the case that due consideration must be taken of changed circumstances. This is particularly true when it comes to questions related to memory, including reliance on memory, citation by memory, and so forth.

When appropriate caution is exercised, is there anything of value to be learned from modern experiences? My answer is in the affirmative, and, I feel, it is not my answer alone. Several major researchers in this area provide autobiographical accounts related to memory. For example, E. P. Sanders recalls—to the exact date (18 April 1947)—an (unintentionally?) dispiriting remark from one of his teachers, to the effect that "we do not need to memorize."[40] Further, J. Ross Wagner relates that "when I recite the psalm [Ps 23] for my four-year-old, I purposefully modernize the language in order to communicate the meaning of the psalm in terms he can understand."[41] The Montgomery-to-Orlinsky letter with which I began this essay points in the same direction. More broadly, the *New York Times Magazine* article cited earlier[42] reveals that there are striking similarities (as well, admittedly, as differences) between how at least some people today commit written material to memory and how their predecessors accomplished similar feats in antiquity.

Even where these modern examples part company with the ancient exemplars, or perhaps exactly where they part company, we can recognize both our proximity to those who came thousands of years before us and the distance that separates us. My preference is to emphasize the former while not neglecting the latter.

---

39. See Leonard Greenspoon, "Biblical Translators in Antiquity and in the Modern World: A Comparative Study," *HUCA* 60 (1989), 91–113; and idem, "At the Beginning: The Septuagint as a Jewish Bible Translation," in *"Translation Is Required": The Septuagint in Retrospect and Prospect* (ed. Robert J. V. Hiebert; SBLSCS 56; Atlanta: Society of Biblical Literature, 2010), 159–69.
40. Sanders, "Paul between Judaism and Hellenism," 78.
41. Wagner, *Heralds of the Good News*, 23 n. 83.
42. See note 30.

Paul and Memory

No one, so far as I know, doubts that Paul read and knew well the Jewish Scriptures in the Greek language. So far as I am concerned, there is no reason to suspect that he did not also know Scripture in Hebrew.[43] His choice to make regular use of an existing text in Greek rather than making his own translation from the Hebrew (which he probably did on occasion) may have been determined by existing practice in the churches with which he was in communication, or by Paul's recognition of the general suitability of the existing translation, or any number of factors.

But Paul's reliance on an existing text in Greek was the starting, not the ending point for his citation of Scripture. Whether or not we wish to allow for inadvertent mistakes on Paul's part, it should now be clear that we must allow for Paul's rewording of earlier texts on the basis of the experience of Jesus' life and death. Is this procedure more likely to have occurred through Paul's immediate use of written sources (whether full text or abstracts), through the practice and application of memory, or a combination of these and perhaps other methods?

My research in a number of areas leads me to be leery of "either-or" solutions. Thus, for example, I am unconvinced by arguments that the origins of the Septuagint must be located in either royal initiative (on the part of Ptolemy II, his librarian, or both) or the needs of the Alexandrian community, for whom fluency in Hebrew was fast becoming a rarity. Rather, it was a confluence of interests, both internal and external to the Jewish community, that led to the Greek translation.[44]

In my view, a similar multiplicity of approaches or resources should be envisioned for Paul.[45] As I see it, he was at home in researching "biblical" scrolls, with all the inconveniences and labors such an approach entailed. And he was comfortable with using lists either specially prepared for—or by—him or ready-made beforehand. And he not only knew the Greek text (or large parts of it) by memory but he had also mentally catalogued it, placing similar passages side by side in his "memory bank" in such a way

---

43. *Pace* Stanley.
44. See now Greenspoon, "At the Beginning."
45. See Wagner, *Heralds of the Good News*, 25–26, and the two examples from antiquity (2 Macc 2:25 and Augustine, *De doctrina Christianana* 2.30–31) that he cites (26–27).

that he could easily withdraw passages that had been deposited near each other.

I am particularly drawn to this last view of Paul, not to the exclusion of the others but because it fits with the picture of a man who, armed with vast intellectual and theological resources, stepped down from any (and every) possible ivory tower into the realities, as messy as they were, of the world he inhabited. That world didn't always stop, any more than ours does, to allow the individual the "leisure" of going back (literally) to the sources. The measure of this man was, to a large degree, dependent on what he could recall at the moment. And for this purpose, Paul's memory was well suited and well used.

Bibliography

Barton, Stephen C., Loren T. Stuckenbruck, and Benjamin G. Wold, eds. *Memory in the Bible and Antiquity*. Tübingen: Mohr Siebeck, 2007.

Beale, G. K., and D. A. Carson, eds. *Commentary on the New Testament Use of the Old Testament*. Grand Rapids: Baker Academic, 2007.

Carruthers, Mary. "How to Make a Composition: Memory-Craft in Antiquity and in the Middle Ages." Pages 15–29 in *Memory: History, Theories, Debates*. Edited by Susannah Radstone and Bill Schwarz. New York: Fordham University Press, 2010.

Ellis, E. Earle. *Paul's Use of the Old Testament*. Edinburgh: Oliver & Boyd, 1957.

Fisk, Bruce N. "Influence and Scriptural Knowledge among the Christians of Rome." Pages 157–85 in *As It Is Written: Studying Paul's Use of Scripture*. Edited by Stanley E. Porter and Christopher D. Stanley. SBLSymS 50. Atlanta: Society of Biblical Literature, 2008.

Foer, Joshua. "Secrets of a Mind-Gamer: How I Trained My Brain and Became a World-Class Memory Athlete." *New York Times Magazine*. February 15, 2011.

Greenspoon, Leonard. "At the Beginning: The Septuagint as a Jewish Bible Translation." Pages 159–69 in *"Translation Is Required": The Septuagint in Retrospect and Prospect*. Edited by Robert J. V. Hiebert. SBLSCS 56. Atlanta: Society of Biblical Literature, 2010.

———. "Biblical Translators in Antiquity and in the Modern World: A Comparative Study." *HUCA* 60 (1989): 91–113.

Harris, William V. *Ancient Literacy*. Cambridge: Harvard University Press, 1989.

Hezser, Catherine. *Jewish Literacy in Roman Palestine*. TSAJ 81. Tübingen: Mohr Siebeck, 2001.

Jaffee, Martin S. *Torah in the Mouth: Writing and Oral Tradition in Palestinian Judaism 200 BCE—400 CE*. Oxford: Oxford University Press, 2001.

Jellicoe, Sidney. *The Septuagint in Modern Study*. Oxford: Oxford University Press, 1968. Repr., Winona Lake, Ind.: Eisenbrauns, 1978.

Mackay, E. Anne ed. *Orality, Literacy, Memory in the Ancient Greek and Roman World*. Leiden: Brill, 2007.

Marrou, Henri. *A History of Education in Antiquity*. New York: Sheed & Ward, 1956.

Porter, Stanley E. "Paul and His Bible: His Education and Access to the Scriptures of Israel." Pages 97–124 in *As It Is Written: Studying Paul's Use of Scripture*. Edited by Stanley E. Porter and Christopher D. Stanley. SBLSymS 50. Atlanta: Society of Biblical Literature, 2008.

Porter, Stanley E., and Christopher D. Stanley, eds. *As It Is Written: Studying Paul's Use of Scripture*. SBLSymS 50. Atlanta: Society of Biblical Literature, 2008.

Sanders, E. P. "Paul between Judaism and Hellenism." Pages 74–89 in *St. Paul Among the Philosophers*. Edited by John D. Caputo and Linda Martin Alcoff. Bloomington: Indiana University Press, 2009.

Small, Jocelyn Penny. *Wax Tablets of the Mind: Cognitive Studies of Memory and Literacy in Classical Antiquity*. London: Routledge, 1997.

Stanley, Christopher D. *Arguing with Scripture: The Rhetoric of Quotations in the Letters of Paul*. New York: T&T Clark, 2004.

———. *Paul and the Language of Scripture: Citation Technique in the Pauline Epistles and Contemporary Literature*. SNTSMS 74. Cambridge: Cambridge University Press, 1992.

———. "Paul's 'Use' of Scripture: Why the Audience Matters." Pages 125–55 in *As It Is Written: Studying Paul's Use of Scripture*. Edited by Stanley E. Porter and Christopher D. Stanley. SBLSymS 50. Atlanta: Society of Biblical Literature, 2008.

———. "'Pearls before Swine': Did Paul's Audience Understand His Biblical Quotations?" *NovT* 41 (1999): 124–44.

Swete, Henry Barclay. *An Introduction to the Old Testament in Greek*. Rev. ed. New York: Ktav 1968.

Wagner, J. Ross. *Heralds of the Good News: Isaiah and Paul "in Concert" in the Letter to the Romans*. NovTSup 101. Brill: Leiden, 2002.

Identity, Memory, and Scriptural Warrant: Arguing Paul's Case

Jeremy Punt

1. Introduction: Identity and Continuity[1]

In a recent study on early Christian identity, a basic question was not really addressed, partly because it was not a focal interest of the study and partly because of conventional views in this regard.[2] While the contributors acknowledged in various ways, some tacitly and others explicitly,[3] that textual traditions had influenced the New Testament authors' concerns with identity, a further set of questions remained unanswered. What was the rationale for the constitutively important role of Israel's Scriptures in the formation of the new Jesus-centered movement, which in many cases entailed that they be read against their own traditions? Why and how were the Scriptures incorporated within the Jesus-follower movement and presented as the founding platform for the emerging Christian

---

1. An earlier version of this essay appeared in *Journal of Early Christian History* 1 (2011) and is used here with the editor's permission.

2. Bengt Holmberg, ed., *Exploring Early Christian Identity* (WUNT 226; Tübingen: Mohr Siebeck, 2008). The appropriateness of the use of the term "early Christian" (and "early Judaism"), which Holmberg takes pains to defend (ibid., 3-5; cf. Anders Runesson, "Inventing Christian Identity: Paul, Ignatius, and Theodosius I," in Holmberg, *Exploring Early Christian Identity*, 59-92), is hotly debated. In opposition to the use of terms like "Christian" or "Judaism" in the first century, see Judith M. Lieu, *Neither Jew nor Greek: Constructing Early Christianity* (Studies of the New Testament and Its World; London: T&T Clark, 2002), 191-209; idem, *Christian Identity in the Jewish and Graeco-Roman World* (Oxford: Oxford University Press, 2004).

3. S. Byrskog, "Memory and Identity in the Gospels: A New Perspective," in Holmberg, *Exploring Early Christian Identity*, 33-57; Runesson, "Inventing Christian Identity," 81-82.

way?[4] How were these Scriptures seen to provide grounding and legitimation for the followers of Jesus—what they stood for (identity and community), what they believed in (convictions), and how they lived their lives (ethos)? The interplay between texts,[5] memory, and identity appears to provide some of the answers, as will be shown in the (largely theoretical) discussion that follows.

As a working description,[6] the term "identity" is used here in the sense of "a complex phenomenon of fundamental beliefs, embodied in myth, rites, and ethos of living communities, evolving and institutionalizing over time in interplay with local realities."[7] Three important aspects of identity are important when discussing Paul's early Jesus-follower communities. First, identity is not a matter of essentialism but of construction.[8] In this sense it is like the term "culture," for which a variety of descriptions, definitions, and approximations can be found in the literature. Second, in discussions of identity, there is a major tension between stability and change.

---

4. Or, to put it another way, "This, indeed, was the dilemma with which Christians struggled: how to claim the continuity with the past without admitting the Jews' own claim, which would entail losing a sense of separate identity" (Lieu, *Christian Identity*, 83).

5. The word "texts" here is broadly conceived, including both oral and written materials, textual traditions or transmissions, narratives, etc. The focus on texts does not translate simplistically into an ideas-based approach since it is not primarily the contents but rather the function of the texts that is important. In this way other aspects of material culture as well as the embodied nature of first-century life, strongly guided by attitudes to bodiliness and gender, can also be accounted for; cf. Lieu, *Christian Identity*, 25.

6. A rather modern term, "identity" entered the English language toward the end of the sixteenth century, evoking notions of "sameness and difference, of commonalities and boundaries, and of individual and/or group" (Lieu, *Neither Jew nor Greek*, 191). Important to consider in the debate about identity, which has grown large and voluminous, is the contribution made by the French philosopher Paul Ricoeur, who suggests that narrative identity can be understood according to either the notion of sameness (*idem*) or that which concerns the self or one's own group (*ipse*) ("Narrative Identity," *Philosophy Today* 35 [1991]: 73–81). Although definitions and descriptions differ, what is clear is that the term identity consists of "ideas of boundedness, of sameness and difference, of continuity, perhaps of a degree of homogeneity, and of recognition by self and others" (Lieu, *Christian Identity*, 12).

7. Holmberg, *Exploring Early Christian Identity*, v.

8. "Identity—self-sameness through time—is always a relation between past and present established through the media of memory" (J. K. Olick, "Products, Processes, and Practices: A Non-reificatory Approach to Collective Memory," *BTB* 36 (2006): 8.

Recognition of the constructedness of identity comprises both an acknowledgement of the perceived and claimed origins of identity and attention to those devices by which change is managed and continuity asserted.[9] In the present case, attention is focused on the way that the Scriptures of Israel, as one element employed in an uneven and complex historical setting, were operationalized through memory, and how this process contributed to the construction and ongoing negotiation of group identity.[10]

Third, identity continues over time, or at least claims to do so. Continuity is never "just there," available in some unmitigated form, existing in and of itself, waiting to be collected and claimed, because identity is not a predefined essence, a packaged and contained entity with fixed boundaries and definite silhouette. Continuity is always constructed within identity—even if variously by different people or groups laying claim to the same continuity—and is called, not infrequently, "history." The relationship between the identity of people and their sense of past, as seen in the histories that they construct, is always both reciprocal and dynamic, the constant tugging between an experienced continuity and the sense of constant change and decay.[11] The present essay explores this interaction between continuity and discontinuity, the reciprocity involved and the resulting tension and contestation in the construction and negotiation of identity as it occurred in the early community of Christ-followers through the Scriptures of Israel mediated by (as?) memory.[12]

2. Memory and Identity: Cultural Memory[13]

The importance of memory for social identity in groups has been dis-

---

9. Cf. Lieu, *Christian Identity*, 14.

10. Thus, rather than attempting to describe the parameters and "content" of identity in first-century Pauline communities, the focus here is on the processes of constructing, maintaining, and adjusting (or negotiating) such identity, concentrating on Paul's use of Scriptures and the role of memory in these processes.

11. Cf. Lieu, *Christian Identity*, 22, 62.

12. A long series of caveats is in order when dealing individually with the topics of memory, history, and identity, and all the more so when all three are juxtaposed. Such caveats (e.g., the fruitlessness of seeking "objective history/historiography," distinctions between individual and collective memory, acceptance of the diversity and complexity of "early Christian identity," etc.) will be dealt with as they are encountered in the discussion below.

13. Cultural memory is "a collective concept for all knowledge that directs behav-

cussed vigorously over the last few decades.[14] Cultural memory plays an important role in the construal and maintenance of group identity, with groups providing the setting and social patterns for coherent and enduring memories.[15] The culture of recollection is a form of social obligation determining the identity or self-assessment of a group,[16] since every group needs to define itself with the help of memory in order to bring about communion. Collective memory refers to a group's internal perspective, its current, generalized, and popularized notions of the past. The idea was developed by Maurice Halbwachs, though his conception focused on change and showed no concern for the identity of the group.[17] Jan Ass-

---

ior and experience in the interactive framework of a society and one that obtains through generations in repeated societal practice and initiation" (Jan Assmann, "Collective Memory and Cultural Identity," *New German Critique* 65 [1995]: 126). The significance of Maurice Halbwachs's work on collective memory (see note 14) is acknowledged for reframing memory as a variety of products and practices, a dynamic process incorporating individual and collectivist approaches (cf. Olick, "Products, Processes, and Practices," 12).

14. Recent studies in social anthropology and related fields, including pioneering work done by Maurice Halbwachs (1877–1945), provide many useful theoretical frameworks and concepts. The study of social identity and its reliance upon categorizing, construing, and negotiating similarities and differences within and between groups was boosted by the work of scholars like Henri Tajfel (1919–1982). For its application to Pauline hermeneutics, cf. Jeremy Punt, "Jude and the Others: Hermeneutics, Identity, Conflict," *South African Baptist Journal of Theology* 17 (2008): 149–62; idem, "Hermeneutics in Identity Formation: Paul's Use of Genesis in Galatians 4," *HTS Teologiese Studies/Theological Studies* 67 (2011): 1–9, doi:10.4102/hts.v67i1.846.

15. Although individuals are the carriers of memory, the memory of individuals cannot exist without the social frames which given collectives define. Recollections (intimate or otherwise) are formed only through communication and interaction within the scope of a social group. This implies that the individual can only remember what fits into the social frames of his or her present and that historical facts are transposed into memory figures to be substantiated by specific place and specific time; cf. Jan Assmann, "Cultural Memory: Script, Recollection, and Political Identity in Early Civilizations," *Historiography East and West* 1 (2003): 154–77.

16. A social group constituted as memory communion will safeguard its past by focusing on two elements: its unique character and duration. In its self-image it will accentuate external distinctions while minimizing internal disparities (Assmann, "Cultural Memory").

17. Maurice Halbwachs, *On Collective Memory* (ed. and trans. Lewis A. Coser; The Heritage of Sociology; Chicago: University of Chicago Press, 1992); cf. Assmann, "Cultural Memory," 162–69; Santiago Guijarro, "Cultural Memory and Group Identity in Q," *BTB* 37 (2007): 92. Halbwachs insisted that history was not memory, since

mann built upon and developed these ideas further, differentiating within collective memory as a generic category two further types of group-related memory, which he called "communicative" and "cultural" memory. While communicative memory approximates Halbwachs's notion of collective memory in focusing on everyday matters and being diachronically restricted, cultural memory is differentiated by its distance from the past.[18]

Collective memory provides a centripetal force for a group and concomitantly serves as a powerful marker of social differentiation.[19] Such boundary drawing and self-identification is what constitutes identity.[20] Memory is important to a group's sense of identity, since the culture of recollection is a form of social obligation that determines the identity and self-assessment of a group:[21] "Memory is not the cause of life, not its effect, nor even an isolable feature of it, but its very form—relationality in time."[22] Socially patterned individual memory allows groups to establish their continuity, unity, and particularity through consensus about the past. The collective memory of a group and its sense of identity are reciprocally

---

memory is always related to the identity of a living group, while history began when the past was no longer claimed as the collective memory of a particular living social group. Yet history is not unrelated to memory, since history is objectified memory. For Assmann, too, historiography starts where memory ends; when the past is no longer remembered, history sets in. History is the product of historiography and is abstract, and so is the opposite of memory that is always collective, i.e., group-specific and identity-concrete ("Cultural Memory," 169–72; cf. Guijarro, "Cultural Memory," 92). See further the section below titled "Memory and/against History."

18. Understandably, the nomenclature in this area is contested: e.g., D. C. Duling uses collective memory interchangeably with social memory (referring to smaller social units) and cultural memory (referring to larger social units); see "Social Memory and Biblical Studies: Theory, Method, and Application," *BTB* 36 (2006): 2–4.

19. Halbwachs, *On Collective Memory*, 38–45.

20. Bradley R. Braxton, *The Tyranny of Resolution: 1 Corinthians 7:17–24* (SBLDS 181; Atlanta: Society of Biblical Literature, 2000). In social-identity theory, categorization and stereotyping are important for identifying the self and the other, the in-group and the other groups.

21. Assmann, "Cultural Memory."

22. Olick, "Products, Processes, and Practices," 8; cf. Israel Rosenfield, "Memory and Identity," *New Literary History* 26 (1995): 197–203. Although Rosenfield (202) focuses on individual memory, her statement that "memory, then, is not a set of stored images that can be remembered by an independent 'I'; memory is a set of ever-revolving procedures," is true of cultural memory, too.

related, with memory and identity feeding off of one another so that those who belong to the same group share (or at least ascribe to) the same past.[23]

Unlike communicative memory and its focus on proximity and the present, cultural memory is concerned with notions and events of the past, which it actively props up through cultural formations such as texts, rituals, monuments, and institutional communication (recitation, practice, observance).[24] Such cultural products are the result of collective experience that is relevant for the identity of a particular group or society.[25] Cultural memory includes "that body of re-usable texts, images and rituals specific to each society in each epoch, whose cultivation serves to stabilize and convey that society's self-image."[26] In short, the culture of recollection[27] deals with staking out social horizons of meaning and time.[28] Written texts play a vital role in this process.

---

23. Assmann, "Cultural Memory," 162–69; cf. Guijarro, "Cultural Memory," 92. Although Assmann agrees with Martin Walser that memories arise from within the individual, he insists that memories that connect with society "make their way into the interstices of communication and, if only they are significant enough, they end up in the visible *outer* world of symbols, texts, rituals, and monuments, and form the basis of a cultural memory that can last hundreds or thousands of years" (Jan Assmann, *Religion and Cultural Memory: Ten Studies* [trans. R. Livingstone; Cultural Memory in the Present; Stanford, Calif.: Stanford University Press, 2006], 178).

24. Assmann refers to these matters as "figures of memory," which he claims form the basis for the entire Jewish calendar. "In the flow of everyday communications such festivals, rites, epics, poems, images, etc., form 'islands of time,' islands of a completely different temporality suspended from time. In cultural memory, such islands of time expand into memory spaces of 'retrospective contemplativeness'" ("Collective Memory," 129).

25. Sites of memory "where memory crystallizes and secretes itself" (Pierre Nora, "Between Memory and History: *Les Lieux de Mémoire*," *Representations* 26 [1989]: 7) would include places (e.g., archives, museums, palaces, cemeteries, memorials), concepts and practices (e.g., commemorations, generations, mottos, rituals), and objects (e.g., inherited property, commemorative monuments, manuals, emblems, basic texts and symbols). Cf. French historian Pierre Nora's work on the construction of the French past, where he insists that sites of memory should not be idealized, first and foremost because they are mere substitutes for *mileux de mémoire* or real environments of memory ("Between Memory and History," 7).

26. Assmann, "Collective Memory," 132; cf. Guijarro, "Cultural Memory," 93.

27. The culture of recollection is not tantamount to tradition, as the latter tends to stress continuity, progression, and resumption. Assmann's notion of "cultural memory," however, is typified by emotive attachment as well as a deliberate refer-

3. Cultural Memory, Identity, and Texts[29]

Memory was maintained, stimulated, and refreshed by various artifacts in early times that, notwithstanding the oral cultural setting, included narratives *and* written resources—in short, texts. "Being that can be remembered is text."[30] Identity or a sense of self, both among individuals and among groups, is commonly constructed by and through narrative, through the stories told by people about and among themselves, suggesting a link between identity and narrative, identity and text.[31] Texts, and oral-mediated texts[32] in particular, are webs "of meaning and meaning-effects that depend on the cultural signs encoded in the text and that condition the experience of it during and after the performance. To the extent that it contains traces of a cultural system of other written and oral texts, it is a reservoir of collective memory and affects the hearers' negotiation of how they remember the past socially and construe their social identity."[33]

---

ence to the past that overcomes the breach by allowing for both memory and oblivion ("Cultural Memory," 154–77).

28. People reconstruct the past in their memory, and the culture of recollection supplies them with different forms and means of relating to the past. A break with the past, most basically in the form of death, brings about the necessity of relating to the past and so stands at the beginning of the culture of recollection (Assmann, "Cultural Memory").

29. Narratives and texts are collapsed into one another, since the argument here is not about issues of literacy but rather about the invocation and presence of certain traditions underwritten by narratives or texts in the communities addressed by Paul.

30. Assmann, *Religion and Cultural Memory*, ix, in analogy to Gadamer's dictum on hermeneutics, "Being that can be understood is language." For Assmann (*Religion and Cultural Memory*, ix), "The theory of cultural memory explores the textuality of the past within the linguistic framework of our experiences of the world that hermeneutics has decoded for us."

31. Cf. Olick, "Products, Processes, and Practices," 5–6.

32. The vibrancy and creativity of the literary productivity among the early followers of Jesus is present also in Paul, as attested, e.g., in his remark in 1 Thess 5:27 imploring the recipients to ensure the reading of the letter to the whole community.

33. Samuel Byrskog, "Christology and Identity in an Intertextual Perspective: The Glory of Adam in the Narrative Substructure of Paul's Letter to the Romans," in *Identity Formation in the New Testament* (ed. Bengt Holmberg and Mikael Winninge; WUNT 227; Tübingen: Mohr Siebeck, 2008), 4. Collective memory, therefore, entails more than a context where prototypes from the past can be used to negotiate social identity (also P. F. Esler, *Conflict and Identity in Romans: The Social Setting of Paul's Letter* [Minneapolis: Fortress, 2003]). For the distinction between *mneme* (remem-

Among the early Christ-followers, texts assumed a central role not just in documenting what it meant to be Christian but also in shaping the very meaning of Christianity.[34] Indeed, "if ever there was a case of the construction of reality through text, such a case is provided by early Christianity."[35] Not only were texts carried in memory but public memory was cultivated and nurtured by a canon.[36] While we should be careful about claiming precedence for texts over group formation, the Scriptures informed the collective memory of Jews, Jesus-followers, and Christians for many centuries[37] in a process of which distinctive traces can be discerned in the New Testament.

Two problems in particular must be considered in any accounting of the textual construction of "Christianity," although some aspects of both problems may be more apparent than real. First, this approach privileges literary sources, and by extension also the elites who produced such documents, while also tending to mute the voices of the majority of people as well as the meanings that were transacted through other social means (goods and practices, icons and images) that constituted and populated everyday life.[38] Marginalized communities, on the other hand, construct

---

bered knowledge that is present consciously or otherwise) and *anamnesis* (scrutinizing activities aimed at recollection of past items for their present value), see P. Ricoeur, *Memory, History, Forgetting* (trans. K. Blamey and D. Pellauer; Chicago: University of Chicago Press, 2004), 7–21; W. Kelber, "The Generative Force of Memory: Early Christian Traditions as Processes of Remembering," *BTB* 36 (2006): 15–22, esp. 18.

34. Lieu, *Christian Identity*, 7. Lieu is speaking of the centuries following the New Testament era, but her comments are true of these texts as well. According to Lieu, highlighting the textually constructed nature of early Christianity works against the misplaced tendency to find "some essential and abiding reality independent of texts" (8).

35. Averil Cameron, *Christianity and the Rhetoric of Empire: The Development of Christian Discourse* (Sather Classical Lectures 57; Berkeley: University of California Press, 1991), 21.

36. Different aggregations and intensities characterize the binding and reflexive character of a heritage: "One society bases its self-image on a canon of sacred scripture, the next on a basic set of ritual activities, and the third on a fixed and hieratic language of forms in a canon of architectural and artistic types" (Assmann, "Collective Memory," 132).

37. Doron Mendels, "Introduction," in *On Memory: An Interdisciplinary Approach* (ed. Doron Mendels; New York: Lang, 2007), 9–18, esp. 12.

38. "Literary texts tend to be more exclusive than social experience; individuals and groups interact socially who textually are denied such intercourse" (Lieu, *Christian Identity*, 9). See also the section below titled "Memory and/against History."

their own narratives that subvert the hegemonic constructions of history and culture imposed by the dominant in society. Memory is important in the shaping of these narratives, allowing the reclamation of a suppressed past while at the same time enabling a revisioning of that past which is vital to (re)gaining control over the life and future of both the individual and the group.[39] The issue of authorial agency and textual ownership will require further attention below.

Secondly, dependence on texts or literary devices for the construction of identity in a world with at best a ten percent literacy figure may sound problematic, but it forms only part of a broader set of complexities. In contrast to the other aspects of material culture, the ready availability of texts from the first-century world only partly explains their use in the study of identity in antiquity. The constructive role of texts in the ancient world, and in the Roman Empire in particular,[40] requires attention to the way they influenced their audiences, even when, for the most part, they would have been heard rather than read.[41] Even functionally illiterate people valued literacy in imperial times.

Narrative supports the activation of identity through memory, but, as social constructions, memories can also be reconstructed in the form of narratives in the pursuit of change and new meaning. Narrative recollects even as it aspires to create new stories, new histories. Textual narrative links memory and identity through its twofold operation of creating story while making use of formal convention. As fragmented notions are connected into a coherent whole, memory acquires agency. Memory is closely aligned with imagination, because memory relates to absence. "The imaginative capacity of memory to recover and reinvent images and ideas of absent places bridges the locales, supplying a crucial sense of self."[42]

---

39. Amritjit Singh, Joseph T. Skerrett Jr., and Robert E. Hogan, "Introduction," in *Memory, Narrative, and Identity: New Essays in Ethnic American Literatures* (ed. Amritjit Singh, Joseph T. Skerrett Jr., and Robert E. Hogan; Boston: Northeastern University Press, 1994), 19.

40. For example, Fergus Millar's dictum, "The emperor was what the emperor did" points to the emperors' involvement in giving justice while on military campaigns and, as circumstances allowed, engaging in extensive communication by means of letters and decrees. *The Emperor in the Roman World (31 BC–AD 337)* (London: Duckworth, 1977), 6, 9.

41. Lieu, *Christian Identity*, 9–10.

42. Debra Shostak, "Maxine Hong Kingston's Fake Books," in Singh, Skerrett, and Hogan, *Memory, Narrative, and Identity*, 234.

Along with other early Jesus-follower communities, the Pauline communities exhibited distinct connections between their social memory and the narrative basis of that memory, including the memory of Jesus' words and deeds, which they related to the life of the movement. The process of acquiring social identity in these communities included being socialized into the memories of the group[43] and so learning to identify with its collective past.[44] Just as the Jesus traditions were invoked and claimed in the Pauline communities as part of their construction and negotiation of identity,[45] so also their connection to the "collective past" was established through a connection to the Scriptures of Israel. This is especially evident in Paul's use of texts to present Abraham as the father of faith in some of his communities. Before we examine this aspect of Paul's practice, however, a brief word on the relation between memory and history would be appropriate.

4. Memory and/against History: Issues of Power [46]

Paul's use of the Scriptures of Israel cannot be equated with historiography, not even as a first-century version of it, and is therefore better discussed in

---

43. Not only was this process more complicated and less linear than what is often contemplated but the relationship between the author of the texts and the communities from which these texts emerged and to which they are directed is also complex, so that simple equations of the identity of the author and the originating and receiving communities should be avoided. The present argument requires only that the identity of Paul and the communities that he addresses cohered at least broadly.

44. Byrskog, "Memory and Identity," 57.

45. As we see, for example, in 1 Thess 1:6-10; Phil 2:6-11 (cf. Col 1:15-23); 1 Cor 11:23-26. Locally conditioned texts convey some trains of thought that connect them with others; cf. Lieu, *Christian Identity*, 22.

46. The use of postcolonialism as a "critique of history" (Robert J. C. Young, *Postcolonialism: An Historical Introduction* [London: Blackwell, 2001]) is contentious, and bound to recall the Hegelian notion of equating history with civilization or progress. Western imperialism claims to have a civilizing mission with strong pedagogical leanings, aimed at the "undeveloped" nations of the world, and subscribes to the "teleological promise of linear time" (Leela Gandhi, *Postcolonial Theory: A Critical Introduction* [New York: Columbia University Press, 1988], 171-72, 174). From this standpoint, history becomes the grand narrative of a totalizing Eurocentrism that conveniently omits European failures and inadequacies and ignores the fact that dominance and resistance were refused by some on both sides. If we are not careful, postcolonial theory with its focus on history as a heuristic category might reimpose a European

relation to memory rather than to history. History should be distinguished from memory, even if a complete separation between the two is neither achievable nor feasible since memory is the womb of history.[47] Memory's unwillingness to distinguish between fact and fiction is a major difference between memory and history.[48] Moreover, history's horizon is determined by availability of resources, while cultural memory's horizon depends on a community's self-identification with and accounting for the past.[49] Without denying history's link to the identity of those writing or reading it,[50] history is different from memory; indeed, it can even stand in opposition to memory. Sometimes history has a more sinister aim:[51] "History is perpetually suspicious of memory, and its true mission is to suppress and destroy it.… History's goal and ambition is not to exalt but annihilate what has in reality taken place."[52] In our contemporary context, history has won

---

imperial notion of history by presenting colonialism as a single and valid historicizing category and so erasing all of the diversity and alterity of colonized nations (cf. the views of Anne McClintock as described in Gandhi, *Postcolonial Theory*, 171–72, 174).

47. Ricoeur, *Memory, History, Forgetting*. Elsewhere Ricoeur differentiates sharply between history and archives: "History was not an issue of archives. With archives we are confronted with the trace, the trace which has been kept. This is completely alien to the mentality of the Jews and even the early church" ("The Self in the Mirror of the Scriptures," in *The Whole and Divided Self* [ed. D. E. Aune and J. McCarthy; New York: Crossroad, 1997], 243).

48. Assmann, *Religion and Cultural Memory*, 179.

49. Ibid.

50. Jim Sharpe, "History From Below," in *New Perspectives on Historical Writing* (ed. Peter Burke; University Park: Pennsylvania State University Press, 1991), 24–41.

51. If "history" is primarily an academic category, called to life and given structure in primarily elitist institutions, it is questionable whether it will allow the "opaque and contradictory processes which characterise the politics of the people" (as the Subaltern Studies collective is described in Gandhi, *Postcolonial Theory*, 172). Historical accounts further marginalize those who are already marginalized, e.g., by employing the coercion/retaliation binary (Gandhi, *Postcolonial Theory*, 173).

52. Nora, "Between Memory and History," 9; cf. Georgia M. Keightley, "Christian Collective Memory and Paul's Knowledge of Jesus," in *Memory, Tradition, and Text: Uses of the Past in Early Christianity* (SemeiaSt 52; Atlanta: Society of Biblical Literature, 2005), 129–50; Olick, "Products, Processes, and Practices," 6–8. This is not to claim that memory can be equated with "what really happened" but rather to point to some differences between history and memory. According to Nora, there is in fact a *fundamental opposition* between memory and history: "Memory is life, borne by living societies founded in its name. It remains in permanent evolution, open to the dialectic of remembering and forgetting. Memory is a perpetually actual phenomenon, a bond

its victory over memory by usurping it: "Memory has been promoted to the center of history."[53]

In order not to drive the dissimilarity between memory and history too far, a mediating approach might be to understand New Testament texts from a *people's-history* point of view.[54] Unlike history in general, where the focus is all too often on the elite—the "great men" as shapers of history and world events—people's history shifts the perspective to the non-elite, viewing them as significant to history[55] and trying to understand them in the light of their own experiences and reactions to such experiences.[56] In situations characterized by asymmetric power relationships, people tend to construct narratives that vigorously challenge the dominant group or entity's attempt to destroy or counteract a marginalized group by obliterating or appropriating its collective history.[57] Such a history "from below" has to contend with all aspects of life and thus employs interdisciplinary approaches[58] for its research.

---

tying us to the eternal present; history is a presentation of the past. ... Memory is absolute, while history can only conceive the relative" ("Between Memory and History," 8–9).

53. Nora, "Between Memory and History," 24.

54. Sharpe, "History From Below," 24–41; cf. Richard A. Horsley, "Unearthing a People's History," in *Christian Origins* (ed. Richard A. Horsley; vol. 1 of *A People's History of Christianity*; Minneapolis: Fortress, 2005), 1–20.

55. As part of a new approach to history and historiography, history from below, which focuses on the experiences of ordinary people rather than the great (male) figures of history, exhibits several other characteristics of a new historical perspective. (1) History is seen as concerned with more than politics, including every type of human activity. (2) History is not simply a narrative of events; it also includes an analysis of structures. (3) Historiography must move beyond a chronicling approach that favors documents to encompass other evidence attesting to human activities. (4) Historiography should allow for a wider range of questions and events, including both collective movements and individual actions, trends, and events. (5) Historians must recognize that neutral, unbiased historiography is impossible and acknowledge the reality of cultural relativism. (6) Historiography must be broadened beyond the realm of professional historians and become more interdisciplinary. See Peter Burke, "Overture: The New History; Its Past and Its Future," in Burke, *New Perspectives on Historical Writing*, 1–23.

56. Sharpe, "History From Below," 26.

57. Terry Dehay, "Narrating Memory," in Singh, Skerrett, and Hogan, *Memory, Narrative, and Identity*, 26–44.

58. Drawing upon poststructuralist theory, a postcolonial commitment to the subaltern as the subject of history requires both a new historicism and a recognition of

Beyond the obvious problem of a dearth of evidence and sources, the notion of a people's history is by no means unproblematic, requiring caution and even criticism. One problem concerns the identity of "the people"—are they the poor, the subordinates, the marginalized? It is not always clear whether the focus is on those excluded from power or on people engaged in grassroots politics. A related problem concerns the criteria that should be used to determine such groups of people, since economic, political, and cultural divisions do not necessarily coincide in societies. In addition, a history that focuses on popular culture soon has to face questions about the definitions and varied uses of terms like "popular" and "culture."[59] In the end, what holds such historiographic strategies together is their concern for the experience of ordinary people and their impact on the course of events in history.

Despite these problems, it seems clear that a people's-history approach is more suitable than traditional historical methods for studying Paul and his communities, since their social status and activities place them below the radar of traditional historiography. As a leader of such communities, Paul invoked memories that gave (new) life to tradition, establishing a tradition that gave authority to memory.[60] The resulting reciprocity requires us to reach beyond and behind Paul's version of memory and events to

---

heterogeneity which ascribes value to difference although it cannot always be named, i.e., knowing and valuing difference in and for itself. Rather than searching for origins, historicism has to investigate present and future conditions while acknowledging the sociohistorical embeddedness of the subject-effects. Secondly, heterogeneity in the postcolonial context views the colonized body as the subject of history; the Other is an *effect* and not some kind of essence. Consciousness is only the effect, albeit with *strategic* usefulness, of a plural and hybrid subject who is in a position to appropriate different discursive strategies and turn them against one another. Annamaria Carusi, "Post, Post and Post: Or, Where Is South African Literature in All This?" in *Past the Last Post: Theorizing Post-colonialism and Post-modernism* (ed. I. Adam, and H. Tiffin; New York: Harvester Wheatsheaf, 1981), 95–108.

59. Burke, "Overture," 10; Sharpe, "History From Below," 26–29; cf. Joseph Marchal, *The Politics of Heaven: Women, Gender, and Politics in the Study of Paul* (Minneapolis: Fortress, 2008), 26–33, 140 n. 86.

60. In Paul's use of texts, the power of literacy and the coercive potential of possessing the Scriptures is apparent. "Their [texts'] embeddedness and social functions are paradigmatic; but these become alive as we discover the way texts construct readers and 'reality' through acts of power, by silence and marginalization, as well as by unarticulated assumptions, by the values and hierarchies engendered, and by the authoritative voice claimed" (Lieu, *Christian Identity*, 25).

come closer to the different experiences of social reality that are revealed and invoked by Paul in his letters.[61]

5. Identity and Memory: Re-membering the Scriptures

5.1 The Founding Importance of Scriptures

A number of indicators suggest the importance of the Scriptures of Israel to the Pauline and other Jesus-follower communities. In the first place, the preservation of the Scriptures of Israel, presumably in Greek, along with other Jewish writings by the early followers of Jesus already constituted a primary, assertive act of remembering.[62] Secondly, any commonality or unity that existed within the first-century Jesus-follower movement was situated in and traced through myth and ethos, not through common structures of leadership,[63] at least in the early years when the Jesus-follower communities were being formed, as attested by the time-span of slightly more than a decade covered by Paul's letters.[64]

A third issue concerns the relationship between the Jesus traditions and the Scriptures of Israel in the identity formation of the early Jesus-followers. Samuel Byrskog concludes that the combination of historical and biographical approaches in the Gospels is an attempt to align the contemporary receivers of the Gospels with the decisive, identity-forming fact of their alignment with Jesus Christ in history.[65] In Paul's case, however,

---

61. "[M]emories are not one-way tracks.... If the past casts a shadow on the present through memory, the present also imposes on the past by means of memory" (Ben Xu, "Memory and the Ethnic Self: Reading Amy Tan's *The Joy Luck Club*," in Singh, Skerrett, and Hogan, *Memory, Narrative, and Identity*, 265).

62. Cf. Lieu, *Christian Identity*, 75; Ricoeur, "The Self in the Mirror," 206.

63. Cf. Mikael Telbe, "The Prototypical Christ-Believer: Early Christian Identity Formation in Ephesus," in Holmberg, *Exploring Early Christian Identity*, 115–38.

64. I include only the seven authentic Pauline letters, since the Deutero-Paulines (2 Thessalonians, Colossians, Ephesians, and the Pastorals) evidence a later development of the ongoing Pauline tradition(s). A study of memory and identity within the Deutero-Paulines falls outside the scope of this investigation.

65. Such connection is achieved by linking the Gospels' *Sitz im Leben* to the social memory of the groups of early Jesus-followers. According to Byrskog ("Memory and Identity," 33–57), the gospel *chreia* served a mnemonic purpose, bridging past and present while contributing to the groups' sense of belonging to the past and sharing a Christ-centered identity. Plotting the role of the Gospels in the construction of

these traditions did not occupy the same place or exhibit the same intensity as his use of the Scriptures, despite the importance that he attached to the coming of Jesus and his death and resurrection for grounding his understanding of the Gospel and his knowledge of at least some Jesus traditions.[66] "More important for Christian identity, then, was this prior history that found its climax in Jesus than any subsequent one that took its start from him."[67] For Paul, the Jesus narratives and traditions did not provide a history, nor did he use them as foundational in his letters.[68]

5.2 MEMORY AND RE-MEMBERING: POWER AND VULNERABILITY

In its use of texts to construe identity, memory exercises its power in a number of ways. Remembering assembles a historical narrative that provides a coherent continuity out of the discontinuities of past human experience. But it does more than explain the present; it also justifies the present.[69] In the process, memory often glosses over or even hides the complex

---

Christian identity becomes more complex, however, as the early communities become increasingly aware of the (unexpressed or not reflected upon) link between the Gospels and their own contemporary communities and turn to legitimating their own beliefs and practices through the story of Jesus (Lieu, *Christian Identity*, 87–88).

66. Although focusing more on the New Testament Gospel traditions, Kelber ("The Generative Force of Memory," 15–22) rightly bemoans the disregard for memory in New Testament studies. However, he appears to gloss over the involvement of the Scriptures in giving memory content, assisting in the continuous negotiation of the understanding the life and significance of Jesus, and providing a hermeneutical map for such understanding. Rather than claiming that "the Jesus tradition commenced not with archives, but from remembering" (Kelber, "The Generative Force of Memory," 18), it is more accurate to say that the tradition was invoked and re-membered through textual archives.

67. Lieu, *Christian Identity*, 94.

68. With the possible exception of 1 Cor 11:23–26. This tendency continues well into the second century, with Apostolic Fathers and apologists showing a relative lack of interest in the life of Jesus as found in the Synoptic Jesus traditions. Lieu (*Christian Identity*, 89) refers to the moral traditions found in the *Didache*, which connect far more strongly with the Torah than the Jesus traditions. The exception in the New Testament is the Acts of the Apostles, which stresses the continuity between Jesus and the church. Keightley ("Christian Collective Memory," 129–50) argues that Paul's familiarity with the Jesus traditions can be traced primarily to his participation in rituals practiced by the early followers of Jesus.

69. Lieu, *Christian Identity*, 62.

origins of certain traditions and conventions. In other words, forgetting is just as important as remembering. This fact is evident in the adage that history is written by the victors, as well as in the increasing acknowledgment that all historical constructions are perspectival, selective, and informed by needs and vested interests. The exclusion of the Other of history often amounts to selective amnesia.[70] In the construction of a narrative of identity, both remembering and forgetting are acts of power that regulate inclusion as well as exclusion.[71]

At the same time, memory is both fragile and vulnerable for a number of reasons, including the complex relationship between identity and time, which requires the maintenance of similarity while accommodating change; the encounter with others and otherness, which can constitute a threat to a group's sense of identity; and the heritage of founding violence which attends the inception of any historical community.[72] Moreover, cultural memory disallows any notion of the past as free from the pain of value judgments. The content and structure of what is remembered in cultural memory does not require the focus to be on "what actually happened." Instead, it centers on the meaning of the past for the present and how the present continues to exist in such remembrances.[73]

Returning to Paul, it is clear that the apostle used texts from the Jewish tradition to foster, structure, maintain, and negotiate identity within his communities of Jesus-followers.[74] For the majority of them, the Scriptures of Israel would not have been part of their previous traditions or cultures.[75]

---

70. In certain contexts the forgetting of texts is prearranged and remembering is privileged, as in the case of Qumran: "Where the experience of marginalization from actual power might seem to undermine certainty, an interpretation of Scripture that is available only by special divine revelation establishes an alternative identity, albeit one that is persuasive only to those already within" (Lieu, *Christian Identity*, 34).

71. Cf. Lieu, *Christian Identity*, 64.

72. Ricoeur, *Memory, History, Forgetting*, 81–83.

73. Assmann, *Religion and Cultural Memory*, 180.

74. "When dealing with apothegms and other traditions, Paul shows us the same willingness to paraphrase and even to encode for memory that a Pharisee might have utilized in learning Rabbinic tradition" (Alan F. Segal, *Life after Death: A History of the Afterlife in Western Religion* [New York: Doubleday, 2004], 400).

75. The point here is not to claim that Paul was unique (space does not allow for a comparative study) but rather to underline how he adopted the Jewish literary tradition as a distinctive choice against the better-known Graeco-Roman cultural and literary traditions (cf. Lieu, *Christian Identity*, 36).

This contrasted with the vital role of the Scriptures of Israel in Second Temple Judaism, where they marked out the identity of the Jewish people.[76] Fortunately, Paul's negotiation of the identity of the early Jesus-follower communities through the Scriptures did not depend upon meticulous exegesis (in the modern sense) of the Jewish Scriptures. Instead, he read the texts as a form of memory. Reading texts as memory underlines that remembering the self is not about the restoration of some original self but rather about re-membering, of putting past and present selves together, moment by moment, in a process of provisional (re)construction.[77] Such processes are at play in Paul's invocation of texts linked to the figure of Abraham in the Scriptures, where we see a complex interplay between texts, memory, and identity.

5.3 Pauline Texts and Practices: Abraham Texts[78]

In Gal 3:1–4:11 and Rom 4:1–25, Paul enlisted texts and interpretations pertaining to Abraham as part of his arguments. When Paul claims that the words he quotes from Gen 15:6 about Abraham (ἐπίστευσεν δὲ ᾿Αβραὰμ τῷ

---

76. Many examples can be cited, but, as we see from the *Letter of Aristeas*, much importance was given to the Scriptures of Israel as written texts that were available amid world literature as markers of Jewish identity; cf. Lieu, *Christian Identity*, 31–36.

77. On the one hand, "Christian thought, behaviour, attitudes, values, and self-understanding were forged textually," but on the other hand, "the multiple self-representations we encounter in the texts are themselves constructs" (Cameron, *Christianity and the Rhetoric of Empire*, 21, 32). So too "the Scriptures of Israel are themselves the expression of, and the consequence of, a process by which a coherent remembering of a common past and a shared experience of divine presence has been forged out of the inchoate multiple pasts, largely lost to us, of disparate peoples" (Lieu, *Christian Identity*, 67).

78. Paul's choice of Scriptures indicates that his inclusion of some texts was as important as his exclusion of others. Paul used a variety of traditions from Scripture, but his explicit citations come predominantly from four sets of traditions or "books" from the Scriptures of Israel: twenty-eight citations from Isaiah, twenty from the Psalms, fifteen from Genesis, and fifteen from Deuteronomy. No other book is cited more than five times. For a list of Old Testament books from which Paul quotes, including the number of times he uses each book, see Dietrich-Alex Koch, *Die Schrift als Zeuge des Evangeliums: Untersuchungen zur Verwendung und zum Verständnis der Schrift bei Paulus* (BHT 69; Tübingen: Mohr Siebeck, 1986), 33. Cf. Jeremy Punt, "Paul, Hermeneutics and the Scriptures of Israel," *Neot* 30 (1996): 377–425.

θεῷ καὶ ἐλογίσθη αὐτῷ εἰς δικαιοσύνην, Rom 4:3; cf. Gal 3:6)[79] apply equally to himself and his contemporaries[80] (οὐκ ἐγράφη δὲ δι' αὐτὸν μόνον ... ἀλλὰ καὶ δι' ἡμᾶς, Rom 4:23–24), the Scriptures not only inform his memory of the situation but also generate and legitimate new possibilities of self-understanding.[81] The Scriptures are the starting and orientation point for his argument here, as is often the case in Paul's letters. As we see elsewhere in the New Testament, Paul's quotations are introduced with brief introductory formulas such as γέγραπται (e.g., Gal 3:10) or ἡ γραφὴ λέγει (e.g., Rom 4:3) that he apparently thought needed no further explanation.[82] These formulae are indicative of the importance of the Scriptures in Paul's recollection of the past and their perceived significance for the present.[83]

In his letters to the Galatians and the Romans, however, Paul's claim upon the Scriptures of Israel was contentious, since others in the communities to which the letters were addressed also laid claim to these texts and traditions and drew conclusions that differed from Paul's. In Romans, various parts of the letter focus strongly on people with Jewish roots (e.g., Rom 2–3, 9–11), while historical evidence suggests a notable Jewish presence in the city even after Claudius's edict of 49 C.E. As far as Galatians is concerned, the contentious nature of Paul's claim on the Scriptures was even more accentuated given the difference of opinion between Paul and

---

79. Except for the spelling of "Abraham" in the LXX (Ἀβραμ), Paul's quote corresponds exactly to the wording found in Gen 15:6.

80. Cf. 1 Cor 10:11, "They were written also to serve as warnings for us" (ἐγράφη δὲ πρὸς νουθεσίαν ἡμῶν). See the discussion in Anthony C. Thiselton, *First Corinthians: A Shorter Exegetical and Pastoral Commentary* (Grand Rapids: Eerdmans, 2006), 152–55.

81. The same is claimed for the formation of Scripture in Second Temple Judaism after 70 C.E.; cf. Lieu, *Christian Identity*, 34.

82. A wide range of intertextual links with the Scriptures of Israel is found in the Pauline letters, including explicit quotation, implicit allusion, symbolism, and conceptual links. Cf. R. B. Hays, *Echoes of Scripture in the Letters of Paul* (New Haven: Yale University Press, 1989); Punt, "Paul, Hermeneutics and the Scriptures of Israel."

83. It is important to investigate the particular narrative of self-understanding that is presented in the scriptural narratives, but the focus here is on how such narratives "provoke further retellings or re-memberings in new settings" (Lieu, *Christian Identity*, 68). In other words, the focus is not on the long history of debate about the patriarchal narratives and whether Paul correctly understood the identity cues constructed by and conveyed in the Genesis texts but rather on how Paul took clues and utilized notions from the Abraham narrative for his own purposes, and what these purposes were.

the other apostles (Gal 1–2) and the presence of the Judaizers (e.g., Gal 2:14), who were promoting the active pursuit of a Jewish life even though their roots may have been elsewhere.[84]

While Abraham is central to Paul's arguments in both instances, the argument in Gal 3–4 soon shifts to a concern with Abraham's descendants,[85] whereas in Rom 4 the focus remains squarely on Abraham. Nevertheless, in both texts the story of Abraham as mediated through Paul's use of the Scriptures is presented as the basis for the identity of the Pauline communities in Galatia and Rome. Here we see how texts can be used to mediate identity and how identity likewise formats or re-members texts. Even more than reciprocity, we see the *reflexivity* of cultural memory at work. Cultural memory provides a framework for interpreting the past as well as defining the self-image of the group, which in turn becomes a resource for explaining or revising the existing cultural memory: cultural memory is reflexive.[86] Certain textual narratives such as those about Abraham were central in Paul's memory, though not simply as reservoirs of meaning. For Paul, texts were part of an ongoing identity negotiation process in which earlier texts were reworked and re-membered for new and different pur-

---

84. Here we may already have the earliest example of a case where a claimed history serves the purpose of legitimation and drawing boundaries, not so much against Judaism as against "competing claimants to a common identity" (cf. Lieu, *Christian Identity*, 96; contra Runesson, "Inventing Christian Identity," 87, who disavows the idea that Christians and Jews in the first century claimed shared origins).

85. Cf. also Gal 4:21–5:1, where Paul reconstructs the place of Abraham's wives in the history of Israel and relates them to the followers of Jesus (Punt, "Hermeneutics in Identity Formation", 3–8; cf. Lieu, *Christian Identity*, 79–80). For a similar identity reconstruction operation, see Josephus, *Ant.* 1.12.2–4 (§§214–221); 3.9.3 (§213), where the contemporary Arabs became the descendant of Ishmael (cf. Lieu, *Christian Identity*, 69). Such interpretive moves are common in both the history of exegesis and rewritings of history (80).

86. Assmann, "Collective Memory," 132–33. Of the six important functions that Assmann identified for cultural memory within communities and groups, the final one is reflexivity. Cultural memory is reflexive in three ways: (a) practice-reflexive in reinterpreting social practices through proverbs and rituals; (b) self-reflexive in drawing on itself to explain, justify, and control; and (c) reflexive of its own image through its preoccupation with its own social system (Assmann, "Collective Memory," 132). Assmann's six functions of cultural memory overlap, but his basic emphases remain useful.

poses[87] in changed circumstances.[88] In this way, Paul's invocation and reworking of the Scriptures provided a memory map for plotting his own and his communities' identities.[89]

In recalling the Abraham stories in Gal 3–4 and Rom 4, Paul traced a common thread from the past to the experienced realities of the present through both continuities and breaches, so Paul's story about Abraham is neither stable nor closed.[90] In defining his communities' identity, Paul's use of memory to invoke and employ texts and his use of texts to invoke and structure memory created a reciprocally interlinked and complex situation. Texts became vehicles for memory, while memory not only invoked texts but also directed the use, meaning, and application of such texts.

5.3.1. Scriptures Related/Mediated through Memory: Re/constructing Identity

In the oral context of the first century, collective or cultural memory established, kept alive, and transmitted scriptural traditions. Jan Assmann has

---

87. Elsewhere in the New Testament, the author of 2 Peter calls on his readers not to forget but to remember (3:8), listing scriptural stories that illustrate God's judgment while providing both negative and positive models, a point that is made explicit in 2 Pet 2:6. The letter of James also contains many invocations of scriptural figures such as Abraham and others.

88. This applies not only to Paul but also to the use of the Scriptures in the rest of the New Testament. In some cases, texts arise as the products of a period when traditions are under transition. Historical, political, cultural, and societal processes of change can place religious identities under stress, and texts emerging from such times testify to the ways in which people coped with such situations. At other times, texts take up other texts and rework and reinterpret them so that they become formative—in an interactive way—for the religious identities negotiated by communities. The relationship between biblical texts and identity is analogous to the complex reciprocal relationship between text and context: literary texts do not merely reflect historical reality—they play a vital role in the construction of both past and present realities.

89. Many scholars insist that Gal 3:10–14 exhibits the familiar practice of resolving an apparent contrast between two texts, the one (Deut 27:26) insisting on nomistic obedience in lieu of being cursed and the other (Hab 2:4) claiming life through justification by faith, by reference to a third text (Deut 27:26) that speaks of a curse resting on a crucified person. Paul, however, plots the situation in terms of the Abraham narratives, arguing that Deut 27:26 can be applied to Christ as a way to mediate Abraham's blessing (ἡ εὐλογία τοῦ Ἀβραάμ) to the nations (εἰς τὰ ἔθνη).

90. Cf. Lieu, *Christian Identity*, 97.

identified six important functions for cultural memory within communities and groups. The primary function is what he calls "the concretion of identity" or, more simply, the *construction* of identity. "Cultural memory preserves the store of knowledge from which a group derives an awareness of its unity and peculiarity."[91] It is through this knowledge that the boundaries of the group are established and distinctions made between insiders and outsiders, providing resources for the members' awareness of unity and particularity. In both Galatians and Romans, Paul textually recalled the figure of Abraham, insisting on his importance in the past and present. Yet Paul himself made no explicit claim to physical descent from Abraham. While a vague notion of lineage might have been present in the Jewish part of the community in Rome, the rest of the community could not even claim that much—and certainly not the Galatian community (cf. later, in Gal 4:21–5:1).[92] Physical descent is not the basis for the claims that Paul makes (cf. Gal 3:29);[93] rather, an appeal to memory hides his complex relationship to the Abraham narratives.

No memory can fully preserve the past, which makes *reconstructing*[94] a vital function of memory. Memory relates its knowledge to a contemporary situation according to the requirements of newer generations.[95] Paul's invocation of the Abraham narratives is matched or even exceeded by the way he redescribes, or retools, Abraham for his purposes. In appropriating Abraham for the followers of Jesus, he asserts that they rather than the Jews were truly following in Abraham's footsteps.[96] Not only did he claim authenticity for the new movement; he also asserted that it simultaneously

---

91. Assmann, "Collective Memory," 130.

92. Jeremy Punt, "Revealing Rereading. Part 1: Pauline Allegory in Gal 4:21–5:1," *Neot* 40 (2006): 87–100; Jeremy Punt, "Revealing Rereading. Part 2: Paul and the Wives of the Father of Faith in Galatians 4:21–5:1," *Neot* 40 (2006): 101–18.

93. Genealogies are powerful devices for legitimizing claims to continuity; cf. Lieu, *Christian Identity*, 78. In Matthew, Abraham grounds the genealogy of Jesus (Matt 1:1), while Luke goes beyond Abraham to Adam (Luke 3:34–38) and Hebrews makes Abraham central to the genealogy of faith (Heb 11:8–19).

94. Reconstruction is enabled through two modes of cultural memory: as potentiality (the archive's accumulated resources constituting an interpretative horizon) and as actuality (the objectivized meaning given meaning and relevance by the contemporary context) (Assman, "Collective Memory," 130).

95. Ibid.

96. As Lieu (*Christian Identity*, 84–86) shows, "The argument from antiquity remains a fundamental weapon in the armoury of Christian apologetic." Soon it

represented and restored the ancient and original truth of God's interaction with people. Apart from Gen 15:6, he invokes parts of two other LXX texts, Gen 17:5 (πατέρα πολλῶν ἐθνῶν τέθεικά σε) and Gen 15:5 (οὕτως ἔσται τὸ σπέρμα σου), in Rom 4:17–18 (cf. Gal 3:16) and applies them to the audience of Romans. For Paul, the new movement (based on a new covenant; cf. his citation of Jer 31:31 in 1 Cor 11:25) was not really new but, rather, a reincarnation of the original. This view raised questions about the validity of the claims of other (Jewish) groups.

One function of cultural memory that Assmann did not include in the six characteristics that he identified[97] is memory's involvement in *contesting* identity through narrative. The dominant discourse in a society tends to be the discourse of the dominant. In such a context, marginalized discourses can only survive if they successfully modify or replace those that they challenge. Thus textuality comprises more than an articulation of identity, since textuality is also the field on which identity is contested.[98] Memory is also implicated in this contestation of identity, since memory is involved in structuring identity. This becomes clear when we examine three other functions of cultural memory that are useful for describing how Paul's memory was mediated through the Scriptures.

5.3.2. Memory Related/Mediated through the Scriptures: Formation, Organization, and Normativity

In addition to accounting for how memory enabled and often facilitated the currency and value of the Scriptures of Israel, cultural memory helps us to see how for Paul these writings contributed to, enabled, and even co-constituted the memory of the group. Even in Paul's oral environment, memory conveyed through texts played an important role in the recollection of what had been said and what had happened in the past, and so

---

became not only a matter of self-justification but also of antagonism, manifest in accusations of Jewish obduracy and discontinuity.

97. Assmann, "Collective Memory," 125–133.

98. Lieu, *Christian Identity*, 30; cf. 61: "Texts construct a world; they do this out of multiple worlds, including textual ones, that they and their authors and readers already inhabit and experience as 'reality'; that new world itself becomes part of subsequent 'reality' within and out of which new constructions may be made. Yet this is not a self-generating system: constructions and worlds interact and clash with others, whether they are seen as congenial or as alien."

helped to construe his cultural memory. Scriptures were used as both a model and a resource for subsequent rememberings.[99] But the use of allusive texts and language that outsiders fail to understand is important in another way: such texts provide and strengthen the bond between group members. Allusive texts can serve an important function in assisting with the drawing of group boundaries and reinforcing feelings of belonging to a group.[100]

Assmann identifies three additional characteristics of cultural memory—formation, organization, and obligation—that are useful for describing Paul's invocation of memory through the Scriptures. In the first place, cultural memory has the capacity for *formation* or objectification, generating a transportable, collective shared meaning that does not depend only on writing.[101] As is evident in Paul's extended contemplations in Gal 3:1–4:11 and Rom 4:1–25, Abraham[102] became a scripturally defined figure in the Pauline letters.[103] Paul expected his audiences to share in the story of Abraham and to emulate him as an example of faith. In other words, Paul wanted them to derive their contemporary identity from his recollection of Abraham's past, reflecting the way his own memory was construed through and carried by the Scriptures.

Secondly, memory contributes to *organization*, which according to Assmann implies a "cultivated" specialization and institutional support of communication.[104] Consistent with our earlier discussion of the construc-

---

99. Ibid., 67.

100. Cf. D. C. Allison Jr., *Scriptural Allusions in the New Testament: Light from the Dead Sea Scrolls* (North Richland Hills, Tex.: Bibal, 2000), 7.

101. Assmann, "Collective Memory," 130–31.

102. Abraham is mentioned by name nineteen times in the Pauline letters: Rom 4:1, 2, 3, 9, 12, 13, 16; 9:7; 11:1; 2 Cor 11:22; Gal 3:6, 7, 8, 9, 14, 16, 18, 29; 4:22. Further references to Abraham are found throughout the New Testament: in all four Gospels, Acts, Hebrews, James, and 1 Peter. Ricoeur refers to Abraham as "a more or less fictional character" ("The Self in the Mirror," 222).

103. Lieu, *Christian Identity*, 37. Other important figures, events, or *topoi* can be identified in the Pauline letters; on Paul's use of the exodus tradition, see, e.g. Sylvia Keesmaat, *Paul and His Story: (Re)interpreting the Exodus Tradition* (JSNTSup 181; Sheffield: Sheffield Academic Press, 1999).

104. Assmann, "Collective Memory," 131. In the context where a group maintains a special relationship with certain texts, three dimensions of cultivation can be identified: cultivation of the text (textual transmission processes), cultivation of meaning (comprising all of the various dimensions of hermeneutical activity), and cultivation

tion of narratives and the contestation of identity between dominant and marginalized discourses, Paul's focus on the faith of Abraham leaves out of consideration his acts of unfaithfulness (cf. Rom 4:20), which ranged from twice offering his wife to the king of Egypt to using his own machinations to accomplish the divine promise about offspring. Paul also ignores Sarah's prominent role in a number of other situations in Abraham's life and Abraham's rather dismissive attitude toward another wife and her son.[105] Here we see both the positive and the negative aspects of collective memory. On the one hand, narratives can be liberating, as the products of memory (and their meaning) are shaped through selection, elaboration, and shifts in context.[106] But memory can also use these same processes in a more ominous manner. Problems of belonging and not belonging, of visibility and invisibility, are always part of the construction and maintenance of identity. But such processes also entail the exercising of power[107] and strategies of exclusion through forgetting, whether as deliberate amnesia, selective memory, or remembering otherwise.

Finally, memory entails *obligation* insofar as a normative self-image is propped up by a requisite value set and differentiations in importance[108] "which structure the cultural supply of knowledge and symbols."[109] Our earlier discussion of the tension between memory and history is crucial here, since cultural memory, unlike history, *formatively* appeals to certain values in structuring its body of knowledge while also *normatively* entail-

---

of mediation (retranslation of the text through its incorporation in education and upbringing).

105. Cf. Punt, "Revealing Rereading. Part 1"; Punt, "Revealing Rereading. Part 2."
106. Shostak, "Maxine Hong Kingston's Fake Books," 235–38.
107. "Remembering as well as forgetting—that is, the construction of the narrative of identity—are both acts of power and means of maintaining power; if they include, they of necessity will also exclude" (Lieu, *Christian Identity*, 65), and, at a deeper level, "Through its cultural heritage a society becomes visible to itself and to others. Which past becomes evident in that heritage and which values emerge in its identificatory appropriation tells us much about the constitution and tendencies of a society" (Assmann, "Collective Memory," 133).
108. In history, such perspectival evaluation of a heritage is frowned upon (Assmann, "Collective Memory," 131).
109. Assmann, "Collective Memory," 131–32. "The binding character of the knowledge preserved in cultural memory has two aspects: the *formative* one in its educative, civilizing, and humanizing functions and the *normative* one in its function of providing rules of conduct" (132).

ing certain forms of conduct. The *formative* influence of Paul's patriarchalism is evident in his fabrication of Abraham's narrative (i.e., his omission of Abraham's lack of faith and Sarah's important role in Abraham's life), while the *normative* nature of his appeal, in Gal 3–4, to living a life of freedom and his statements about justification and its existential impact on all followers of Jesus, in Rom 4, is readily apparent.

6. Conclusion: Pauline Texts as Cultural Formation

The Scriptures of Israel were the primary, though not the sole, constituent artifacts in Paul's cultural memory. They were indispensable for his thinking about group identity and cohesion, as well as instrumental in his construing and reconstructing identity. His selective recalling of the Abraham narrative through the texts of the Scriptures was vital for positioning his arguments. But "memory is not just a narrative, even though it does have to take a narrative form; it is more importantly an existential relation between the past and the present, projecting a future as well."[110] The notion of cultural memory, which attempts to link the three elements of memory (the contemporized past), culture, and the group (or community),[111] puts Paul's use of the Scriptures of Israel into perspective, particularly their use in negotiating the identity of the early communities of Jesus followers.

One question remains to be considered: to what extent did Paul, consciously or otherwise, engage in cultural formation? Did he intend that his use of the Scriptures for the sake of cultural memory would leave a lasting legacy in the form of practices, documents, and so on that would become cultural artifacts? Even if Paul himself did not deliberately position his letters as artifacts of cultural memory, we know from the Deutero-Paulines that his initial efforts in using the Scriptures to negotiate identity soon resulted in his letters becoming cultural markers for the developing Christian community. Ironically, the emerging Pauline supremacy in early Christian theologies relegated the Scriptures to the theological backwaters,[112] where their use was filtered through a Pauline framework.

---

110. Xu, "Memory and the Ethnic Self," 266.
111. Assmann, "Collective Memory," 129.
112. In the centuries after Paul, users of the new Christian literary corpus, which included the writings of Paul and others that were associated with him, assumed an increasingly more tense position towards the Scriptures of Israel. "The thrust of the development of what was to become the New Testament was that these texts should

Over the centuries, a decidedly Pauline framework increasingly became and remained the grounding artifact in Christian cultural memory.[113] The unfortunate result was that Christians largely forgot about how Scriptures, memory, and identity had converged in Paul's arguments.

Bibliography

Allison, Dale C., Jr. *Scriptural Allusions in the New Testament: Light from the Dead Sea Scrolls*. North Richland Hills, Tex.: Bibal, 2000.

Assmann, Jan. "Collective Memory and Cultural Identity." *New German Critique* 65 (1995): 125–33.

———. "Cultural Memory: Script, Recollection, and Political Identity in Early Civilizations." *Historiography East and West* 1 (2003): 154–77.

———. *Religion and Cultural Memory: Ten Studies*. Cultural Memory in the Present. Translated by R. Livingstone. Stanford, Calif.: Stanford University Press, 2006.

Braxton, Bradley R. *The Tyranny of Resolution: 1 Corinthians 7:17–24*. SBLDS 181. Atlanta: Society of Biblical Literature, 2000.

Burke, Peter. "Overture: The New History; Its Past and Its Future." Pages 1–23 in *New Perspectives on Historical Writing*. Edited by Peter Burke. University Park: Pennsylvania State University Press, 1991.

Byrskog, Samuel. "Christology and Identity in an Intertextual Perspective: The Glory of Adam in the Narrative Substructure of Paul's Letter to the Romans." Pages 1–18 in *Identity Formation in the New Testament*. Edited by Bengt Holmberg and Mikael Winninge. WUNT 227. Tübingen: Mohr Siebeck, 2008.

———. "Memory and Identity in the Gospels: A New Perspective." Pages 33–57 in *Exploring Early Christian Identity*. Edited by Bengt Holmberg. WUNT 226. Tübingen: Mohr Siebeck, 2008.

---

act as the primary hermeneutical key for the preservation and interpretation of the Jewish Scriptures" (Lieu, *Christian Identity*, 51).

113. Another lasting effect of the identity-formation process among the early Jesus-followers was the construction of definite boundary lines positing insiders and outsiders, a situation which has over the course of the centuries acquired an even more menacing if not belligerent tone than it had in the first century c.e. "If the danger of all identity-construction is its tendency to 'demonize' the other, a tendency the Christian tradition has not avoided, then the importance of the often apparent chaos of the study of early Christianity is its demonstration of the shifting identity of the other, now you, now me" (Lieu, *Christian Identity*, 209).

Cameron, Averil. *Christianity and the Rhetoric of Empire. The Development of Christian Discourse.* Sather Classical Lectures 57. Berkeley: University of California Press, 1991.
Carusi, Annamaria. "Post, Post and Post. Or, Where Is South African Literature in All This?" Pages 95–108 in *Past the Last Post: Theorizing Post-colonialism and Post-modernism.* Edited by I. Adam and H. Tiffin. New York: Harvester Wheatsheaf, 1991.
Dehay, Terry. "Narrating Memory." Pages 26–44 in *Memory, Narrative, and Identity: New Essays in Ethnic American Literatures.* Edited by Amritjit Singh, Joseph T. Skerrett Jr., and Robert E. Hogan. Boston: Northeastern University Press, 1994.
Duling, Dennis C. "Social Memory and Biblical Studies: Theory, Method, and Application." *BTB* 36 (2006): 2–4.
Esler, Philip F. *Conflict and Identity in Romans: The Social Setting of Paul's Letter.* Minneapolis: Fortress, 2003.
Gandhi, Leila. *Postcolonial Theory: A Critical Introduction.* New York: Columbia University Press, 1998.
Guijarro, Santiago. "Cultural Memory and Group Identity in Q." *BTB* 37 (2007): 90–100.
Halbwachs, Maurice. *On Collective Memory.* Edited, translated, and with an introduction by Lewis A. Coser. The Heritage of Sociology. Chicago: University of Chicago Press, 1992.
Hays, Richard B. *Echoes of Scripture in the Letters of Paul.* New Haven: Yale University Press, 1989.
Holmberg, Bengt. *Exploring Early Christian Identity.* WUNT 226. Tübingen: Mohr Siebeck, 2008.
———. "Understanding the First Hundred Years of Christian Identity." Pages 1–32 in *Exploring Early Christian Identity.* Edited by Bengt Holmberg. WUNT 226. Tübingen: Mohr Siebeck, 2008.
Horsley, Richard A. "Unearthing a People's History." Pages 1–20 in *Christian Origins.* Vol. 1 of *A People's History of Christianity.* Edited by Richard A. Horsley. Minneapolis: Fortress, 2005.
Keesmaat, Sylvia C. *Paul and His Story: (Re)interpreting the Exodus Tradition.* JSNTSup 181. Sheffield: Sheffield Academic Press, 1999.
Keightley, Georgia M. "Christian Collective Memory and Paul's Knowledge of Jesus." Pages 129–50 in *Memory, Tradition, and Text: Uses of the Past in Early Christianity.* SemeiaSt 52. Atlanta: Society of Biblical Literature, 2005.

Kelber, Werner. "The Generative Force of Memory: Early Christian Traditions as Processes of Remembering." *BTB* 36 (2006): 15–22.

Koch, Dietrich-Alex. *Die Schrift als Zeuge des Evangeliums: Untersuchungen zur Verwendung und zum Verständnis der Schrift bei Paulus.* BHT 69. Tübingen: Mohr Siebeck, 1986.

Lieu, Judith M. *Christian Identity in the Jewish and Graeco-Roman World.* Oxford: Oxford University Press, 2004.

———. *Neither Jew nor Greek: Constructing Early Christianity.* Studies of the New Testament and Its World. London: T&T Clark, 2002.

Marchal, Joseph A. *The Politics of Heaven: Women, Gender, and Empire in the Study of Paul.* Paul in Critical Contexts. Minneapolis: Fortress, 2008.

Mendels, Doron. Introduction to *On Memory: An Interdisciplinary Approach.* Edited by Doron Mendels. New York: Lang, 2007.

Millar, Fergus N. *The Emperor in the Roman World (31 BC–AD 337).* London: Duckworth, 1977.

Nora, Pierre. "Between Memory and History: *Les Lieux de Mémoire.*" *Representations* 26 (1989): 7–24.

Olick, J. K. "Products, Processes, and Practices: A Non-Reificatory Approach to Collective Memory." *BTB* 36 (2006): 5–14.

Punt, Jeremy. "Hermeneutics in Identity Formation: Paul's Use of Genesis in Galatians 4. *HTS Teologiese Studies/Theological Studies* 67 (2011): 1–9. doi:10.4102/hts.v67i1.846.

———. "Jude and the Others: Hermeneutics, Identity, Conflict." *South African Baptist Journal of Theology* 17 (2008): 149–62.

———. "Paul, Hermeneutics and the Scriptures of Israel." *Neot* 30 (1996): 377–425.

———. "Revealing Rereading. Part 1: Pauline Allegory in Gal 4:21–5:1." *Neot* 40 (2006): 87–100.

———. "Revealing Rereading. Part 2: Paul and the Wives of the Father of Faith in Galatians 4:21–5:1." *Neot* 40 (2006): 101–18.

Ricoeur, Paul. *Memory, History, Forgetting.* Translated by K. Blamey and D. Pellauer. Chicago: University of Chicago Press, 2004.

———. "Narrative Identity." *Philosophy Today* 35 (1991): 73–81.

———. "The Self in the Mirror of the Scriptures." Pages 201–20 in *The Whole and Divided Self.* Edited by D. E. Aune and J. McCarthy. New York: Crossroad, 1997.

Rosenfield, Israel. "Memory and Identity." *New Literary History* 26 (1995): 197–203.

Runesson, Anders. "Inventing Christian Identity: Paul, Ignatius, and Theodosius I." Pages 59–92 in *Exploring Early Christian Identity*. Edited by Bengt Holmberg. WUNT 226. Tübingen: Mohr Siebeck, 2008.

Segal, Alan F. *Life after Death: A History of the Afterlife in Western Religion*. New York: Doubleday, 2004.

Sharpe, Jim. "History From Below." Pages 24–41 in *New Perspectives on Historical Writing*. Edited by Peter Burke. University Park: Pennsylvania State University Press, 1991.

Shostak, Debra. "Maxine Hong Kingston's Fake Books." Pages 233–60 in *Memory, Narrative, and Identity: New Essays in Ethnic American Literatures*. Edited by Amritjit. Singh, Joseph T. Skerrett Jr., and Robert E. Hogan. Boston: Northeastern University Press, 1994.

Singh, Amritjit, Joseph T. Skerrett Jr., and Robert E. Hogan. "Introduction." Pages 3–25 in *Memory, Narrative, and Identity: New Essays in Ethnic American Literatures*. Edited by Amritjit Singh, Joseph T. Skerrett Jr., and Robert E. Hogan. Boston: Northeastern University Press, 1994.

Telbe, Mikael. "The Prototypical Christ-Believer: Early Christian Identity Formation in Ephesus." Pages 115–38 in *Exploring Early Christian Identity*. Edited by Bengt Holmberg. WUNT 226. Tübingen: Mohr Siebeck, 2008.

Thiselton, Anthony C. *First Corinthians: A Shorter Exegetical and Pastoral Commentary*. Grand Rapids: Eerdmans, 2006.

Xu, Ben. "Memory and the Ethnic Self: Reading Amy Tan's *The Joy Luck Club*." Pages 261–77 in *Memory, Narrative, and Identity: New Essays in Ethnic American Literatures*. Edited by Amritjit Singh, Joseph T. Skerrett Jr., and Robert E. Hogan. Boston: Northeastern University Press, 1994.

Young, Robert J. C. *Postcolonialism: An Historical Introduction*. London: Blackwell, 2001.

Paul among the Storytellers: Reading Romans 11 in the Context of Rewritten Bible

Bruce N. Fisk

Only a generation ago it was possible for a ranking Pauline scholar to offer a learned treatise on Paul's relationship to Palestinian Judaism and say virtually nothing about how Scripture functioned in either context. Times have changed. The quest for Paul's "Jewishness" inspired by E. P. Sanders (among others),[1] combined with the increasing availability of primary sources and the literary turn in late twentieth-century biblical scholarship, meant it was inevitable that Paul's use of Scripture would come to be compared closely with the way Scripture functioned among the tradents of Second Temple Judaism. Thus today the claim that Paul's use of Scripture bears a family resemblance to that of other Second Temple tradents requires little or no defense. The following claims represent the current consensus.

1. Oral tradition. As a trained Pharisee, Paul inherited a rich tradition of oral biblical interpretation (1 Cor 10:4; cf. Gal 1:14; Acts 22:3). As James Kugel has elegantly demonstrated, these early oral traditions included a "common store of biblical exegesis" as well as a set of common orientations, sensibilities, understandings of canon, and concerns for contemporary relevance.[2]

---

1. E.g., Joseph Bonsirven, *Exégèse rabbinique et exégèse paulinienne* (Paris: Beauchesne et ses fils, 1939); W. D. Davies, *Paul and Rabbinic Judaism: Some Rabbinic Elements in Pauline Theology* (New York: Harper & Row, 1948); Joseph A. Fitzmyer, "The Use of Explicit Old Testament Quotations in Qumran Literature and in the New Testament," *NTS* 7 (1961): 297–333.

2. James Kugel, *In Potiphar's House: The Interpretive Life of Biblical Texts* (Cambridge: Harvard University Press, 1994), 266.

2. Biblical commentary. Paul's appeals to Scripture were not principally driven by his desire to *explain* the OT. The *commentary* genre was, after all, relatively undeveloped in Paul's day.[3] However much his oral discourses and synagogue sermons included running biblical commentary, Paul's apostolic correspondence was less expositional than it was theological, pastoral, and rhetorical.

3. Exegetical rules. Paul does not expound Scripture by systematically applying pre-existing exegetical rules. More determinative than received techniques were his newly formed convictions about the centrality of Jesus' death and resurrection in God's plan for both Israel and the nations.[4]

4. Worldview. Although Paul's approach to Scripture tended to be charismatic and imaginative, he remained firmly grounded in prevailing Jewish theology, including its eschatological expectations, its assumptions about biblical and historical continuity, and its assurance of God's covenant faithfulness.

Paul the Storyteller

No one claims that the role of Scripture in pre-rabbinic Judaism was monolithic or that Paul's "Jewishness" precluded "Hellenistic" influences on his biblical interpretation.[5] What *is* broadly acknowledged is that Paul's varied uses of Scripture—including his assumptions, citation techniques, hermeneutical strategies, and rhetorical appeals—lie well within the broad spectrum of Jewish exegetical literature produced during the Second Temple period. Paul, all agree, did not invoke Scripture in a hermeneu-

---

3. I define *commentary* as explanatory composition that demarcates clearly between authoritative *traditum* and its *traditio*. (I take this pair of terms from Michael Fishbane, *Biblical Interpretation in Ancient Israel* [Oxford: Oxford University Press, 1985], 6 and passim, who in turn credits D. Knight.) Early exemplars are Philo's allegories and Qumran's pesher mode of interpretation. As for whether such works were *typical* of early Jewish interpretation, see further Kugel, *In Potiphar's House*.

4. Richard Hays, *Echoes of Scripture in the Letters of Paul* (New Haven: Yale University Press, 1989), 12–13, 160–61 and passim.

5. Francis Watson, *Paul and the Hermeneutics of Faith* (Edinburgh: T&T Clark, 2004), 18; Bruce N. Fisk, "Paul: Life and Letters," in *The Face of New Testament Studies* (ed. Scot McKnight and Grant R. Osborne; Grand Rapids: Baker, 2004), 301–6; Hans J. Schoeps, *Paul* (Philadelphia: Westminster, 1961), 26, 37, 47; Donald A. Hagner, "Paul in Modern Jewish Thought," in *Pauline Studies* (ed. Donald A. Hagner and Murray J. Harris; Exeter: Paternoster, 1980), 143–65.

tical vacuum: the *Scripture* that Paul knew, and to which he frequently appealed, was always *Scripture-interpreted*. Israel didn't simply drink from a rock; it "drank from a *spiritual, following* rock" (1 Cor 10:4). The fact that Paul could cite as Scripture a Greek translation of the "original" illustrates nicely the fuzzy boundary between *traditum* and *traditio*—between Scripture and commentary.[6] Sharp distinctions between Paul's text and its interpretation, then, may be anachronistic and historically naive. Paul is certainly more than the sum of his postbiblical influences,[7] but his often-novel Christo- and ecclesio-centric readings of Scripture do not emerge *ex nihilo*. If Paul the interpreter was sometimes more radical than some of his peers, if he had his own unique exegetical spin, it was not because he stood *outside* the Jewish exegetical tradition but because, standing *within* it, he read his text tradition by a different light: the radiance of the resurrection of a crucified messiah.[8]

The aim of this paper is to offer further evidence that on this matter of interpreting Israel's Scriptures, there are good reasons to bring Paul into conversation with his Jewish contemporaries. More narrowly, it will contend that Paul's letters share several notable features with the genre known to us, since Geza Vermes, as "rewritten Bible." Members of this collection—Jubilees, Genesis Apocryphon, Pseudo-Philo's *Liber Antiquitatum Biblicarum*, Josephus's *Antiquities*, Philo's *Moses*—model their

---

6. Reflecting the current consensus on Paul's principle relationship with the Greek Old Testament are Dietrich-Alex Koch, *Die Schrift als Zeuge des Evangeliums: Untersuchungen zur Verwendung und zum Verstandnis der Schrift bei Paulus* (BHT 69; Tübingen: Mohr-Siebeck, 1986); Christopher D. Stanley, *Paul and the Language of Scripture: Citation Technique in the Pauline Epistles and Contemporary Literature* (SNTSMS 74; Cambridge: Cambridge University Press, 1992); and J. Ross Wagner, *Heralds of the Good News: Isaiah and Paul "in Concert" in the Letter to the Romans* (NovTSup 101; Leiden: Brill, 2002).

7. See Fisk, *Do You Not Remember? Scripture, Story, and Exegesis in the Rewritten Bible of Pseudo-Philo* (Sheffield: Sheffield Academic Press, 2001), 77–78; Hays, *Echoes of Scripture*, 11.

8. This point emerged clearly in the post-*Echoes* dialogue between Richard Hays, Craig Evans, and James Sanders. In substantial agreement with Evans, Hays writes, "Paul's discourse is performed within the linguistic symphony (or cacophony, as the case may be) of his culture." See Craig A. Evans and James A. Sanders, eds., *Paul and the Scriptures of Israel* (JSNTSup 83; Sheffield: JSOT Press, 1993). The quotation is from Richard Hays, *The Conversion of the Imagination: Paul as Interpreter of Israel's Scripture* (Grand Rapids: Eerdmans, 2005), 165, where Hays's response is reprinted. Cf. Donald Hagner, "Paul in Modern Jewish Thought," 157–59.

narrative framework on Scripture's historical books but only rarely do they distinguish postbiblical traditions from biblical material. Their biblical exegesis is thus implicit and unmarked, advanced through narrative embellishments, omissions, and alterations. Often they assume their readers' knowledge of the biblical precursor.[9] These works of so-called rewritten Bible (RB) represent a vibrant early stage of Jewish biblical interpretation inspired by, and extended from, the exegesis latent within the Hebrew Bible itself.[10] RB remains an underutilized resource in the task of assessing Paul's appropriations of Scripture in his Jewish context. Indeed, Pseudo-Philo—arguably the least sectarian and most "Palestinian" of the bunch—may rank among the most illuminating of Paul's hermeneutical conversation partners. Both Paul and Pseudo-Philo wrote to assure readers that God's rule was intact and that God's plan was unfolding as it should, both advanced these claims through lively engagement with Scripture, and both believed that God's intimate, sustained involvement in Israel's affairs meant that meaningful correspondences *in history* were inevitable.[11] But whereas Pseudo-Philo found those corre-

---

9. E.g., 1QapGen 21:5; Jub. 31:2; *L.A.B.* 2:1, 9:3, 12:5, 18:5.

10. Shown preeminently by Fishbane, *Biblical Interpretation*. On the generic features, exemplars, and modes of exegesis in "rewritten Bible," see Bruce N. Fisk, "Rewritten Bible in Pseudepigrapha and Qumran," in *Dictionary of New Testament Background* (ed. Craig A. Evans and Stanley E. Porter; Downers Grove, Ill.: InterVarsity Press, 2000), 947–48.

11. Cf. Frederick J. Murphy, *Pseudo-Philo: Rewriting the Bible* (Oxford: Oxford University Press, 1993), 16, 226; Howard Jacobson, *A Commentary on Pseudo-Philo's Liber Antiquitatum Biblicarum* (2 vols.; Leiden: Brill, 1996), 241; Richard Bauckham, "The *Liber Antiquitatum Biblicarum* of Pseudo-Philo and the Gospels as 'Midrash,'" in *Gospel Perspectives III: Studies in Midrash and Historiography* (ed. R. T. France and D. Wenham; Sheffield: JSOT Press, 1983), 33–76. N. T. Wright traces these themes across Second Temple literature in *The New Testament and the People of God*, vol. 1: *Christian Origins and the Question of God* (Minneapolis: Augsburg Fortress, 1992), 215–23. As with Paul, Pseudo-Philo's claims about correlations *in history* reflect his hermeneutical convictions *about Scripture*, i.e., that it is a coherent and self-interpreting narrative. Scripture was not simply a fund of wisdom sayings, rhetorical devices, and theological symbols; for both tradents it was an important weapon in their exegetical arsenals. Thus both communicated their beliefs about God and covenant not only *explicitly* but also *implicitly* in the way they read and interpreted Israel's Scripture (cf. Hays, *Echoes of Scripture*, 147, 157). For efforts to compare Pseudo-Philo with other NT authors, see Eckart Reinmuth, *Pseudo-Philo und Lukas* (WUNT 74: Tübingen: Mohr Siebeck, 1994; Bauckham, "Pseudo-Philo and the Gospels," 33–76; Craig A. Evans, "Luke and

spondences between episodes in the sacred past, Paul made connections between Israel's past and its present, between the stories of Scripture and the new story of Jesus.

Toward these ends, we shall consider closely Paul's use of biblical narrative in Rom 11:1–7, noting how he draws on compositional techniques and hermeneutical strategies found also in RB. This is not to offer RB as the new "hermeneutical key" to Paul (replacing *midrash*, the favorite of a previous generation).[12] It is, however, a call to give full attention to the narratival dimensions of both Scripture and Paul's use of it, including those features of his use that he shares with contemporaries who likewise trade in the currency of Israel's stories. And it is to suggest that we are likely to read Paul differently when we approach him as a storyteller, a species of novelist rather than as, say, a legistic sage, an impassioned rhetor, or an ad hoc pastoral troubleshooter.

A People Abandoned?

Romans 10 ends with Paul's gaze fixed on Israel's disobedience and rebellion. Chapter 11 begins with Paul denying what might seem to be the dark corollary—that God has now abandoned faithless, sinful Israel and turned to the Gentiles whose salvation, Paul has argued, Scripture has foreseen and foretold.[13] Paul's case that God has not rejected τὸν λαὸν αὐτοῦ rests on two (arguably interlocking) arguments. He points first to himself (11:1b), then to the Scriptures (11:2b). The emphatic καὶ γάρ, *for indeed*,[14] and the litany of self-designations—Ἰσραηλίτης, ἐκ σπέρματος Ἀβραάμ,

---

the Rewritten Bible: Aspects of Lucan Hagiography," in *The Pseudepigrapha and Early Biblical Interpretation* (ed. Craig A. Evans and James A. Sanders; JSPSup 14; Sheffield: JSOT Press, 1993), 170–201.

12. "Midrash" describes a genre of rabbinic literature, but it can also refer to a hermeneutical approach that spans many genres, in which sense RB and midrash are not at all mutually exclusive. See Hays, *Echoes of Scripture,* 10–14, for an assessment of the various ways in which "midrash" has functioned (often unsuccessfully) to illuminate Paul's use of Scripture.

13. Wagner, *Heralds of the Good News,* 220, describes how Paul has "brazenly subverted into prophecies of God's redemption of *Gentiles*" scriptural texts that originally foretold Israel's redemption. Cf. Rom 9:25–26; 10:15, 20–21.

14. For this emphatic construction elsewhere in Paul, see Rom 15:3; 1 Cor 8:5; 11:9; 12:13, 14; 14:8; 2 Cor 2:10, 3:10, 5:2, 5:4, 13:4; Phil 2:27; 1 Thess 3:4, 4:10; 2 Thess 3:10. (Rom 16:2 may be nonemphatic.)

φυλῆς Βενιαμίν—suggest that Paul means to present himself as compelling "empirical evidence"[15] in the case for God's faithfulness to the line of Jacob. The point is not that Paul *speaks as* a Jew but that Paul *is* one—an Israelite from Abraham's seed and Benjamin's line.[16] Unlike many of Paul's Roman readers, Paul himself is no Gentile transplant; Israel's ancient story is his family history.[17] As we shall see, this self-reference may be what calls to mind another solitary figure—the prophet Elijah—whose life, like Paul's, testified similarly to God's faithfulness to Israel.

Paul's double refusal to contemplate God's abandonment of Israel has drawn considerable attention, both in terms of its implicit theology and its echoes of antecedent Scripture.

μὴ ἀπώσατο ὁ θεὸς τὸν λαὸν αὐτοῦ; μὴ γένοιτο. ...
οὐκ ἀπώσατο ὁ θεὸς τὸν λαὸν αὐτοῦ ὃν προέγνω.

To the trained ear, the use of ἀπωθέομαι ("repudiate," "reject") to describe God's stance toward Israel would recall a cluster of scriptural texts in which abandonment is seen as a real possibility, even a foregone conclusion. Among these, 4 Kgdms 21:14 stands out for its intensity and its use of several other words relevant to Paul's argument: καὶ ἀπώσομαι τὸ ὑπόλειμμα

---

15. Cf. Wagner, *Heralds of the Good News,* 220, 232.

16. Similarly, E. Elizabeth Johnson, "Romans 9–11: The Faithfulness and Impartiality of God," in *Romans* (vol. 3 of *Pauline Theology*; ed. David M. Hay and E. Elizabeth Johnson; Minneapolis: Augsburg Fortress, 1995), 231–32; Francis Watson, *Paul, Judaism, and the Gentiles* (Grand Rapids: Eerdmans, 2007), 304, 334–35. Contra James D. G. Dunn, *Romans 9–16* (WBC 38B; Waco, Tex.: Word, 1988), 635. Note the use of λέγω or λαλῶ in Rom 3:5; 1 Cor 9:8, 10:15; 2 Cor 11:17, 23; Gal 3:15. Paul's use of εἰμί puts the focus on his identity, not his perspective. Hays takes Paul's self-reference principally to indicate "that Paul, as a Jew, should never be suspected of suggesting such an appalling idea" (*Echoes of Scripture,* 69). But the focus of Paul's subsequent argument, as Hays's parenthetical remark acknowledges, is on the survival of a remnant of faithful Jews within unfaithful Israel. Reading Paul's language in v. 1 as conceptually linked to the remnant theology of vv. 2–6, rather than as a disconnected, purely rhetorical intrusion, is to be preferred.

17. On the likelihood that Paul's Roman readers were predominantly Gentile converts, see Bruce N. Fisk, "Synagogue Influence and Scriptural Knowledge Among the Christians of Rome," in *As It Is Written: Studying Paul's Use of Scripture* (ed. Stanley E. Porter and Christopher D. Stanley; SBLSymS 50; Atlanta: Society of Biblical Literature, 2008), 157–85, esp. 166–69.

τῆς κληρονομίας μου καὶ παραδώσω αὐτοὺς εἰς χεῖρας ἐχθρῶν.[18] Likewise, the double use of ἀπωθέομαι in Ps 43:10, 24 [MT 44:9, 23] is striking, particularly since Paul invokes this psalm by citing an adjacent verse (43:23 [MT 44:22]) in Rom 8:36.

Ps 43:10
νυνὶ δὲ ἀπώσω καὶ κατῄσχυνας ἡμᾶς καὶ οὐκ ἐξελεύσῃ ἐν ταῖς δυνάμεσιν ἡμῶν·
But now you have rejected and shamed us and you will not go out with our forces.

Ps 43:24
ἐξεγέρθητι· ἵνα τί ὑπνοῖς, κύριε; ἀνάστηθι καὶ μὴ ἀπώσῃ εἰς τέλος.
Get up! Why are you sleeping, Lord? Arise and do not reject [us] forever.

The psalmist, inhabiting a bleak world from which all signs of the divine presence have vanished, urges God to abandon Israel no longer. Paul, in Romans 8–11, dares respond on God's behalf.[19] The double denial of Romans 11:1–2, then, is not simply the next step in Paul's argument; it is a backward glance at the tumultuous history of Israel and a decisive refutation of every Israelite who doubted God's faithfulness.

---

18. See also Jer 2:37, ὅτι καὶ ἐντεῦθεν ἐξελεύσῃ, καὶ αἱ χεῖρές σου ἐπὶ τῆς κεφαλῆς σου· ὅτι ἀπώσατο κύριος τὴν ἐλπίδα σου, καὶ οὐκ εὐοδωθήσῃ ἐν αὐτῇ; 2 Chr 35:19d (MT 2 Kgs 23:27), καὶ εἶπεν κύριος Καί γε τὸν Ιουδαν ἀποστήσω ἀπὸ προσώπου μου, καθὼς ἀπέστησα τὸν Ισραηλ, καὶ ἀπωσάμην τὴν πόλιν, ἣν ἐξελεξάμην, τὴν Ιερουσαλημ, καὶ τὸν οἶκον, ὃν εἶπα Ἔσται τὸ ὄνομά μου ἐκεῖ; Ezek 5:11, διὰ τοῦτο Ζῶ ἐγώ, λέγει κύριος, εἰ μὴ ἀνθ᾽ ὧν τὰ ἅγιά μου ἐμίανας ἐν πᾶσιν τοῖς βδελύγμασίν σου, κἀγὼ ἀπώσομαί σε, οὐ φείσεταί μου ὁ ὀφθαλμός, κἀγὼ οὐκ ἐλεήσω (note the hints of hope in the context, esp. Ezek 5:13 and 6:8); Ezek 11:16, διὰ τοῦτο εἰπόν Τάδε λέγει κύριος ὅτι Ἀπώσομαι αὐτοὺς εἰς τὰ ἔθνη καὶ διασκορπιῶ αὐτοὺς εἰς πᾶσαν τὴν γῆν, καὶ ἔσομαι αὐτοῖς εἰς ἁγίασμα μικρὸν ἐν ταῖς χώραις, οὗ ἂν εἰσέλθωσιν ἐκεῖ (here God promises future restoration [vv. 16b–17] in terms of protection during exile and regathering to the land); and Hos 9:17, ἀπώσεται αὐτοὺς ὁ θεός, ὅτι οὐκ εἰσήκουσαν αὐτοῦ, καὶ ἔσονται πλανῆται ἐν τοῖς ἔθνεσιν. See further Dunn, *Romans*, 634; Wagner, *Heralds of the Good News*, 227 nn. 30–32.

19. On the relationship between Ps 43 (MT 44) and the argument of Romans, see especially Hays, *Echoes of Scripture*, 57–61.

Twin Prophets, Twin Messiahs

The closest scriptural parallels to Rom 11:1a, 2a are found in 1 Sam 12:22 and Ps 93:14, both of which deny that God has repudiated Israel. Paul's language may be indebted to both.[20]

1 Kgdms

    ὅτι   οὐκ   ἀπώσεται   κύριος   τὸν λαὸν αὐτοῦ
    διὰ τὸ ὄνομα αὐτοῦ τὸ μέγα, ὅτι ἐπιεικέως κύριος προσελάβετο ὑμᾶς αὐτῷ εἰς λαόν.

Ps 93:14

    ὅτι   οὐκ   ἀπώσεται   κύριος   τὸν λαὸν αὐτοῦ
    καὶ τὴν κληρονομίαν αὐτοῦ οὐκ ἐγκαταλείψει

Rom 11:1

              μὴ   ἀπώσατο   ὁ θεὸς   τὸν λαὸν αὐτοῦ;

Rom 11:2

              οὐκ   ἀπώσατο   ὁ θεὸς   τὸν λαὸν αὐτοῦ
                                                                  ὃν προέγνω.

The first passage records Samuel's oracle in response to the people's ill-conceived, faithless demand for an earthly king (1 Sam 8:5-6, 19; 10:19; 12:12). Samuel's reply to their request (1 Sam 12:20-25) would need only minor revisions before Paul could level it at unbelieving Israel in his day.[21]

1 Kgdms 12:20-25

    καὶ εἶπεν Σαμουηλ πρὸς τὸν λαόν Μὴ φοβεῖσθε· ὑμεῖς πεποιήκατε τὴν πᾶσαν κακίαν ταύτην, πλὴν μὴ ἐκκλίνητε ἀπὸ ὄπισθεν κυρίου καὶ δουλεύσατε τῷ κυρίῳ ἐν ὅλῃ καρδίᾳ ὑμῶν καὶ μὴ παραβῆτε ὀπίσω τῶν μηθὲν ὄντων, οἳ οὐ περανοῦσιν οὐθὲν καὶ οἳ οὐκ ἐξελοῦνται, ὅτι οὐθέν εἰσιν. ὅτι οὐκ ἀπώσεται κύριος τὸν λαὸν αὐτοῦ διὰ τὸ ὄνομα αὐτοῦ τὸ μέγα, ὅτι ἐπιεικέως κύριος προσελάβετο ὑμᾶς αὐτῷ εἰς λαόν. καὶ ἐμοὶ μηδαμῶς τοῦ ἁμαρτεῖν τῷ κυρίῳ ἀνιέναι τοῦ προσεύχεσθαι περὶ ὑμῶν, καὶ δουλεύσω τῷ κυρίῳ καὶ δείξω ὑμῖν τὴν ὁδὸν τὴν ἀγαθὴν καὶ τὴν

---

20. For a detailed discussion, see Wagner, *Heralds of the Good News*, 221-24, and further below.

21. Similarly Hays, *Echoes of Scripture*, 69.

εὐθεῖαν· πλὴν φοβεῖσθε τὸν κύριον καὶ δουλεύσατε αὐτῷ ἐν ἀληθείᾳ καὶ ἐν ὅλῃ καρδίᾳ ὑμῶν, ὅτι εἴδετε ἃ ἐμεγάλυνεν μεθ' ὑμῶν, καὶ ἐὰν κακίᾳ κακοποιήσητε, καὶ ὑμεῖς καὶ ὁ βασιλεὺς ὑμῶν προστεθήσεσθε.

1 Sam 12:20–25

> Do not be afraid; you have done all this evil, yet do not turn aside from following the Lord, but serve the Lord with all your heart; and do not turn aside after useless things that cannot profit or save, for they are useless. For the Lord will not cast away his people, for his great name's sake, because it has pleased the Lord to make you a people for himself. Moreover as for me, far be it from me that I should sin against the Lord by ceasing to pray for you; and I will instruct you in the good and the right way. Only fear the Lord, and serve him faithfully with all your heart; for consider what great things he has done for you. But if you still do wickedly, both you and your king will be swept away.

The situations of Paul and Samuel are symmetrical. Both are frustrated by the faithlessness of their people, both are convinced that God would not ultimately abandon his people in spite of their obstinacy, and both are committed to intercede on Israel's behalf. Paul's mention of his Benjamite lineage (11:1) would have encouraged biblically schooled readers to think of another Benjamite, Saul, whose rise to the throne (1 Sam 9–11) provides the context for Samuel's oracle (12:20–25), to which Paul here may be alluding. Samuel's words come after the people finally acknowledge their guilt for demanding a king (1 Sam 12:19; cf. 10:16, 24–25; 11:15; 12:1) and in response to their fearful appeal to Samuel to pray for them.

Insofar as Paul alludes to the story of Samuel and Saul of which the oracle in 1 Sam 12:22 is both the moral and the climax, he appears to view events in his own day in its light. Israel's "chronic failure to trust God alone"[22] and God's abiding covenant loyalty tie the two episodes together, as does the centrality in each story of Israel's anointed King. Both Samuel and Paul enjoin Israel to acknowledge its newly appointed King Messiah. Whereas Israel in Samuel's day demonstrated disbelief by *demanding* a Messiah, Israel now shows its disbelief by *rejecting* one.[23]

---

22. Wagner, *Heralds of the Good News,* 229.
23. For Saul as *Christos*, see 1 Sam 9:16; 10:1; 12:3, 5.

Samuel	Paul
Israel demands a King Messiah	God raises up a King Messiah
God appoints Saul over Israel	Israel rejects Jesus
Saul prays for Israel's salvation	Paul prays for Israel's salvation (Rom 10:1)
Samuel proclaims God's loyalty	Paul proclaims God's loyalty

Pseudo-Philo's revision of 1 Sam 8–12 in *L.A.B.* 56–57 offers several instructive parallels. First, in *L.A.B.* Israel does not ground its request for a king in an inappropriate desire to be *like other nations* as she did in 1 Sam 8:5, 20. On the contrary, Israel's request derives from its zeal to obey a biblical command.

L.A.B. 56:1 (Jacobson)

> Behold now you are old, and your sons do not walk in the ways of the Lord.[24] Now appoint over us a king to judge us, because the word that Moses spoke to our fathers in the wilderness must be fulfilled, "Appoint from your brothers a king over you."
> Ecce nunc tu senuisti, et filii tui non ambulant in viis tuis. Et nunc constitue super nos regem qui nos diiudicet, quoniam completum est verbum quod dixit Moyses patribus nostris in heremo dicens: Constituendo constitue de fratribus tuis super te principem.

1 Sam 8:5 (NRSV)

> You are old and your sons do not follow in your ways; appoint for us, then, a king to govern us, like other nations.
> אַתָּה זָקַנְתָּ וּבָנֶיךָ לֹא הָלְכוּ בִּדְרָכֶיךָ עַתָּה שִׂימָה־לָּנוּ מֶלֶךְ לְשָׁפְטֵנוּ כְּכָל־הַגּוֹיִם׃

---

24. D. Harrington ("Pseudo-Philo: A New Translation and Introduction," in *The Old Testament Pseudepigrapha* [2 vols.; ed. J. H. Charlesworth; Garden City, N.Y.: Doubleday, 1985]); and M. R. James (*The Biblical Antiquities of Philo* [London: SPCK, 1917]), follow *L.A.B.* MS Δ here, which in turn reflects the biblical precursor (1 Sam 8:5): *in viis tuis* ("in your ways"). Jacobson (*Commentary*, 2:1148–49) proposes harmonization as the reason to prefer an original *Domini*.

Deut 17:15 (NRSV)
> You may indeed set over you a king whom the LORD your God will choose. One of your own community you may set as king over you; you are not permitted to put a foreigner over you, who is not of your own community.

שׂוֹם תָּשִׂים עָלֶיךָ מֶלֶךְ אֲשֶׁר יִבְחַר יְהוָה אֱלֹהֶיךָ בּוֹ מִקֶּרֶב אַחֶיךָ תָּשִׂים עָלֶיךָ מֶלֶךְ לֹא תוּכַל לָתֵת עָלֶיךָ אִישׁ נָכְרִי אֲשֶׁר לֹא־אָחִיךָ הוּא׃

The citation of Deut 17:15 ("Appoint from your brothers a king over you") nicely illustrates Pseudo-Philo's penchant for intruding secondary texts into his primary narrative.[25] This practice is both Pseudo-Philo's preferred way of demonstrating the unity and harmony of Scripture and an important means by which he advances his interpretations. Secondary texts in Pseudo-Philo transform the primary story even as they themselves are transformed.[26] The remarkable thing here is that *L.A.B.* turns the apodosis of a condition in the biblical precursor into a freestanding command. Whereas Moses's words in Deuteronomy, far from endorsing monarchy, sought to constrain the institution once it arose, Deut 17:15 in Pseudo-Philo has become a divine charge that Israel was compelled to obey.[27] This semantic reversal, accomplished largely by omitting the con-

---

25. See Fisk, *Do You Not Remember?* (the title of which alludes to this practice); idem, "One Good Story Deserves Another: The Hermeneutics of Invoking Secondary Biblical Episodes in the Narratives of Pseudo-Philo and the *Testaments of the Twelve Patriarchs*," in *The Interpretation of Scripture in Early Judaism and Christianity* (ed. Craig A. Evans; JSPSup 33; Sheffield: Sheffield Academic Press, 2000), 217–38; idem, "Gaps in the Story, Cracks in the Earth: The Exile of Cain and the Destruction of Korah in Pseudo-Philo (*Liber Antiquitatum Biblicarum* 16), in *Of Scribes and Sages: Early Jewish Interpretation and Transmission of Scripture* (ed. Craig A. Evans; Edinburgh: T&T Clark, 2004), 20–33. James Kugel (*In Potiphar's House*, 261) calls this practice "back-referencing," though the direction is not always backward, canonically or chronologically.

26. See Fisk, "One Good Story," esp. 220–21.

27. In this reading, Pseudo-Philo aligns with several latter rabbinic sources. See references in Jacobson, *Commentary*, 2:1149. There is textual uncertainty about whether to read *completum est verbum* ("the word *has been* fulfilled"; so Δ, Harrington, James, Murphy) or *complendum est verbum* ("the word *must be* fulfilled"; π, Cazeaux ["il faut que s'accomplisse la parole"], tentatively Jacobson). The people see themselves either witnessing or enacting scriptural fulfillment.

text, means that a biblical injunction to appoint only the ruler whom God chose has become an explicit command to appoint a king.

Deut 17:14-15 (MT)

כִּי־תָבֹא אֶל־הָאָרֶץ אֲשֶׁר יְהוָה אֱלֹהֶיךָ נֹתֵן לָךְ וִירִשְׁתָּהּ וְיָשַׁבְתָּה בָּהּ
וְאָמַרְתָּ אָשִׂימָה עָלַי מֶלֶךְ כְּכָל־הַגּוֹיִם אֲשֶׁר סְבִיבֹתָי׃
שׂוֹם תָּשִׂים עָלֶיךָ מֶלֶךְ אֲשֶׁר יִבְחַר יְהוָה אֱלֹהֶיךָ בּוֹ מִקֶּרֶב אַחֶיךָ תָּשִׂים
עָלֶיךָ מֶלֶךְ לֹא תוּכַל לָתֵת עָלֶיךָ אִישׁ נָכְרִי אֲשֶׁר לֹא־אָחִיךָ הוּא׃

Deut 17:14-15 (LXX)

Ἐὰν δὲ εἰσέλθῃς εἰς τὴν γῆν, ἣν κύριος ὁ θεός σου δίδωσίν σοι ἐν κλήρῳ, καὶ κληρονομήσῃς αὐτὴν καὶ κατοικήσῃς ἐπ' αὐτῆς καὶ εἴπῃς Καταστήσω ἐπ' ἐμαυτὸν ἄρχοντα καθὰ καὶ τὰ λοιπὰ ἔθνη τὰ κύκλῳ μου,
καθιστῶν καταστήσεις <u>ἐπὶ σεαυτὸν ἄρχοντα</u>, ὃν ἂν ἐκλέξηται κύριος ὁ θεός σου αὐτόν. ἐκ τῶν ἀδελφῶν σου καταστήσεις <u>ἐπὶ σεαυτὸν ἄρχοντα·</u> οὐ δυνήσῃ καταστῆσαι ἐπὶ σεαυτὸν ἄνθρωπον ἀλλότριον, ὅτι οὐκ ἀδελφός σού ἐστιν.

L.A.B. 56:1

Constituendo constitue de fratribus tuis <u>super te principem</u>.

According to 1 Sam 8:7-8 (cf. 12:12, 17; Deut 17:14), Israel's stated desire to be *like other nations* was an explicit rejection of theocratic rule.

οὐ σὲ ἐξουθενήκασιν, ἀλλ' ἢ ἐμὲ ἐξουδενώκασιν τοῦ μὴ βασιλεύειν ἐπ' αὐτῶν. κατὰ πάντα τὰ ποιήματα, ἃ ἐποίησάν μοι ἀφ' ἧς ἡμέρας ἀνήγαγον αὐτοὺς ἐξ Αἰγύπτου ἕως τῆς ἡμέρας ταύτης καὶ ἐγκατέλιπόν με καὶ ἐδούλευον θεοῖς ἑτέροις, οὕτως αὐτοὶ ποιοῦσιν καὶ σοί.
It is not you they have scorned but they have rejected me from ruling over them. In accord with all the deeds which they did to me from the day I led them up out of Egypt until this day they have forsaken me and served other gods. Thus they have done even to you.[28]

---

28. Similarly Josephus, *Ant.* 6.38, in which God consoles a fretful Samuel, ὡς οὐκ

Because Israel had scorned God's rule (ἐξουθενέω, ἐξουδενέω) and consistently forsaken God (ἐγκαταλείπω), God would not heed (ἐπακούω) Israel's cry when their king became oppressive.

1 Kgdms 8:18
> καὶ βοήσεσθε ἐν τῇ ἡμέρᾳ ἐκείνῃ ἐκ προσώπου βασιλέως ὑμῶν, οὗ ἐξελέξασθε ἑαυτοῖς, καὶ οὐκ ἐπακούσεται κύριος ὑμῶν ἐν ταῖς ἡμέραις ἐκείναις, ὅτι ὑμεῖς ἐξελέξασθε ἑαυτοῖς βασιλέα.
> And you will cry out in that day before your king whom you chose for yourselves, and yet your Lord will not listen in those days, because you chose for yourself a king.

Pseudo-Philo's rewritten account once again exercises creative license. Gone is any suggestion that Israel rejected God's rule, any hint that Israel was following a well-established pattern of infidelity. There is only the slightest suggestion that Israel will reap what she has sown (L.A.B. 56:3; cf. 1 Sam 12:17–20a). These omissions simultaneously remove the most problematic aspects of the Samuel episode and supply in their place a positive biblical warrant for the nation's shift to monarchical rule. Pseudo-Philo, that is, brazenly replaces vice with virtue, a hermeneutical move comparable to some of Paul's transformations, such as his surprising reading of Hos 1:10 and 2:23 in Rom 9:24–26 wherein the prophet's references to Israel's restoration become promises of Gentile inclusion.[29] For both Paul and Pseudo-Philo, the exegesis of a specific text is fueled not only by theological commitments but also by the hermeneutical assumption that Israel's Scriptures are coherent and self-interpreting.

Samuel's response to the people's request for a king in Pseudo-Philo includes another type of creative reclamation. According to L.A.B. 56:2, Israel was simply guilty of poor timing. Their request for a king was not wrong; it just came too early:

> And when Samuel heard talk of a kingdom, he was very sad in his heart and said, "Behold now I see that it is not yet the time [*non est adhuc tempus*] for us to have an everlasting kingdom and to build

---

ἐκεῖνον ὑπερηφανήσαντας ἀλλ' ἑαυτόν ("since it was not him whom they had spurned, but God Himself").

29. See especially Wagner, *Heralds of the Good News*, 79–85.

the house of the LORD our God, for these people are seeking a king before the proper time [*petentibus regem ante tempus*]."

This revision may reflect the tradition found in later rabbinic sources that Israel erred by requesting a king *before* (*ante*) erecting a temple.[30] More likely, the move is simply meant to alleviate the awkwardness of God handpicking a king who turns out so bad (1 Sam 9:16). In this case, the nation's demand for a king is no longer a sign of collective infidelity. Either way, there is no veiled threat of abandonment (cf. 1 Sam 12:15, 25); the covenantal relationship between God and Israel remains intact and unquestioned. All the vicissitudes of Saul's reign are subsumed under the divine plan (*L.A.B.* 56:3; contra 1 Sam 9:16, 15:11). Samuel has no need to deliver the sort of ominous oracle we find in 1 Sam 12:20–25, nor to assure the people that "the Lord will not abandon his people" (12:22; cf. Rom 11:1–2).

In contrast to *L.A.B.*, the story of Samuel and Saul floats beneath the surface of Paul's letter with only a few narrative tips visible above the waterline. Paul shares Pseudo-Philo's zeal for the irrevocability of God's promises to Israel, but the way each tradent defends Israel's privileged position differs sharply. Pseudo-Philo's bold rewriting of the Samuel episode has the people zealous to conform to the Scriptures, not the nations, and it downgrades their distrust in God to mere impatience. By contrast, Paul's allusion to the Samuel story—if allusion it is—invites his readers to imagine themselves taken up into Israel's story or, at the least, to recognize a fundamental historical symmetry between past and present. Unlike Pseudo-Philo, Paul does not reduce or minimize Israel's sin; their disobedience and obstinacy (10:21) continue into the present. A remnant, but only a remnant, remains faithful (11:5).

Covenantal Theology as Hermeneutical Impulse

The other biblical text that bears striking similarities to Rom 11:1–2 is Ps 93:14 (MT 94:14). Wagner has identified points of correspondence between Paul's argument and the psalmist's lament—chief among them the shared conviction that God will ultimately vindicate his righteous ones—and contends for the originality of the variant reading τὴν κληρονομίαν in Rom

---

30. See references in Louis Ginzberg, *The Legends of the Jews* (trans. Henrietta Szold; 6 vols.; Philadelphia: Jewish Publication Society of America, 1909–1928; repr., Baltimore: Johns Hopkins University Press, 1998), 4:230.

11:1, which makes an allusion to Ps 93:14 in Rom 11:1-2 all but assured, since now both Paul and the psalmist use λαός and κληρονομία in back-to-back clauses.[31]

Rom 11:1-2
Λέγω οὖν, μὴ ἀπώσατο ὁ θεὸς τὴν κληρονομίαν αὐτοῦ; μὴ γένοιτο· ... οὐκ ἀπώσατο ὁ θεὸς τὸν λαὸν αὐτοῦ ὃν προέγνω.

Ps 93:14
ὅτι οὐκ ἀπώσεται κύριος τὸν λαὸν αὐτοῦ καὶ τὴν κληρονομίαν αὐτοῦ οὐκ ἐγκαταλείψει.

Whether we read κληρονομία or λαός in 11:1, however, Paul's argument turns on the conviction that Israel's god will keep his promises to Abraham and remain ever faithful to the people he has chosen for himself. Thus the beginning of Rom 11 foreshadows its end.

Rom 11:28
κατὰ δὲ τὴν ἐκλογὴν ἀγαπητοὶ διὰ τοὺς πατέρας· ἀμεταμέλητα γὰρ τὰ χαρίσματα καὶ ἡ κλῆσις τοῦ θεοῦ.
In accord with election, beloved on account of the fathers; for God's gifts and calling are irrevocable.

This belief that God's loyalty to Israel was tied to Israel's status as God's possession is not only rooted deeply in Israel's Scriptures (e.g., Deut 7, 32); it is also widespread across the literature of Second Temple Judaism.[32]

---

31. Wagner, *Heralds of the Good News*, 222 (cf. 224-26), against NA[27]. On favoring the variant reading in 11:1, Wagner follows Mark Given, "Restoring the Inheritance in Romans 11:1," *JBL* 118 (1999): 89-96. Given contends that Paul chose κληρονομία under the influence of Ps 93 (92-93) and that *inheritance* language puts greater stress on the permanence of the relationship between God and Israel (94-95).

32. See again Wagner, *Heralds of the Good News*, 226-28, and the references in notes 26-31; E. P. Sanders, *Paul and Palestinian Judaism* (Philadelphia: Fortress, 1977), passim; idem, *Judaism: Practice and Belief, 63 BCE-66 CE* (Philadelphia: Trinity Press International, 1992), 262-78; idem, "The Covenant as a Soteriological Category and the Nature of Salvation in Palestinian and Hellenistic Judaism," in *Jews, Greeks and Christians: Religious Cultures in Late Antiquity* (ed. Robert Hamerton-Kelly and Robin Scroggs; Leiden: Brill, 1976), 11-44. Josephus tellingly replaces Jewish covenant theology with themes of divine providence, retribution, and human virtue, on which

We can scarcely sense the depth of Paul's convictions on the matter unless we read his letters in this context. Pss. Sol. 7, to take one example, assures Israel of God's continued care in the face of Gentile (i.e., Roman) oppression. Although the present distress reflects God's righteous discipline of sinful Israel, discipline will one day give way to mercy, and to judgment upon the nations. *God, in other words, has not abandoned his people.* Note the phrase οὐκ ἀπώσῃ in verse 8.

Pss. Sol. 7:1-3, 5-10
> Μὴ ἀποσκηνώσῃς ἀφ' ἡμῶν, ὁ θεός, ἵνα μὴ ἐπιθῶνται ἡμῖν οἳ ἐμίσησαν ἡμᾶς δωρεάν. ὅτι ἀπώσω αὐτούς, ὁ θεός· μὴ πατησάτω ὁ πούς αὐτῶν κληρονομίαν ἁγιάσματός σου. σὺ ἐν θελήματί σου παίδευσον ἡμᾶς καὶ μὴ δῷς ἔθνεσιν ... ὅτι σὺ ἐλεήμων καὶ οὐκ ὀργισθήσῃ τοῦ συντελέσαι ἡμᾶς. Ἐν τῷ κατασκηνοῦν τὸ ὄνομά σου ἐν μέσῳ ἡμῶν ἐλεηθησόμεθα, καὶ οὐκ ἰσχύσει πρὸς ἡμᾶς ἔθνος. ὅτι σὺ ὑπερασπιστὴς ἡμῶν, καὶ ἡμεῖς ἐπικαλεσόμεθά σε, καὶ σὺ ἐπακούσῃ ἡμῶν. ὅτι σὺ οἰκτιρήσεις τὸ γένος Ισραηλ εἰς τὸν αἰῶνα καὶ οὐκ ἀπώσῃ. καὶ ἡμεῖς ὑπὸ ζυγόν σου τὸν αἰῶνα καὶ μάστιγα παιδείας σου. κατευθυνεῖς ἡμᾶς ἐν καιρῷ ἀντιλήψεώς σου τοῦ ἐλεῆσαι τὸν οἶκον Ιακωβ εἰς ἡμέραν ἐν ᾗ ἐπηγγείλω αὐτοῖς.

> Do not move away from us, O God, lest those who hate us without cause should attack us. For you have rejected them, O God; do not let their feet trample your holy inheritance. Discipline us as you wish, but do not turn (us) over to the gentiles ... For you are kind, and will not be angry enough to destroy us. While your name lives among us, we shall receive mercy and the gentile will not overcome us. For you are our protection, and we will call to you, and you will hear us. For you will have compassion on the people forever and you will not reject (them); and we are under your yoke forever, and (under) the whip of your discipline. You will direct us in the time of your support, showing mercy to the house of Jacob on the day when you promised (it) to them.

---

see Harold Attridge, *The Interpretation of Biblical History in the Antiquitates Judaicae of Flavius Josephus* (Missoula, Mont.: Scholars Press, 1976), 79-92 passim.

The same cry for mercy sounds in Pss. Sol. 9, and with it the same assurance that God's choice of Abraham's children is irrevocable. Once again, the phrase οὐκ ἀπώσῃ εἰς τὸν αἰῶνα is reminiscent of Paul's diction.

Pss. Sol. 9:8–11
> Καὶ νῦν σὺ ὁ θεός, καὶ ἡμεῖς λαός, ὃν ἠγάπησας· ἰδὲ καὶ οἰκτίρησον, ὁ θεὸς Ισραηλ, ὅτι σοί ἐσμεν, καὶ μὴ ἀποστήσῃς ἔλεός σου ἀφ᾽ ἡμῶν, ἵνα μὴ ἐπιθῶνται ἡμῖν. ὅτι σὺ ᾑρετίσω τὸ σπέρμα Αβρααμ παρὰ πάντα τὰ ἔθνη καὶ ἔθου τὸ ὄνομά σου ἐφ᾽ ἡμᾶς, κύριε, καὶ οὐκ ἀπώσῃ εἰς τὸν αἰῶνα. ἐν διαθήκῃ διέθου τοῖς πατράσιν ἡμῶν περὶ ἡμῶν, καὶ ἡμεῖς ἐλπιοῦμεν ἐπὶ σὲ ἐν ἐπιστροφῇ ψυχῆς ἡμῶν. τοῦ κυρίου ἡ ἐλεημοσύνη ἐπὶ οἶκον Ισραηλ εἰς τὸν αἰῶνα καὶ ἔτι.
>
> And now, you are God and we are the people whom you have loved; look and be compassionate, O God of Israel, for we are yours, and do not take away your mercy from us, lest they set upon us. For you chose the descendants of Abraham above all the nations, and you put your name upon us, Lord, and it will not cease forever. You made a covenant with our ancestors concerning us, and we hope in you when we turn our souls toward you. May the mercy of the Lord be upon the house of Israel forevermore.

Pseudo-Philo, roughly contemporary with Paul, is not only consumed with defending the irrevocability of God's covenant with Israel;[33] his covenant theology is a fundamental hermeneutical impulse.[34] Thus in Pseudo-Philo's account of the exodus (*L.A.B.* 10:2), when the people are trapped between the sea and the Egyptian army, rather than blaming Moses for bringing them into the desert to die (cf. Exod 14:11–12), the people invoke God's promise to Abraham (Gen 12:7).

> Ob hoc nos eduxit Deus, aut hec sunt testamenta que disposuit patribus nostris dicens: Semini verstro dabo terram quam vos

---

33. See also *L.A.B.* 4:5; 7:4; 8:3; 9:3, 7; 11:1, 3, 5; 12:9-10; 13:6; 22:7; 23:1–2, 11; 28:2, 5; 30:4, 7; 32:8, 12–14. For the key Latin terms in *L.A.B.*, see Murphy, *Pseudo-Philo*, 244, 293, 307; and Fisk, *Do You Not Remember*, 45–46.

34. Jacobson, *Commentary*, 1:241, declares it the "single predominant theme" in *L.A.B.* Cf. Leopold Cohn, "An Apocryphal Work Ascribed to Philo of Alexandria," *JQR* 10 (1898): 322; Eckart Reinmuth, "'Nicht vergeblich' bei Paulus und Pseudo-Philo, Liber Antiquitatum Biblicarum," *NovT* 33 (1991): 111.

habitatis, ut nunc quod placitum est ante conspectum suum faciat in nobis?

Is it for this that God has brought us forth, or are these the covenants that he established with our fathers, saying, "To your seed will I give the land in which you dwell' that now he might do with us whatever is pleasing in his sight"?[35]

Likewise, *L.A.B.* 15:4 embellishes Num 14:2-4—the people's reaction to the ten spies—by recalling (cynically) God's promise, this time to Moses at the burning bush (Exod 3:8, 17, etc.).

Plebes autem ... conturbati sunt valde, et locuti sunt dicentes: Numquid hec sunt verba, que locutus est nobis Deus dicens: Inducam vos in terram fluentem lacte et melle. Et quomodo nunc elevat nos ut incidamus in rompheam, et mulieres nostre erunt in captivitatem?

But the people ... were very disturbed and said, "Are these the words that God spoke to us, saying, 'I will bring you into a land flowing with milk and honey'? And how does he now bring us up so that we should fall upon the sword and our wives be taken into captivity?"

Insofar as the people at Kadesh explicitly challenged God's trustworthiness, their culpability is greater in *L.A.B.* than it is in the biblical precursor, but so also is their awareness of God's promises.[36]

Pseudo-Philo's rewriting of the call of Gideon is similarly revealing. In Judg 6:13, Gideon's anguish is expressed in terms of divine abandonment.

καὶ εἶπεν πρὸς αὐτὸν Γεδεων Ἐν ἐμοί, κύριε, καὶ εἰ ἔστιν κύριος μεθ᾽ ἡμῶν, ἵνα τί εὗρεν ἡμᾶς πάντα τὰ κακὰ ταῦτα; καὶ ποῦ ἐστιν πάντα τὰ θαυμάσια αὐτοῦ, ὅσα διηγήσαντο ἡμῖν οἱ πατέρες ἡμῶν λέγοντες Οὐχὶ ἐξ Αἰγύπτου ἀνήγαγεν ἡμᾶς κύριος; καὶ νῦν ἀπώσατο ἡμᾶς καὶ παρέδωκεν ἡμᾶς ἐν χειρὶ Μαδιαμ.

---

35. On the people's citation of the *land* promise (Gen 12:7) when sheer physical survival was the immediate need, see Fisk, *Do You Not Remember*, 156-57.

36. For a fuller discussion, see Fisk, *Do You Not Remember*, 195-99.

וַיֹּאמֶר אֵלָיו גִּדְעוֹן בִּי אֲדֹנִי וְיֵשׁ יְהוָה עִמָּנוּ וְלָמָּה מְצָאַתְנוּ כָּל־זֹאת וְאַיֵּה
כָל־נִפְלְאֹתָיו אֲשֶׁר סִפְּרוּ־לָנוּ אֲבוֹתֵינוּ לֵאמֹר הֲלֹא מִמִּצְרַיִם הֶעֱלָנוּ
יְהוָה וְעַתָּה נְטָשָׁנוּ יְהוָה וַיִּתְּנֵנוּ בְּכַף־מִדְיָן:

Gideon's cry of dereliction becomes, in Pseudo-Philo's hands (35:2), a declaration of Israel's divine election, couched in language drawn from Deut 7:6 (cf. 14:2).[37]

> [Gedeon] dixit ei: "... Incidit enim Israel in angustias; ... Et ubi sunt mirabilia que narraverunt nobis patres nostri dicentes: Dominus elegit Israel singularem pre omnibus populis terre? Et ecce modo tradidit nos, et oblitus est sponsionum quas dixit patribus nostris."
>
> [Gideon] said to him, "... Israel has fallen into distress ... And where are the wonders that our fathers described to us, saying, 'The LORD has chosen Israel alone before all the peoples of the earth'? And behold now he has delivered us up and forgotten the promises that he told our fathers."

The centrality of election in Pseudo-Philo's theology is likewise affirmed by the angel's response to Gideon (*L.A.B.* 35:3):

> Non traditi estis in vanum ... secundum quod reliquistis sponsiones quas accepistis a Domino, invenerunt vos mala hec.... Sed ipse miserebitur sicut nemo miseretur generi Israel, etiam non propter vos sed propter eos qui dormierunt.
>
> "You have not been delivered up without reason...; because, as you have abandoned the promises that you have received from the LORD, these evils have found you out.... But he will have mercy, as no one else has mercy, on the race of Israel, though not on account of you but on account of those who have fallen asleep."

As these rewritten narratives demonstrate, Pseudo-Philo's assurance of Israel's survival is predicated on his confidence in God's faithfulness to the ancient promises.[38] Israel's privilege is tied not to national virtue or

---

37. Similarly Jacobson, *Commentary*, 2:913.
38. For further examples, see *L.A.B.* 9:4, 13:10, 18:11, 19:2, 21:5, 23:13, 49:3. Note-

merit but to God's elective choice and honor. However much it might seem to Pseudo-Philo's readers that Israel's oppressors were going unchecked, future events will rescue God's people and vindicate God's faithfulness. Resonances between Pseudo-Philo's covenantal theology and Paul's are not difficult to hear, as the following pairs of texts illustrate.

(1) *L.A.B.* 13:10

They will forget the covenants that I have established with their fathers; but nevertheless I will not forget them forever ... because I am faithful in my ways [fidelis sum in viis meiis].

Rom 3:3–4

What if some were unfaithful? Will their faithlessness nullify the faithfulness of God [τὴν πίστιν τοῦ θεοῦ]? By no means! Although everyone is a liar, let God be proved true [γινέσθω δὲ ὁ θεὸς ἀληθής].

(2) *L.A.B.* 39:6

Even if our sins be overabundant, still his mercy will fill the earth.

Rom 5:20

But where sin increased, grace abounded all the more.

(3) *L.A.B.* 9:4

Nor will he cast forth the race of Israel in vain upon the earth; nor did he establish a covenant [testamentum] with our fathers in vain [nec in vanum disposuit testamentum patribus nostris].

---

worthy is *L.A.B.* 49:6, which recounts the people's prayer of desperation during the time of Phinehas: "LORD God of Israel, why have you abandoned your people in the victory of their enemies, and in the time of distress why have you neglected your inheritance? ... For if the ordinances that you have established with our fathers are true, saying, 'I will multiply your seed,' and they will experience this, then it would have been better to say to us, 'I am cutting off your seed,' than to neglect our root." Note the pairing of "your people" and "your inheritance" (cf. Rom 11:1–2) and how the people invoke the patriarchal promise—most likely Gen 22:17 (cf. Gen 26:4, 24)—to challenge God's apparent abandonment.

L.A.B. 39:7
> LORD, look upon the people that you have chosen, and may you not destroy the vine that your right hand has planted, in order that this nation, which you have had from the beginning and always preferred and for which you made dwelling places and brought into the land you promised may be for you as an inheritance.

Rom 9:4–6a
> They are Israelites, and to them belong the adoption, the glory, the covenants [αἱ διαθῆκαι], the giving of the law, the worship, and the promises; to them belong the patriarchs, and from them, according to the flesh, comes the Messiah, who is over all, God blessed forever. Amen. It is not as though the word of God has failed [οὐχ οἷον δὲ ὅτι ἐκπέπτωκεν ὁ λόγος τοῦ θεοῦ].

(4) *L.A.B.* 49:3
> For I know that God will not reject us forever [scio enim quia non in finem nos abiciet Deus].

Rom 11:2
> God has not rejected his people whom he foreknew.

(5) *L.A.B.* 12:9
> Even if you plant another vine, this one will not trust you [nec hec tibi credet], because you have destroyed the former one.

Rom 11:19–21
> You will say, Branches were broken off so that I might be grafted in.... They were broken off because of their unbelief, but you stand only through faith.... For if God did not spare the natural branches, perhaps he will not spare you.

Notwithstanding uncertainties about the purpose of Romans and the views of Paul's opponents, we know much more about Paul's social context (theology, audiences, opponents) than we do about Pseudo-Philo's. We have copies of Paul's personal correspondence as well as non-Pauline texts (e.g., Acts) that refer explicitly to Paul, his contemporaries, and his churches. Almost everything we know about Pseudo-Philo comes from the rewritten narrative itself (now, alas, two languages removed from the original). Does Pseudo-Philo's covenant theology help us reconstruct his original audience? Were some members of Pseudo-Philo's community, weary of Roman domination or traumatized by Jerusalem's destruction, inclined to doubt God's faithfulness to Israel?[39]

Roughly contemporary with *L.A.B.*, 4 Ezra and 2 Baruch confirm the presence of communities struggling to reconcile covenant promises with post-70 realities.[40] Pseudo-Philo's recurring defense of Israel's irrevocable status and final restoration may suggest a similar historical context.[41] Nevertheless, the fact that there is no consensus on the date of *L.A.B.* relative to 70 C.E.,[42] coupled with the likelihood that *L.A.B.* (whatever its date of composition) preserves much older interpretive traditions,[43] makes it precarious to argue that Pseudo-Philo shaped his narrative explicitly to

---

39. Thus Frederick J. Murphy, "The Eternal Covenant in Pseudo-Philo," *JSP* 3 (1988): 54: "It would not be surprising if at that time [1st c. C.E.] many Jews wondered about the fulfillment of the promises to the fathers, or even thought in terms of Israel's annihilation." Cf. idem, "God in Pseudo-Philo," *JSJ* 19 (1988): 17; Rhonda Burnette-Bletsch, "At the Hands of a Woman: Rewriting Jael in Pseudo-Philo," *JSP* 17 (1998): 54–56, 63–64; Jacobson, *Commentary*, 242, 253.

40. See, e.g., 4 Ezra 3:1–2, 28–36; 4:23–24; 5:21–30; 6:55–59; 8:15–19; 10:19–24; 2 Bar. 3:1–9; 82:1–9; 85:1–9. Cf. Michael E. Stone, "Apocalyptic Literature," in *Jewish Writings of the Second Temple Period: Apocrypha, Pseudepigrapha, Qumran Sectarian Writings, Philo, Josephus* (ed. M. E. Stone; CRINT 2.2; Minneapolis: Augsburg Fortress, 1984), 433n273.

41. For thematic comparisons of 2 Baruch with *L.A.B.* and 4 Ezra, see Gwendolyn B. Sayler, *Have the Promises Failed? A Literary Analysis of 2 Baruch* (SBLDS 72; Chico, Calif.: Scholars Press, 1984), 41–91, 115–23, 148–50; P.-M. Bogaert, *L'Apocalypse Syriaque de Baruch* (SC 144/145; Paris: Cerf, 1969), 248–52. Cf. also George W. E. Nickelsburg, *Jewish Literature between the Bible and the Mishnah* (Philadelphia: Fortress, 1981), 288–90, 293–94. Other responses to the events of 70 C.E. also defended divine trustworthiness, whether explicitly or implicitly (e.g., Josephus, *J.W.* 4.104, 323, 366–371; 6.110, 285–288, 310–315, 411; 7.327–332, 358–360; Apoc. Ab. 25:4–27:12; cf. Matt 21:41–44; Luke 21:20–24).

42. See Fisk, *Do You Not Remember*, 34–40. Nancy Calvert-Koyzis (*Paul, Monotheism and the People of God: The Significance of Abraham for Early Judaism and Christianity* [JSNTSup 273; Edinburgh: T&T Clark, 2004], 42–44) is an example of those who regard Pseudo-Philo's interest in good and bad leaders as evidence that he sought a way out of Roman oppression, perhaps during or shortly after the first Jewish War.

43. As I seek to demonstrate in Bruce N. Fisk, "Pseudo-Philo, Paul, and Israel's Rolling Stone: Early Points Along an Exegetical Trajectory," in *Israel in the Wilderness: Interpretations of the Biblical Narratives in Jewish and Christian Traditions* (ed. Kenneth E. Pomykala; Leiden: Brill, 2008), 117–36.

console Jews after the fall of the Temple.[44] Indeed, Pseudo-Philo's unusual interest in the period of the Judges may suggest that his social context is one of "faith fatigue" due to foreign occupation, rather than of "faith crisis" due to devastation and exile.

But if the social setting and occasion of *L.A.B.* remain elusive, we may yet conclude that Paul and Pseudo-Philo faced roughly analogous historical dislocations.[45] Like *L.A.B.*, Romans is (in part) a defense of divine faithfulness,[46] a response to a crisis at least as troubling as political upheaval or military dislocation. As Richard Hays observes, "Paul's problem arises instead from a different sort of historical phenomenon, not the occupation of Israel by a Gentile military power but the apparent usurpation of Israel's favored covenant status by congregations of uncircumcised Gentile Christians."[47] Analogous to Pseudo-Philo's composition, Paul wrote Romans in response to unforeseen and unwelcome historical developments—chief among them the widespread Jewish rejection of Jesus. To make his case for God's abiding faithfulness, Paul turns to Israel's Scriptures, where he finds covenantal promises to Israel wending

---

44. On the merits and risks of "mirror-reading" a text to discern its social setting, see John M. G. Barclay, "Mirror-Reading a Polemical Letter: Galatians as a Test Case," *JSNT* 31 (1987): 78–79. Barclay's criteria for reconstructing the opponents of a polemical text include *frequency, consistency,* and *historical plausibility* (84–85). Whatever the inherent dangers of mirror-reading Paul's letters, they are surely multiplied with works such as *L.A.B.*

45. On the way social disruption and crises could provide the social setting and catalyst for biblical interpretation, see Fishbane, *Biblical Interpretation*, 411–14; Fisk, *Do You Not Remember*, 129, 264–67.

46. On divine faithfulness as a central theme in Romans, see Hays, *Echoes of Scripture*, 34, 38–41, 53, 57–59, 63–70; E. Elizabeth Johnson, "Romans 9–11: The Faithfulness and Impartiality of God," in Hay and Johnson, *Romans*, 211–39; J. C. Beker, *Paul the Apostle: The Triumph of God in Life and Thought* (Minneapolis: Fortress, 1980), 77; idem, "The Faithfulness of God and the Priority of Israel in Paul's Letter to the Romans," in *The Romans Debate* (ed. Karl P. Donfried; rev. ed.; Peabody, Mass.: Hendrickson, 1991), 330–32; William S. Campbell, "Romans III as a Key to the Structure and Thought of the Letter," in Donfried, *The Romans Debate*, 262–64; A. J. M. Wedderburn, *The Reasons for Romans* (Minneapolis: Fortress, 1991), 108–114; N. T. Wright, "Romans and the Theology of Paul," in *1992 Society of Biblical Literature Seminar Papers* (Chico, Calif.: Scholars Press, 1992), 188–10, 210; Sylvia C. Keesmaat, "Exodus and the Intertextual Transformation of Tradition in Romans 8.14–30," *JSNT* 54 (1994): 41.

47. Hays, *Echoes of Scripture*, 40. Cf. Eckart Reinmuth, "Nicht vergeblich," 123.

between stories of national unfaithfulness.⁴⁸ Paul's appeals to this story are driven by theological convictions rather than exegetical techniques, but the creativity with which Paul appropriates Scripture is not distinctively Christian nor distinctively Pauline; it is, rather, a standard feature of early Jewish exegesis of the sort we encounter in works of rewritten Bible.

Paul Rewrites the Bible

To examine further this fraternal bond between Paul-as-storyteller and the authors of RB, we turn to Rom 11:2b–5, where we catch Paul in the act of "rewriting" the biblical story of Elijah.⁴⁹ Unlike many works of early Biblical interpretation,⁵⁰ Paul draws clear lines between *traditum* and *traditio*: verse 2 deploys a typical citation formula (ἢ οὐκ οἴδατε ἐν Ἠλίᾳ τί λέγει ἡ γραφή;), while verse 4 treats the biblical text as an oracle (ἀλλὰ τί λέγει αὐτῷ ὁ χρηματισμός;) uttered by the mysterious God whom Elijah encountered at the Horeb cave.⁵¹ Unless ἢ οὐκ οἴδατε is purely formulaic,

---

48. Richard Hays observes that Scripture in Romans testifies to God's "unbroken faithfulness to Israel" with "an extraordinary—indeed, almost monotonous—thematic consistency" (*Echoes of Scripture*, 73).

49. For the textual history of 3 Kgdms 19:10, 18, as it relates to Paul's usage, see Christopher D. Stanley, "The Significance of Romans 11:3–4 for the Text History of the LXX Book of Kingdoms," *JBL* 112 (1993): 43–54. My remarks about Paul's creative use of the text presuppose his work.

50. E.g., *L.A.B.*, Genesis Apocryphon, Jubilees, Josephus's *Antiquities*, 1QH, Sirach, Psalms of Solomon, 1 En. 6–11, and the testamentary literature.

51. The word χρηματισμός, a New Testament *hapax*, is difficult. The cognate verb χρηματίζω is used of divine instructions in the New Testament (Matt 2:12; 22; Luke 2:26; Acts 10:22; Heb 8:5; 11:7) and in Josephus (*Ant.* 5.42; 10.13). LSJ suggests "*oracular response, divine injunction* or *warning*" for our passage and a few others, including 2 Macc 2:4. On the semantic range of cognates in Philo (esp. χρησμός, "oracular response"), see Y. Amir, "Authority and Interpretation of Scripture in the Writings of Philo," in *Mikra: Text, Translation, Reading and Interpretation of the Hebrew Bible in Ancient Judaism and Early Christianity* (CRINT 2.1; Minneapolis: Augsburg Fortress, 1988), 429–31. A. T. Hanson ("The Oracle in Romans XI.4," *NTS* 19 [1973]: 300–302) argues that the word highlights "the localization, the awesomeness and probably the indirectness of the divine communication" (301). According to Paul E. Dinter, "The Remnant of Israel and the Stone of Stumbling in Zion According to Paul (Romans 9–11)" (Ph.D. diss., Union Theological Seminary, 1979), 43, the word "oracle" reflects the "lively, even personified, sense in which [Paul] perceived the Scriptures." On Paul's depiction of scriptural citations as a *spoken* utterance, see comments and references in Watson, *Paul and the Hermeneutics of Faith*, 45.

Paul assumed his readers knew something of the Elijah story.⁵² Accordingly, he supplies no context for Elijah's litany of complaints, nor does he explain why "Israel" committed these offenses nor why Elijah's head count of the faithful is off by 6,999. Although what Paul assumed about the biblical literacy of his readers is of considerable interest to scholars these days,⁵³ these assumptions are not often examined alongside those of his Jewish contemporaries like *Jubilees*, the Genesis Apocryphon, and Pseudo-Philo. *L.A.B.* routinely assumes biblical literacy among its readers, most notably when it alludes to biblical episodes and details that the author has omitted from his rewritten account. The following examples could be multiplied in *L.A.B.* and elsewhere in the RB corpus.

L.A.B.	rewrites	a biblical story	omitted earlier.
L.A.B. 9:5	Exod 1	the story of Tamar (Gen 38:24)	*L.A.B.* 8
L.A.B. 11:15	Exod 24	the Tree of Life	*L.A.B.* 1–2 (Gen 2:9; 3:22)
L.A.B. 15:6	Num 14	the third day of creation (Gen 1:9)	*L.A.B.* 1
L.A.B. 16:2	Num 16	Cain's murder of Abel (Gen 4)	*L.A.B.* 1
L.A.B. 18:5–6	Num 22	the Aqedah (Gen 22) and Jacob's wrestling match (Gen 32)	*L.A.B.* 8

---

52. On this formula in Paul, see Rom 6:16; 1 Cor 3:16; 5:6; 6:2, 3, 9, 15, 16, 19; 9:13, 24; cf. ἢ ἀγνοεῖτε in Rom 6:3 and esp. 7:1, which refers to his readers' knowledge of the law (γινώσκουσιν γὰρ νόμον λαλῶ). 1 Corinthians 6:16 is the only other place where Paul uses this idiom to introduce a "known" biblical passage: [ἢ] οὐκ οἴδατε ὅτι ὁ κολλώμενος τῇ πόρνῃ ἓν σῶμά ἐστιν; Ἔσονται γάρ, φησίν, οἱ δύο εἰς σάρκα μίαν.

53. See esp. Christopher D. Stanley, *Arguing with Scripture: The Rhetoric of Quotations in the Letters of Paul* (Edinburgh: T&T Clark, 2004), 43, 55–56, 66–71; ibid., "The Significance of Romans 11:3–4," 47; Wagner, *Heralds of the Good News*, 232–33 (cf. 54); Fisk, "Synagogue Influence," 158.

I have argued elsewhere that Pseudo-Philo's allusions to unnarrated material do important hermeneutical work for him. Here we observe only that this compositional technique is effective only if readers already know the story.[54]

Paul's selective rewriting of the Elijah narrative (Rom 11:2-5) shares several compositional features with works of RB. One such feature is catchword linkage or *gezerah shawah*.[55] Both verses from 1 Kings that Paul cites contain cognates of λείπω: ὑπελείφθην (11:3) and κατέλιπον (11:4). In order to link the Elijah narrative to his own situation, Paul describes fellow Jesus-believing Jews with the cognate λεῖμμα (11:5). But all of this—his appeal to Elijah and his own diction—has surely been inspired by Isaiah (10:22-23; 1:9), to whose remnant theology Paul has recently appealed (Rom 9:27-29).[56]

Ἠσαΐας δὲ κράζει ὑπὲρ τοῦ Ἰσραήλ, Ἐὰν ᾖ ὁ ἀριθμὸς τῶν υἱῶν Ἰσραὴλ ὡς ἡ ἄμμος τῆς θαλάσσης, <u>τὸ ὑπόλειμμα</u> σωθήσεται· λόγον γὰρ συντελῶν καὶ συντέμνων ποιήσει κύριος ἐπὶ τῆς γῆς. καὶ καθὼς προείρηκεν Ἠσαΐας, Εἰ μὴ κύριος Σαβαὼθ <u>ἐγκατέλιπεν</u> ἡμῖν σπέρμα, ὡς Σόδομα ἂν ἐγενήθημεν καὶ ὡς Γόμορρα ἂν ὡμοιώθημεν.

Similarly noteworthy is Paul's abbreviation of οἱ υἱοὶ Ἰσραήλ (בְּנֵי יִשְׂרָאֵל MT) to Ἰσραήλ so as to align the biblical text more closely with his usage in 10:19, 21, and throughout Rom 9–10.[57] The "Israel" of Paul's day thus

---

54. For other examples of authors assuming biblical knowledge, see note 9 above.
55. See Craig A. Evans, *Ancient Texts for New Testament Studies* (Peabody, Mass.: Hendrickson, 2005), 219; E. Earle Ellis, *The Old Testament in Early Christianity* (Grand Rapids: Baker, 1991), 87–89.
56. See Ronald E. Clements, "'A Remnant Chosen by Grace' (Romans 11:5): The Old Testament Background and Origin of the Remnant Concept," in Hagner and Harris, *Pauline Studies*, 106–21; Dinter, "Remnant of Israel," 40–43; Hays, *Echoes of Scripture*, 69–70; Wagner, *Heralds of the Good News*, 233, and esp. 106–117 on the remnant theme in Paul, Isaiah, and Jewish thought more broadly. Note that the omitted line of 1 Kgs 19:10, 14, according to the LXX, has Elijah charge Israel with abandoning (ἐγκαταλείπω) God. For other examples, see the use of λογίζομαι to link Gen 15:6 and Ps 32:1–2 in Rom 4:3. (Λογίζομαι occurs seven times in eight verses.) See further Hays, *Echoes of Scripture*, 55. Likewise, see Paul's use of καλέω in Rom 9:24–26 to summon Hos 2:23 and 1:10.
57. Cf. Dinter, "Remnant of Israel," 38: "The line of Paul's argument flows directly from the citation/statement in 10:21, where he characterized Israel as a 'disobedient

stands in direct continuity with Elijah's Israelites. Catchword linkages such as these are common in rewritten biblical narratives. L.A.B. 16:2-3, for example, uses the catchword *deglutio* ("swallow"; LXX, καταπίνω) from Num 16:30, 32, 34 to tie Korah's rebellion to Abel's murder (Gen 4:1-16): the ground "swallowed" Korah's men just as it had "swallowed" Abel's blood.[58] Examples could be multiplied.

A second feature common to Paul and early Jewish biblical interpretation is *strategic omission*.[59] Paul's goal is not to rehearse biblical history, so we would expect his biblical references to be economical and concise. They are. Paul cites only two verses from the lengthy episode in 1 Kings: Elijah's complaint (Rom 11:3; 1 Kgs 19:10, 14) and part of God's reply (Rom 11:4; 1 Kgs 19:18). For crucial context and details, as Wagner observes, Paul's readers are on their own.

> Paul treats the story as one familiar to his hearers, one whose relevance to his present argument requires no explanation, and he invites them by his mild rebuke to reflect on the narrative and to draw from it the same conclusions he has drawn.[60]

Several elements of the biblical precursor are conspicuous by their absence. For example, we hear nothing about Elijah's virtue and zeal (1 Kgs 19:10a, 14a); Paul's point is not about Elijah's exemplary character[61] but about Israel's nondisqualification. Romans 11:3 likewise fails to record Elijah's charge that Israel had forsaken *God* or *God's covenant*.

3 Kgdms 19:10
καὶ εἶπεν Ηλιου Ζηλῶν ἐζήλωκα τῷ κυρίῳ παντοκράτορι, ὅτι ἐγκατέλιπόν σε οἱ υἱοὶ Ισραηλ· τὰ θυσιαστήριά σου κατέσκαψαν καὶ

---

and contrary people' (Isa 65:2). It is this *laos* and their fate that Paul now considers in 11:1-12."

58. See further Fisk, "Gaps in the Story."

59. Most famously, see Josephus's omission of the golden-calf episode (*Ant.* 3.99-101). Cf. Pseudo-Philo's omission of awkward elements of the Shechem episode (Gen 34) in *L.A.B.* 8:7. The exegetical impact of such omissions must not be overlooked.

60. Wagner, *Heralds of the Good News*, 232-33. Wagner grants that Paul "may be mistaken with regard to the 'hearer competence' of some in his audience" (ibid., 232 n. 51), but he suggests that the introductory formula, ἢ οὐκ οἴδατε ἐν Ἠλίᾳ, implies that Paul assumed some prior knowledge.

61. Contrast Josephus, *Ant.* 8.328-354, on which see below.

τοὺς προφήτας σου ἀπέκτειναν ἐν ῥομφαίᾳ, <u>καὶ ὑπολέλειμμαι ἐγὼ μονώτατος, καὶ ζητοῦσι τὴν ψυχήν μου</u> λαβεῖν αὐτήν.

3 Kgdms 19:14

καὶ εἶπεν Ηλιου Ζηλῶν ἐζήλωκα τῷ κυρίῳ παντοκράτορι, ὅτι ἐγκατέλιπον τὴν διαθήκην σου οἱ υἱοὶ Ισραηλ· τὰ θυσιαστήριά σου καθεῖλαν καὶ τοὺς προφήτας σου ἀπέκτειναν ἐν ῥομφαίᾳ, <u>καὶ ὑπολέλειμμαι ἐγὼ μονώτατος, καὶ ζητοῦσι τὴν ψυχήν μου</u> λαβεῖν αὐτήν.

Rom 11:2b-3

ἢ οὐκ οἴδατε ἐν 'Ηλίᾳ τί λέγει ἡ γραφή, ὡς ἐντυγχάνει τῷ θεῷ κατὰ τοῦ 'Ισραηλ; Κύριε, τοὺς προφήτας σου ἀπέκτειναν, τὰ θυσιαστήριά σου κατέσκαψαν, <u>κἀγὼ ὑπελείφθην μόνος καὶ ζητοῦσιν τὴν ψυχήν μου</u>.

If Paul's goal was merely to summarize and characterize Elijah's speech, this element (ἐγκατέλιπόν σε οἱ υἱοὶ Ισραηλ) would be the obvious one to include since (1) it is the first charge listed in both verse 10 and verse 14, (2) it is the most foundational of all the charges, and (3) it arguably provides the closest parallel to events in Paul's day. All of this suggests that the omission is intentional and not without significance: the charge that Israel had violated the covenant is precisely what Paul did *not* wish to emphasize.[62] Thus Paul's rewritten narrative makes his case for him better than would the biblical precursor itself.

Third, Paul, like his fellow tradents, engages in *aggadic embellishment*: he quietly intrudes the reflexive pronoun ἐμαυτῷ into the story of Rom 11:4.[63]

---

62. Paul also skips over 1 Kgs 19:15-17, since this pertains to the installation of kings, the commissioning of Elisha, and divine judgment on the infidels who have so upset Elijah. This omission is predictable but not insignificant, for it fundamentally alters the focus of God's response.

63. Paul's addition of ἐμαυτῷ may have been influenced by 1 Sam 12:22: ὅτι ἐπιεικέως κύριος προσελάβετο ὑμᾶς <u>αὐτῷ</u> εἰς λαόν. The Vulgate has *derelinquam mihi*, apparently by attraction to *reliqui mihi* in Rom 11:4.

1 Kgs 19:18 MT
>I have left / will leave (וְהִשְׁאַרְתִּי)in Israel seven thousand, all the knees which did not bow to Baal.

3 Kgdms 19:18
>*You* will leave [καταλείψεις][64] in Israel seven thousand men, all the knees which did not bow to Baal.

Rom 11:4
>*I* left *for myself* [κατέλιπον ἐμαυτῷ] seven thousand men who did not bow the knee to Baal.

The key word in God's response to Elijah, καταλείπω, describes God's action of *leaving* the seven thousand faithful. Unless Paul's *Vorlage* differed at this point from both MT and LXX traditions, we must conclude that he has added the word ἐμαυτῷ, thus altering the semantic force of the governing verb and the entire clause.[65] In the *traditum* God promised to keep seven thousand nonapostates alive; in Paul's new *traditio* God has *already* set apart seven thousand *for himself*. As "coauthor" of a new sacred text,[66] Paul uses Scripture to establish his claim that the remnant's election is grounded in God's covenant faithfulness,[67] a move that clearly supports his argument (v. 6). The survival of the remnant in Elijah's day

---

64. Targum, Peshitta, and the Lucianic text all support the MT והשארתי (hiphil perfect, first-person singular); cf. Wagner, *Heralds of the Good News*, 235 n. 60; C. E. B. Cranfield, *Romans 9–16* (ICC; Edinburgh: T&T Clark, 1979), 546. The LXX employs καταλείπω to render a hiphil of שאר some twenty-three times, but here the imperatival future (second-person singular) significantly alters the focus: the divine word is no longer a promise (MT) but is now a command addressed to Elijah (LXX). It is difficult to know whether Paul's *Vorlage* followed the MT here, but clearly the LXX reading would have undermined his point.

65. The assessment of James D. G. Dunn (*Romans 9–16*, 637) that this is "a good example of elaborative or paraphrastic translation" (637) does not do justice to the hermeneutical significance of Paul's revision here. Ernst Käsemann's remark (*Commentary on Romans* [trans. Geoffrey W. Bromiley; Grand Rapids: Eerdmans, 1980], 299) is similarly inadequate: "Whether another LXX version had some influence here or whether Paul made the changes himself is a moot question."

66. The phrase is Fishbane's. See *Biblical Interpretation*, 87; Fisk, *Do You Not Remember*, 55–56 n. 3.

67. Cf. Dunn, *Romans 9–16*, 637.

was due, says Paul, to divine grace, *not* to the merits of the faithful. It was not enough simply to observe that a parallel remnant exists "in the present time" (οὕτως ... καὶ ἐν τῷ νῦν καιρῷ λεῖμμα ... γέγονεν).[68] Paul also needed to say that this remnant came about "in accordance with (God's) gracious election" (κατ᾽ ἐκλογὴν χάριτος).[69] Thus, Paul's version of 1 Kgs 19:18 in verse 4 supports both halves of Paul's argument in verse 5.

	11:4 (1 Kgs 19:18)	11:5
remnant	κατέλιπον	λεῖμμα
election/grace	ἐμαυτῷ	κατ᾽ ἐκλογὴν χάριτος

In other words, the Elijah narrative advances Paul's remnant theology in part because of transformations that Paul has introduced into the biblical precursor.[70] Paul's answer to charges of divine abandonment is bound up with God's ἐκλογή (11:5, 7, 28; cf. 9:11) and χάρις (11:5, 6a, b, c, 29), attributes that his *rewritten* version of the ancient story brings into focus. God's gracious election in the past grounds Paul's hope for the salvation of his kinsfolk in the future (11:12, 15, 23, 25–32).

Paul among the Tradents

These features—catchword linkage, strategic omission and creative embellishment—also characterize Josephus's rewriting of 1 Kgs 19:9–18 (*Ant.* 8.350–352).[71]

ἐρομένης δέ τινος αὐτὸν φωνῆς ἐξ ἀδήλου τί παρείη καταλελοιπὼς τὴν πόλιν ἐκεῖσε, διὰ τὸ κτεῖναι μὲν τοὺς προφήτας τῶν ξενικῶν θεῶν,

---

68. This was his point in citing Isa 10:22 (cf. ὑπόλειμμα) at Rom 9:27.
69. Cf. Cranfield, *Romans*, 547; J. W. Aageson, "Typology, Correspondence, and the Application of Scripture in Romans 9–11," *JSNT* 31 (1987): 58.
70. Mark Seifrid, "Romans," in *Commentary on the New Testament Use of the Old Testament* (ed. G. K. Beale and D. A. Carson; Grand Rapids: Baker, 2008), 669, notes correctly that Paul thus interprets 1 Kings in light of Isaiah's remnant theology (cf. Rom 9:27–29), but he appears to underestimate Paul's own creativity in this reading strategy.
71. Greek text and English translation from *Josephus: Jewish Antiquities, Books VII–VIII* (trans. R. Marcus; Loeb Classical Library; Cambridge: Harvard University Press, 1968).

πεῖσαι δὲ τὸν λαὸν ὅτι μόνος εἴη θεὸς ὁ ὤν, ὃ ἀπ' ἀρχῆς ἐθρήσκευσαν, ἔφησε· ζητεῖσθαι γὰρ ἐπὶ τούτῳ πρὸς τιμωρίαν ὑπὸ τῆς γυναικὸς τοῦ βασιλέως. πάλιν δὲ ἀκούσας προελθεῖν εἰς τὸ ὕπαιθρον τῇ ἐπιούσῃ (γνώσεσθαι γὰρ οὕτως τί δεῖ ποιεῖν), προῆλθεν ἐκ τοῦ σπηλαίου μεθ' ἡμέραν καὶ σεισμοῦ τε ἐπακούει καὶ λαμπρὰν πυρὸς αὐγὴν ὁρᾷ. καὶ γενομένης ἡσυχίας φωνὴ θεία μὴ ταράττεσθαι τοῖς γινομένοις αὐτὸν παρακελεύεται, κρατήσειν γὰρ οὐδένα τῶν ἐχθρῶν αὐτοῦ.... "διαφθερεῖ δὲ τοῦ ἀσεβοῦς ὄχλου τοὺς μὲν Ἀζάηλος τοὺς δὲ Ἰηοῦς."

But a voice which came from someone, he knew not whom, asked him why he had left the city to come to that spot, whereupon he said that it was because he had killed the prophets of the strange gods and had convinced the people that the only true God was the Eternal, whom they had worshipped from the beginning; it was for this reason that he was being sought for punishment by the wife of the king. And again he heard a voice telling him to come out into the open air on the morrow, for so he should learn what he must do. The next day, therefore, he came out of the cave and heard the earth rumble and saw a brilliant fiery light. And, when all became quiet, a divine voice exhorted him not to be alarmed by what was happening, for none of his enemies should have him in their power.... "But," said the voice, "of the impious people Azaelos shall destroy some, and Jehu others."

Josephus condenses Elijah's answer in 1 Kgs 19:10 from six propositions to two, *strategically omitting* all references to Israel (Jezebel) killing the true prophets (cf. 1 Kgs 18:4, 13) and abandoning worship of the true God. Josephus's Elijah highlights, rather, another killing: his own act of killing the Baal prophets (1 Kgs 18:40). It is unlikely, however, that Josephus's replacement of Israel's "bad" killing with Elijah's "good" was arbitrary. Elijah's response in 1 Kings contains a biblical catchword—an allusion to the zeal that drove Phinehas to execute the idolatrous Zimri and his Midianite consort in Num 25.[72]

---

72. The significance of this word, and its connection to Num 25, is confirmed by 1 Macc 2:24, 26–27: καὶ εἶδεν Ματταθιας καὶ ἐζήλωσεν, καὶ ἐτρόμησαν οἱ νεφροὶ αὐτοῦ, καὶ ἀνήνεγκεν θυμὸν κατὰ τὸ κρίμα καὶ δραμὼν ἔσφαξεν αὐτὸν ἐπὶ τὸν βωμόν· ... καὶ ἐζήλωσεν τῷ νόμῳ, <u>καθὼς ἐποίησεν Φινεες τῷ Ζαμβρι υἱῷ Σαλωμ</u>. καὶ ἀνέκραξεν Ματταθιας ἐν τῇ πόλει φωνῇ μεγάλῃ λέγων Πᾶς ὁ ζηλῶν τῷ νόμῳ καὶ ἱστῶν διαθήκην ἐξελθέτω ὀπίσω μου. Cf. Josephus's rewritten account of Mattathias's speech in *Ant.*

3 Kgdms 19:10 (cf. 14)

Ζηλῶν ἐζήλωκα τῷ κυρίῳ παντοκράτορι

Num 25:11, 13b

Φινεες ... κατέπαυσεν τὸν θυμόν μου ἀπὸ υἱῶν Ισραηλ ἐν τῷ ζηλῶσαί μου τὸν ζῆλον ἐν αὐτοῖς, καὶ οὐκ ἐξανήλωσα τοὺς υἱοὺς Ισραηλ ἐν τῷ ζήλῳ μου ... ἐζήλωσεν τῷ θεῷ αὐτοῦ καὶ ἐξιλάσατο περὶ τῶν υἱῶν Ισραηλ.

As Josephus interprets 1 Kings, he appears to have understood Ζηλῶν ἐζήλωκα in light of Num 25, as a reference to Elijah's righteous slaughter of the prophets of Baal (1 Kgs 18:40).[73] Josephus's revised account strengthens his case for Israel's merits, just as Paul's rewritten Elijah narrative strengthens his case for God's faithfulness.

We conclude with three additional points about Paul's relationship to the story he is telling. First, insofar as Paul is interpreting his own experience through the lens of the ancient story, he may see himself in the figure of Elijah. The apocalyptic significance of Elijah was well known, and Paul's language in Rom 11:5—οὕτως οὖν καὶ ἐν τῷ νῦν καιρῷ (cf. 3:26)—suggests an eschatological orientation. Thus Käsemann suggests that Paul appealed to Elijah because he also "seemed to be alone among his people and had to bewail the unbelief of Israel."[74] Dunn presses the correspondence further:

> Paul as an Israelite (11:1) echoes Elijah's complaint against Israel. To that extent Paul sees himself, with a mixture of self-assertion and self-mockery, as a latter-day Elijah..., appealing to God to vindicate his understanding of Israel's role within God's saving purpose over against the bulk of his fellow countrymen, and expecting a similar rebuke and reassurance that God's purpose for Israel is still "on course".[75]

12.271: "εἴ τις ζηλωτής ἐστιν τῶν πατρίων ἐθῶν καὶ τῆς τοῦ θεοῦ θρησκείας, ἐπέσθω," φησίν, "ἐμοί."

73. Several other differences between Josephus and his biblical precursor stand out. Elijah makes no claim to be the sole faithful Israelite (but see *Ant.* 8.338, where Elijah claims to be God's only *prophet*). Josephus makes only passing reference to the earthquake and fire (1 Kgs 19:11–12). There is, in his account, no covenant crisis and no divine rebuke, only consolation. The remnant language of 1 Kgs 19:18 is replaced with God's promise to protect Elijah.

74. Käsemann, *Romans*, 301.

75. Dunn, *Romans*, 637.

It is not often observed that Paul seems to have structured his composition to mirror the dialogical and rhetorical shape of the biblical narrative in which Elijah's repeated charge of divine abandonment (19:10, 14) is decisively refuted by God (19:15–18).

1 Kgs 19	**Rom 11**	**Structure**
10a: Elijah's errant claim	1a: Implicit errant claim	Israel is abandoned
10b–13: Elijah's self-reference	1b: Paul's self-reference	Counter-example
14: Claim repeated	2a: Claim repeated	Israel is abandoned
15–18: God's response	5: Paul's response	A remnant remains

Did Paul see himself as a parallel figure—a solitary prophet compelled to ask, in a moment of national distress, whether God has allowed his people to perish? Although the similarities between the two men are striking, Elijah's words correspond less to Paul's than to those of his imaginary interlocutor, whose question appears in Rom 11:1a. Likewise, Paul's response corresponds less to Elijah's than to God's.[76] So if an Elijah typology is present, it is submerged and fractured: as the embattled prophet, Paul is Elijah; as the defender of God's faithfulness, Paul is Elijah's harshest critic, who cares not for himself (Rom 9:3) but for fellow Israelites who continue in unbelief.

Second, more briefly, if Paul's principal concern was to reconcile the relatively small number of Jews who had embraced Jesus as Messiah with his conviction that God was still operating within the boundaries of faithfulness established by the OT, the Elijah narrative allows Paul to explain the presence of a faithful remnant *coexisting within the covenant people as*

---

76. Cf. Wagner, *Heralds of the Good News*, 234, who doubts that Paul wrote with an "Elijah complex": "Rather than identifying with Elijah's view of the remnant, Paul emphatically rejects it as a profound misperception of the depth of God's commitment to preserve his people. In 11:4, he appeals to the divine response to Elijah precisely to insist that he himself is *not* the sole Israelite who has believed the gospel, but that by God's grace there exists even now a significantly larger 'remnant' of Israel."

a whole at a particular point in Israel's history. As it was in Elijah's day, so it is in his own.[77]

Third, we might wonder whether Paul saw correspondences between unbelieving Israel in his day and rebellious Israel in Elijah's, as Dunn implies[78] and Sanday and Headlam declare: "The spiritual condition is the same. The nation as a whole has rejected God's message, now as then."[79] If Paul saw a correspondence between these two faithless majorities, and not just between the two believing minorities, he has again suppressed it well. Perhaps only those accustomed to Paul's allusive use of Scripture will ask whether this might be one of the "suppressed ... points of resonance between the two texts."[80] If Paul did mean to link these two groups—those who formerly rejected Yahweh and those who now have failed to embrace Messiah—it would mean that "in the present time" acceptable worship was only possible for those who confessed Jesus as Lord and believed that God had raised him from the dead (10:9).

Two biblical references in the context lend weight to this proposal. First, Paul's critique of unbelieving Israel in Rom 10:16-21 incorporates Deut 32:21, the context of which clearly has the sin of idolatry in view. The portion of Deut 32:21 *not* cited in 10:19 reads, "They made me jealous with what is no god; provoked me with their idols." What Paul does cite makes sense only when heard as an ironic inversion of the part that he leaves out: the reason God conscripted a *non-nation* to *make* Israel *jealous* is because Israel *made* God *jealous* by a *non-god*, that is, by idolatrous worship (cf. Deut 32:16-17). Second, Isa 65:1-2, cited in Rom 10:20-21, begins an extended indictment of Israel's apostasy and false worship (vv. 1-12). These two OT passages share the verb כָּעַס in the MT,

---

77. I bracket the question of whether Paul identified the multiethnic church of his day with the "remnant," on which see E. P. Sanders, *Jesus and Judaism* (Philadelphia: Fortress Press, 1985), 95-98; idem, *Paul, the Law, and the Jewish People* (Philadelphia: Fortress Press, 1983), 175-76; James W. Watts, "The Remnant Theme: A Survey of New Testament Research, 1921-1987," *PRSt* 15 (1988), 109-29. Paul Dinter ("Remnant of Israel," 219-25) marshals evidence (e.g., 1QM 14:8-9; 13:8-9; CD 1:4; 1QH 6:7-8; 4QpIsa[a,c]) that the Qumran community saw itself as the remnant. Similarly, James W. Aageson, *Written Also for Our Sake* (Philadelphia: Westminster John Knox, 1993), 94-95.

78. Dunn, *Romans*, 637.

79. William Sanday and A. C. Headlam, *The Epistle to the Romans* (ICC; Edinburgh: T&T Clark, 1898), 311.

80. Hays, *Echoes of Scripture*, 20.

which is rendered by παραζηλόω ("provoke to jealousy") in Deut 32:21 and παροξύνω ("provoke to wrath") in Isa 65:3.[81]

If Paul's implicit message *is* that Jews who reject his gospel are guilty, like ancient Baal-worshipers, of covenant violation, his explicit argument is that the fate of his nonbelieving kinsmen, *unlike* that of ancient Baal worshipers, is not sealed. The unfaithful majority has not stumbled so as to fall (11:11); they are not consigned to judgment but may repent and be regrafted into the tree (11:24). Thus any negative typological function that Paul may have attributed to the people of Israel in the Elijah narrative is ultimately subverted. Elijah's kin may have "forsaken the covenant" and incurred divine judgment, but Paul's kin stand in line for God's mercy, if only they do not "continue in their unbelief."

Paul's appropriation of the Elijah narrative is both exegetical and revisionary. He interprets the sacred *traditum* by transforming it, even while absorbing it into his new *traditio*. In this respect, Paul's storytelling, like his covenantal framework and social-historical agenda, has much in common with what we find in works of RB. But if Paul's rewritings of the biblical precursor can be strikingly revisionary, his audience, then as now, would quite possibly have regarded many of his subtle revisions as mere explication. Like other early Jewish interpreters, Paul's transformations of Scripture—even his radical ones—were embedded in and disguised as biblical citations and straightforward commentary. The hermeneutical tension between reiteration and transformation in Paul's letters, between continuity and change, constitutes an illuminating and largely unexploited point of comparison between Paul and those among his Jewish contemporaries who *rewrote* the Bible.

Bibliography

Aageson, James W. "Typology, Correspondence, and the Application of Scripture in Romans 9–11." *JSNT* 31 (1987): 51–72.

---

81. Whether this was the "transgression" of 11:11–12 is not clear. Other suggestions include (1) Israel's rejection of the gospel (based upon ἀπιστία in 11:20, 23, εὐαγγέλιον in 11:28, and the thrust of Rom 10; cf. Cranfield); (2) Israel's rejection/crucifixion of Jesus (if καταλάσσω in 5:10 illuminates the phrase καταλλαγὴ κόσμου in 11:15; cf. K. Barth, Cranfield); (3) Israel's failure to understand its own role and the role of the law (cf. Dunn); and (4) hostility to Paul's Gentile mission (cf. 11:28; L. Gaston).

———. *Written Also for Our Sake*. Philadelphia: Westminster John Knox, 1993.

Amir, Y. "Authority and Interpretation of Scripture in the Writings of Philo." Pages 429–31 in *Mikra: Text, Translation, Reading, and Interpretation of the Hebrew Bible in Ancient Judaism and Early Christianity*. Edited by Martin J. Mulder. CRINT 2.1. Minneapolis: Augsburg Fortress, 1988.

Attridge, Harold. *The Interpretation of Biblical History in the Antiquitates Judaicae of Flavius Josephus*. Missoula, Mont.: Scholars Press, 1976.

Barclay, John M. G. "Mirror-Reading a Polemical Letter: Galatians as a Test Case." *JSNT* 31 (1987): 73–93.

Bauckham, Richard. "The *Liber Antiquitatum Biblicarum* of Pseudo-Philo and the Gospels as 'Midrash.'" Pages 33–76 in *Gospel Perspectives III: Studies in Midrash and Historiography*. Edited by R. T. France and D. Wenham. Sheffield: JSOT Press, 1983.

Beker, J. C. "The Faithfulness of God and the Priority of Israel in Paul's Letter to the Romans." Pages 330–32 in *The Romans Debate*. Edited by Karl P. Donfried. Rev. ed. Peabody, Mass.: Hendrickson, 1991.

———. *Paul the Apostle: The Triumph of God in Life and Thought*. Minneapolis: Fortress, 1980.

Bogaert, P.-M. *L'Apocalypse Syriaque de Baruch*. SC 144/145. Paris: Cerf, 1969.

Bonsirven, Joseph. *Exégèse rabbinique et exégèse paulinienne*. Paris: Beauchesne et ses fils, 1939.

Burnette-Bletsch, Rhonda. "At the Hands of a Woman: Rewriting Jael in Pseudo-Philo." *JSP* 17 (1998): 53–64.

Calvert-Koyzis, Nancy. *Paul, Monotheism and the People of God: The Significance of Abraham for Early Judaism and Christianity*. JSNTSup 273. Edinburgh: T&T Clark, 2004.

Campbell, William S. "Romans III as a Key to the Structure and Thought of the Letter." Pages 262–64 in *The Romans Debate*. Edited by Karl P. Donfried. Rev. ed. Peabody, Mass.: Hendrickson, 1991.

Clements, Ronald E. "'A Remnant Chosen by Grace' (Romans 11:5): The Old Testament Background and Origin of the Remnant Concept." Pages 106–21 in *Pauline Studies*. Edited by D. A. Hagner and M. J. Harris. Grand Rapids: Eerdmans, 1980.

Cohn, Leopold. "An Apocryphal Work Ascribed to Philo of Alexandria." *JQR* 10 (1898): 277–332.

Cranfield, C. E. B. *Romans*. 2 vols. ICC. Edinburgh: T&T Clark, 1979.

Davies, W. D. *Paul and Rabbinic Judaism: Some Rabbinic Elements in Pauline Theology.* New York: Harper & Row, 1948.

Dinter, Paul E. "The Remnant of Israel and the Stone of Stumbling in Zion According to Paul (Romans 9–11)." Ph.D. diss., Union Theological Seminary, 1979.

Dunn, James D. G. *Romans.* 2 vols. WBC 38A/B. Waco, Tex.: Word, 1988.

Ellis, E. Earle. *The Old Testament in Early Christianity.* Grand Rapids: Baker, 1991.

Evans, Craig A. *Ancient Texts for New Testament Studies.* Peabody, Mass.: Hendrickson, 2005.

———. "Luke and the Rewritten Bible: Aspects of Lucan Hagiography." Pages 170–201 in *The Pseudepigrapha and Early Biblical Interpretation.* Edited by C. A. Evans and J. A. Sanders. JSPSup 14. Sheffield: JSOT Press, 1993.

Evans, Craig A., and James A. Sanders, eds. *Paul and the Scriptures of Israel.* JSNTSup 83. Sheffield: JSOT Press, 1993.

Fishbane, Michael. *Biblical Interpretation in Ancient Israel.* Oxford: Oxford University, 1985.

Fisk, Bruce N. *Do You Not Remember? Scripture, Story, and Exegesis in the Rewritten Bible of Pseudo-Philo.* Sheffield: Sheffield Academic Press, 2001.

———. "Gaps in the Story, Cracks in the Earth: The Exile of Cain and the Destruction of Korah in Pseudo-Philo (*Liber Antiquitatum Biblicarum* 16)." Pages 20–33 in *Of Scribes and Sages: Early Jewish Interpretation and Transmission of Scripture.* Edited by Craig A. Evans. Edinburgh: T&T Clark, 2004.

———. "One Good Story Deserves Another: The Hermeneutics of Invoking Secondary Biblical Episodes in the Narratives of Pseudo-Philo and the *Testaments of the Twelve Patriarchs.*" Pages 218–38 in *The Interpretation of Scripture in Early Judaism and Christianity.* Edited by Craig A. Evans. JSPSup 33. Sheffield: Sheffield Academic Press, 2000.

———. "Paul: Life and Letters." Pages 301–6 in *The Face of New Testament Studies.* Edited by Scot McKnight and Grant R. Osborne. Grand Rapids: Baker, 2004.

———. "Pseudo-Philo, Paul and Israel's Rolling Stone: Early Points Along an Exegetical Trajectory." Pages 117–36 in *Israel in the Wilderness: Interpretations of the Biblical Narratives in Jewish and Christian Traditions.* Edited by Kenneth E. Pomykala. Leiden: Brill, 2008.

———. "Rewritten Bible in Pseudepigrapha and Qumran." Pages 947–48 in *Dictionary of New Testament Background*. Edited by Craig A. Evans and Stanly E. Porter. Downers Grove, Ill.: InterVarsity Press, 2000.

———. "Synagogue Influence and Scriptural Knowledge Among the Christians of Rome." Pages 157–85 in *As It Is Written: Studying Paul's Use of Scripture*. Edited by Stanley E. Porter and Christopher D. Stanley. SBLSymS 50. Atlanta: Society of Biblical Literature, 2008.

Fitzmyer, Joseph A. "The Use of Explicit Old Testament Quotations in Qumran Literature and in the New Testament." *NTS* 7 (1961): 297–333.

Ginzberg, Louis. *The Legends of the Jews*. 6 vols. Philadelphia: Jewish Publication Society, 1909–1928. Repr., Baltimore: Johns Hopkins University Press, 1998.

Given, Mark D. "Restoring the Inheritance in Romans 11:1." *JBL* 118 (1999): 89–96.

Hagner, Donald A. "Paul in Modern Jewish Thought." Pages 143–65 in *Pauline Studies*. Edited by Donald A. Hagner and M. J. Harris. Exeter: Paternoster, 1980.

Hanson, Anthony T. "The Oracle in Romans XI.4." *NTS* 19 (1973): 300–302.

Harrington, Daniel. "Pseudo-Philo: A New Translation and Introduction." Pages 297–377 in vol. 2 of *The Old Testament Pseudepigrapha*. Edited by J. H. Charlesworth. Garden City, N.Y.: Doubleday, 1985.

Hays, Richard B. *The Conversion of the Imagination: Paul as Interpreter of Israel's Scripture*. Grand Rapids: Eerdmans, 2005.

———. *Echoes of Scripture in the Letters of Paul*. New Haven: Yale University Press, 1989.

Jacobson, Howard. *A Commentary on Pseudo-Philo's Liber Antiquitatum Biblicarum*. 2 vols. Leiden: Brill, 1996.

James, M. R. *The Biblical Antiquities of Philo*. London: SPCK, 1917.

Johnson, E. Elizabeth. "Romans 9–11: The Faithfulness and Impartiality of God." Pages 211–39 in *Romans*. Vol. 3 of *Pauline Theology*. Edited by David M. Hay and E. Elizabeth Johnson. Minneapolis: Augsburg Fortress, 1995.

Käsemann, Ernst. *Romans*. Grand Rapids: Eerdmans, 1980.

Keesmaat, Sylvia C. "Exodus and the Intertextual Transformation of Tradition in Romans 8.14–30." *JSNT* 54 (1994): 29–56.

Koch, Dietrich-Alex. *Die Schrift als Zeuge des Evangeliums: Untersuchun-*

gen zur Verwendung und zum Verstandnis der Schrift bei Paulus. BHT 69. Tübingen: Mohr-Siebeck, 1986.

Kugel, James. *In Potiphar's House: The Interpretive Life of Biblical Texts*. Cambridge: Harvard University Press, 1994.

Murphy, Frederick J. "The Eternal Covenant in Pseudo-Philo." *JSP* 3 (1988): 43–57.

———. "God in Pseudo-Philo." *JSJ* 19 (1988): 1–18.

———. *Pseudo-Philo: Rewriting the Bible*. Oxford: Oxford University, 1993.

Nickelsburg, George W. E. *Jewish Literature between the Bible and the Mishnah*. Philadelphia: Fortress, 1981.

Reinmuth, Eckart. "'Nicht vergeblich' bei Paulus und Pseudo-Philo, Liber Antiquitatum Biblicarum." *NovT* 33 (1991): 97–123.

———. *Pseudo-Philo und Lukas*. WUNT 74. Tübingen: Mohr Siebeck, 1994.

Sanday, William, and A. C. Headlam. *The Epistle to the Romans*. ICC. Edinburgh: T&T Clark, 1898.

Sanders, E. P. "The Covenant as a Soteriological Category and the Nature of Salvation in Palestinian and Hellenistic Judaism." Pages 11–44 in *Jews, Greeks and Christians: Religious Cultures in Late Antiquity*. Edited by Robert Hamerton-Kelly and Robin Scroggs. Leiden: Brill, 1976.

———. *Jesus and Judaism*. Philadelphia: Fortress Press, 1985.

———. *Judaism: Practice and Belief 63 BCE–66 CE*. Philadelphia: Trinity Press International, 1992.

———. *Paul and Palestinian Judaism*. Philadelphia: Fortress Press, 1977.

———. *Paul, the Law and the Jewish People*. Philadelphia: Fortress Press, 1983.

Sayler, Gwendolyn B. *Have the Promises Failed? A Literary Analysis of 2 Baruch*. SBLDS 72. Chico, Calif.: Scholars Press, 1984.

Schoeps, Hans J. *Paul*. Philadelphia: Westminster, 1961.

Seifrid, Mark. "Romans." Pages 607–94 in *Commentary on the New Testament Use of the Old Testament*. Edited by G. K. Beale and D. A. Carson. Grand Rapids: Baker, 2008.

Stanley, Christopher D. *Arguing with Scripture: The Rhetoric of Quotations in the Letters of Paul*. Edinburgh: T&T Clark, 2004.

———. *Paul and the Language of Scripture: Citation Technique in the Pauline Epistles and Contemporary Literature*. SNTSMS 74. Cambridge: Cambridge University Press, 1992.

———. "The Significance of Romans 11:3–4 for the Text History of the LXX Book of Kingdoms." *JBL* 112 (1993): 43–54.

Stone, Michael E. "Apocalyptic Literature." Pages 383–442 in *Jewish Writings of the Second Temple Period: Apocrypha, Pseudepigrapha, Qumran Sectarian Writings, Philo, Josephus*. Edited by M. E. Stone. CRINT 2.2. Minneapolis: Augsburg Fortress, 1984.

Wagner, J. Ross. *Heralds of the Good News: Isaiah and Paul "in Concert" in the Letter to the Romans*. NovTSup 101. Leiden: Brill, 2002.

Watson, Francis. *Paul and the Hermeneutics of Faith*. London: T&T Clark, 2004.

———. *Paul, Judaism, and the Gentiles*. Grand Rapids: Eerdmans, 2007.

Watts, James W. "The Remnant Theme: A Survey of New Testament Research, 1921–1987." *PRS* 15 (1988): 109–29.

Wedderburn, A. J. M. *The Reasons for Romans*. Minneapolis: Fortress, 1991.

Wright, N. T. *Christian Origins and the Question of God*. Vol. 1 of *The New Testament and the People of God*. Minneapolis: Augsburg Fortress, 1992.

———. "Romans and the Theology of Paul." Pages 184–214 in *1992 Society of Biblical Literature Seminar Papers*. Atlanta: Scholars Press, 1992.

Part 2
Text and Context

Does Paul Respect the Context of His Quotations?

Steve Moyise

Introduction

It is clear from even a cursory glance at the literature on Paul's use of Scripture that studies tend to fall into one of two camps: some regard him as a great exegete, laying bare the meaning of Scripture in the light of the Christ-event,[1] while others view him as an expert in rhetoric, using Scripture to support positions that may have been reached on other grounds. Both sides recognize the importance of the Christ-event for Paul's interpretations, but they differ as to its role. The former sees Scripture as a genuine object of study, able to "speak" to the reader's situation when interpreted in the light of the Christ-event. Thus even a text like Deut 25:4 ("You shall not muzzle an ox while it is treading out the grain") can speak to the congregation when properly interpreted (1 Cor 9:9). The latter regards the Christ-event as primary and Scripture as "speaking" only when its "voice" coincides with Paul's rhetorical concerns. When it does not, as in the case of circumcision, it is simply set aside (Gal 5:2). Though the use of the word "respect" is problematic, as we will see below, it is commonly used to distinguish the two camps just outlined: the former assert that Paul respects the context of his quotations/allusions, the latter that he does not.

What Is Meant by "Respect"?

It is easy to show that "respect" is not a very precise term for such a debate. In a modern publishing context, I am obliged to quote a scholar's words

---

1. I use this term to speak not only of Christ's life, death, and resurrection but also what followed, namely, the birth of the Church and especially the inclusion of the Gentiles.

with accuracy even if I disagree with them. Changing the wording of a quotation, especially if it strengthens my argument, is regarded as a lack of respect for the author that undermines my credibility as a scholar. In the ancient world, by contrast, such alterations were common. For example, while the complexities of textual transmission make it difficult to know the precise form of Paul's sources, most scholars accept that Paul is responsible for removing the pronoun μου ("my") from his quotation of Hab 2:4 (Rom 1:17; Gal 3:11) and adding the word πᾶς ("every") to his quotation of Isa 28:16 (Rom 10:11). In modern publishing terms, Paul has not respected the wording of his quotations.

It would be anachronistic, however, to judge Paul by such standards. It would be the equivalent of saying that modern scholars are slavish imitators because they reproduce the wording of their quotations exactly. This is a modern convention that we all follow even when we regard the words as potentially misleading, as when we detect the presence of metaphor or irony in a text. Our conventions require that we proceed in stages: the words are quoted exactly as they appear in the publication; evidence is offered for the presence of metaphor or irony; an interpretation is offered. Of course, this academic convention is hardly what takes place in the majority of sermons, where preachers frequently move directly from text to contemporary application. Neither was it a convention in Paul's day. It is clear from writers such as Philo and Josephus, as well as from the Dead Sea Scrolls, that first-century authors were quite willing to fuse some of these stages by offering an interpretation in the form of a modified quotation. For Paul, the inclusion of the Gentiles suggests that the ὁ πιστεύων ("The one who believes") in Isa 28:16 means "everyone who believes," and he makes this point plain in Rom 10:11 by adding πᾶς ("every").[2]

This has implications for both sides of the debate. For those who think that Paul is a great exegete, the assertion that Paul always respects the context of his quotations and allusions needs qualification: the word "respect" is not being used in its modern publishing sense. It is therefore necessary to clarify the way that the word is being used. On the other hand, for those who focus on Paul's use of Scripture as a means of persuasion rather than

---

2. That this is deliberate is shown by the fact that he has earlier quoted the text without the πᾶς (Rom 9:33), when the emphasis was on those who have stumbled rather than those who believe. It is also to be noted that he will shortly quote from Joel 2:32 (LXX 3:5), where "Everyone [πᾶς] who calls on the name of the Lord shall be saved" (Rom 10:13). This confirms that it is the teaching of Scripture as well as revelation.

exposition, the claim that Paul does not respect the context of his quotations and allusions needs to do more than point out a few minor changes of wording. In both cases, a line needs to be drawn and arguments offered as to whether Paul does or does not cross it. And herein lies the problem: there is no agreement as to where this line should be drawn.

Attempts to Draw a Line

For those who advocate "respect," it is often argued that Paul's meaning, while sometimes different from the actual words quoted, is nevertheless faithful to their wider context. And if that does not appear to be true for the half dozen or so verses on either side of the quoted text, the field is widened to the chapter, the book, or in some cases, one of the major divisions of the Hebrew Bible, such as the Pentateuch. For example, it is difficult to see how Paul can be said to respect the context of Deut 27:26 and Lev 18:5 in Gal 3:10–12, since these texts emphasize the absolute importance of the law while Paul asserts that "the law does not rest on faith" (Gal 3:12). Francis Watson, however, argues that the earlier reference to Abraham (Genesis) in Gal 3:6–9 and the later reference to Sinai (Exodus) in Gal 3:19–20 shows that Paul has in mind a "construal" of the whole Pentateuch. Watson may be right, but if this is where the line is to be drawn, it is difficult to see how Paul (or his contemporaries) could ever cross it, so the assertion of "respect" becomes meaningless.[3]

Those who deny that Paul respects the context of his quotations and allusions can go beyond pointing out a few minor changes or wording by showing that some of the meanings that Paul derives from the texts could not possibly have been in the mind of the original author (or editor). For example, Paul uses Isa 52:5 in Rom 2:24 as an accusation against the Jews: "The name of God is blasphemed among the Gentiles because of you." It is widely acknowledged that this is not the meaning of the words in their immediate context (Isa 52:3–6), or even in the wider context of Isaiah 51–52.[4] However, Richard Hays points out that Paul quotes Isa 52:7 ("How

---

3. See Steve Moyise, "How Does Paul Read Scripture?," in Craig A. Evans and H. D. Zacharias, eds., *Early Christian Literature and Intertextuality 1* (New York: T&T Clark, 2009), 184–96.

4. "According to both the Hebrew original and the LXX, it was Israel's misfortune that led to the reviling of God's name by the nations. Paul, however, interprets the LXX phrase 'on account of you' as 'because of your fault,' thereby converting what

beautiful upon the mountains...") in Rom 10:15, clearly demonstrating that he is aware of the salvation context of Isa 52:5: "If he reads Isa 52:5 as a reproach, it is a reproach only in the same way that the historical event to which it refers was a reproach."[5] According to Hays, then, Paul is demonstrating not a lack of respect for the context but a deliberate hermeneutical strategy. Paul will show in Rom 10 that he fully endorses the salvation message of Isa 52, but for hermeneutical reasons, he chooses to delay it:

> The letter's rhetorical structure lures the reader into expecting Israel's final condemnation, but the later chapters undercut such an expectation, requiring the reader in subsequent encounters with the text to understand the Isaiah quotation more deeply in relation to its original prophetic context.[6]

But is this a sufficient answer? Hays is surely correct that Paul is aware of what he is doing, but I am not sure that "subsequent encounters with the text" would lead readers to view it as a deeper understanding of the "original prophetic context." It seems that Hays is using the phrase "original prophetic context" to mean the "historical event to which it refers," namely, the exile. If this is so, then it may be that Paul has in mind other exilic texts which do accuse Israel, such as Ezek 36:22: "It is not for your sake, O house of Israel, that I am about to act, but for the sake of *my holy name, which you have profaned among the nations* to which you came." It may even be this text that led the LXX translator to add ἐν τοῖς ἔθνεσιν ("among the nations") and δι' ὑμᾶς ("for your sake") to his rendering of Isa 52:5, which simply says, "continually, every day, my name is scorned" (ותמיד כל היום שמי מנאץ).[7] Essentially, then, what Paul has done is to provide a context (Rom 2:17–24) that suggests to the reader that δι' ὑμᾶς should be taken to mean "because of you" rather than "for your sake." For some, this shows

---

was originally an oracle of compassion towards Israel into one of judgment" (Brendan Byrne, *Romans* [Collegeville, Minn.: Liturgical Press, 1996], 101). For a discussion of this quotation, see Steve Moyise, *Evoking Scripture: Seeing the Old Testament in the New* (London: T&T Clark, 2008), 33–48.

5. Richard B. Hays, *Echoes of Scripture in the Letters of Paul* (New Haven: Yale University Press, 1989), 45.

6. Ibid., 46.

7. There is of course the possibility that the LXX is dependent on a pre-MT reading that has not survived.

a lack of respect for the original, while others find such scripturally based explanations an adequate defence of Paul's respect for context.[8]

Scriptural or Rhetorical Explanations?

The example above suggests that at the heart of this debate is the question of whether Paul derives his interpretations *mainly* through "inner-biblical exegesis" or from the rhetorical exigencies of his and his reader's situation. The answer is not straightforward, for those who advocate "respect" usually begin with the assumption that there must be an innerbiblical explanation and then go to great lengths to find one. Thus Timothy Berkley suggests that behind Rom 2:17–29 lies a hidden exegesis of Jer 7:9–11, 9:23–24, and Ezek 36:16–27. We have already noted the relevance of Ezek 36:22, but Berkley find in the two Jeremiah passages sufficient warrant for the rest of Paul's accusations. Jeremiah 7:9–11 accuses Israel of theft, murder, adultery, swearing falsely, and idolatry, while Jer 9:23–24, a text that Paul explicitly quotes elsewhere (1 Cor 1:31; 2 Cor 10:17), adds boasting to the list. Berkley argues that it is through the mutual interpretation of these three "reference" texts that Paul can indict the Jews of his day with these crimes. Thus Isa 52:5 does not stand alone; in fact, Berkley argues that it is the least important of the texts, serving simply to provide a convenient summary of Paul's exegesis.[9]

This explanation raises at least two questions. First, if it is true that Paul did precisely what Berkley says he did, how can this be seen as respecting the context of Isa 52:5? It may respect the context of Jer 7:9–11 and 9:23–24 and Ezek 36:16–27 and thereby confirm Paul as a serious exegete, but, in using the words of Isa 52:5 as a convenient summary, Paul has in fact taken the latter text out of context. This does not necessarily imply a lack of respect *if* Paul's readers could have understood what he was doing. Just

---

8. "Paul's citations and allusions to Isaiah are not plundered from random raids on Israel's sacred texts. Rather, they are the product of sustained and careful attention to the rhythms and cadences of individual passages as well as to larger themes and motifs that run throughout the prophet's oracles" (J. Ross Wagner, *Heralds of the Good News: Isaiah and Paul "in Concert" in the Letter to the Romans* [NovTSup 101; Leiden: Brill, 2002], 356).

9. Timothy W. Berkley, *From a Broken Covenant to Circumcision of the Heart: Pauline Intertextual Exegesis in Romans 2.17–29* (SBLDS 175; Atlanta: Society of Biblical Literature, 2000), 139.

as adding πᾶς ("every") to his quotation of Isa 28:16 (Rom 10:11) does not constitute a lack of respect because readers would have recognized this as a deliberate addition, neither does using Isa 52:5 as a convenient summary text if it is recognized as part of a literary strategy.

This brings me to my second question: How likely is it that Paul's readers could have discerned Berkley's "hidden exegesis"? The question can be posed in general terms regarding levels of literacy in the first century or in terms of specific evidence from Paul's letter. Christopher Stanley has frequently made the point that it is difficult to imagine members of the churches having the wherewithal to discern the sophisticated theories being proposed by modern scholars. The more educated among them would have known the stories about Abraham, Moses, and David and possibly a number of the church's key texts (Ps 2, Dan 7, Isa 53), but hardly the intricate textual details on which such theories often depend.[10] Although he does not specifically comment on Berkley's proposal, it is clear that he would regard it as virtually impossible for first-century members of the church to discern such an interpretive strategy.

Of course, that is not to say that it would have been impossible for Paul. It is clear from his letters as a whole that he has a deep knowledge of the Scriptures, and it is quite possible that the texts mentioned by Berkley could have come to mind as he moved toward his conclusion that "no human being will be justified in his sight by deeds prescribed by the law" (Rom 3:20). But unless his readers could have discerned this, they would have been unable to recognize the hidden exegesis behind Paul's "summarizing quotation." In other words, there is nothing to suggest to them that the quotation of Isa 52:5 is part of a literary convention. They would naturally assume that the words present an accusation against the Jews, and they would thus be misled. As Stanley says, if any of them had possessed the ability to find an Isaiah scroll and look up the quotation (which he doubts), they would have "found themselves more confused than helped."[11]

Berkley is in fact ambivalent about whether Paul's readers would be able to discern his exegesis. For example, in discussing Rom 2:17 ("But if you call yourself a Jew"), he maintains that the "address Ἰουδαῖος now takes on a significance it would not have if the OT texts Paul is drawing

---

10. Christopher D. Stanley, *Arguing with Scripture: The Rhetoric of Quotations in the Letters of Paul* (New York: T&T Clark, 2004), 45.

11. Ibid., 147.

from were not taken into consideration."[12] But there is then a footnote that says: "This is not to assume that the original readers were aware of Paul's references to those texts. But for those who were they give a greater understanding of how this passage fits into the larger whole of the epistle."[13] Thus, according to Berkley, Paul has kept hidden what would have been most useful (his dependence on Jeremiah and Ezekiel) and made explicit (Isa 52:5) what is merely a summarizing text. The suggestion that Paul's allusions might carry more profundity than his explicit quotations is worthy of consideration, but it seems perverse to suggest that he would deliberately hide that which would have been the most illuminating.

Of course, Paul might have done what many a teacher has done and assumed his readers possess more knowledge and insight than was actually the case.[14] This opens up the possibility that in Paul's mind the context of Isa 52:5 has been respected because it is part of a complex inner-biblical exegesis, even though this would have been lost on his readers. However, few scholars would wish to attribute such poor communication skills to Paul. Most argue that the congregation would have contained at least a few educated members who could have discerned Paul's reasoning—perhaps after multiple readings and study—and explained it to the rest of the congregation.[15] Thus a reference to Scripture is regarded as an invitation to explore more of the context than is explicitly cited. It is assumed that this will be helpful—indeed, vital—for understanding Paul's letter.

Stanley suggests we start at the other end. If it is unlikely that Paul's readers would have discerned the complex inner-biblical exegesis suggested by Berkley or the broader hermeneutical strategy suggested by Hays, then perhaps these proposals tell us more about the imagination of these scholars than Paul's actual intentions. Stanley suggests that by "framing his quotations in such a way that their 'meaning' could be determined from the context of his letter, Paul did his best to insure that his quotations

---

12. Berkley, *From a Broken Covenant*, 119.
13. Ibid., 119 n. 30.
14. "Either Paul was rhetorically inept in failing to take account of the literary capabilities of his audiences or Hays and his followers have misjudged what Paul was doing with his biblical references. We cannot have it both ways." Christopher D. Stanley, "Paul's Use of Scripture: Why the Audience Matters" in *As It Is Written: Studying Paul's Use of Scripture* (ed. Stanley E. Porter and Christopher D. Stanley; SBLSymS 50; Atlanta: Society of Biblical Literature, 2008), 146.
15. Wagner, *Heralds of the Good News*, 36–9.

would be understood in the manner in which he intended them."[16] Paul is not inviting his readers to locate the quotation and use its "context" to understand what he is saying. As Stanley says, to do so in this case would have left them "more confused than helped." Instead, Paul is asking them to follow his line of reasoning in the letter and accept his interpretations of Scripture as correct.

This approach is helpful in that it allows us to further clarify the terms of the debate. On the one hand, some scholars are attempting to reconstruct Paul's thought processes. Paul makes it clear that he understands Isa 52:5 as an accusation against the Jews, so a sequence of reasoning is sought which will explain this. And since we all know that human thought processes are complex, we should not be surprised if the explanation for Paul's interpretation turns out to be complex. Of course, the more complex the theory becomes, the less likely it is that his readers would have been able to discern it. But this is not a problem for scholars in this camp. The goal of their study is to discover how Paul reached his conclusions, not to determine whether his original readers would have understood this process. The question of "respect" for this type of study is largely synonymous with whether a plausible sequence of exegetical steps can be found that explains how Paul got from scripture text to interpretation.

On the other side are scholars who argue that we must also take account of what Paul was wishing to communicate to his readers. The processes that led to Paul's interpretations were no doubt complex, but they are not what he was trying to communicate. The latter can only be discerned by attending to the specific signals that Paul has placed in the text. Studies that follow this approach aim not to reconstruct Paul's thought processes but rather to figure out what he wanted his readers to notice. We can therefore clarify the difference between the interpretations of Berkley, Hays, and Stanley in the following terms.

- Berkley: Readers are expected to notice that the accusations of Rom 2:17–23 are part of a hidden exegesis behind the explicit quotation of Isa 52:5.
- Hays: Readers are expected to notice that the quotation of Isa 52:7 in Rom 10:15 implies that the earlier quotation of Isa 52:5 was not taken out of context but is part of a particular hermeneutical strategy.

---

16. Stanley, *Arguing with Scripture*, 176.

- Stanley: Readers are expected to notice that Paul's introductory formula ("For, as it is written") confirms that the rather unpleasant accusations against the Jews in Rom 2:17-23 are in fact the verdict of Scripture, and that is all there is to it.

Each approach has its weaknesses. (1) Berkley himself suggests that the links that he discerns are so "hidden" that Paul can hardly have expected his readers to notice them. But his footnote indicating that such a recognition would have greatly benefited those who did notice them seems to undermine his whole position. Paul either intends to keep it hidden or does not. (2) The weakness of Hays's proposal is that Paul has not made it easy for readers to spot the significance of the Isa 52:7 quotation in Rom 10:15. For one thing, it belongs to a section (Rom 10:5-21) that contains nearly a dozen quotations from Scripture, so it is difficult to see why this one would be singled out. Moreover, if Paul had wanted his readers to explicitly notice that the words Ὡς ὡραῖοι οἱ πόδες τῶν εὐαγγελιζομένων [τὰ] ἀγαθά ("How beautiful are the feet of those who bring good news") closely follow the earlier quotation, it would have helped if he had included more of it, especially as Nah 1:15 is almost identical. (3) The weakness of the third suggestion is that it implies both a strong authoritarian streak in Paul's rhetoric and a lack of curiosity in his readers. Surely someone in Paul's congregations would have been curious as to whether Scripture actually says what Paul is claiming. And would not Paul want to encourage his readers to "search the scriptures" rather than closing them down?

Thus none of the theories is entirely convincing, though I am inclined to think that it comes to a choice between the second and the third, with a slight preference for the third. Of course, one cannot generalize from this one example to broad statements about Paul's use of Scripture. For example, it is likely that the sustained treatment of Abraham in Gal 3 and Rom 4 requires readers to draw significantly on the Genesis stories in order to make sense of Paul's argument. But it is interesting that Paul's opening quotation in Romans (Hab 2:4; Rom 1:17) raises questions similar to those raised by Isa 52:5, and to this we will now turn.

Does Paul Expect His Readers to Use the Context of Hab 2:4 in Rom 1:17?

The discovery of the Habakkuk commentary at Qumran demonstrates that at least one ancient Jewish community was very interested in the continuous interpretation of this text. Although the interpretations are not what we would call "contextual," the author(s) clearly thought that Hab 2:1–3 and Hab 2:5–7 could speak to their community as much as the highly charged words of Hab 2.4. This is the assumption behind Rikki Watts's study of Rom 1:16–17. Watts suggests that the explicit quotation of Hab 2:4 in Rom 1:17 acts as a trigger for a host of other parallels between the two writings.[17] For example, he thinks the accusations of Rom 2:17–23 ("do you steal? ... do you commit adultery? ... do you rob temples?") parallel the "puffed up and arrogant Chaldean (Hab 2:4a), who steals and is an idolater."[18] He suggests that Paul's critique of the law in Rom 2:1–3:20 has similarities with Habakkuk's complaint that "the law becomes slack and justice never prevails" (Hab 1:4). Indeed, Watts says that Paul's lament in Rom 7:24 ("How wretched I am! Who will deliver me from this body of sin?") *"sounds surprisingly close* to Habakkuk's first lament where, distressed at the ineffectiveness of the law (1.3b–4), he too cries out for help (1.2–3b)."[19] In a similar way, Paul's principle in Rom 2:9 that "there will be anguish and distress for everyone who does evil, the Jew first and also the Greek" mirrors Habakkuk's word against Judea (Hab 1:12) and his later words against the Chaldeans (Hab 2:5–20). Watts also points to a correspondence between Habakkuk's combination of a song of praise (Hab 3:2–15) and a call for perseverance (Hab 3:16–17) with Paul's exclamations of praise (Rom 5:6–11, 8:28–39, 11:33–36) and calls for perseverance (Rom 4:18–21, 5:1–5, 8:18–27). Finally, noting that Habakkuk ends with the affirmation "The Lord is my strength" (Hab 3:19), Watts thinks that Paul "echoes this language" in Rom 1:16 and even that *"it might explain* why Romans alone of Paul's letters concludes with a doxology (16:25–27): 'Now to the one who is able to strengthen you....'"[20]

I find this totally unconvincing. If we had doubts as to whether Paul's readers would find echoes of Jeremiah and Ezekiel behind Rom 2:17–23, they look positively convincing next to Watts's assumption that the readers would draw comparisons with the "puffed up and arrogant Chaldean (Hab. 2:4a), who steals and is an idolater." Paul's critique of the law in Rom

---

17. Rikki E. Watts, "'For I Am Not Ashamed of the Gospel': Romans 1:16–17 and Habakkuk 2:4," in *Romans and the People of God* (ed. S. K. Soderlund and N. T. Wright; Grand Rapids: Eerdmans, 1999), 3–25.
18. Ibid., 17.
19. Ibid., emphasis added.
20. Ibid., 24, emphasis added.

2:1–3:20 is very different from Habakkuk's concern that "the wicked surround the righteous" and "justice never prevails," as Watts himself acknowledges ("True, the emphasis is different"). His opening sentence is telling: "Although Paul gives no explicit indication that he has in view Habakkuk's complaint about the Law's ineffectiveness, it is noteworthy that he is especially concerned with this issue."[21] In my view, the first part of this statement ("Paul gives no explicit indication") applies to all of his suggestions. Habakkuk's word of judgement against Judea (1:12), followed by a much longer section against the Chaldeans (2:5–20), is hardly a convincing parallel to Paul's succinct statement ("the Jew first and also the Greek"). The combination of perseverance and praise is also far too common to suggest that Habakkuk was in Paul's mind, especially as the order in Rom 5:1–11 and 8:18–39 is perseverance followed by praise, the reverse of Hab 3:2–17. Lastly, the case for seeing Hab 3:19 (κύριος ὁ θεὸς δύναμίς μου) behind Rom 16:25 (τῷ δὲ δυναμένῳ ὑμᾶς στηρίξαι) is no stronger than any other text that combines "God" and "strength," such as LXX Ps 17:33, 45:1, or 67:36. The suggestion that Hab 3:19 might be the *reason* that Paul wrote the doxology (if it is in fact genuine) is surely incredible.

In fact, neither NA[27] nor UBS[4] note any further allusions to Habakkuk in Romans, and only two in the rest of the Pauline corpus. These are both in 1 Corinthians, namely, Hab 3:19 in 1 Cor 1:24 and Hab 2:18 in 1 Cor 12:2. The first concerns Paul's affirmation that, for those who are called, Christ is the "power of God and the wisdom of God" (θεοῦ δύναμιν καὶ θεοῦ σοφίαν). The first part of this could be an allusion to Habakkuk's affirmation that God is his strength, or power (κύριος ὁ θεὸς δύναμίς μου), though it is not regarded as such by UBS[4]. The case for an allusion is not strong, for the agreement only extends to two (very common) words, and the constructions are quite different (nominative in Habakkuk, genitive in Paul). Indeed, Paul is stating a fact (for believers, Christ *is* the power of God), whereas Habakkuk is making a personal affirmation that, despite his troubles, God will be his strength, or power. The supposed allusion is not distinctive enough to suggest that Paul wished his readers to specifically think of Habakkuk's struggles.

The case for seeing an allusion to Habakkuk in 1 Cor 12:2 is stronger and is supported by NA[27] and UBS[4]. Paul reminds the Corinthians that, when they were pagans (ἔθνη), they were led astray by dumb idols (τὰ

---

21. Ibid., 17.

εἴδωλα τὰ ἄφωνα). One of the indictments found in Habakkuk 2 is that the people trust in dumb idols (εἴδωλα κωφά). Here we only have one word in common, and it is difficult to see why Paul would change κωφός τo ἄφωνος when his only other use of ἄφωνος is to make the point that "nothing is without sound" (1 Cor 14:10). Nevertheless, though verbal agreement is missing, there is undoubtedly a strong conceptual link (the foolishness of trusting in idols that cannot even speak), but such an idea is not unique to Habakkuk. LXX Ps 113:13 and 134:16 speak of idols which "have a mouth but will not speak" (στόμα ἔχουσιν καὶ οὐ λαλήσουσιν), and there is little reason to suggest that priority should be given to Habakkuk over these verses. It appears that Paul is drawing on a common *topos* that idol worshippers seek answers from objects that are unable to speak. Habakkuk 2:18 may have contributed to the development of such a tradition, but this does not mean that Paul was specifically pointing to Habakkuk.

Hays and Watson adopt a different approach.[22] Neither tries to establish specific verbal parallels between Romans and Habakkuk, but both insist that Paul has used the text with the utmost seriousness. For Hays, the key is that the book of Habakkuk is a well-known *locus classicus* for the theme of theodicy. There is of course a considerable difference between the "problem" in Habakkuk and the "problem" in Romans. Habakkuk is concerned about the "military domination of the Chaldeans ... over an impotent Israel," whereas Paul's concern is the "apparent usurpation of Israel's favored covenant status by congregations of uncircumcised Gentile Christians."[23] In that sense, the parallel is off center and thus metaphorical (a trope). But Hays insists that there is sufficient similarity to deny that Paul is "circumventing the text's original referential sense." Instead, he maintains that Paul "draws on that sense—indeed, on at least two different traditional readings of it—as a source of symbolic resonance for his affirmation of the justice of God's ways in the present time."[24]

Watson's argument is very different. He first notes the close lexical correspondence between assertion and citation. Normally, when Paul cites texts, there is a close semantic correspondence between assertion and Scripture text, but not a close lexical correspondence.[25] Here, the par-

---

22. This section draws on Moyise, *Evoking Scripture*, 49–62.
23. Hays, *Echoes of Scripture*, 40.
24. Ibid., 41.
25. He cites Rom 3:9-10 as typical of Paul's method. Paul asserts that "we have already charged that all, both Jews and Greeks, are under the power of sin," then sup-

ticular genitive expression (ἐκ πίστεως) is unlikely to have been formulated by Paul and only later discovered in Hab 2:4. In fact, the assertion of Rom 1:17a is virtually a paraphrase of Hab 2:4: "*The one who is righteous* (that is, with a *righteousness* of God, revealed in the gospel) *by faith* (since this righteousness is received *by faith* and is intended for faith) *will live*."[26] The theme of "righteousness by faith" will be picked up in Rom 4 when Paul discusses Abraham, who "believed God and it was reckoned to him as righteousness" (Gen 15:6). Before that, Paul pursues an argument designed to demonstrate that "no human being will be justified in his sight by works of the law" (Rom 3:20). Watson suggests that the widely debated genitive phrase ἐξ ἔργων νόμου ("of works of law") has been constructed in contrast to ἐκ πίστεως. In other words, Paul's exegesis *begins* with Hab 2:4; it is not simply an afterthought.

This does not mean that Paul wishes his readers to see their situation in the light of the historical Habakkuk. The point is that these words, like the words in Gen 15:6, stand in Scripture and are in tension with texts like Lev 18:5, which promise life through obedience to the law. Paul's exegesis makes this tension explicit, so that the "voice of the prophet and the voice of the law represent the positive and negative side of the total scriptural testimony to the Pauline gospel."[27] It is undoubtedly a radical interpretation, but what is notable about Rom 1:16–17 is that Paul does not simply impose a Christological interpretation onto the words of Hab 2:4. Of course, faith for Paul is "entirely and exclusively bound up with God's saving action in Christ"[28] and he will make this explicit in Rom 3:21–22. But this does not mean that Paul thought that this is what Habakkuk had in mind, since the text presupposes a reader who lives in the time of fulfilment and so can interpret what has previously remained mysterious ("For there is a vision for the appointed time," Hab 2:3). In other words, Paul is not attending to the "literal sense" as understood by modern historical criticism, but his reading is literal insofar as he is responding to the text in a way that the text authorizes.

---

ports it ("as it is written") by the text, "There is no one who is righteous, not even one." Conceptually, the cited text is in close agreement with the assertion, but there is virtually no lexical correspondence.

26. Watson, *Paul and the Hermeneutics of Faith*, 48.
27. Ibid., 66.
28. Ibid., 161.

Moving in a different direction, Michael Shepherd has recently argued that the context for understanding Paul's quotation is not the individual book of Habakkuk but "The Twelve" (cf. Sir 49:10). He begins by noting that Hab 2:4 falls between the eschatological theophanies of Nah 1:2–8 and Hab 3:3–15. He then points out that the issue faced by Habakkuk is encapsulated in Hab 1:5, which he describes as a temptation to "lack faith" (לא תאמינו) in the "work" (פעל) of God. Next, he observes that the message of Hab 2:1–4 is fundamentally eschatological, as indicated by the use of מועד ("appointed time") and קץ ("the end"), terms that are taken up in Dan 10–12. He also notes that Hab 2:4 is linked to Hab 1:5 not only by the repetition of the root אמן, which he understands as "faith" rather than "faithfulness," but also by the strange use of עפל ("to swell"), which reverses the first two consonants of פעל ("work"). Finally, pointing to Habakkuk's confession that he has "feared" God's work (Hab 3:2), Shepherd argues that "fear" and "believe" fall within the same semantic field. From these points, he concludes that the "composition of Habakkuk is about justification by faith in the eschatological and messianic work of God,"[29] which is precisely Paul's meaning in Rom 1:17.

What, then, do we say? Does Paul respect the context of Hab 2:4? Watts, Hays, Watson, and Shepherd all think so, but for very different reasons. Watts thinks that the many parallels between the two works show that Paul intended to evoke the whole book. To my mind, none of his suggested parallels are convincing, nor do they figure in the arguments of Hays, Watson, or Shepherd, or in the tables in NA[27] and UBS[4]. It seems to me that Watts is convinced that Paul always respects the context of his quotations and therefore cites a series of tenuous parallels to support this contention. If "respect for context" requires us to believe that Paul engaged in such complex and veiled allusions to other parts of Habakkuk, then I must conclude that Paul has not respected the context of Hab 2:4.

For Hays, it is not the presence of specific allusions but the overall theme of Habakkuk—namely, theodicy—that is important. This coheres with his view that Romans is not primarily about salvation but about God's faithfulness. This is probably not unconnected with his view that the phrase πίστις Ἰησοῦ should be taken as the "faithfulness of Jesus" rather than "faith in Jesus."[30] Each time Paul returns to the theme of theo-

---

29. Michael B. Shepherd, *The Twelve Prophets in the New Testament* (Studies in Biblical Literature 140; New York: Lang, 2011), 51.

30. In the second edition of Hays's 1983 work, he notes an impressive list of

dicy in Romans (2:11, 3:3–4, 3:25–26, 9:6 etc.), says Hays, readers will remember the opening quotation and think of Habakkuk, though not of specific verses or phrases. It is difficult to evaluate this claim. On the one hand, Hays rightly notes that Romans begins with a statement about the importance of the prophets ("the gospel of God, which he promised beforehand through his prophets," Rom 1:2), and the first explicit quotation comes from the prophet Habakkuk. On the other hand, the lack of any further allusions to this text could suggest that it is the theme of theodicy (if Hays is correct) rather than Habakkuk that is important to Paul. In this case, it cannot be said that Paul disrespects the context of Habakkuk, since the book is indeed about theodicy, but Paul's main interest appears to lie elsewhere.

For Watson, Paul is not inviting his readers to think specifically of Habakkuk, but he does wish to engage them in the serious task of establishing the meaning of ὁ δίκαιος ἐκ πίστεως ζήσεται. It is not necessary to agree with Watson's far-reaching conclusion that Paul finds a fundamental antithesis in Scripture to acknowledge how important these words are to him. They are cited in Galatians and discussed and paraphrased in Romans, and they appear to be the basis for Paul's ἐκ πίστεως / ἐξ ἔργων νόμου language. But does this constitute respect for the context of Hab 2:4? It does if we take "context" to be the role or function of the words in Scripture as a whole, since Paul is explicitly relating them (if Watson is correct) to two of its most important themes: life through legal obedience and life through faith. As with Hays, this is not what historical critics would regard as "respecting the context" of Hab 2:4, but neither is it an arbitrary or ad hoc use of this text.

Shepherd is rather different. He does not offer any evidence that Paul read Hab 2:4 in relation to the theophanies of Nah 1:2–8 and Hab 3:3–15 or that he specifically linked it with Hab 1:5 and 3:2. Rather, he thinks that this is what the editor-compiler of "The Twelve" did. So his argument is not that Paul agrees with the meaning of Hab 2:4 but that the meaning of

---

scholars who have now adopted the subjective genitive interpretation: B. Byrne, D. Campbell, C. B. Cousar, C. A. Davis, G. N. Davies, T. L. Donaldson, L. Gaston, B. R. Gaventa, M. D. Hooker, G. Howard, L. T. Johnson, L. E. Keck, B. W. Longenecker, R. N. Longenecker, J. L. Martyn, F. J. Matera, P. T. O'Brian, M. L. Soards, S. K. Stowers, B. Witherington, S. K. Williams, N. T. Wright. A critique by J. D. G. Dunn is included as an appendix. See Richard B. Hays, *The Faith of Jesus Christ: The Narrative Substructure of Galatians 3:1–4:11* (2nd ed.; Grand Rapids: Eerdmans, 2002).

Hab 2:4 agrees with Paul. Integral to Shepherd's thesis is the belief that the meanings assigned to quotations in the New Testament are always identical to their original meanings. For example, Paul's interpretation of Hos 13:14 as a reference to resurrection (1 Cor 15:55) is correct because "the hope of a renewed state of Israel in which the reader would not actually take part" would hardly be of comfort to his Gentile Christian readers.[31] Similarly, in his discussion of Paul's quotation of Joel 2:32 in Rom 10:13, he says that "there is no reason to think that salvation in Paul is different from salvation in Joel unless the reader creates a false dichotomy between physical deliverance and spiritual deliverance."[32] In short, the issue of whether Paul respects the context of his quotations is not a question for Shepherd. He operates with the assumption that the two meanings are identical, even when the LXX differs from the Hebrew, and so has nothing to contribute to our discussion.

Conclusion

I began this essay by noting that, while "respect for context" is a frequently debated topic and scholars usually align themselves with one side or the other, there is no agreed definition of the word "respect." I conclude with a series of observations that I hope will help to clarify the terms of this debate.

- If "respect for context" means absolute fidelity to the language of the original, then Paul does not always respect the context of his quotations.
- If "respect for context" means relating his interpretations to the *historical* situation of the original authors, then Paul does not always (or even often, perhaps) respect the context of his quotations.
- If "respect for context" means drawing on the surrounding verses of the quotations, then Paul does not always (or often) respect the context of his quotations.

On the other hand,

---

31. Shepherd, *The Twelve Prophets*, 25
32. Ibid., 31

- If "respect for context" means a serious engagement with the actual words of the quotation and relating them to similar texts elsewhere in Scripture, then Paul does sometimes (or often) respect the context of his quotations.
- If "respect for context" means discerning the meaning of a quotation by relating it to the main contours of Scripture or a major section of Scripture, then Paul does sometimes (or often) respect the context of his quotations.[33]

Bibliography

Berkley, Timothy W. *From a Broken Covenant to Circumcision of the Heart: Pauline Intertextual Exegesis in Romans 2.17–29.* SBLDS 175. Atlanta: Society of Biblical Literature, 2000.

Byrne, Brendan. *Romans.* Collegeville, Minn.: Liturgical Press, 1996.

Hays, Richard B. *Echoes of Scripture in the Letters of Paul.* New Haven: Yale University Press, 1989.

———. *The Faith of Jesus Christ: The Narrative Substructure of Galatians 3:1–4:11.* 2nd ed. Grand Rapids: Eerdmans, 2002.

Moyise, Steve. *Evoking Scripture: Seeing the Old Testament in the New.* London: T&T Clark, 2008.

———. "How Does Paul Read Scripture?" Pages 184–96 in vol. 1 of *Early Christian Literature and Intertextuality.* Edited by Craig A. Evans and H. D. Zacharias. New York: T&T Clark, 2009.

Shepherd, Michael B. *The Twelve Prophets in the New Testament.* Studies in Biblical Literature 140. New York: Lang, 2011.

Stanley, Christopher D. *Arguing with Scripture: The Rhetoric of Quotations in the Letters of Paul.* New York: T&T Clark, 2004.

———. "Paul's Use of Scripture: Why the Audience Matters." Pages 125–55 in *As It Is Written: Studying Paul's Use of Scripture.* Edited by Stanley E. Porter and Christopher D. Stanley. SBLSymS 50. Atlanta: Society of Biblical Literature, 2008.

Wagner, J. Ross. *Heralds of the Good News: Isaiah and Paul "in Concert" in the Letter to the Romans.* NovTSup 101. Leiden: Brill, 2002.

---

33. It should be noted, however, that it is only in specific theological circles that "respect for context" is defined in these terms. A more general audience would understand the phrase within our first category and hence conclude that Paul does not always (perhaps often) respect the context of his quotations.

Watson, Francis. *Paul and the Hermeneutics of Faith*. London: T&T Clark, 2004.

Watts, Rikki E. "'For I Am Not Ashamed of the Gospel': Romans 1:16–17 and Habakkuk 2:4." Pages 3–25 in *Romans and the People of God*. Edited by S. K. Soderlund and N. T. Wright. Grand Rapids: Eerdmans, 1999.

Respect for Context and Authorial Intention: Setting the Epistemological Bar

Mitchell Kim

The degree of Paul's respect for the original context of his Old Testament allusions and quotations is a matter of ongoing debate. In his essay in this volume, Steve Moyise argues that "'respect' is not a very precise term" to convey the types of complex and daring interpretations that Paul offers of Old Testament texts. The imprecision of the phrase "respect for context" is a subset of a muddled conception of authorial intention more broadly; Stanley Porter comments rightly that "biblical scholars need a more precise definition of intentionality."[1]

Philosopher Michael Polanyi provides resources to define authorial intention more precisely with his category of "latent knowledge." Latent knowledge reminds us that "we know more than we can tell." Consequently, authorial communicative intention should not be limited to the conscious and focused attention of the author at the time of writing but rather encompasses a whole body of assumed knowledge. Polanyi's concept of latent knowledge helps to legitimize this broader understanding; latent knowledge is simply part of the wider nature of all human knowing.

Using Polanyi's ideas as a framework, I will seek to clarify what it might mean for Paul to respect the context of his Old Testament allusions and quotations. This chapter will proceed in four stages. First, I will argue that Steve Moyise and others have set the epistemological bar too high by suggesting that Paul respects the context of his Old Testament quotations only if there is exact agreement between the explicit sense of the source

---

1. Stanley E. Porter, "Allusions and Echoes," in *As It is Written: Studying Paul's Use of Scripture* (ed. Stanley E. Porter and Christopher D. Stanley; SBLSymS 50; Atlanta: Society of Biblical Literature, 2008), 35.

text and the quoting text. Modern authors often apply previous texts in ways that draw out the latent sense of earlier texts. In so doing, they respect the original context of the earlier text but draw out latent senses of that text for new settings. Next, I will seek to reset the epistemological bar for determining proper "respect for context." While Moyise assumes that drawing out the latent sense of an earlier text is inferior to relying on the explicit sense, Michael Polanyi's view of latent knowledge establishes the legitimacy of drawing out the latent sense. Third, I will apply these insights to a test case, the use of Hos 2:23 in Rom 9:26, examining how Paul draws out a latent but not explicit sense of this earlier text. Before offering final comments and conclusions, I will ask whether my approach sets the epistemological bar too low in defining respect for the context of Old Testament quotations.

Setting the Epistemological Bar Too High? Respect for Context and Authorial Intention

What does it mean for Paul to respect the context of an Old Testament quotation? Steve Moyise struggles with the anachronistic nature of this question.

> In a modern publishing context, I am obliged to quote a scholar's words with accuracy even if I disagree with them. Changing the wording of a quotation, especially if it strengthens my argument, is regarded as a lack of respect for the author that undermines my credibility as a scholar.... It would be anachronistic, however, to judge Paul by such standards.[2]

Consequently, the assertion that Paul respects the context of his quotations would mislead a modern audience, who might judge this process with standards different from those from Paul's time. This sort of argument is not new. In 1964, Richard T. Mead said:

> To use our current, scholarly sense of respect for context is to make unfair, modernized demands upon the biblical materials. The simple fact that such respect tends to appear as a function of only certain kinds of

---

2. Steve Moyise, "Does Paul Respect the Context of His Quotations?" 97–98 in this volume.

Old Testament uses suggests quite plainly that historical contextuality was not cherished on principle in New Testament times.³

For both Moyise and Mead, discussions of whether Paul "respects the context" of his quotations in this sense are misleading and unhelpful.

At what level, then, should the epistemological bar be set for judging whether Paul "respects the context" of his quotations? Moyise criticizes those whose idea of "context" extends to "the chapter, the book, or in some cases, one of the major divisions of the Hebrew Bible, such as the Pentateuch." According to Moyise, "the assertion of 'respect' becomes meaningless" when context is defined so broadly. He also insists that "some of the meanings that Paul derives from the [OT] texts could not possibly have been in the mind of the original author (or editor)."⁴ In other words, a later text "respects the context" of an earlier text only when its use of that text corresponds to its explicit, historical sense. Similarly, Mead suggests that violation of an Old Testament context happens when the historical Old Testament situation is "thoroughly disregarded (e.g., Matt 2:18, weeping at Ramah refers to the slaughter of the innocents under Herod) and/or when novel subjects or objects are substituted into the interpretation (e.g., 1 Cor. 14:21, where Paul replaces the Assyrians of Isa. 28:11–12 with speakers in tongues)."⁵ Consequently, for both Mead and Moyise, Paul can only be seen as respecting the context of an Old Testament quotation if he uses that quotation in the same sense of its original. Sensitivity to the historical context and accuracy of quotation suggest that the explicit sense of the original is in fact being maintained. To sum up Mead and Moyise's understanding of "respect for context," we can use the following definition (D¹): respect for context means that the earlier texts are used in their explicit, historical sense. Moyise assumes this definition when he says, "If 'respect for context' means relating his interpretations to the *historical* situation of the original authors, then Paul does not always (or even often, perhaps) respect the context of his quotations."⁶

But does this not set the epistemological bar too high? A "modern audience" does not necessarily understand "respect for context" in this

---

3. Richard T. Mead, "A Dissenting Opinion about Respect for Context in OT Quotations," *NTS* 10 (1964): 288.
4. Moyise, "Respect the Context," 99.
5. Mead, "Dissenting Opinion," 281.
6. Moyise, "Respect the Context," 112.

way. John Kotre's biography about Andrew Greeley, *The Best of Times, the Worst of Times*, takes its title from the opening lines of Charles Dickens's *A Tale of Two Cities*. Kotre explores the life of a Catholic priest and sociologist at the University of Chicago, and he applies this famous quote to the context of late twentieth century America. Does this violate the context of the original because the historical situation of the French Revolution in Paris and London is "thoroughly disregarded"? Or does this "violation" actually pay a compliment to the earlier work by applying its description in a new setting? Kotre obviously thinks the latter, as his acknowledgements pays tribute to "one Charles Dickens for providing the title to a volume that is very much a tale of two cities—and of a man caught between them."[7] Here D^1 clearly sets the epistemological bar too high.

In short, a later text may legitimately borrow a latent sense of an earlier text and apply it in a different context, contrary to D^1. Perhaps the problem is not so much an anachronistic application of "respect for context" as a fuzzy and imprecise understanding of the latent sense of the earlier text. This problem emerges not only when New Testament authors engage in surprising interpretations of Old Testament quotations but also in the identification of Old Testament echoes and/or allusions. Jeannine Brown says that New Testament authors often "echo or evoke an Old Testament text or idea without being fully aware that they have done so."[8] This latent awareness of an Old Testament text is made explicit in the echoes and allusions to that text, since authors mean "more than they are fully attending to." In the next section, I will seek to clarify this fuzzy and imprecise category of latent knowledge by drawing from the work of Michael Polanyi and discussing its relation to the question of authorial intention.

Resetting the Epistemological Bar: Michael Polanyi's Account of Latent Knowledge

Michael Polanyi (1891–1976), former fellow of Merton College, Oxford, was a scientist turned philosopher whose objections to the reigning positivist view of science led him to articulate the role of personal commitment and tacit knowledge to science. In his Gifford Lectures, he explored

---

7. John Kotre, *The Best of Times, the Worst of Times* (Chicago: Nelson-Hall, 1978), vii.

8. Jeannine Brown, *Scripture as Communication* (Grand Rapids: Baker, 2007), 108.

the structure of tacit knowledge, a concept that reminds us that *"we can know more than we can tell."*[9]

One type of tacit knowledge is latent knowledge, which, according to Polanyi provides "an articulate interpretative framework on which we rely as a representation of a complex situation, drawing from it ever new inferences regarding further aspects of that situation."[10] Polanyi applies this idea to textual interpretation in his discussion of metaphors. He cites the following metaphor that Shakespeare used to describe the defiance of King Richard II before his enemies:

> Not all the waters of the rough rude sea
> Can wash the balm from off an anointed king.

Shakespeare is not saying that kings have a physical anointing balm spread over their bodies that is impermeable to water. This literal meaning is subsidiary to the intention of the metaphor, which communicates the inviolability of the kingship that Richard II possesses.[11] Shakespeare assumes his reader's knowledge of the absence of any such physically impermeable balm so that the reader may interpret the metaphor accurately. The reader unconsciously shifts from the obvious meaning to a subsidiary meaning in an integrative and imaginative act that immediately understands the point of the metaphor. This act integrates the widely divergent ideas of the metaphor and unites them into a coherent whole on the basis of latent knowledge.

What happens when the absence of latent knowledge prevents the reader from understanding a metaphor? The basic point of Shakespeare's metaphor can still be understood without any knowledge of anointing balms. The overall context suggests a reference in some way to the stability of the king's throne. Understanding the nature of anointing balms enhances and strengthens the metaphor so that it communicates more

---

9. Michael Polanyi, *The Tacit Dimension* (Garden City, N.Y.: Doubleday, 1966), 4–10.

10. Michael Polanyi, *Personal Knowledge: Towards a Post-critical Philosophy* (Chicago: University of Chicago Press, 1958), 74.

11. Michael Polanyi and Harry Prosch, *Meaning* (Chicago: University of Chicago Press, 1975), 77–79; Polanyi quotes from William Shakespeare, *Richard II*, act 3, scene 2.

fully; a minimal understanding of the passage, nevertheless, is still possible even without this latent knowledge.

The importance of latent knowledge can also be understood from the process of language acquisition. When I moved to Japan from the United States in the fourth grade, I was overwhelmed by the squiggles on the signs and the inarticulate garble of syllables in the marketplace. My mother took me to a private tutor to learn Japanese, and the grammar and basic vocabulary of Japanese became the object of my attention. After some time, I began to venture out in my neighborhood to play with other Japanese children. At first my attention was focused on recalling the proper words for ball, game, run, and play and forming coherent sentences in order to communicate. As the words and grammatical structures were internalized and became latent in my mind, the words began to connect more naturally, and I could communicate with fluency and ease. The knowledge of the vocabulary and grammar of the Japanese language had moved to the place of latent knowledge, where they were no longer the focus of my attention but were simply assumed, as my attention was focused on playing and joking with my friends.

Such latent knowledge is not only important for the learning of a language: "education is *latent* knowledge, of which we are aware subsidiarily in our sense of intellectual power based on this knowledge."[12] Education provides a conceptual framework by which we understand the world and assimilate new experiences. The importance of such latent knowledge recently became evident for me when I was training our church's small-group leaders to facilitate discussions about the book of Revelation. Although I had given them texts to study in advance and a commentary to help them interpret this book, I had not adequately educated them in the latent knowledge necessary to understand its genre. One leader said, "I read the text, and I don't understand what I'm reading. I read the commentary, and it all just goes over my head. However, only when I listen to you preach do I understand what's going on in this text."

The problem here is clear. I had failed to adequately educate this small-group leader in how to read the book of Revelation. As a result, her reading only led to confusion, and the words on the page of the commentary made no sense to her because she lacked the latent knowledge to make such information coherent. Only further training in the process of bibli-

---

12. Polanyi, *Personal Knowledge*, 103.

cal interpretation and the genre of Revelation could provide the necessary latent knowledge that would allow her to make sense of the text in front of her.

How, then, does this account of latent knowledge help us develop a more robust understanding of authorial intention? Let us return to Jeannine Brown's observation that New Testament authors "echo or evoke an Old Testament text or idea without being fully aware that they have done so." Brown suggests that we need a broader view of authorial intention that includes "those sub-meanings that an author may not be attending to or fully aware of as he or she writes, yet that fit the overall pattern of meaning the author willed to communicate and shared in the text."[13] Stanley Porter objects to Brown's view on the grounds that she fails to "utilize any clear notion of authorial intention."[14] It is precisely here that Michael Polanyi's account of latent knowledge can help us to develop a more robust understanding of authorial intention. In fact, Brown's contention that authors mean "more than they are fully attending to" in their communicative intention[15] is remarkably similar to Polanyi's understanding of tacit knowledge, which reminds us that *"we can know more than we can tell."*[16]

The idea of latent knowledge helps us to see that inattentive intentionality should not be regarded as some inferior mode of reference; indeed, it is part and parcel of all communicative intentions. We always intend more than what we are fully attending to. In writing these words, I am not fully attending to the grammatical structures of the English language or the acceptable canons of academic discourse or the tapping of my fingers upon the keyboard; my attention is focused on the articulation of a fuller account of authorial intention. Yet it is my latent knowledge of grammar, academic discourse, and typing that make this communication possible. To reduce authorial intention to conscious authorial attention

---

13. Brown, *Scripture as Communication*, 108, 110.

14. Porter, "Allusions and Echoes," 35.

15. Brown, *Scripture as Communication*, 108. This distinction between authorial intention and attention is taken from Kevin J. Vanhoozer, who argues that meaning should not be limited to "the author's focal awareness" but can also cover things of which "the author was only tacitly aware (or unaware), too." *Is There a Meaning in This Text? The Bible, the Reader, and the Morality of Literary Knowledge* (Grand Rapids: Zondervan, 1998), 259.

16. Polanyi, *Tacit Dimension*, 4–10.

is unnecessarily reductionistic. We always intend more than the focus of our attention.

In a similar manner, biblical authors possess a latent knowledge of Scriptural texts even when their attention is focused elsewhere. The fact that they are not consciously attending to these texts does not make them irrelevant to the interpretation of their writings. Rarely do we focus upon the interpretative frameworks by which we make sense of the world, yet they operate just the same. The reader need not share the entirety of the author's latent knowledge for the author to achieve his or her communicative intent, but such knowledge would obviously add further resonances and nuances that could aid interpretation. An elucidation of this latent knowledge brings about a richer and deeper understanding of the meaning and significance of biblical references.

A number of recent works have argued for a wider understanding of the role of Old Testament scriptures in the New Testament—an understanding that extends beyond isolated quotations and allusions. Drawing on C. H. Dodd's seminal insights into the role of context in Old Testament quotations and allusions, a number of authors have argued that entire books of the New Testament were shaped by certain Old Testament passages that provide an interpretative framework for understanding the objects of focal attention.[17] For example, Paul struggles with the failure of the Jews to believe the gospel and argues in Romans 9–11 that "it is not as though the word of God [regarding Israel] has failed" (9:6). J. Ross Wagner suggests that in this section Paul traces a "web of intratextual connection" from different parts of Isaiah based on a Christian "radical rereading" of the entire book of Isaiah.[18] A full understanding of the nature of Paul's "radical rereading" of Isaiah may not be necessary to understand Paul's argument in these chapters, just as an intimate knowledge of anatomy may not be necessary to understand a doctor's diagnosis of cancer. However, Wagner's work shows that an understanding of this latent knowledge can deepen the reader's understanding of Paul's argument in this section.

---

17. C. H. Dodd, *According to Scriptures: The Substructure of New Testament Theology* (London: Nisbet, 1952). The role of Isaiah's New Exodus in Mark and Acts is explored by Rikki E. Watts, *Isaiah's New Exodus and Mark* (WUNT 2/88; Tübingen: Mohr Siebeck, 1997); and David W. Pao, *Acts and the Isaianic New Exodus* (WUNT 2/130; Tübingen: Mohr Siebeck, 2000).

18. J. Ross Wagner, *Heralds of the Good News: Isaiah and Paul "in Concert" in the Letter to the Romans* (NovTSupp 101; Leiden: Brill, 2002), 184, 154.

To sum up, authorial communicative intention should not be limited to conscious and focused attention, since it necessarily encompasses a whole body of assumed knowledge that is not the focus of the conscious attention of the author. Ignorance of such latent knowledge on the part of the reader does not entirely prevent the communication of the author's intentions from being realized, but it does reduce the reader's comprehension of the full scope of that meaning.

With this understanding in view, what does it mean for an author to respect the context of an earlier quotation? If we recognize not only the explicit but also the latent meanings of a text, then a later text must embrace the explicit and the latent meanings—or both—of an earlier text in order to be seen as legitimately respecting the context of that text. This can be expressed in the following definition (D^2): respect for context means that the earlier texts are used consistently with the explicit and/or latent senses of the former. This definition includes not only "a serious engagement with the actual words of the quotation and relating them to similar texts elsewhere in Scripture"[19] but also an engagement that is consistent with their explicit or latent senses, or both.

Respect for Context and the Use of Hosea 2:23 in Romans 9:26: A Test Case

As a test case, I will explore Paul's use of Hos 2:23 in Rom 9:25. Did Paul respect the context of Hosea? In Rom 9, Paul struggles with the status of unbelieving Israel in the plan of God in light of the acceptance of the gospel by the Gentiles. He argues that God has "endured with much patience vessels of wrath prepared for destruction, in order to make known the riches of his glory for vessels of mercy, which he has prepared beforehand for glory—even us whom he has called, not from the Jews only but also from the Gentiles?" (Rom 9:22–24). This statement is then grounded in two quotations from Hos 2:23 and 1:10 in Rom 9:25–26. We will focus on the first of these quotations. The texts can be seen below.

Hos 2:25 LXX: καὶ ἐλεήσω τὴν Οὐκ-ἠλεημένην καὶ ἐρῶ τῷ Οὐ-λαῷ-μου Λαός μου εἶ σύ, καὶ αὐτὸς ἐρεῖ Κύριος ὁ θεός μου εἶ σύ.

---

19. Moyise, "Respect the Context," 113.

Rom 9:25: ὡς καὶ ἐν τῷ Ὡσηὲ λέγει· <u>καλέσω τὸν οὐ λαόν μου λαόν μου καὶ τὴν οὐκ ἠγαπημένην ἠγαπημένην</u>·

Hos 2:23 (2:25 LXX): And <u>I will have mercy on No Mercy, and I will say to Not My People, 'You are my people'</u>; and he shall say, 'You are my God.'"

Rom 9:25: As indeed he says in Hosea, "Those who were <u>not my people I will call 'my people,' and her who was not beloved I will call 'beloved.'</u>"

While Paul clearly uses Hos 2:23 in Rom 9:25 to describe the inclusion of the Gentiles, the context of Hos 2:23 is surprising. Hosea 2:23 refers to God's mercy upon the ten northern tribes of Israel, not the inclusion of the Gentiles. The application of a prophecy about the ten northern tribes of Israel to the Gentiles is shocking. J. Ross Wagner says that Paul gives a "radical rereading" of earlier texts to show how "Hosea's moving depiction of God's passionate commitment to his people Israel is refracted and refocused into a prophecy of the 'riches of God's glory' now showered upon *Gentile* 'vessels of mercy.'"[20] Richard Hays says that Paul provides a "scandalous inversion" of the earlier text, "as though the light of the gospel shining through the text has illuminated a latent sense so brilliant that the opaque original sense has vanished altogether."[21]

To return to our earlier question, did Paul respect the context of Hos 2:23 in Rom 9:25? According to D[1], the opacity of the "original sense" suggests that its context is not respected; Moyise opines that many modern readers would be unlikely to associate "respect for context" with an interpretation where "the opaque original sense has vanished altogether."[22] However, even Hays wonders whether "the opaque original sense has vanished altogether." God calls his people "*not only from the Jews* but also from the Gentiles" (Rom 9:24), and Rom 9–11 looks forward not only to the salvation of the Gentiles but also to the salvation of "all Israel" (Rom

---

20. Wagner, *Heralds of the Good News*, 83.
21. Richard B. Hays, *Echoes of Scripture in the Letters of Paul* (New Haven: Yale University Press, 1989), 66–67.
22. Steve Moyise, "Does Paul Respect the Context of His Quotations? Hosea as Test-Case," in *What Does the Scripture Say? Studies in the Function of Scripture in Early Judaism and Christianity* (ed. C. A. Evans and H. D. Zacharias; New York: T&T Clark, 2012), 1–12.

11:25–26).[23] According to D², if Paul is illuminating a latent sense in the original context (as Hays rightly recognizes), he continues to respect the context of the original quotation. Paul does not concoct an interpretation based on a meaning that is absent from the original but rather highlights an original, albeit overlooked, latent sense. Paul's use of Hos 2:23 might be surprising and shocking, but it is still respectful of the original context since it is consistent with a latent sense in the original. Consequently, if "respecting the context" includes not only the explicit original sense but also the latent senses of the original, then Paul respects the context of his original context here.

If Paul had disregarded both the explicit and latent senses of Hos 2:23, then he would have failed to respect the context of the original text. However, as long as Paul at least takes into account a latent sense of the original, then he legitimately respects the context of the original.

Setting the Epistemological Bar Too Low?

One might object that D² sets the epistemological bar too low. Would this not allow Paul to take any latent sense and apply it to his own context while still clearing the bar of "respecting the context"? For example, the explicit sense of Hos 2:23 refers to YHWH's mercy on the ten northern tribes of Israel. A latent sense might include how YHWH's covenant with his people includes his covenant with creation, by which YHWH promises to bless the earth so that it "shall answer the grain, the wine, and the oil, and they shall answer Jezreel" (Hos 2:21–22). Interpreters in a rural context could take this latent sense to argue that YHWH not only adopts the Gentiles but also promises that their land will perpetually yield grain, wine, and oil.

However, respecting the context does not in itself legitimize an interpretation. While this "rural" reading of Hos 2:23 might respect the context according to D², respecting the context is not a sufficient condition for a legitimate interpretation. The legitimacy of an interpretation depends not only on whether or not it respects the earlier context but also on a host of other factors. Paul's use of Hos 2:23 in Rom 9:26 is surprising given the explicit sense of the former, but Paul draws on Hos 2:23 because of his christocentric convictions. Consequently, "the 'embarrassing' uses of the OT by the NT become a fruitful field for uncovering

---

23. Hays, *Echoes of Scripture*, 67.

the theological presuppositions of Christian leaders and thinkers in the apostolic period."[24]

The relationship between a fuller meaning and its earlier antecedents can be exemplified by the relationship of an apple and its seed. The differences between a Golden Delicious and a Macintosh apple seed may not be apparent from observing the seed alone. However, the Golden Delicious apple is latent within its seed, even though its distinctive fruit will only be seen when the tree is fully grown. Nevertheless, a person highly trained in apple seeds might be able to detect the differences between a Golden Delicious and Macintosh apple even while it is still in seed form. For example, if a Golden Delicious apple seed usually has more lines down the middle than a Macintosh apple seed, an apple seed expert might reasonably guess what apple would grow from that seed. Yet the distinctive appearance of the Golden Delicious apple is caused not by the lines on the seed but by a host of other factors that come into play in the growth of the apple. The relationship between the seed's lines and the apple is one of correlation and not causation.

Similarly, the relationship between an earlier and a later text may be one of correlation and not causation. The importance of this is seen in an exchange between Steve Moyise and G. K. Beale on this question of the respect for context. While G. K. Beale argued that Paul respected the context of the earlier texts in light of Paul's own presuppositions, Moyise responded by saying that "if 'respect for context' simply means 'understandable given the author's presuppositions,' then it surely becomes a truism."[25] Beale replied that Paul's presuppositions were based in the Old Testament and were a legitimate extension of the meaning of Old Testament texts.[26] Moyise argued in turn that these presuppositions do not "explain" Paul's use of Scripture but merely "rationalize" his use of the Old Testament. To explain Paul's use of Scripture, such presuppositions ought

---

24. R. T. France, "Relationship between the Testaments," in *Dictionary of the Theological Interpretation of the Bible* (ed. Kevin J. Vanhoozer et al.; Grand Rapids: Eerdmans, 2005), 668.

25. Steve Moyise, "The Old Testament in the New: A Reply to Greg Beale," *IBS* 21 (1999), 56–57. Admittedly, much of their discussion grows out of differences in the use of the Old Testament in the book of Revelation more specifically, but the title and overall thrust of their articles suggest a wider application beyond that specific book.

26. G. K. Beale, "Questions of Authorial Intent, Epistemology, and Presuppositions and Their Bearing on the Study of the Old Testament in the New: A Rejoinder to Steve Moyise," *IBS* 21 (1999): 167–72.

to tell us why he chose certain texts, which lenses are to be applied to what texts, and why the wording of certain texts is changed.[27]

Moyise's comments confirm that he has set the epistemological bar too high. Is this what "explain" really means? Explanation does not entail prediction. I can explain how John Kotre applies Charles Dickens's line "it was the best of times, it was the worst of times" to twentieth-century America without predicting that this line might be applied in that manner. Similarly, explaining the New Testament use of the Old does not entail that certain presuppositions predict how the Old Testament will be interpreted; it simply describes how the Old Testament is being interpreted by the New Testament authors. Explanation is descriptive, not prescriptive.

Consequently, D^2 does not set the epistemological bar too low for respecting the context of Paul's Old Testament quotations. This definition provides a criterion by which we can know when an author is or is not respecting the context of his or her Old Testament quotations, even if by itself it does not legitimize the propriety of certain interpretations. Legitimizing interpretations is a different question altogether.

Conclusion

In this paper I have sought to clarify the terminology surrounding the idea of "respecting the context" in a biblical quotation or allusion. My comments do not answer the question of whether the New Testament authors always respect the context of their Old Testament quotations. Such a categorical statement can only be answered by an in-depth exploration of every Old Testament quotation in the New Testament. I have sought to define "respect for context" by legitimizing the inclusion of latent senses of earlier texts in the range of possible interpretations which may be seen as respecting the context, and I have shown how this works in the case of Paul's use of Hos 2:23 in Rom 9:26. My hope is that this clarification of definitions might further the discussion of whether Paul respects the context of his Old Testament quotations and allusions.

---

27. Steve Moyise, "Seeing the Old Testament through a Lens," *IBS* 23 (2001): 36–41.

Bibliography

Beale, G. K., ed. *The Right Doctrine from the Wrong Texts?* Grand Rapids: Baker, 1994.

Brown, Jeannine. *Scripture as Communication.* Grand Rapids: Baker, 2007.

Dodd, C. H. *According to Scriptures: The Substructure of New Testament Theology.* London: Nisbet, 1952.

France, R. T. "Relationship between the Testaments." Pages 666–72 in *Dictionary of the Theological Interpretation of the Bible.* Edited by Kevin J. Vanhoozer et al. Grand Rapids: Eerdmans, 2005.

Hays, Richard B. *The Conversion of the Imagination: Paul as Interpreter of Israel's Scripture.* Grand Rapids: Eerdmans, 2005.

———. *Echoes of Scripture in the Letters of Paul.* New Haven: Yale University Press, 1989.

Hübner, Hans. *Vetus Testamentum in Novo.* 3 vols. Göttingen: Vandenhoeck & Ruprecht, 1997–2003.

Koch, Dietrich-Alex. *Die Schrift als Zeuge des Evangeliums: Untersuchengen zur Verwendung und zum Verständnis der Schrift bei Paulus.* BHT 69. Tübingen: Mohr, 1986.

Moyise, Steve. "Does Paul Respect the Context of His Quotations and Does It Matter?" Paper presented at the Annual Meeting of the Society of Biblical Literature. Boston, November 2008. Online: http://www.westmont.edu/%7Efisk/paulandscripture/moyise%20paper%202008.pdf.

———. "Does Paul Respect the Context of His Quotations? Hosea as Test-Case." Pages 1–12 in *What Does the Scripture Say? Studies in the Function of Scripture in Early Judaism and Christianity.* Edited by C. A. Evans and H. D. Zacharias. New York: T&T Clark, 2012.

———. *Paul and Scripture: Studying the New Testament Use of the Old Testament.* Grand Rapids: Baker, 2010.

———. *Seeing the Old Testament in the New.* Edinburgh: T&T Clark, 2008.

Pao, David W. *Acts and the Isaianic New Exodus.* WUNT 2/130. Tübingen: Mohr Siebeck, 2000.

Polanyi, Michael. *Personal Knowledge: Towards a Post-critical Philosophy.* Chicago: University of Chicago Press, 1958.

———. *The Tacit Dimension.* Garden City, N.Y.: Doubleday, 1966.

Polanyi, Michael, and Harry Prosch. *Meaning.* Chicago: University of Chicago Press, 1975.

Porter, Stanley E., ed. *Hearing the Old Testament in the New.* Grand Rapids: Eerdmans, 2006.

Porter, Stanley E., and Christopher D. Stanley, eds. *As It Is Written: Studying Paul's Use of Scripture.* SBLSymS 50. Atlanta: Society of Biblical Literature, 2008.

Stanley, Christopher D. *Arguing with Scripture: The Rhtetoric of Quotations in the Letters of Paul.* New York: T&T Clark, 2004.

———. " 'Pearls Before Swine': Did Paul's Audiences Understand His Biblical Quotations?" *NovT* 41 (1999): 124–44.

Vanhoozer, Kevin J. *Is There a Meaning in This Text? The Bible, the Reader, and the Morality of Literary Knowledge.* Grand Rapids: Zondervan, 1998.

Wagner, J. Ross. *Heralds of the Good News: Isaiah and Paul "in Concert" in the Letter to the Romans.* NovTSup 101. Leiden: Brill, 2002.

Watson, Francis. *Paul and the Hermeneutics of Faith.* New York: T&T Clark, 2005.

Watts, Rikki E. *Isaiah's New Exodus and Mark.* WUNT 2/88. Tübingen: Mohr Siebeck, 1997.

Wright, N. T. *The Climax of the Covenant: Christ and the Law in Pauline Theology.* Edinburgh: T&T Clark, 1991.

LATENCY AND RESPECT FOR CONTEXT: A RESPONSE TO MITCHELL KIM

Steve Moyise

INTRODUCTION

Much of the discussion about the apostle Paul's "respect for context" has assumed that the meaning of the Old Testament text is relatively clear. In this model, the task of the scholar is to evaluate the proximity or lack of proximity between Paul's interpretations and the original meaning of the texts. By drawing on the concept of latent meaning, Mitchell Kim has drawn our attention to the fact that the original meanings are far from clear. It is a common experience that people "say more than they know," so that hindsight can lead to an acknowledgment of "that's what I really meant." Kim's suggestion is that "authorial intention" should not be limited to the conscious thoughts of the author but should embrace a number of latent meanings that may only become apparent in the fullness of time. On this understanding, Paul can be said to "respect the context" of his quotations if it can be shown that he is illuminating a latent, though previously overlooked, sense of the original.

Kim is aware that this could be seen as setting the "epistemological bar" too low: "Would this not allow Paul to take any latent sense and apply it to his own context while still clearing the bar of 'respecting the context'?" He answers this by drawing a distinction between "respect for context" and "legitimacy," and illustrates his point by comparing Paul's reading of Hos 2:21–22 with a hypothetical "rural" interpretation of the same text. The explicit sense of this text speaks of God's mercy on the northern tribes of Israel, but a latent sense might well extend this to the Gentiles of a later period. In a similar way, a "rural" interpretation might see here a latent indication that Yahweh will cause crops to grow well for the faithful. In Kim's analysis, both of these interpretations can be said to be respecting the context of the original. This does not mean, however, that both are legitimate interpretations, since legitimacy, according to Kim, depends on a "host of other factors." In the case of Paul's use of Hos 2:23, it is his "christocentric application" that sets it apart from other interpretations.

In this response, I will consider three questions. First, is a theory of latent meaning as author-centered as Kim suggests? If texts come to us with a number of latent meanings, do not readers have to choose which meaning to adopt? Second, has the debate about "respect for context" really been about legitimacy? Has the debate been energized because a denial of "respect for context" is thought to undermine Paul's conclusions and hence the credibility of the church? Third, does a theory of latent meanings offer support for Paul's respect for context, as Kim suggests, or does it simply show that the question is more complicated than is often assumed?

LATENT MEANING AND THE ROLE OF THE READER

Since Paul offers a "christological interpretation" of Scripture,[1] it has made sense to many interpreters to turn to "reader-centered" theories of interpretation in order to understand what Paul is doing. I myself have used the concept of intertextuality to argue that textual meaning is not something that is intrinsic to a text but must be understood as "text in relation to."[2] Textual meaning is something that occurs when readers try to situate the text within their own "encyclopaedia" (Eco) of knowledge and experience. Thus my explanation of Paul's use of Hos 1:10 and 2:23 in Rom 9:26 would begin by pointing out that Paul was commissioned by God to preach to the Gentiles, a vision that has dominated his life and thought.[3] From the point of view of God's covenant, Gentiles are indeed "not my people," though that was not the explicit referent of Hos 1:10 and 2:23. But Paul has now witnessed large numbers of Gentiles turning to God through faith in

---

1. Hays would call it ecclesiological, since it speaks not so much about the person of Christ as the composition of the people of God. For our purposes, however, the point is simply that the interpretation comes about when the text is interpreted in the light of later events.

2. Steve Moyise, *Evoking Scripture: Seeing the Old Testament in the New* (London: T&T Clark, 2008), 125–41.

3. See Steve Moyise, "Does Paul Respect the Context of his Quotations? Hosea as Test-Case," in *What Does the Scripture Say? Studies in the Function of Scripture in Early Judaism and Christianity* (ed. C. A. Evans and H. D. Zacharias; New York: T&T Clark, 2012), 1–12.

Christ and becoming "children of God" (Gal 3:26). It is thus "obvious" to Paul that a text that speaks of "not my people" becoming "children of the living God" (Hos 1:10) has to be speaking to his situation.

This is not an interpretation that was likely to arise until Gentiles turned to God in great numbers. I believe that Mark Goodwin is mistaken in trying to find a precedent for it in contemporary Judaism.

> The Jewish and early Christian evidence thus suggests that "sons of the living God" was a text already linked to Gentiles and Gentile conversion.... Paul, then, in Rom 9:26, can apply Hos 2:1 LXX to Gentile converts with no explanation or clarification because the application was already familiar. Paul operates with a precedent that links Hos 2:1 LXX with Gentile converts and can thus assume his reader's familiarity with this association.[4]

The evidence that Goodwin offers is the fact that the term "living God" occurs in a number of texts connected with idol polemic (e.g., LXX Dan 5:23, 6:10). From this he deduces that the identification of Hosea's "not my people" with Gentiles was common in Paul's day. However, there is no evidence that anyone before Paul had interpreted Hos 1:10 and 2:23 in this manner, and it is pure speculation to say that such an identification was "already familiar." As Ross Wagner and Richard Hays have indicated, such an interpretation would have appeared "scandalous" and "shocking" to non-Christian Jews.[5]

Mark Seifrid offers a different type of explanation by suggesting that when Israel became "not my people," they effectively became a Gentile nation ("fallen and condemned human beings"), so that the promise of restoration directly prefigures the inclusion of the Gentiles.[6] I would prefer to put the matter in terms of intertextuality. Thus the combination of the promise of restoration for the northern tribes and the suggestion that they were now outside the covenant like the Gentiles had the potential to be taken as a promise of Gentile inclusion *once that had become a reality*. It is not that the meaning of Hos 1:10 and 2:23 can be "objectively" described as a reference to Gentile inclusion but rather that, when the

---

4. Mark J. Goodwin, *Paul, Apostle of the Living God: Kerygma and Conversion in 2 Corinthians* (Harrisburg, Pa.: Trinity Press, 2001), 153.

5. Quoted in Kim's essay in this volume (p. 124).

6. Mark D. Seifrid, "Romans," in *Commentary on the New Testament Use of the Old Testament* (ed. G. K. Beale and D. A. Carson; Grand Rapids: Baker, 2007), 647–50.

text is read in the light of what Paul thinks God is doing in the present, his interpretation becomes understandable and perhaps even inevitable. As George Aichele notes, the act of interpretation "makes the meaning of the text seem obvious by providing a set of conventional codes that allows the reader to recognize the text as a work, to identify it, and to make sense out of it."[7]

It should be noted that this does not imply that readers can make texts mean whatever they like. This is a common objection to "reader-centered" approaches, but it is mistaken. We could not talk about interpretation at all if there were not a text to interpret. The point is that texts do not present themselves to readers as transparent packages of meaning; readers have to do something in order to interpret them. Intertextuality suggests that what they do is relate them to other intertexts, which might be actual texts or, more generally, events, cultural phenomena, or personal experiences and commitments. Thus the main reason (though not the only reason) that Paul's interpretations differ from those at Qumran is that they are relating the texts to a different set of intertexts, especially their belief that God has a particular purpose for their own community.

Kim wishes to refute such "reader-centered" accounts of interpretation in favor of an "author-centered" account. He is aware that restricting authorial intention to the conscious thoughts of the original author would make it very difficult to assert that this is what we find in Paul's interpretations of Scripture, so he expands the definition to include what he calls latent meanings. In Kim's view, readers do not *construct* meaning by relating texts to other intertexts but *discover* latent meanings that have always been there. He illustrates this with a story about a church-group leader who was finding it difficult to understand the book of Revelation. The answer was to provide her with the necessary background to understand the nature of the book. Armed with that "latent knowledge," she could begin to understand the text as it was intended to be understood.

This story, however, is amenable to another interpretation. Prior to Kim's intervention, the group leader was unable to obtain a coherent understanding of the text; it was just "words on a page." So Kim taught her "how to read the book" by suggesting that she adopt insights from biblical interpretation and genre studies. In other words, he told her that she

---

7. George Aichele, "Canon as Intertext: Restraint or Liberation?" in *Reading the Bible Intertextually* (ed. Richard B. Hays, S. Alkier, and L. A. Huizenga; Waco, Tex.: Baylor University Press, 2009), 143.

should read Revelation in the light of a different set of intertexts. Of course, Kim would argue that these intertexts are more suited to understanding the book of Revelation than what she was previously using (presumably some sort of literalist approach), but the point remains: her interpretation of the text changed when she *chose* (or was persuaded) to relate it to a different set of intertexts. So can this really be said to be an author-centered understanding of interpretation? Put another way, if texts come to us with a number of latent meanings, as Kim suggests, then readers must choose which meaning to adopt in any given situation.

I should add that I found it rather confusing that Kim should describe the information that he imparted to the group leader as "latent knowledge." To whom is it latent? The point of his essay is that texts can have latent meanings because authors are not fully aware of their intentions; they say more than they know. How then does this relate to the latent knowledge that Kim imparted to the group leader so that she could better understand the text? Are we to understand that he imparted those details from the "shared encyclopedia" of the first century that the author would have known but was not actually attending to at the time of writing? If so, I cannot imagine how he could possibly know this. My guess is that he is referring either to the general background of the first century or to insights from modern biblical interpretation. If it is the former, it is unclear why the commentary that she was using could not provide it; if the latter, then we are back to readers adopting a reading strategy based on later events.

Legitimacy

Although Kim's paper is not about legitimacy, his statement that "respect for context" is not the same as legitimacy is important. Indeed, one suspects that much of the energy that has gone into this debate is precisely because it is commonly thought to be about legitimacy. Those who claim that Paul does not respect the context of his quotations are often thought to be denying the legitimacy of his interpretations and (perhaps more worrisomely) the foundations of the Church. However, this does not follow. One might believe that the Christ-event is the clearest manifestation of God's purposes for humankind and thus deduce that Paul's interpretations are legitimate, even though they might offend modern ideas of "scientific" exegesis. Or one might think that Paul was led to his interpretations by direct revelation from God (Gal 1:12) and are legitimate for that reason.

Either way, "respect for context" is a modern criterion that is not to be equated with "legitimacy."

In a similar way, those who argue for "respect for context" are often thought to be conservative Christians who wish to defend their beliefs at any cost. But again this does not follow. It is possible to see patterns between Old Testament narratives (slavery and freedom) and sections of Paul's writing (Rom 8) and declare that, on balance, "respect for context" is a more accurate description of Paul's interpretation than its opposite. Such an evaluation need not involve a "faith" decision, though of course it might. Kim helpfully draws a distinction between "respect for context" and "legitimacy" and asserts that the latter would depend on a "host of factors." I think that most scholars would agree with this, though there would be much debate about what those factors are and how they might be applied. Having said that, my guess is that, when Kim says that he taught the group leader "how to read the book," he was in fact talking about legitimacy. I do not get the impression that he was introducing her to a range of latent meanings, each of which could legitimately be said to "respect the context" of the original.

Latency and Respect for Context

Kim suggests that if we take a broader view of authorial intention by incorporating the concept of latent meanings, then Paul does indeed respect the context of his quotations. To my mind, this is a category mistake. Using the concept of latent meaning does not tilt the evidence in favour of Paul; it simply shows that the debate is much more complicated than is often assumed. In fact, it is probably the nail in the coffin for the debate itself. If texts come with multiple (latent or potential) meanings and there is always some debate about Paul's own meaning, then trying to correlate these under the rubric of "respect" is unlikely to succeed. I think we can see this when Kim tries to apply the idea to Paul's use of Hos 1:10 and 2:23 in Rom 9:26. After citing Wagner and Hays regarding the "scandalous" and "shocking" nature of Paul's interpretation, he then offers a reason for why it does not constitute a lack of respect.

> According to D^2, if Paul is illuminating a latent sense in the original context (as Hays rightly recognizes), he continues to respect the context of the original quotation. Paul does not concoct an interpretation absent

from the original but highlights an original, albeit overlooked, latent sense.

The key word here is "if." How do we decide whether a particular interpretation is illuminating a latent sense or not? No criteria are offered as to how one might do this (unless the agreement of Hays is a criterion). Kim's final sentence ("concoct an interpretation absent from the original") is clearly apologetic, as if these were the only alternatives.[8] The same is true of his "apple and seed" analogy.

> The differences between a Golden Delicious and a Macintosh apple seed may not be apparent from observing the seed alone. However, the Golden Delicious apple is latent within its seed, even though its distinctive fruit will only be seen when the tree is fully grown. Nevertheless, a person highly trained in apple seeds might be able to detect the differences between a Golden Delicious and Macintosh apple even while it is still in seed form.

I cannot see how anyone could disagree with this, but where does it get us? I could cite the same analogy and say that an expert in apple seeds might look at the apple that I am gazing at (Rom 9:26) and declare that it *does not* come from either a Golden Delicious seed (Hos 1:10) or a Macintosh seed (Hos 2:23). The analogy is false because, in the realm of biblical studies, we do not have the equivalent of a microscope that would provide the evidence for making such a decision. "Latent meaning" is one possible way of explaining diversity of interpretation, but it does not offer any criteria for deciding whether a particular meaning is "latent" or not. So on a theoretical level, I can agree with Kim that *if* one could show that Rom 9:26 is drawing on a latent meaning of Hos 1:10 and 2:23 and *if* one could produce an expert that could demonstrate that Rom 9:26 is the genuine fruit of Hos 1:10 and 2:23, then we could conclude that Paul respects the context of his quotations. The problem is that we cannot do either of these things.[9]

---

8. Since Kim wishes to emphasize the rights of authors rather than the freedom of readers in the act of interpretation, I find it surprising that he should use a term like "concoct an interpretation," which he will not find in any of my writings and which I would vehemently deny. Perhaps Kim would say that he has discerned a latent meaning in my writings of which I was unaware, but I think a more likely explanation is that he is reading my work through the lens of his own theological commitments.

9. This is similar to an exchange I had with Greg Beale some years ago. Beale

Conclusion

It seems to me that Kim's essay has two targets in mind. The first is those who assert that Paul does not respect the context of his quotations because his interpretations differ from the original meaning of the texts. By introducing the idea of latent meaning, he shows that the situation is more complicated than that, and I agree. However, I do not think he has done anything to tilt the balance in favour of Paul's respect for context, since he does not cite any criteria by which we might judge whether a particular meaning is latent or not. He is in fact agreeing with me that "respect" is a rather imprecise term for such a debate. His second target is those who seek to understand Paul's interpretations through a "reader-centered" rather than "author-centered" approach. He assumes that the former leads to the conclusion that Paul "concocted" his own interpretations, and perhaps there are some deconstructionists who would say this. However, that is not my position. I have no doubt that Paul has seriously attended to the words of Hos 1:10 and 2:23, but I also think that his theological outlook and rhetorical situation have significantly affected how he reads them. In the end, I do not think a theory of latent meaning can sufficiently account for the diversity of interpretations that we find in Paul's letters. Paul the reader is also a factor in the interpretative process.

---

wanted to assert that the author of Revelation respects the contexts of his allusions and offered the analogy of a decorative bowl of fruit. His point was that, while the fruit (Old Testament allusions) now exist in a different context (Revelation) and have a different function, they never lose their identity as particular fruit from a particular tree. I challenged this by saying that texts are *not* like a decorative bowl of fruit, for individual fruits have hard boundaries that prevent them from interacting with other fruit. I suggested that if one was going to use such an analogy, Old Testament allusions in the book of Revelation are more like a fruit salad, where the apples and pears have been peeled, cored, and diced and float around in syrup. My point was that the differences outweigh the similarities. My chief concern, however, was to deny the validity of the analogy; the Old Testament allusions in the book of Revelation are *not* like a decorative bowl of fruit! See Steve Moyise, "Intertextuality and the Study of the Old Testament in the New Testament" in *The Old Testament in the New Testament* (ed. Steve Moyise; JSNTSup 189; Sheffield: Sheffield Academic Press, 2000), 31–32. The articles mentioned in Kim's essay are further responses to the debate. It is worth noting that the debate was about the book of Revelation, where the question about "respect for context" is rather different from Paul's explicit statement that Hosea spoke about the inclusion of the Gentiles.

Bibliography

Aichele, George. "Canon as Intertext. Restraint or Liberation?" Pages 139–56 in *Reading the Bible Intertextually*. Edited by Richard B. Hays, S. Alkier, and L. A. Huizenga. Waco, Tex.: Baylor University Press, 2009.

Goodwin, Mark J. *Paul, Apostle of the Living God: Kerygma and Conversion in 2 Corinthians*. Harrisburg, Pa.: Trinity Press, 2001.

Moyise, Steve. "Does Paul Respect the Context of his Quotations? Hosea as Test-case." Pages 1–12 in *What Does the Scripture Say? Studies in the Function of Scripture in Early Judaism and Christianity*. Edited by Craig A. Evans and H. D. Zacharias. New York: T&T Clark, 2012.

———. *Evoking Scripture: Seeing the Old Testament in the New*. London: T&T Clark, 2008.

———. "How Does Paul Read Scripture?" Pages 184–96 in *Early Christian Literature and Intertextuality 1*. Edited by Craig A. Evans and H. D. Zacharias. London: T&T Clark, 2009.

———. "Intertextuality and the Study of the Old Testament in the New Testament." Pages 14–41 in *The Old Testament in the New Testament*. Edited by Steve Moyise. JSNTSup 189. Sheffield: Sheffield Academic Press, 2000.

Seifrid, Mark D. "Romans." Pages 607–94 in *Commentary on the New Testament Use of the Old Testament*. Edited by G. K. Beale and D. A. Carson. Grand Rapids: Baker, 2007.

PART 3
BEYOND THE *HAUPTBRIEFE*

Paul's Reliance on Scripture in 1 Thessalonians

E. Elizabeth Johnson

Though in 1 Thessalonians Paul uses what we recognize as biblical language and some phrases that seem to echo the Bible, nowhere in this letter does he quote Scripture as he does elsewhere. This essay seeks to understand how the scattered echoes and allusions to Scripture in 1 Thessalonians inform the shape of Paul's apocalyptic theology, regardless of whether those echoes and allusions would have been recognized by his Thessalonian listeners.

It is instructive to compare the letter to the Romans, which in the Nestle-Aland 27 text is peppered with italicized words and sentences indicating quotations from or allusions to the Bible, with 1 Thessalonians, which has no italics at all. Marginal references to biblical allusions in the letter are also relatively few, numbering only twenty-four on seven pages of text, roughly three to a page, compared with 288 on the thirty-two pages of Romans, about nine per page.[1] Although Professor Nestle and his descendants can locate a word or two here and there from the LXX that show up also in Paul's letter to Thessalonica, they can find no quotations. Neither can I. Edgar Krentz think that 1 Thess 2:14–16, Paul's indictment of those who "killed ... the prophets," is the "only reference to the OT in the Letter," although he offers no specifics.[2]

---

1. "Of the approximately one hundred explicit citations of the OT in the Pauline corpus, almost all appear in the *Hauptbriefe*. In fact, among the uncontested letters of Paul, not only are the explicit citations confined to the *Hauptbriefe*, but fully half are found in Romans alone" (James M. Scott, "Paul's Use of Deuteronomic Tradition," *JBL* 112 [1993]: 645).

2. Edgar N. Krentz in *HarperCollins Study Bible* (ed. Wayne A. Meeks et al.; San Francisco: HarperCollins, 1993), 2221. Presumably, Krentz has in mind texts like 1 Kgs 18:13 and 19:10, 14; Neh 9:26; or 4 Ezra 1:32. It is telling that Nestle does not

In view of the pagan past of the Thessalonian Christians,³ it is scarcely surprising that the apostle does not quote the Jewish Bible to them. He nevertheless presumes that his listeners share with him some fundamental notions that we recognize as biblical.⁴ In order to understand this letter, one must have a rudimentary grasp of whom Paul refers to as θεός,⁵ whom Paul designates as χριστός and κύριος,⁶ who or what God's πνεῦμα is,⁷ the necessary connection between ethics and religion, particularly the notion of the "will of God,"⁸ and the nature of God's coming judgment.⁹ Paul also refers in this letter to the apostolic preaching that established the church as "the word of the Lord" (e.g., 1:8; 4:15), a phrase that commonly describes divine revelations and prophetic speech.¹⁰

General Biblical Language and Ideas in 1 Thessalonians

Whether they learned it directly from the Bible¹¹ or not, the Thessalonians apparently understood something of what Scripture says to Paul and other first-century Jews like him. This letter is rife with what Ciampa describes as "scriptural language and ideas."¹² Even if they did not know the Decalogue—Paul does not refer to it in 1 Thessalonians—they certainly know

---

point to the same passages. Identifying Bible verses in 1 Thessalonians is a remarkably creative enterprise.

3. 1 Thess 1:9 precludes their having been synagogue hangers-on of any sort, *pace* Abraham J. Malherbe, *The Letters to the Thessalonians: A New Translation with Introduction and Commentary* (AB 32B; New York: Doubleday, 2000), 58–62.

4. Paul also presumes his listeners' familiarity with other essentials of his Christian proclamation—that Jesus died, that God raised him from the dead, and that he will come again at the last day to rescue us from "the impending wrath" (1:10).

5. 1 Thess 1:1, 3, 4, 8, 9; 2:2, 4, 8, 9, 10, 12 ,13, 14; 3:2, 9, 11, 13, 14; 4:3, 5, 8, 9, 14, 16; 5:9, 18, 23.

6. χριστός: 1 Thess 1:1, 3; 2:7, 14; 3:2; 4:16; 5:9, 18, 23, 28; κύριος: 1 Thess 1:3, 6, 8; 2:15, 19; 3:11, 12, 13; 4:2, 6, 15, 16, 17; 5:2, 9, 23, 27, 28.

7. 1 Thess 1:5, 6; 4:8.

8. 1 Thess 4:3; 5:18.

9. 1 Thess 1:10; 2:16; 4:6; 5:2.

10. Gen 15:1; Exod 9:20; Num 3:16; Isa 1:10; Jer 1:2; Ezek 1:3; etc.

11. I assume a rather broad "canon" here, in view of Paul's wide-ranging use of texts from both the Tanak and other Second Temple literature.

12. Roy E. Ciampa, "Scriptural Language and Ideas," in *As It Is Written: Studying Paul's Use of Scripture* (ed. Stanley E. Porter and Christopher D. Stanley; SBLSymS 50; Atlanta: Society of Biblical Literature, 2008), 41–57.

the equivalent of the first commandment. They have "turned to God from idols," and they "serve the living and true God" (1:9). To "turn to God from idols" echoes[13] numerous biblical exhortations to turn to Israel's God and away from all others.[14] The epithet "living God" is ubiquitous in scripture,[15] as is "true God,"[16] and the two are adjacent at Jer 10:10: "the LORD is the true God; he is the living God and the everlasting King." There is no particular reason, however, to think the Thessalonians knew that Paul is referring to his (their?) holy book when he describes God in that way. There is not even any compelling reason to think the apostle himself consciously alludes to Scripture when he speaks of God like this. It is simply one of the ways Jews refer to God.

Depending on how long Paul stayed in Thessalonica when he founded the church and how long the congregation had existed when Paul writes—estimates range from a few weeks to a few months—there may have been a measure of time for him to teach them from the Bible. We simply have no way of knowing. Surely Stanley is correct to say it is "historically implausible" that the Thessalonians knew very much about Scripture.[17] Malherbe's observation about 1 Thess 4:5 is typical of the entire letter: "The epithet that Gentiles do not know God comes from the OT (Job 18:21; Ps 78[79]:6; Jer 10:25), but Paul does not appear to have any particular OT passage in mind."[18] The idea that the Thessalonians are loved and called by God[19] is part and parcel of Israel's identity as the covenant people; a Jew need not point specifically to the story of Abraham's election or a particular text about God's love for Israel to know that God loves and calls. The idea that

---

13. Despite Stanley E. Porter's carefully nuanced distinction between an "echo" and an "allusion" ("Allusions and Echoes," in Porter and Stanley, *As It Is Written*, 29–40), I am afraid that I use the two interchangeably here. The difference does not finally seem to be sufficient to distinguish among the few texts that Paul seems to invoke in 1 Thessalonians.

14. Lev 19:4; Deut 11:28; 30:10; Ps 85:8; Isa 45:22; Ezek 6:9; 14:6; 18:30; 33:11; Jon 3:8; Mic 7:17; 4 Ezra 15:20.

15. Deut 5:26; Josh 3:10; 1 Sam 17:26, 36; 19:16; Pss 42:2; 84:3; Isa 37:4, 17; Jer 10:10; 23:36; Dan 6:20, 26; Hos 1:10; Esth 6:13, 16; Bel 1:5, 25 (and, by contrast, 1:6, 24), 3 Macc 6:28; 4 Macc 5:24.

16. 2 Chr 15:3; Jer 10:10; Wis 12:27; 3 Macc 6:18.

17. Christopher D. Stanley, "Paul's 'Use' of Scripture: Why the Audience Matters," in Porter and Stanley, *As It Is Written*, 133.

18. Malherbe, *The Letters to the Thessalonians*, 230.

19. 1 Thess 1:4; 2:13; 5:24.

the Thessalonians are called into the realm of God (1 Thess 2:12) likewise recalls one of the ways in which Christian Jews described God's sovereignty, though Elliott is right to remind us that "empire" is also a category that evokes powerful images from the everyday lives of people living in a Roman city like Thessalonica.[20]

What "Christ" means to Paul is beyond the scope of this discussion, though the word derives from the Bible's descriptions of "anointing" as a means of setting someone apart for a divine purpose. The multivalent character of the act of anointing, and therefore of Messiah as a concept, was likely beyond the reach of former pagans.[21] Thus there is every reason to think that the non-Jews in Paul's audience would have understood his designation of Jesus as χριστός without reference to the Bible. They probably would have regarded it as one of Jesus' names.[22]

The Spirit of God is another category that runs throughout Israel's Scriptures,[23] though non-Jews, too, were well aware of spirits and spiritual beings.[24] Stoics, in particular, spoke of the universal, cosmic character of πνεῦμα that holds the universe together, and that conviction is frequently reflected in Jewish discussions of the Spirit.[25] When Paul speaks of God's πνεῦμα (4:8), or simply τὸ πνεῦμα (5:19), he very likely thinks of God's creative (Gen 1:2) and electing Spirit (1 Sam 16:13) that inspires prophecy (1 Sam 10:6) and recreates Israel (Ezek 37:5). The Thessalonians, however, did not need to know these stories to understand what Paul means when he says that God has given them πνεῦμα αὐτοῦ (1 Thess 4:8) or urges them not to quench τὸ πνεῦμα (5:19). That believers, too, have a πνεῦμα (5:23) that can be sanctified by being made whole and blameless would have been understandable to the Thessalonians with or without any particular knowledge of the Bible.

God's wrath (1 Thess 1:10), God's vengeance on wrong-doers (4:6), and the "day of the Lord" (5:2) are other concepts that betray biblical ori-

---

20. Neil Elliott, "'Blasphemed among the Nations': Pursuing an Anti-imperial 'Intertextuality' in Romans," in Porter and Stanley, *As It Is Written*, 213–33.

21. Ciampa, "Scriptural Language and Ideas," 51–52.

22. James D. G. Dunn, *The Theology of Paul the Apostle* (Grand Rapids: Eerdmans, 2006) 197.

23. Gen 1:2, 41:38; Num 24:2; 1 Sam 10:10, 11:16; etc.

24. Hermann Kleinknecht, "πνεῦμα, κ.τ.λ.," *TDNT* 6:331–59.

25. Jon R. Levison, *The Spirit in First-Century Judaism* (Leiden: Brill, 1997) 133–37.

gins.²⁶ The ideas are rooted in Israel's—and Judaism's—conviction that God requires just behavior from the people of God. This intimate connection of religion with ethics is distinctive of first-century Jews and therefore of Christians like Paul.²⁷ Again, though, there is little indication in 1 Thessalonians that Paul is referring to Scripture specifically to make these points. He simply reminds them of what he has previously told them about right living (4:1). He does, however, claim that his ethics are not of his creation but rather come directly from God: they are literally "God-taught" virtues (4:9).

Proposed Allusions

Most of Nestle-Aland's marginal references in 1 Thessalonians do little more than point to isolated vocabulary in Paul's letter that also appears in earlier texts. Some proposals are not particularly convincing. The phrase τῆς ὑπομονῆς τῆς ἐλπίδος/τὴν ἐλπίδα τῆς ὑπομονῆς, for example, occurs in both 1 Thess 1:3 and 4 Macc 17:4. There is no indication, though, that Paul meant to invoke specifically the image of the enduring patience of the martyrs' mother or that he presumes the Thessalonians know the story. There are enough stories of patient suffering and martyrdom among Jews and Christians (e.g., 1 Thess 2:13–16; 3:3b–4) that if Paul had wished to point to 4 Maccabees, he might have been more explicit in this letter. There is, of course, no way to know. It seems much more likely that the triad of virtues for which he gives thanks in 1 Thess 1:3 ("faithful work and loving labor and hopeful endurance in our Lord Jesus Christ"), which he uses again in 1 Thess 5:8 in the same order and in a different order in 1 Cor 13:13, is part of his original preaching. That preaching was of course heavily shaped by Israel's Scripture, a point to which we shall return.

The suggestion of another biblical allusion in the letter is even less persuasive. At 1 Thess 5:3, Paul says, "When they say, 'There is peace and security,' then sudden destruction will come upon them, as labor pains come upon a pregnant woman, and there will be no escape!" Nestle points to Jer 6:14 and the false prophets who cry, "'Peace, peace,' when there is

---

26. E.g., Exod 4:14; 32:10–11; Num 11:1, 10; 1 Sam 24:12; Hos 12:3; Joel 1:15; Amos 5:18–20; Obad 15; Zeph 1:14–18.

27. See Wayne A. Meeks, *The Moral World of the First Christians* (LEC 6; Philadelphia: Westminster, 1986), 91–96; and idem, *The Origins of Christian Morality: The First Two Centuries* (New Haven: Yale University Press, 1995).

no peace." Paul, though, manifestly quotes—and mocks—not those seventh-century prophets but contemporary Roman imperial propaganda.[28] Although the apostle himself may well have heard an ironic echo of Jeremiah's indictment in the empire's repeated promise of "peace and security"—I certainly do—he does not draw the parallel in 1 Thess 5:3.

The image of "a thief in the night" to describe the suddenness of the *parousia* in 1 Thess 5:2 is sometimes read as an allusion to Job 24:13–14: "The murderer rises at dusk to kill the poor and needy, and in the night is like a thief." But the phrase could just as well echo the dominical saying in Matt 24:43–44, since the context is much more similar: "But understand this—if the owner of the house had known in what part of the night the thief was coming, he would have stayed awake and would not have let his house be broken into. Therefore you also must be ready, for the Son of Man is coming at an unexpected hour." In view of how remarkably seldom Paul quotes Jesus, even this is merely a guess.

A few other passages in the letter seem somewhat more clearly to reflect biblical texts, though none of them is a direct quotation. Three merit our attention. (1) Paul claims in 1 Thess 2:14–16 that Judean resistance to Christian preaching serves a divine purpose: to "fill up the full measure of their sins" (τὸ ἀναπληρῶσαι αὐτῶν τὰς ἁμαρτίας). Verbal similarities suggest an echo of the assurance from God to Abram in Gen 15:16 that "the iniquity of the Amorites is not yet complete" (ἀναπεπλήρωνται αἱ ἁμαρτίαι). Second Maccabees makes similar use of the Genesis story: "For in the case of the other nations the Lord waits patiently to punish them until they have reached the full measure of their sins" (ἐκπλήρωσιν ἁμαρτιῶν, 6:14). A still-later text, the *Testament of Levi*, apparently also has the Genesis episode in view when it describes God's vengeance on Shechem, son of Hamor, for his rape of Dinah and multiple subsequent sins:[29] "the wrath of the Lord came upon them to the uttermost" (6:11).[30] It is interesting that

---

28. See Abraham Smith, "Unmasking the Powers: Toward a Postcolonial Analysis of 1 Thessalonians," in *Paul and the Roman Imperial Order* (ed. Richard A. Horsley; New York: Continuum, 2004), 63; Holland Lee Hendrix, "Archaeology and Eschatology at Thessalonica," in *The Future of Early Christianity: Essays in Honor of Helmut Koester* (ed. Birger A. Pearson; Minneapolis: Fortress, 1991), 114.

29. I.e., his being circumcised, his intention to rape Sarah and Rebecca as he had Dinah, his persecution of Abram "when he was a stranger," and so on.

30. Jeffrey S. Lamp lists five possible explanations for the similarities: (1) Paul quotes T. Levi 6:11; (2) T. Levi quotes 1 Thess 2:16; (3) 1 Thess 2:14-16 is an interpolation; (4) T. Levi 6:11 is an interpolation; and (5) Paul and T. Levi independently

three unrelated Jewish authors use the same language, apparently drawn from the same text in Genesis 15, to make a similar point about divine judgment—that it waits until wickedness builds to a particular level of offense. Significantly, all three authors substitute their own enemies for the Amorites in the original Genesis context: Paul says that God's wrath falls on the Judeans who "killed both the Lord Jesus and the prophets, and drove us out" (1 Thess 2:15); 2 Maccabees says that God punishes Gentiles but "does not deal in this way with us [i.e., Israel], in order that he may not take vengeance on us afterward when our sins have reached their height" (6:13b–14); and the *Testament of Levi* substitutes the story of Shechem from Genesis 33 for God's promise of judgment on the Amorites (6:1–11). All three of these references may rise to the level of Porter's definition of an allusion, since each one seems to "bring an external person, place, or literary work into [a] contemporary text."[31]

(2) A similar case occurs at 1 Thess 5:8, where Paul urges his listeners to "put on the breastplate of faith and love, and for a helmet the hope of salvation." This is one of the clearest allusions to Scripture in the letter, invoking the picture in Isa 59:17 of God who "put on righteousness like a breastplate, and a helmet of salvation on his head; he put on garments of vengeance for clothing, and wrapped himself in fury as in a mantle" in preparation for the nation's redemption from exile.[32] What is curious here

---

quote a common source ("Is Paul Anti-Jewish? *Testament of Levi* 6 in the Interpretation of 1 Thessalonians 2:13–16," *CBQ* 65 [2003]: 408–27, citing Tjitze Baarda, "The Shechem Episode in the Testament of Levi: A Comparison with Other Traditions," in *Sacred History and Sacred Texts in Early Judaism: A Symposium in Honour of A. S. van der Woude* [ed. J. N. Bremmer and F. García Martínez; Kampen: Kok Pharos, 1992], 11–73, esp. 63). Such an assumption of complex literary relationships seems unnecessary when a common tradition—perhaps oral?—offers an equally plausible theory.

In a different vein entirely, Scott argues that a more general use of biblical theology, specifically what Scott calls the "Deuteronomic View of Israel's History," informs the apostle's thought in 1 Thess 2:14–16 ("Paul's Use of Deuteronomic Tradition," 649; cf. Donald A. Hagner, "Paul's Quarrel with Judaism," in *Anti-Semitism and Early Christianity: Issues of Polemic and Faith* (ed. Craig A. Evans and Donald A. Hagner; Minneapolis: Fortress, 1993], 133–34). If that is the case, a narrative of Israel's sin and God's judgment, rooted in Scripture but not explicitly citing it, informs Paul's expectation of judgment on those who oppose his mission. He makes a similar point in Rom 9:14–18—that Pharaoh's oppression of Israel demonstrates God's power by highlighting God's freedom to harden and to have mercy—with an interpretation of Exod 9:16.

31. Porter, "Allusions and Echoes," 40.
32. Paul quotes from Isa 59 also in Romans. Romans 3:15–17 cites Isa 59:7–8,

is the way Paul uses the image to talk not about God's being armed against enemies but about Christians' protecting themselves from the dangers of wickedness by donning God's armor. The same image occurs in three other texts: the Wisdom of Solomon, Ephesians, and the Babylonian Talmud.

> The Lord will take his zeal as his whole armor, and will arm all creation to repel his enemies; he will put on righteousness as a breastplate, and wear impartial justice as a helmet; he will take holiness as an invincible shield, and sharpen stern wrath for a sword, and creation will join with him to fight against his frenzied foes. (Wis 5:17–20)

> Therefore take up the whole armor of God, so that you may be able to withstand on that evil day, and having done everything, to stand firm. Stand therefore, and fasten the belt of truth around your waist, and put on the breastplate of righteousness. As shoes for your feet put on whatever will make you ready to proclaim the gospel of peace. With all of these, take the shield of faith, with which you will be able to quench all the flaming arrows of the evil one. Take the helmet of salvation, and the sword of the Spirit, which is the word of God. (Eph 6:13–17)

> Raba said: The following was told me by the suckling who perverted the way of his mother, in the name of R. Eleazar. What is the meaning of the verse, *And he put on righteousness as a coat of mail*? It tells us that just as in a coat of mail every small scale joins with the others to form one piece of armour, so every little sum given to charity combines with the rest to form a large sum. R. Hanina said: The same lesson may be learnt from here: *And all our righteousness is as a polluted garment*. Just as in a garment every thread unites with the rest to form a whole garment, so every farthing given to charity unites with the rest to form a large sum. (b. B. Bat. 9b)[33]

All four of these discussions take place in contexts of moral exhortation rather than descriptions of God's saving power. Although there is no particular reason to think that the writer of Ephesians knows 1 Thessalonians, even if Eph 6:13–17 were influenced by 1 Thess 5:8, Wisdom and the Babylonian Talmud would still offer two other unrelated uses of the picture of divine armor in Isaiah to exhort the hearers to proper moral life.

---

somewhat selectively, as part of the catena of verses that attest the sinfulness of the entire world.

33. *Baba Bathra* (trans. Israel W. Slotki; London: Soncino, 1935).

This suggests the existence of some kind of Jewish paraenetic tradition that interpreted Isa 59:17 as hortatory. Richard suggests that this tradition grew up in apocalyptic contexts, "precisely because life itself and particularly the end-time struggle were seen as a contest between the spheres of light and darkness or good and evil"[34] and thus require more than mere human vigilance or moral fortitude, that is, God's own protection and power.

(3) A final allusion to Scripture may be present in Paul's portrayal of the Day of the Lord, where he speaks of destruction that arrives on non-believers as suddenly as a pregnant mother's labor pains (1 Thess 5:3). The image of childbirth as a metaphor for the wrenching pain of redemption is ubiquitous in both Jewish and Christian apocalyptic literature (1 En. 62:4; 4 Ezra 4:40–42; 16:35–39; Sib. Or. 5.514; 1QH 3:7–10; Gal 4:19; Matt 24:8; Mark 13:8; Rev 12:2). Its roots are in the Hebrew Bible. Psalm 48 paints a picture of God's staring down of God's competitors and their fleeing in terror.

> Within [Zion's] citadels God
>   has shown himself a sure defense.
> Then the kings assembled,
>   they came on together.
> As soon as they saw it, they were astounded;
>   they were in panic, they took to flight;
> trembling took hold of them there,
> pains as of a woman in labor [ὠδῖνες ὡς τικτούσης],
>   as when an east wind shatters the ships of Tarshish. (vv. 3–7; LXX 47:7)

Isaiah may be the first to compare the advent of the Day of the Lord specifically to the onset of childbirth.

> Wail, for the day of the LORD is near;
>   it will come like destruction from the Almighty!
> Therefore all hands will be feeble,
>   and every human heart will melt,
>   and they will be dismayed.
> Pangs and agony will seize them;
>   they will be in anguish like a woman in labor [ὠδῖνες ... ὡς γυναικὸς τικτούσης].

---

34. Earl J. Richard, *First and Second Thessalonians* (SP 11; Collegeville, Minn.: Liturgical Press, 1995), 255.

They will look aghast at one another;
    their faces will be aflame. (13:6-8)

Jeremiah, though, uses the simile most frequently (seven times), expressly linking the terror that precedes imminent destruction with the consequences of idolatry.

> And you, O desolate one, what do you mean that you dress in crimson, that you deck yourself with ornaments of gold, that you enlarge your eyes with paint? In vain you beautify yourself. Your lovers despise you; they seek your life. For I heard a cry as of a woman in labor [ὡς ὠδινούσης], anguish as of one bringing forth her first child, the cry of daughter Zion gasping for breath, stretching out her hands, "Woe is me! I am fainting before killers!" (4:30-31)

> We have heard news of them, our hands fall helpless; anguish has taken hold of us, pain as of a woman in labor [ὠδῖνες ὡς τικτούσης]. (6:24)

> What will you say when they set as head over you those whom you have trained to be your allies? Will not pangs take hold of you, like those of a woman in labor [ὠδῖνες ... καθὼς γυναῖκα τίκτουσαν]? (13:21)[35]

Unlike the echoes of Gen 15:16 at 1 Thess 2:14-16 and Isa 59:17 at 1 Thess 5:8, the phrase ὥσπερ ἡ ὠδὶν τῇ ἐν γαστρὶ ἐχούσῃ in 1 Thess 5:3 does not betray any verbal associations with the prophetic texts that employ the image, with the notable exceptions of the noun ὠδίν and the cognate verb ὠδίνω. The echo here is not of a single text but of a significant theme in Jeremiah, where the image of labor pains serves repeatedly to describe the

---

35. Cf. also 22:23: "O inhabitant of Lebanon, nested among the cedars, how you will groan when pangs come upon you, pain as of a woman in labor!"; 30:5-6: "Thus says the Lord: We have heard a cry of panic, of terror, and no peace. Ask now, and see, can a man bear a child? Why then do I see every man with his hands on his loins like a woman in labor? Why has every face turned pale?"; 48:40-41: "For thus says the Lord: Look, he shall swoop down like an eagle, and spread his wings against Moab; the towns shall be taken and the strongholds seized. The hearts of the warriors of Moab, on that day, shall be like the heart of a woman in labor"; 49:24: "Damascus has become feeble, she turned to flee, and panic seized her; anguish and sorrows have taken hold of her, as of a woman in labor"; 50:43: "The king of Babylon heard news of them, and his hands fell helpless; anguish seized him, pain like that of a woman in labor."

fear that comes suddenly on people when they see the threat of destruction looming on the national horizon. For Paul, what will come suddenly and terribly is the destruction that will sweep away all who have idolatrously trusted in the Empire's "peace and security" rather than turning to God and God's Messiah.

The Apocalyptic Shape of Paul's Gospel

For the most part, it seems that the echoes or allusions that scholars have detected in 1 Thessalonians of the language of Israel's Bible are faint at best. Even the clearest allusions do not require that those who hear Paul's letter know Scripture themselves. Though these passages are reminiscent of the Old Testament, they seem also to have been used by other Jews in similar ways, in roughly contemporary contexts. Thus we see Paul in 1 Thessalonians engaging in some conventional Jewish exegesis that helps him to interpret his apocalyptic message for a church that was founded on that message. Genesis 15:16 helps him to affirm God's justice in the face of opposition to the gospel. Isaiah 59:17 aids his moral exhortation by assuring Christians that their struggle against evil is not theirs alone but is supported by God's own armor. And Jeremiah's metaphor of labor pains to describe sudden fear and destruction give him a picture of the judgment that will fall on outsiders when the Day of the Lord brings redemption to God's elect.

It is not particularly surprising that when we catch Paul in this letter relying on biblical texts, however subtly, we find him in the company of others who inhabit his apocalyptically shaped world. He is, after all, fundamentally an interpreter—in Beker's words, an apocalyptic interpreter—of the Christ event.

> We can say then that the hermeneutical interaction between the coherent center of the gospel and its contingency—that is, the manner in which the one gospel of "Christ crucified and risen" in its apocalyptic setting achieves incarnational depth and relevance in every particularity and variety of the human situation—constitutes Paul's particular contribution to theology.[36]

The same is true of his interpretation of scripture, whether overtly, as in the *Hauptbriefe*, or less visibly, as in 1 Thessalonians.

---

36. J. Christiaan Beker, *Paul the Apostle: The Triumph of God in Life and Thought* (Philadelphia: Fortress, 1980), 35.

First Thessalonians is commonly described as Paul's quintessentially apocalyptic letter, in large measure because of one section in it: 4:13–5:11. In point of fact, however, discussion of the end times constitutes a comparatively smaller portion of the letter than conventional wisdom assumes. Paul's assurance that the Lord will not abandon Christians who have died and his exhortations concerning the Day of the Lord occupy a single page of the letter's seven and a half pages in the Nestle text. Although their anxiety about the destinies of believers who have died is very real, as is the church's anticipation of the trumpet's blast, eschatology is scarcely the primary matter that occupies Paul's attention in this letter, and it should not be uncritically equated with his apocalyptic proclamation.

Although the apocalypse that shapes Paul's message certainly contains news that "the appointed time has grown short" (1 Cor 7:29), it is primarily the revelation of Jesus Christ (Rom 16:25; Gal 1:12; 2:2) and of his cross (2 Cor 12:1–10). It discloses the invasion of God's καινὴ κτίσις (2 Cor 5:17; Gal 6:15) and the consequences of that invasion for the present life of the church that is molded after the model of Jesus' death and resurrection.[37]

It is helpful to consider his use of the word παρουσία, that most conventionally apocalyptic of words, in this letter, because it points as much to the present reality of the church's life in response to Paul's preaching as it does the assurance of Jesus' future appearing. Outside the New Testament, παρουσία commonly denotes the appearance or visit of a ruler among subjects, and it is sometimes used in the New Testament to describe the coming of the risen Lord in glory.[38] Paul is the least consistent New Testament writer in his use of this term. Of twenty-four occurrences of the word, eleven are Paul's; of those, only five refer to the eschatological appearing of Christ. Only in 1 Thessalonians does he use the word to speak exclusively of the Lord's appearing. The only place outside this letter that he mentions Jesus' *parousia* is 1 Cor 15:23: "Christ the first fruits [of resurrection], then at his appearing those who belong to Christ." More frequently, he uses παρεῖναι and παρουσία to describe his own presence among his churches (1 Cor 5:3; 2 Cor 10:2, 11; 11:9; 13:2, 10; Gal 4:13).[39] This makes 1 Thessalonians appear to be more focused on the eschaton than perhaps it ought.

---

37. I am indebted to J. Louis Martyn's remarkably perceptive understanding of this in his treatment of Galatians: "The Apocalyptic Gospel in Galatians," *Int* 54 (2000): 252–53.

38. Albrecht Oepke, "παρουσία, κ.τ.λ.," *TDNT* 5:858–71.

39. See R. W. Funk, "The Apostolic *Parousia*: Form and Significance," in *Christian*

Each reference to Jesus' *parousia* in 1 Thessalonians (1:9–10, 2:19, 3:12–13, 4:15, 5:23) stands at a critical turning point in the letter's structure. The first three mark transitions within the thanksgiving—Paul's gratitude for the Thessalonians' faithfulness to the gospel (1:2–8) and for their faithfulness to the apostolic mission team (2:1–18), and his prayer for their continued faithfulness (3:1–10)—and the fifth initiates the letter's concluding benediction (5:23–28). Only the fourth mention of *parousia*, at 4:15, occurs in a discussion of the end times. The recurrence of this image of the Lord's appearing serves as something like the letter's heartbeat, the steady rhythm that moves it from beginning to end. The apostle sounds a persistent note of reminder throughout 1 Thessalonians that the crucified and risen Christ is both the source of the church's faithfulness and the guarantor of that faithfulness. Jesus' *parousia* carries at once the reality of God's election and the promise of redemption. Jesus is "the one who rescues us from the impending wrath" (1:10), the one who will gather his church to himself at the last trumpet (4:16; cf. 1 Cor 15:52). He is also, however, the one through whom the Thessalonians bring their faithful work, loving labor, and hopeful endurance into the very presence of God (1:3), the one who makes the faithful church a crown of boasting for the apostles (2:19), the one who pours into believers' hearts his own love such that their love becomes known beyond their own fellowship (1:8, 3:12, 4:10), and the one who sanctifies the church and assures its holiness so that it may stand in the presence of the holy God (3:13, 5:23). The assurance of Jesus' *parousia* that suffuses 1 Thessalonians stems from an emphatically apocalyptic conviction that is by no means limited to eschatology.[40]

The central concern of 1 Thessalonians is not simply the church's proper understanding of God's eschatological timetable but the formative function of Christian proclamation. Far more pervasive in 1 Thessalonians than discussion of the end times is this concern for preaching and its effects. Paul variously calls his proclamation "the word," "the word of the Lord," or "the word of God" (1:6, 8; 2:13 [*bis*]; 4:15, 18),[41] "the gospel" (1:5; 2:2, 8, 9; 3:2, 6), "exhortation" or "comfort" (2:3; cf. 2:12; 3:2; 4:1, 10; 5:11),

---

History and Interpretation: Studies Presented to John Knox (ed. W. R. Farmer, C. F. D. Moule, and R. R. Niebuhr; Cambridge: Cambridge University Press, 1967), 249–68.

40. This is *in nuce* the case that I make in "Preaching in 1 Thessalonians," *Journal for Preachers* 28.3 (2005): 20–26.

41. Note also the contrast between God's word and human words in 1 Thess 2:5, 13; 4:8.

"command" (4:2, 11), and "prophecy" (5:20). It is instructive to consider the verbs that he uses when he talks about preaching. He customarily uses verbs of speaking and hearing with εὐαγγέλιον, and he does this in 1 Thess 2:2 and 9. Elsewhere in the letter, though, the gospel is more than the specific words he speaks or his listeners hear. God entrusts the gospel to Paul and his coworkers (2:4), and they in turn hand it over to the Thessalonians (2:8). Nowhere else is there such a clear picture of the preacher as intermediary between God and the church. The only use of the verb εὐαγγελίζομαι in 1 Thessalonians describes not Paul's proclamation but what happens when Timothy reports to him that the Thessalonians have stood firm in the faith despite opposition from their neighbors (3:6). The safety and well-being of the church are themselves "gospel" to the apostle, since "we now live since you stand firm in the Lord" (3:8). Paul thanks God that the gospel "happened" to the Thessalonians "in power and in the Holy Spirit and with complete conviction" rather than in word alone (1:5).[42] The Thessalonians received the word (1:6, 2:13), and it "sounds forth" from them (1:8). Paul says the word of the gospel occurred among the Thessalonians not as a word of flattery or as a disguise for greed (2:5) but in purity and authenticity from those to whom God entrusted it (2:4). The Thessalonians received this word with joy (1:5) and in great tribulation (1:6). The apostles delivered to the church not only the gospel but also their own lives (2:8). The word of the gospel thus is never entirely circumscribed by the words uttered by human preachers because it comes from "the God who

---

42. First Thessalonians has a large concentration of forms of the verb γίνομαι, in addition to texts describing what happens to the word of proclamation. The other instances of γίνομαι rehearse the relationship between the mission team and the Thessalonians who "became" the church in that city: "You became imitators of us and of the Lord" (1:6); "you became a model to all believers" (1:7); "our entrance to you has not become empty" (2:1); "we became infants among you, as a nurse might care tenderly for her own children" (2:7); "you became dear to us" (2:8); "we became holy, just, and blameless to you" (2:10); "you became imitators of the church of God in Judea" (2:14); "I sent [Timothy] so that I might know your faith, lest the tempter tempt you and our labor come up empty" (3:5). These reminders of what "happened" in the formation of the Thessalonian church are clustered in the first three chapters, the thanksgiving period, which points to the importance throughout the letter of the pastoral relationship between the Pauline mission team and the Thessalonian Christians. Paul Schubert's classic study demonstrated that the issues raised in a letter's thanksgiving telegraph at the outset the primary concerns of the letter (*The Form and Function of the Pauline Thanksgiving* [BZNW 20; Berlin: Töpelmann, 1939]).

gives you his Holy Spirit" (4:8). The word that Paul preaches, then, comes to him as the prophets discerned their words of the Lord. It is disclosed as a revelation from God.

This largeness and otherness of the word of proclamation and its power to save determine the several specific consequences of preaching as Paul speaks of it in 1 Thessalonians. Those who hear the word preach it to others (1:8; 4:18). The church encounters resistance and struggle from those who refuse its message; indeed, suffering is to be expected and embraced rather than avoided because that confirms rather than disconfirms the truth of gospel (2:14–16; 3:3–4, 7). The word of the cross, as Paul calls it in 1 Cor 1:18, inevitably subjects those who preach it and those who believe it to the same destiny that their Lord experienced. "We told you ahead of time," he says, "that we were about to be beset by tribulation, and so it has happened and so you know" (1 Thess 3:4). The gospel further reorients the priorities of the Christian community that it creates: it is not the living but the dead whom the Lord of glory summons first to himself (4:16–17). The church is called to care with its ministry not for the strong and hearty of faith but for the weak, the fainthearted, and idlers (5:14). The apostolic mission team itself is shaped by the cruciform message it proclaims.

Paul rehearses the church's relationship with the apostles in chapter 2, highlighting the cruciform character of the church's life.

> Although we might have been able to throw our weight around as apostles of Christ, we became instead infants[43] in your midst, as a wet nurse might care tenderly for her own children. So because we long for you, we are pleased to hand over to you not only the gospel of God but even our own lives, because you have become beloved to us. For you remember, brothers and sisters, our labor and toil, how we worked night and day so that we might not weigh any of you down when we preached to you the gospel of God. You are witnesses, as is God, how we came to you believers in a holy and just and blameless way, as you know, how with

---

43. Beverly Roberts Gaventa's text-critical argument in support of νήπιοι in 2:7 ("Apostles as Babes and Nurses in 1 Thessalonians 2:7," in *Faith and History: Essays in Honor of Paul W. Meyer* [ed. John T. Carroll, Charles H. Cosgrove, and E. Elizabeth Johnson; Atlanta: Scholars Press, 1990], 193–207, and *First and Second Thessalonians*, 26–27) is stronger than Malherbe's case for ἤπιοι ("'Gentle as a Nurse': The Cynic Background to 1 Thess 2," *NovT* [1970]: 203–17; idem, *The Letters to the Thessalonians*, 145–48).

each one of you we were as a father with his own children as we exhorted you and pled with you and testified to you that you might walk in a way that is worthy of the God who calls you into his own glorious realm.... But when we were orphaned from you, brothers and sisters, for a brief season—and only physically, not emotionally—we longed all the more eagerly to see you in person. (2:7–12, 17; my translation)

Paul refers to himself and his colleagues in a single brief paragraph as the infant child, the nursing mother, the brother, the father, and the orphan of the church they have established in Thessalonica. Each of these kinship metaphors—with the exceptions of infant and orphan—occurs commonly in the first century. Philosophers frequently hold up wet nurses as the epitome of instructors who take account of their listeners' frailties, teachers often assume paternal responsibility for their students, and several religious communities use sibling language to refer to themselves. No one but Paul, however, claims both the role of the infant and the nursing mother at the same time. The apostolic mission takes on the astonishing weakness of a newborn and the precarious vulnerability of an orphan, the tender love of a nursing mother and the guiding authority of a father, and the peer relationship of a sibling—all in the same paragraph—because that mission is cruciform in character, shaped by the love and vulnerability of the cross of Christ. This is what Paul elsewhere describes as wisdom revealed in foolishness (1 Cor 1:21) and power made perfect in weakness (2 Cor 12:9). Although the gospel that God has entrusted to the apostles gives them power to "throw [their] weight around" (1 Thess 2:7), that gospel instead shapes their ministry according to the model of Christ crucified.

The cruciform character of Christian life shapes Paul's moral exhortation as well. He urges each of his listeners to "know how to acquire his or her own vessel in holiness and honor" (4:4), that is, to create celibate partnerships like those in view in 1 Cor 7: "So then, the one who marries his own virgin does well; and the one who does not marry will do better" (7:38).[44] To love and honor one's vessel of holiness requires that one respect his or her vow and neither transgress its boundaries nor defraud

---

44. This is the case I make in "A Modest Proposal in Context," in *The Impartial God: Essays in Honor of Jouette M. Bassler* (ed. Robert L. Foster; Sheffield: Sheffield Phoenix Press, 2007), 232–45, building on the argument of Jouette M. Bassler, "Σκεῦος: A Modest Proposal for Illuminating Paul's Use of Metaphor in 1 Thessalonians 4:4," in *The Social World of the First Christians: Essays in Honor of Wayne A. Meeks* (ed. L. Michael White and O. Larry Yarbrough; Philadelphia: Fortress, 1995), 53–66.

one's partner by seeking to set the vow aside (1 Thess 4:6). The radically apocalyptic character of such unconventional households—families that effectively displace the households from which believers have come— also lays on the church the obligation to live quietly among its neighbors, mind its own business, and engage in productive work so as to avoid being dependent on outsiders (4:12). Repeatedly in this letter, Paul describes life together as the church as the granting of precedence to the least among them: the dead will meet the Lord in the air ahead of the living (4:16–17); the disorderly, the discouraged, and the weak are to be the chief concern of the community's patrons (5:14); they are always to "pursue the good for each other and for all" (5:15). The apostle's letter is to be read to "*all* the brothers and sisters," not only to the congregation's leaders (5:27).

Summary

By way of summary, I want to reflect briefly on some of the questions posed to me when I was asked to engage in this study, with appreciation for both the invitation and the task.

Where do we find references to Scripture in 1 Thessalonians? By what criteria can such unmarked references be identified? The criteria proposed by earlier studies for discerning the presence of biblical allusions are somewhat less helpful for the reader of 1 Thessalonians than for readers of other Pauline letters. When Paul offers no direct quotations from Scripture, and when some of his language that reminds us of the Bible may in fact have come from elsewhere, it does not particularly matter whether the apostle had access to an earlier text or if his listeners would have recognized his references. The reminder is valuable, however, that the Bible is the air Paul breathes, the water he swims in, his native language. Sometimes individual words or phrases can in fact signal that he relies on the Bible for much of his vocabulary.

Does Paul seem to be engaging with the broader context of the Old Testament verses to which he refers, or does he use them in a way that bears little relation to their original context? If we were to define context as broadly as possible—that is, including Paul's entire canon rather than the literary contexts of discrete texts—then the answer to this question is affirmative. What is customarily labeled atomistic in Paul's exegesis (e.g., "Does God care for oxen?" in 1 Cor 9:9) assumes a modern respect for literature rather than an apocalyptic conviction that God speaks to him, and to the church, in an unprecedentedly direct manner because of the revelation of Christ and the outpouring of the Spirit. The whole story of God's creative and redemptive work, particularly the death and resurrection of Christ, interprets for him even the smallest phrase from Scripture.

Bibliography

Baarda, Tjitze. "The Shechem Episode in the Testament of Levi: A Comparison with Other Traditions." Pages 11–73 in *Sacred History and Sacred Texts in Early Judaism: A Symposium in Honour of A. S. van der Woude*. Edited by J. N. Bremmer and F. García Martínez. Kampen: Kok Pharos, 1992.

Bassler, Jouette M. "Σκεῦος: A Modest Proposal for Illuminating Paul's Use of Metaphor in 1 Thessalonians 4:4." Pages 53–66 in *The Social World of the First Christians: Essays in Honor of Wayne A. Meeks*. Edited by Michael White and O. Larry Yarbrough. Philadelphia: Fortress, 1995.

Beker, J. Christiaan. *Paul the Apostle: The Triumph of God in Life and Thought*. Philadelphia: Fortress, 1980.

Ciampa, Roy E. "Scriptural Language and Ideas." Pages 41–57 in *As It Is Written: Studying Paul's Use of Scripture*. Edited by Stanley E. Porter and Christopher D. Stanley. SBLSymS 50. Atlanta: Society of Biblical Literature, 2008.

Dunn, James D. G. *The Theology of Paul the Apostle*. Grand Rapids: Eerdmans, 2006.

Elliott, Neil. " 'Blasphemed among the Nations': Pursuing an Anti-imperial 'Intertextuality' in Romans." Pages 213–33 in *As It Is Written: Studying Paul's Use of Scripture*. Edited by Stanley E. Porter and Christopher D. Stanley. SBLSymS 50. Atlanta: Society of Biblical Literature, 2008.

Funk, R. W. "The Apostolic *Parousia*: Form and Significance." Pages 249–68 in *Christian History and Interpretation: Studies Presented to John Knox*. Edited by W. R. Farmer, C. F. D. Moule, and R. R. Niebuhr. Cambridge: Cambridge University Press, 1967.

Gaventa, Beverly Roberts. "Apostles as Babes and Nurses in 1 Thessalonians 2:7." Pages 193–207 in *Faith and History: Essays in Honor of Paul W. Meyer*. Edited by John T. Carroll, Charles H. Cosgrove, and E. Elizabeth Johnson. Atlanta: Scholars Press, 1990.

———. *First and Second Thessalonians*. Interpretation. Louisville: Westminster John Knox, 1998.

Hagner, Donald A. "Paul's Quarrel with Judaism." Pages 128–50 in *Anti-*

Semitism and Early Christianity: Issues of Polemic and Faith. Edited by Craig A. Evans and Donald A. Hagner. Minneapolis: Fortress, 1993.

Hendrix, Holland Lee. "Archaeology and Eschatology at Thessalonica." Pages 107–18 in *The Future of Early Christianity: Essays in Honor of Helmut Koester*. Edited by Birger A. Pearson. Minneapolis: Fortress, 1991.

Johnson, E. Elizabeth. "A Modest Proposal in Context." Pages 232–45 in *The Impartial God: Essays in Honor of Jouette M. Bassler*. Edited by Robert Foster. Sheffield: Sheffield Phoenix Press, 2007.

———. "Preaching in 1 Thessalonians." *Journal for Preachers* 28, no. 3 (2005): 20–26.

Lamp, Jeffrey S. "Is Paul Anti-Jewish? *Testament of Levi* 6 in the Interpretation of 1 Thessalonians 2:13–16." *CBQ* 65 (2003): 408–27.

Levison, Jon R. *The Spirit in First-Century Judaism*. Leiden: Brill, 1997.

Malherbe, Abraham J. "'Gentle as a Nurse': The Cynic Background to 1 Thess 2." *NovT* 12 (1970): 203–17.

———. *The Letters to the Thessalonians: A New Translation with Introduction and Commentary*. AB 32B. New York: Doubleday, 2000.

Martyn, J. Louis. "The Apocalyptic Gospel in Galatians." *Int* 54 (2000): 246–66.

Meeks, Wayne A. *The Moral World of the First Christians*. LEC. Philadelphia: Westminster, 1986.

———. *The Origins of Christian Morality: The First Two Centuries*. New Haven: Yale University Press, 1995.

Porter, Stanley E. "Allusions and Echoes." Pages 29–40 in *As It Is Written: Studying Paul's Use of Scripture*. Edited by Stanley E. Porter and Christopher D. Stanley. SBLSymS 50. Atlanta: Society of Biblical Literature, 2008.

Richard, Earl J. *First and Second Thessalonians*. Sacra Pagina 11. Collegeville, Minn.: Liturgical Press, 1995.

Schubert, Paul. *The Form and Function of the Pauline Thanksgiving*. BZNW 20. Berlin: Töpelmann, 1939.

Scott, James M. "Paul's Use of Deuteronomic Tradition." *JBL* 112 (1993): 645–65.

Smith, Abraham. "Unmasking the Powers: Toward a Postcolonial Analysis of 1 Thessalonians." Pages 47–66 in *Paul and the Roman Imperial Order*. Edited by Richard Horsley. New York: Continuum, 2004.

Stanley, Christopher D. "Paul's 'Use' of Scripture: Why the Audience Matters." Pages 125–55 in *As It Is Written: Studying Paul's Use of Scripture*.

Edited by Stanley E. Porter and Christopher D. Stanley. SBLSymS 50. Atlanta: Society of Biblical Literature, 2008.

The Use of Scripture in Philippians

Stephen Fowl

Introduction

I should begin by confessing that I was and still am a huge fan of Richard Hays's *Echoes of Scripture in the Letters of Paul*.[1] I found his readings compelling, as they often resolve textual conundrums and opening new vistas for thinking about familiar texts. It is one of those books that changes the shape of conversations. Scholars now think of the connections between Paul's letters and the Old Testament in significantly richer, deeper, and more comprehensive ways as the result of this book.

At the same time, and perhaps because of Hays's work, one is forced to ask questions such as: Could the Christians in Corinth, or Galatia, or Rome who first received Paul's letters have seen these connections and heard these echoes? Did Paul intend these letters to be read in such richly allusive ways? If one answers no to these questions, does that change the way we evaluate such readings? I am not the first to raise questions along these lines, nor do I think there are single definitive answers to them.[2]

We today are largely ignorant of how Paul's letters were actually received by their original audiences. We can make judgments about matters such as levels of literacy, access to the text of the LXX in its various forms,

---

1. Richard B. Hays, *Echoes of Scriptures in the Letters of Paul* (New Haven: Yale University Press, 1989).

2. See, for example, the essays in Craig A. Evans and James A. Sanders, eds., *Paul and the Scriptures of Israel* (Sheffield: JSOT Press, 1993) along with Hays's response. See also the incisive article by Christopher D. Stanley, "'Pearls Before Swine': Did Paul's Audiences Understand His Biblical Quotations?" *NovT* 41 (1999): 122–44; and his subsequent monograph, *Arguing with Scripture: The Rhetoric of Quotations in the Letters of Paul* (New York: T&T Clark, 2004).

and the nature of oral performance and reception in the Greco-Roman world. Even here, however, our information is very limited. Were these texts heard multiple times? Heard once and then studied by some? What sort of Scriptural catechesis went on in these first Christian communities? What role did those delivering each epistle play in the interpretation of the epistle? We really know very little of how often these letters were read in their respective congregations and how those occasions were paired with periods of hearing and studying the Old Testament.[3]

In the course of pondering these questions, the one thing that becomes clear is that a phrase like "the original audience of the epistle" is really a heuristic fiction. It does some useful hermeneutical work, and scholars should not abandon it altogether. Nevertheless, no one can speak authoritatively about the ways in which the actual first recipients of Paul's letters engaged with those epistles or the Old Testament over time. One can offer some speculations, but one must also recognize how speculative that work really is.

As a result, when it comes to discussing the use of Scripture in Philippians or any other letter, it is evident that one needs to be quite clear about two related sets of issues. The first concerns the various connections that one might draw between Paul's letters and the Old Testament and how they are made. The second concerns the status of those connections. That is, for whom might these connections have been evident and why? Clarity with regard to each of these matters will substantially enhance our ability to evaluate the varied interpretive work that goes on under the general heading of "the use of Scripture in…". As a way of illustrating the variety of ways in which one might address questions of the use of Scripture in Philippians, I would like to examine three different passages where scriptural texts are either cited or stand in the very near background, though in different ways. In doing this, I will aim to be quite clear about who might be expected to see these connections or hear these allusions.

Identifying three scriptural citations or allusions in Philippians is hard work. Unlike many of his other letters, Philippians does not engage in an ongoing discussion of scriptural texts. Paul does not address prophecies or

---

3. See Harry Y. Gamble, *Books and Readers in the Early Church* (New Haven: Yale University Press, 1995), and J. Ross Wagner, *Heralds of the Good News: Isaiah and Paul "in Concert" in the Letter to the Romans* (NovTSup 101; Leiden: Brill, 2002), 33–36, for a discussion of the various components that would go into an congregation's engagement with a Pauline letter.

promises that are apocalyptically fulfilled in Christ. There are no ongoing dialogues with the law about the status of the law. So we must admit that in some respects Philippians may prove to be anomalous with regard to the Pauline corpus.

Philippians 2:10–11

The first text that I want to look at is Phil 2:10–11 and its use of Isa 45:23. Philippians 2:10–11 explains both the purpose for which God exalted the obedient, humiliated Christ and the gift that God subsequently bestowed on Christ. The purpose of God's exaltation of Christ is that "at the name of Jesus every knee shall bow."[4] The image of bowing the knee seems to be taken from Isa 45:23. In the context of Isaiah and also here in Philippians, it signifies a recognition of authority. It is a way of offering homage to God in the case of Isaiah and, in the case of Philippians, to Jesus. In Rom 14:11, Paul quotes directly from Isa 45:23 to support his claim of God's universal rule and subsequent judgment of all things. In this respect it is interesting to note that the authority and power that Paul attributes to God in Romans he attributes here to Christ by invoking the same Old Testament text.

Philippians interrupts the direct citation of Isa 45:23 with the phrase "in heaven and earth and under the earth." This addition, however, is clearly in line with the sentiments expressed in Isa 45:23. The acclamation of Philippians then continues with Isa 45:23, announcing in 2:11 that "every tongue will confess" that Jesus Christ is Lord.

The language from Isa 45:23 is woven into Phil 2:10–11 without any direct citation from Isaiah such as we find in Rom 14:11. Moreover, the passage is intelligible apart from any recognition of its connection to Isaiah. A reader or hearer of Philippians could in some sense understand the passage without knowing anything about Isaiah. Still, there are at least three perspectives from which one can ask further questions about this text.

---

4. I have translated the Greek preposition ἐν with the English "at." The exact function of this preposition is often debated. Does it refer to the object of worship or the medium? The LXX usage would suggest that worship "in the name of" God is worship offered to God (1 Kgs 8:44; Pss 43:8, 62:5, 104:3). See also Marcus Bockmuehl, *The Epistle to the Philippians* (London: Black, 1998), 145.

The first perspective is Paul's. Since it is clear that Paul is familiar with this text, it is safe to assume that he either recognized the allusion, if the text was preformed material, or made the allusion himself.[5] In this respect it is not crucial to distinguish whether Paul created or quoted the text. Given that, one could argue that Paul made the allusion simply for the joy of making it but did not imagine anything beyond employing a nice turn of phrase. If this is the case, Paul was extremely fortunate because the invocation of Isa 45:23 could, and often does, invite readers familiar with Isaiah to see the story of Christ narrated in 2:6–11 in the light of the larger context of that part of Isaiah. Moreover, doing so seems to be particularly useful for advancing Paul's overall argument in Philippians. God's vindication and exaltation of the obedient, suffering Christ is in line with the vindication of the suffering obedient servant of God in Isa 40–55.[6] Recognizing this further enhances Paul's argument that, should the Philippians adopt the patterns of thinking, feeling, and acting displayed to them by Christ (among others), even in the midst of hostility and suffering, God will vindicate that obedience in ways analogous to God's vindication of Christ.

At this point, it is important to introduce a further distinction when looking at the allusion to Isa 45:23 from Paul's perspective. When looking at matters from Paul's perspective, it is important to try to distinguish authorial motives from an author's communicative intentions:[7] "That is to say, one ought to distinguish between *what* an author is trying to say (which might be called a 'communicative intention') and *why* it is being said (which might be called a motive)."[8] An author might write from any number of motives: a desire for fame and fortune, hopes of acquir-

---

5. Although I argued in *The Story of Christ in the Ethics of Paul* (Sheffield: JSOT Press, 1990), ch. 2, that most of the claims about the life of this text prior to its incorporation into Philippians are little more than unsubstantiated speculation, I am willing, for the sake of argument, to at least grant that possibility here.

6. See Richard Bauckham, *God Crucified* (Grand Rapids: Eerdmans, 1998), and his essay "The Worship of Jesus in Philippians 2:9–11," in *Where Christology Began* (ed. R. P. Martin and Brian Dodd; Louisville: Westminster John Knox, 1998), 128–39, where he argues that Paul has all of Isa 40–55 in mind here.

7. This distinction is initially made by Quentin Skinner, "Motives and Intentions in the Interpretation of Texts," *New Literary History* 3 (1972), 393–408. For biblical scholars, this notion is expertly articulated by Mark Brett, "Motives and Intentions in Gen 1," *JTS* 42 (1991): 1–16. In what follows I am largely indebted to Brett's work.

8. Brett, "Motives and Intentions," 5.

ing tenure, a deep psychological need for self-expression, and so forth. Motives of which an author is not fully conscious may even be at work. Analysis of texts is never enough to uncover an author's motives. In fact, a desire to uncover authorial motives will generally be very difficult to fulfill. In the case of ancient authors, an interest in motives will be almost totally frustrated by our lack of information.

On the other hand, one need not attend to an author's motives in rendering an account of her communicative intentions. Such an account requires attention to matters of semantics, of linguistic conventions operative at the time, and of implication and inference, among other factors. In dealing with biblical writers, attention to these matters is inescapably historical. Indeed, in many respects the practices required to display an author's communicative intentions will be familiar to biblical critics even if they do not characterize their work as offering an account of an author's communicative intention.

Accounting for an author's communicative intention does not depend on having textually mediated access to an autonomous, aware, authorial self. In fact, in the case of the Bible, it probably does not even require the identification of a specific historical character as an author. Rather, in the case of Paul, for example, it depends on knowledge of Greek and the linguistic conventions operative in the first century; an ability to detect and explicate allusions, indirect references, implications, and inferences; and a measure of familiarity with the set of social conventions of which letter writing is a part. The precise ways to mix and match all of these considerations will always be matters of argument and debate. For example, there is no set formula or method that will reveal when one should rely more heavily on semantics than on social conventions or on possible Old Testament allusions. In fact, the great majority of interpretive arguments among biblical scholars can be cast as arguments about how to weigh and evaluate the roles of these pieces of evidence. A great number of factors can determine the outcome of these arguments, but they are not dependent on an accounting of Paul's motives, even if one could know them.

If one is primarily interested in what Paul aimed to communicate, then one has good reason here to suggest that the invocation of Isa 45:23 invites readers and hearers of Philippians to deepen their understanding of Paul's argument by finding that, despite the suffering they might incur through their obedience, God's servants have always found God to be faithful.

In a moment, I want to come back to Paul's perspective with regard to another issue in this text. First, however, I want to look at this text from the perspective of the Philippians who received this letter from Paul. I think that both 2:10-11 and the argument of the epistle as a whole are intelligible without recognizing the reference to Isa 45:23. Moreover, early recognition of this allusion would have required a fairly high level of familiarity with the text of Isaiah. I think that one is justified in assuming that few if any in the church in Philippi had such familiarity. Still, if only one or two members of the congregation could have caught this allusion the first time they heard the epistle, could they not have noted it to the others? And even if no one initially heard the allusion, might it not be the case that further engagement with Isaiah, Philippians, or both could have brought this allusion to their attention? These possibilities seem plausible to me, but scholars must admit that we really do not know very much about how the Philippians or any other congregation engaged Paul's letters or the Old Testament texts over time.

This leads me to suggest that, although the phrase "the original audience" might be a useful way of talking about how a group familiar with the relevant social and linguistic conventions would have understood a word, phrase, or text, it is not really very helpful in reconstructing how a specific group of Christians received, engaged, and interacted with a Pauline letter over time. Given that, how might we make judgments in these matters?

Of course, provisional judgments about literacy levels and access to texts can be helpful here.[9] These considerations may set some useful parameters of plausibility, but they cannot tell us anything about the interactions between the members of a specific first-century Christian community relative to any particular text.[10]

One may get some general help here from other parts of the New Testament. For example, Luke tells us that the resurrected Christ opened the hearts and minds of the disciples so that they could understand the Scriptures (Luke 24:44-45). I do not think this implies that they were infused with a full understanding in an instant. Rather, I take it to mean that their engagement with Scripture was enhanced and directed by the Spirit. Whether one believes this or not, the story presumes that the disciples

---

9. See Gamble, *Books and Readers*, ch. 1.

10. Wagner, *Heralds of the Good News*, 36-37, wonders if reading Paul's letters might have provoked some of the members of his congregations to become fluent in their knowledge of Scripture. He also asks whether, if only one or two members of a congregation had the requisite scriptural knowledge to grasp Paul's allusions, they might be in a position to instruct others.

were engaged with Scripture both before and after the death of Christ. The story of Philip and the Ethiopian in Acts 8 likewise paints a picture of an early disciple who had a facility with Scripture. Thus, at the very least one would have to say that Luke did not find such a prospect implausible. In a similar way, the members of the synagogue in Berea "studied the Scriptures" (Acts 17:10–13), and Timothy is instructed to study to show himself approved (2 Tim 2:15). And if one extrapolates from the role that the Genesis stories of Abraham play in the argument of Galatians, there is some basis for thinking that the congregations in Galatia were engaged with this part of Genesis from at least two different perspectives. Finally, and more specifically, it is clear that by the early third century Origen had clearly noted the connection between Isa 45:23 and Phil 2:10–11.[11]

At best, these are shards of evidence from which one can draw only tentative inferences and very limited conclusions. I will venture a few here. By the time of Origen (184–253 C.E.), there is evidence of a developed theological culture within which at least some Christians are able to recognize, appreciate, and even develop further the sorts of allusions, references, and connections that Paul is able to make. These skills would have been part of the education provided by a γραμματικός.[12] One can assume that churches from Paul's day to Origen's began to develop this theological culture over time. One can also assume that this development would have been sporadic, uneven, and influenced by a host of social, material, and political factors. In short, it would be difficult to work backward from the development of the theological culture evident at the time of Origen and speak with much confidence about the beginnings of such a culture within the Pauline churches. The more advanced one imagines this development to be, the greater the likelihood that the community would have been able to see or hear Paul's allusions.

In the end, there is very little to go on when it comes to making judgments about how the Philippians, or any other Pauline church, would have engaged one of the apostle's letters. Our limited abilities in this respect may indicate that making judgments about the use of Scripture in Philippians from the perspective of the letter's original audience is going to be one of the least interesting and fruitful avenues to pursue.

---

11. Origen, *Or.* 31.3.

12. See the discussion in Lewis Ayres, *Nicea and Its Legacy* (Oxford: Oxford University Press, 2004), 20–40.

The third perspective from which to examine the allusion to Isa 45:23 in Phil 2:1–11 is that of much-later readers. Unlike the Philippians, contemporary interpreters have ready access to the texts that allows them to recognize and even develop their interconnections and allusions. Such an interpretive approach may, but need not, be concerned with the historical questions regarding what Paul might have known and intended and what the original audience may have been capable of understanding and recognizing. As long as interpreters following this path are clear about what they are doing, it is relatively easy to evaluate such work.

The overwhelming majority of contemporary readers of Scripture, by virtue of their Christian convictions, tend to adopt some form of this approach. Moreover, because they treat Scripture as a whole, Christians will interpret scriptural texts in ways that play off, inform, illumine, and regulate each other. At their best, Christians interpret Scripture in ways that enable them to fulfill aims that are larger and more complex than simply interpreting a text.[13] In this light, it is not surprising that interpreting scriptural texts, including their various connections and allusions, might shape and be shaped by factors, questions, and concerns that would not and could not have been known to Paul or the Philippians.

Such an approach can readily be applied to the relation between Phil 2:10–11 and Isa 45:23. In the immediate context of Isa 45:20–25, Yahweh asserts superiority over all other gods. Only Yahweh can save: "I am God, and there is no other." Thus, when Israel and the nations recognize this superiority, "every knee shall bow and every tongue confess." By connecting this language and imagery to Jesus in Phil 2:10–11 and ascribing to Jesus the name κύριος, Paul is, as Richard Bauckham has indicated, including Jesus within the identity of the one God of Israel. In the process, he emphasizes that intentional self-emptying and obedient suffering are compatible with participation in the identity of the one God of Israel.[14] This is an important claim, and it fits well with the overall argument of Philippians.

---

13. In the liturgy of the Word for Palm Sunday, Isa 45:21–25 and Phil 2:5–11 are the readings for Episcopalians, but not in the Revised Common Lectionary, which pairs Phil 2:5–11 with Isa 50:4–9. Although there are no direct textual links between these two texts, I would argue that the echoes between Isa 50 and Phil 2:5–11 connect with the argument of Philippians as a whole as well as or better than those from Isa 45:23.

14. See Bauckham, "The Worship of Jesus," 128–32.

These claims, however, also raise some troubling questions for subsequent generations of readers. To argue that these texts include Jesus within the identity of the one God of Israel without at the same time abandoning a commitment to the singularity of God places on the agenda of subsequent readers a set of questions about how to relate the Son and the Father (and eventually the Spirit) to each other without compromising their divinity or the singularity of the godhead. Although reading Scripture in this light raises such questions, Scripture does not directly resolve them. Nevertheless, for later Christians committed to the whole of Scripture, Paul's claims in Phil 2, along with similar claims such as those made in John 1, raised the issue of how properly to order and organize scriptural discourse about God, Christ, and the Spirit. At their heart, then, the fourth- and fifth-century arguments about Trinitarian doctrine were deeply scriptural, though they would not likely have been imagined by either Paul or the Philippians. Still, it was imperative for Christians to engage in those discussions. In other words, there are times and occasions when Christians need to draw connections between scriptural texts that the authors and audiences of those texts could not have made themselves.

Philippians 1:19

With these theoretical issues in view, there are two other Old Testament texts in Philippians that I would like to examine. The first is the use of a portion of Job 13:16 in Phil 1:19. In 1:18, Paul ends his discussion of various types of preachers with an expression of joy. Most commentators note that 1:18a closes off one thought and 1:18b begins another. Nevertheless, the future tense of the verb in 1:18b links it to the rejoicing in 1:18a even as it also introduces 1:19. In 1:18 we learn that the imprisoned Paul rejoices now in the fact that the gospel is proclaimed despite the motives of some of the proclaimers. He also commits himself to continue his rejoicing into the future. This commitment is based on a certain knowledge that Paul has. The two subsequent clauses, one here in verse 19 and one in verse 20, both introduced by ὅτι, explain the basis for this knowledge. The first clause exactly matches the vocabulary of the LXX of Job 13:16, "This will result in my salvation." Although the amount of textual material here is not large, Job 13:16 and Phil 1:19 are the only places where this precise form of words occurs in Scripture. As with the connection to Isa 45:23 in 2:10–11, Paul does not introduce this biblical reference with any of his standard phrases. The text is perfectly intelligible to anyone who does not know Job

13:16. As Hays notes, however, for someone who does notice and identify the quote, there are some "intriguing resonances," though not exactly the ones Hays proposes.[15]

In chapter 13, Job is in the midst of defending his integrity in the light of his "friends'" accusations that his lamentable situation is the result of some hidden sin in his life. In 13:16, he claims both that he will ultimately be vindicated before God and that those who have spoken falsely will not be welcomed into God's presence.[16] In 13:18, Job again proclaims that the time of his judgment, when he "will be shown to be righteous," is near. Job's convictions about his suffering and vindication are offered in the context of bitter lament for his situation and utter contempt for his friends' theologizing.

Turning to Phil 1, we see Paul recounting his situation in prison. He is there because of his convictions about Christ and his obedience to his apostolic mission. Hence, his suffering is the result not of sin but of his obedience. His discussion of those who preach from false motives indicates that such preaching is taking place in part to increase the pain of his imprisonment. In other words, those who should have been his friends have been acting from false motives. Hays claims that Paul here takes on Job's voice "to affirm confidence in the favorable outcome of his affliction; thereby, he implicitly transfers to himself some of the significations that traditionally cluster around the figure of Job."[17] This comment shows clearly that Hays is interested in Paul's perspective.

From that perspective, there are ample reasons for thinking that Paul's communicative intentions reflected an appreciation of the deep connections between Job and himself that are implicit in his use of Job 13:16 in 1:19. At the same time, close attention to the text of Job 13 indicates that there are significant differences between Job's disposition and Paul's. In fact, given the subsequent movements of the argument of Philippians, one might claim that Paul invokes vocabulary from Job because Paul wants the Philippians to shun Job's disposition toward his suffering and adopt Paul's disposition in its place. Although both figures share a confidence in divine vindication, Job's confidence is cloaked in bitter lament while Paul's is suffused with joy.

---

15. Hays, *Echoes of Scriptures*, 21–24.

16. See also 13:7: "Do not all speak before the Lord? But you speak before him falsely." Cf. Hays, *Echoes of Scriptures*, 22.

17. Ibid., 23.

Paul's use of vocabulary from Job seems to indicate that he sees his situation as analogous to Job's. This analogy of situations helps to generate and sustain in Paul a similar hope to that which Job expresses in 13:16. Given that Paul's admonitions to the Philippians depend to a large degree on the Philippians' ability to see the similarities between their own situation, on the one hand, and a variety of other situations, including Paul's sufferings (cf. 1:29–30), the story of God's activity in Christ (cf. 2:5–11), and the acts of Timothy and Epaphroditus (cf. 2:19–30), on the other hand, we might well take this allusion to Job's sufferings as one more example of the patterns of judgment and perceptual habits that Paul wishes to see formed in the Philippians. The fit between this account of Paul's use of Job and the rest of the argument of the epistle further strengthens Hays's assertions about Paul's perspective. In fact, we can go further and observe that Paul's admonitions to the Philippians to avoid grumbling and dissent in 2:12–18 seem to imply that he desires the Philippians to display a version of Job's confidence without the bitterness of Job. Instead of complaining, Paul invites them to rejoice.

When it comes to the question of whether the Philippians might have detected these connections, we are basically in the same place as we were with Isa 45 and Phil 2. If we imagine them as largely unformed readers who have only one opportunity to recognize an allusion, then it seems unlikely that such readers would have picked up the allusion. If we envision them as fully catechized readers who were well advanced in developing the theological culture that marks at least some in the third century, then we probably are not accurately imagining the church in Philippi anytime in the first century.

Yet even if it is unlikely that the Philippians would have heard Paul's allusions to Job 13:16, it is a separate question whether Christians today should allow these texts from Job to resonate in their ears as they listen to or read Philippians. Christians should read Philippians in the light of all of Scripture without, at the same time, determining in advance what that entails for the interpretation of any text. In this case, attending to the vocabulary from Job in Phil 1:19 and the larger context of the book of Job can provide a theologically edifying context in which to read Philippians. Those who do so will find both similarities and differences between Job and Paul's writing. Christians would be unwise to cut themselves off willfully from such edification.

Philippians 2:12–18

So far, I have looked at two passages from Philippians where one might argue that specific texts from Scripture are invoked or alluded to in fairly direct ways. The manner in which one understands, evaluates, and develops the connections between Philippians and these Old Testament texts depends on one's interpretive aims. I now want to examine a slightly longer passage in Philippians and its connections to a wider complex of Old Testament texts. Here, too, it is important to be clear about one's interpretive aims.

The text that I wish to examine is Phil 2:12-18. I will not offer an extensive account of the entire passage. Instead, I will summarize in order to devote more space to those verses that seem to connect to a complex of Old Testament texts. Paul begins this section with a call to obedience. He recalls his prior relations with the Philippians in order to encourage them to adopt his way of understanding the relationships between the suffering that may come their way as the result of freely willed obedience to God, and God's faithfulness toward and ultimate vindication of that way of life. In addition, Paul assures the Philippians of God's continued care and activity among them.

In 2:14, he adds that the Philippians should "do all things without grumbling and foolish reasoning." The key allusive phrase here is "without grumbling." The only other time Paul uses this phrase is in 1 Cor 10:10, where he cites the grumbling of the Israelites as a negative example not to be emulated by the Corinthians. The Greek terms γογγυσμός and γογγύζω appear a number of times in the LXX with reference to Israel's grumbling against God and Moses.[18] The relatively specific context of this vocabulary in the LXX[19] and Paul's use of the same vocabulary to allude to the same LXX events in 1 Cor 10 may indicate that Paul is also making such an allusion here in Philippians. Nevertheless, this allusion has been a puzzle for modern commentators because it does not seem to have any direct application to the Philippians in the way that it does for the Corinthians.[20] On

---

18. Exod 16:7-12 (six times); 17:3; Num 14:27-29 (three times); 16:41; 17:5 (twice); 17:10.

19. Of the twenty-five uses of γογγύζειν and γογγυσμός in the LXX, sixteen refer to Israel's grumbling in the desert.

20. Some point to the fact that Paul elsewhere addresses internal dissension in the Philippian congregation (4:1-3) to suggest that, rather than alluding to grumbling

closer examination, however, we see that Paul's pattern of reasoning in 1 Corinthians is quite similar to that in Philippians. In the case of 1 Cor 10:10, it is clear that Paul interprets the current life of the Corinthian church in the economy of salvation through the positive and negative examples of God's dealings with Israel in the desert. In Philippians it would appear that Paul engages in a similar activity. He interprets the movements of God's drama of salvation in a way that allows him to draw analogies and spell out implications for the common life of the Philippians. In the case of 2:14, the analogy could be explained as follows. When faced with political and material hardship and opposition, the Israelites grumbled, doubting that God (through Moses) had led them thus far and would likewise lead them out of their present difficulties. It is precisely this attitude that Paul seeks to frustrate in his letter to the Philippians. In 2:13, he reiterates his conviction that God has and will continue to work in the lives of the Philippians, an assertion that he first made in 1:6. The Philippians, therefore, are to avoid exhibiting the response of the Israelites when they are in a similar situation. By alluding to the Israelites' grumbling in the desert, Paul is not seeking to counter present behavior as much as anticipating possible responses to events in the near future.[21]

Avoiding "grumbling and foolish reasoning" will enable the Philippians to be "blameless and innocent, children of God without blemish in the midst of a crooked and perverse generation, in which, they shine as lights in the world." The conjunction of the terms "blameless," "innocent," and "without blemish" gives the very clear impression that Paul is describing the final end toward which God is moving the church at Philippi. Paul is looking forward to that time when God's ultimate "good pleasure" is brought to fruition in the Philippians, a time when the purposes for which God first called them are achieved. This reiterates the movement of the argument of 1:6–10. Moreover, Paul contrasts this holiness toward which God is moving the Philippian Christians with the crookedness and per-

---

against God, Paul is using this term to talk about internal dissent. The language of 4:1–3, however, is different. Moreover, such a suggestion seems deaf to the LXX overtones of grumbling.

21. Chrysostom seems to be on the right track in taking this passage as a warning about future possibilities rather than a direct admonition about current realities. He rightly contrasts the situations of the Corinthians, where grumbling is real and the allusion to the Israelites is direct and explicit, and the Philippians, where grumbling is a possibility to be avoided and the allusion is, correspondingly, less explicit (*Homily* 6).

versity of the present age. On its surface, then, this verse suggests that by avoiding grumbling and foolish reasoning, the Philippians will be brought to that state of holiness for which God called them in contrast to the pagan society around them.

Beneath the surface, however, the clause "children of God without blemish in the midst of a crooked and perverse generation" appears to echo Deut 32:5 with some rather interesting results. While the syntax of the LXX version of Deut 32:5 is obscure, the general thrust of the passage is clear.[22] Israel has failed to perceive God's economy of salvation; they have failed to attend to God's saving deeds and their implications. Hence, in their foolishness, they have ultimately sinned against themselves; they have become a crooked and perverse generation (cf. Deut. 32:1-14). If Paul's communicative intention is to allude to these verses, his point is not to claim that the church in general and the Philippians in particular have replaced Israel.[23] Rather, as in 2:14, he invokes the negative example of Israel as something for the Philippians to avoid if God's best purposes for them are to be fulfilled. With Israel as a negative example, the Philippians should attend wisely to God's economy of salvation. In doing this, they will both avoid grumbling and foolish reasoning and also become holy and blameless children of God in the midst of those who do not rightly recognize and understand God's mighty acts of salvation.

The next two clauses (which actually run into the beginning of 2:16) further display the Philippians' position in a "crooked and perverse generation."[24] Paul claims that in the midst of this corrupt generation the Philippians "shine as lights in the world." This image fits with several others throughout Scripture where the people of God are spoken of as lights in the midst of an unbelieving world. In Isa 42:6 and 49:6, redeemed Israel shines as a light to the Gentiles, drawing them to God. These same verses are glossed by Simeon in Luke 2:29-32 to prophesy the blessings

---

22. A wooden translation of the LXX might read, "They sinned not against him, children of blemish, a crooked and perverse generation." See Bockmuehl, *Philippians*, 156-57, for a discussion of this passage.

23. Bockmuehl, *Philippians*, 157, rightly sees that Moses is not claiming that God has disowned Israel, nor is Paul claiming that the church has replaced Israel.

24. I am following Bockmuehl, *Philippians*, 159; Gordon D. Fee, *The Epistle to the Philippians* (Grand Rapids: Eerdmans, 1995), 246-47; Joachim Gnilka, *Der Philipperbrief* (Freiburg: Herder, 1968), 153; and Peter O'Brien, *Commentary on Philippians* (Grand Rapids: Eerdmans, 1991), 297, who connect the participle "holding fast" in verse 16 with the finite verb "in order that you might be" in verse 15.

that come to both Israel and the Gentiles through Christ. In Acts 13:47, Paul and Barnabas quote Isa 49:6 to justify their mission to the Gentiles.

In their respective commentaries on Philippians, both Fee and Bockmuehl make the interesting suggestion that this clause in 2:15 echoes Dan 12:3, where, in an apocalyptic vision of the resurrection, Daniel is told that "those with understanding shall shine like the brightness of the heavens," and "those who strengthen my words will be like the stars of heaven forever."[25] If we take this allusion seriously, the Daniel text further supports Paul's claims that those who manifest a true understanding of God's saving activity will be brought to their proper end. Further, the phrase "holding fast to the word of life" at the beginning of 2:16 might be seen as an explication of "strengthening the words" of God in the second part of Dan 12:3.[26]

If we look at this from the perspective of Paul's communicative intention, it would appear that in these verses Paul is concerned with keeping the Philippians from following the negative example of Israel in the desert—of misreading the signs of God's activity and, thereby, falling to "grumbling." The aim of avoiding this situation is so that God can lead the Philippians to their true end, which is holiness. In the course of reaching this end, the Philippians will shine in the midst of an unbelieving and hostile world as they order their common life in a manner worthy of the gospel of Christ.[27] The Philippians will hold fast to the word of life as they obediently work out their salvation. More specifically, given that the vocabulary around grumbling seems so closely tied in the LXX to Israel in the desert, and given that Paul uses the trope of Israel's grumbling in 1 Cor, we are probably justified in assuming that Paul was also thinking along these same lines with the Philippians. In addition, both the specificity of the vocabulary and the relatively secure fit between the aims of Deut 32:5 and Paul's larger argument in Philippians support the judgment that Paul intended to allude to Deut 32:5 in Phil 2:15.

The connections to Isa 42:6, Isa 49:6, and Dan 12:3 are less immediately evident. The image of shining as a light in the midst of darkness seems to be relatively widespread. This does not help to tie the Philippians

---

25. See Bockmuehl, *Philippians*, 158; Fee, *Philippians*, 247–48.

26. So Fee, *Philippians*, 247n33.

27. The entire section stretching from 1:27 to 2:18 is really a working out of Paul's admonition to the Philippians to order their common life in a manner worthy of the gospel.

verse to any particular Old Testament text or texts. Further, the apocalyptic context of the Old Testament texts is rather different from that of Philippians. This is not to say that these connections do not edify or generate insight. Rather, I think the argument that Paul intended to communicate such connections is less secure.

What about the Philippians themselves? Again, if one thinks of the Philippians as largely uninstructed in the faith, it is unlikely that they would have picked up these allusions on the first uninstructed hearing. One should not, however, assume that the Philippians had such a static relationship to this epistle and to those who conveyed it. If one grants that the Philippians probably read or heard and subsequently reread or reheard Paul's letter several times and that those who delivered the letter could have instructed the Philippians in the presence and significance of the Old Testament allusions here, then one must grant that in time they, too, might have detected these allusions. Obviously these last considerations do not answer the question of what the original audience might have recognized. They merely make it more probable that over time the Philippians might have come to see the connections between their situation and Israel's.

Regarding the perspective of the Philippians, there is one key difference between this passage and the previous two. In the case of Phil 1:19 and 2:10-11, both texts are intelligible regardless of whether the Philippians would have recognized the Old Testament allusions. With regard to Phil 2:12-18, the issue is a bit more complex. One could argue that the Philippians would have been able to fulfill Paul's admonitions in this passage regardless of whether they picked up any Old Testament allusions. Nevertheless, one of the habits that Paul wants to help form in the Philippians is a sort of Christ-focused practical reasoning. As Paul repeatedly demonstrates in Philippians, one of the keys to cultivating this habit of practical reasoning is developing the ability to read and interpret God's economy of salvation in ways that allow one to see the connections between that economy and one's current situation in order to discern how to live appropriately. Given that this appears to be one of Paul's overarching aims in Philippians, it seems reasonable to assume that part of cultivating such practical wisdom would be developing the ability to see connections both positive and negative between Israel's and the Philippians' situations. If the Philippians were ultimately unsuccessful in discerning Paul's allusions, then his overall aims and hopes for them would have been frustrated. Thus if one is to judge that the Philippians were unlikely ever to have seen or heard the connections to the Old Testament that Paul seems to intend in this passage, then these consequences would have been more significant than they would have been with the other two passages.

I believe that this recognition offers some evidence for answering questions about the Philippians' prospects for seeing or hearing this particular set of Old Testament allusions. Let me explain. I think that the Old Testament allusions in Phil 1:19, 2:10–11, and 2:12–18 enrich and deepen our understanding of these texts. I also think that we have good reason to assume that such allusions were part of Paul's communicative intentions. With regard to 1:19 and 2:10–11, one could argue, even in the face of more sophisticated and optimistic accounts of the Philippians' capacities as the audience of this letter, that it is unlikely that they would have initially seen or heard these allusions. Such an argument would not, however, have significant consequences for our judgments about Paul's overall rhetorical aims in writing Philippians.

If one recognizes that Paul's overall communicative intention in Philippians is not simply to make such allusions but also, at least with regard to 2:12–18, to have them perceived, then one would also have to say that Paul assumed that the Philippians would or ultimately could come to perceive these allusions. That is, one is pushed to conclude that Paul had a fairly high regard for the Philippians' abilities, opportunities, and capacities to perceive his allusive work with the Old Testament. Why otherwise would he risk failure with regard to one of his primary aims for writing in the first place? If one concludes that, even over time and in the light of further study and instruction, the Philippians would not have seen or heard Paul's allusions in this passage, then one is also forced to conclude that an important aspect of Paul's aims in writing Philippians has failed.

Let me be clear about what I am claiming here. I think that it is perfectly possible that any number of Paul's aims in writing to any of his churches might have been frustrated either fully or in part. The fact that we can discern Paul's communicative intentions and the ways in which he hoped for those intentions to shape the faith and practice of the communities to which he wrote does not mean that these aims and purposes were always and fully realized. But I do think that this passage and its role in Paul's overall aims and purposes for the Philippians shows that Paul assumed the Philippians had the prospects and capacities to perceive the allusions in this text. The alternative is to argue that Paul assumed his work would ultimately fail in one of its central aims, the cultivation of a form of Christ-focused practical wisdom, yet he still went ahead and wrote Philippians as he did.

Regardless of how one answers this question about the epistle's first audience, Christians today should take these allusions seriously. It would be extremely odd to argue that Christians should not attend to these allusions despite their potential benefits for Christian life and practice because the epistle's first audience might not have recognized them. No matter how one resolves the historical questions, commenting and reflecting on such allusions would seem to be an essential element of interpreting Scripture theologically. Moreover, cultivating the familiarity with Scripture that will enable one to "hear" these and other allusions is a foundational practice of the Christian life, not because it enhances one's prospects of being a more clever reader of Scripture but because such habits of reading Scripture enhance one's prospects of engaging Scripture in ways that will deepen one's communion with God and others.

With regard to broader questions about the use of Scripture in the New Testament, one has to say that in Philippians Scripture plays a relatively minor role in comparison with its role in Romans, Galatians, or the Corinthian correspondence. As a result, discussions of Philippians have not played a very significant role in the scholarly debates generated by *Echoes of Scripture*. At the same time, this very paucity also allows one to examine some of the more vexing methodological issues in a context where the interpretive issues are less fraught. Less heat may in fact generate more light.

When looking at the use of Scripture in Philippians, the relatively uncluttered scholarly terrain helps one to see that there are at least three perspectives that one can adopt when looking at this issue. Distinguishing between these perspectives can help us to clarify how to evaluate the use of Scripture in any New Testament text.

The first perspective is Paul's own. Here it is important to distinguish between Paul's communicative intention and his motives, as spelled out above. Such a distinction offers a great deal of conceptual clarity. Recognizing such a distinction entails, however, that our claims about Paul and his larger theological and personal hopes, motives, and aims will need to be limited.

When making judgments about the scope of Paul's allusive practices with regard to the Old Testament and how deep we should dig in order to display those allusive practices, there seem to be two important issues to examine. The first is vocabulary. Even when there are no direct indicators that Paul is engaging with an Old Testament text, one might rely on the presence of distinctive vocabulary to make a case that he is in fact doing so.

In Philippians 1:19 and 2:10–11 one finds either exact or close repetitions of the vocabulary of specific Old Testament texts that could indicate that Paul intended to communicate some sort of connection between what he wrote in Philippians and what was already written in Job and Isaiah. With regard to 2:12–18, the case is less conclusive, though the use of "grumbling" in 2:14 and its relatively focused use in the LXX together with some close correspondences between 2:15 and Deut 32:5 support the claim that Paul is both interpreting the Philippians' situation in the light of Israel's past relations with God and inviting the Philippians to do likewise as part of their growth in Christ-focused practical wisdom. This might be further supported by the similar use of "grumbling" language in 1 Cor 10:10.

The second factor that one should consider in offering judgments about Paul's allusive practices has to do with the fit between what is going on in the wider Old Testament context and what Paul is arguing in any particular epistle. If one wishes to argue that Paul uses specific vocabulary to invoke a specific Old Testament verse or two and that he wishes to draw on further and deeper connections between that text and its wider context, then one's argument is enhanced to the degree that one can show how such allusions help to advance arguments Paul is already making in the epistle. For example, consider the allusion to Job 13 in Phil 1:19. In this section of Philippians, Paul is already offering an evaluation of his situation in prison. He is offering himself as an example of how to comport oneself in the face of suffering that is taken on in obedience to God. He is also displaying for the Philippians a particular confidence in God's providential care. All of this is leading up to and supporting his admonition in 1:27–30 that the Philippians should order their common life in a manner worthy of the gospel in the face of opposition. The wider contours of Job's discussion with his friends in Job 13 both reflect and deepen these convictions about God's providence and Paul's ultimate vindication. At the same time, an awareness of Job's disposition of bitterness allows for a sharp contrast with Paul's commitment to rejoice. This fit between the wider context of Job and Paul's argument in Phil 1 provides a basis, then, for arguing that Paul meant to communicate by means of these deeper and wider allusions. When speaking of Paul's communicative intentions, one is limited to arguing in this way. The alternative is to offer highly speculative arguments about what Paul's motives were.

In all of this, however, it is important to remember that one should proportion the level of conviction about Paul's practice with the amount and aptness of the vocabulary and the level and degree of congruence between the Old Testament context and the epistolary argument. In other words, the strength of one's recognition of an allusion or echo should be proportional to the strength of the evidence. In this respect Philippians offers scholars a valuable opportunity to test arguments in an environment where there is less at stake from an interpretive standpoint.

The third perspective from which one can examine the use of Scripture in Philippians is that of contemporary readers. Although there are a variety of interests that contemporary readers might bring to this question, I have focused on Christian readers who are interested in theological reading, broadly conceived. My presupposition is that this category includes the vast majority of people who might attend to this issue. Such a perspective is freed from vexing questions about levels of literacy and accessibility of Old Testament texts in the ancient world. This perspective would still be constrained by the plausibility of any particular interpretive argument relative to the specific theological interests that one is pursuing.

The most challenging way of addressing the issue of the use of Scripture in Philippians is to focus on the Philippians as an audience. Of course, one can say this about any other epistle's original audience. The term "original audience" generally refers to some sort of construct of linguistic, material, and cultural conventions that one has good reason to think that speakers of Greek in the middle part of the first century might have shared. It is not so much a judgment about any particular individual or group as a summary of generalities. I still think that this is a useful construction. When scholars speak of the "original audience" in this sense, they are, for the most part, displaying the same sort of interest as someone who explains what an author's communicative intentions were.

Things become much more complicated, however, when someone wants to make specific historical claims about the particular audience of an epistle. For example, one can claim that if an author writes with a particular set of communicative intentions, then one can assume that the author, who in this case had a good knowledge of the audience, presumes that the audience has the capacities needed to grasp those communicative intentions. But this is not a guarantee of success.

In a similar way, we have some idea about literacy levels in the first century, but such observations are very general and speculative. We also have information about the cost and accessibility of books, but we have little precise information about what a particular group who had an intense commitment to a set of books might do in order to obtain copies of them.[28] We know that Christians from the earliest days of the church catechized new believers, but our information about these processes of formation is much better for later centuries than for the first century. Without question, Paul's epistles were read to their respective congregations, but there is no real information about a congregation's relationship to those texts and to the Old Testament over time. Thus although scholars may have an intense interest in the perspective of an epistle's original audience, one simply must recognize that there is little to say.

As frustrating as this may be, it might also be useful to ask who, other than a very small group of scholars, would be interested in such a question. From the perspective of contemporary readers of Philippians, it is not clear that, even if one could know a great deal about how actual Philippian Christians read Paul's letter, it would have very much regulative force for one's own interpretations.

From the perspective of contemporary scholars interested in the use of Scripture in Paul's letters, the example of Philippians is not particularly rich in material for examination. I hope that I have shown, however, that it provides an occasion for increased clarity and rigor with regard to the issues that one might discuss when addressing the question. I also hope that it will encourage us as scholars to formulate our interests in ways that are directed toward those questions that we can most fruitfully answer.

Bibliography

Abasciano, Brian. "Diamonds in the Rough: A Reply to Christopher Stanley Concerning the Reader Competency of Paul's Original Audiences." *NovT* 49 (2007): 156–61.
Ayres, Lewis. *Nicea and Its Legacy*. Oxford: Oxford University Press, 2004.
Bauckham, Richard. *God Crucified*. Grand Rapids: Eerdmans, 1998.
———. "The Worship of Jesus in Philippians 2:9–11." Pages 128–39 in *Where Christology Began*. Edited by R. P. Martin and Brian Dodd. Louisville: Westminster John Knox, 1998.
Bockmuehl, Marcus. *The Epistle to the Philippians*. London: Black, 1998.
Brett, Mark. "Motives and Intentions in Gen 1." *JTS* 42 (1991): 1–16.

---

28. See Brian Abasciano, "Diamonds in the Rough: A Reply to Christopher Stanley concerning the Reader Competency of Paul's Original Audiences," *NovT* 49 (2007): 156–61.

Evans, Craig A., and James A. Sanders, eds. *Paul and the Scriptures of Israel*. Sheffield: JSOT Press, 1993.

Fee, Gordon D. *The Epistle to the Philippians*. Grand Rapids: Eerdmans, 1995.

Fowl, Stephen. *The Story of Christ in the Ethics of Paul*. Sheffield: JSOT Press, 1990.

Gamble, Harry Y. *Books and Readers in the Early Church*. New Haven: Yale University Press, 1995.

Gnilka, Joachim. *Der Philipperbrief*. Freiburg: Herder, 1968.

Hays, Richard B. *The Echoes of Scripture in the Letters of Paul*. New Haven: Yale University Press, 1989.

O'Brien, Peter. *Commentary on Philippians*. Grand Rapids: Eerdmans, 1991.

Skinner, Quinten. "Motives and Intentions in the Interpretation of Texts." *New Literary History* 3 (1972): 393–408.

Stanley, Christopher D. *Arguing with Scripture: The Rhetoric of Quotations in the Letters of Paul*. New York: T&T Clark, 2004.

———. "'Pearls Before Swine': Did Paul's Audiences Understand His Biblical Quotations?" *NovT* 41 (1999): 124–44.

Wagner, J. Ross. *Heralds of the Good News: Isaiah and Paul "in Concert" in the Letter to the Romans*. NovTSup 101. Leiden: Brill, 2002.

Writing "in the Image" of Scripture: The Form and Function of References to Scripture in Colossians

Jerry L. Sumney

Prolegomena

Discussion of Paul's use of Scripture has grown exponentially since the publication of Richard Hays's *Echoes of Scripture in the Letters of Paul* twenty years ago. His work has stimulated important discussions of methods for identifying and interpreting allusions, as well as of analyses of Paul's hermeneutic. Even though I will treat Colossians as a pseudonymous work, the recent work on Paul's use of Israel's Scriptures demands that one stake out some initial positions about identifying allusions and their use in the broader Greco-Roman culture.

A number of interpreters have set out criteria for identifying allusions. Some focus on the author's intent, others on whether the readers would have recognized the allusions. This study will focus on the author's intent, while crediting the author with enough rhetorical acumen to use allusions in ways that would effectively advance the letter's argument. Christopher Beetham is among the most recent interpreters to set out criteria for identifying allusions and distinguishing them from echoes and parallels. He argues that a passage may be identified as an allusion only if it meets four criteria: (1) it is an intentional citation, (2) it has a single identifiable source, (3) it is distinctive enough in its new context to be recognizable to alert readers (though audience recognition is not necessary for a reference to be an allusion), and (4) the author expects the readers to know the original context of the originating text.[1] His cri-

---

1. Christopher A. Beetham, *Echoes of Scripture in the Letter of Paul to the Colossians* (BIS 96; Leiden: Brill, 2008), 18–19.

teria for an echo are: (1) it may be conscious or unconscious on the part of the author, (2) it must have a single identifiable source, (3) the author does not intend to direct the audience to the originating text, and (4) its effectiveness is not determined by whether the precursor was understood by the readers.

Such stringent criteria offer helpful standards, but some of them seem to assume things about both the author and the readers that are questionable, even though commonly held. For that reason, I will examine some of these criteria as a starting point for discussing the issue of methodology. My first point concerns the thing to which an allusion alludes. Stanley Porter defines an allusion as a "nonformal invocation by an author of a text (or person, event, etc.) that the author could reasonably have been expected to know."[2] This definition broadens the category of allusion by including not just specific texts but also persons and events. With this definition, the author does not need to have a specific text in mind, only the characteristic ideas associated with a particular person or event. Studies of the use of Homer in a variety of types of literature suggest that ancient authors employed allusions in this broader way. For example, Plato sometimes alludes to a particular character from Homer without seeming to have a particular text in mind.[3] Such allusions depend on the audience's ability to recognize particular characteristics of that person but not any specific text. Similarly, classical playwrights borrow Homeric allusions and similes without alluding to the specific texts in which they appear.[4] Such a broad definition of allusions does, however, make identifying distinctions between allusions and echoes more difficult, as Porter's definition of "echo" shows.[5] Still, New Testament authors who allude to events such as

---

2. Stanley Porter, "The Use of the Old Testament in the New Testament: A Brief Comment on Method and Terminology," in *Early Christian Interpretation of the Scriptures of Israel: Investigations and Proposals* (ed. Craig A. Evans and James A. Sanders; JSNTSup 148; Sheffield: Sheffield Academic Press, 1997), 95.

3. Andrea Capra, "Protagoras' Achilles: Homeric Allusions as a Satirical Weapon (Pl. Prt. 340A)," *Classical Philology* 100 (2005): 275-76.

4. Richard Garner, *From Homer to Tragedy: The Art of Allusion in Greek Poetry* (New York: Routledge, 1990), 47, 184-86; T. C. W. Stintson, "The Scope and Limits of Allusion in Greek Tragedy," in *Greek Tragedy and Its Legacy: Essays Presented to D. J. Conacher* (ed. M. Cropp, E. Fantham, and S. E. Scully; Calgary, Alberta: University of Calgary Press, 1986), 67-102. Stintson notes that some allusions are simply ornamental (68).

5. Stanley Porter defines an echo as a reference that invokes "thematically related

the exodus do not need to have a specific text in mind to invoke themes associated with the originating text(s) and events.

Beetham's criteria also embody the commonly held assumption that allusions should manifest resonance with what critical scholarship calls the original context.[6] Given the methods employed by ancient authors, this seems questionable. The interpretive methods of the ancient world often seem unconcerned about such an original context. As scholars from W. D. Davies onward have noted, the more important context is that of the interpreter in the environment of its use.[7] This is evident in both Judaism and the broader Greco-Roman environment. It is often the story as it is used within a tradition that determines the meaning of the allusion in the new text.[8] Thus, while arguments may be built on interpretations that ground themselves in the originating texts,[9] allusions serve a broader range of purposes within arguments than providing a specific original textual basis for a given point.[10]

Some who acknowledge the importance of the use of a text, event, or person in the first-century environment devote a significant amount of study to the original context of the passage in the Hebrew Bible.[11] The

---

language of some more general notion or concept" ("Allusions and Echoes," in *As It Is Written: Studying Paul's Use of Scripture* [ed. Stanley E. Porter and Christopher D. Stanley; SBLSymS 50; Atlanta: Society of Biblical Literature, 2008], 39).

6. An extreme version of this tendency is that of Walter C. Kaiser Jr., who argues that quotations of Old Testament passages that establish a doctrinal point in the New Testament were used in accordance with "the single truth-intention of the original author" in the originating context (*The Uses of the Old Testament in the New* [Chicago: Moody Press, 1985], 14, 228).

7. E.g., W. D. Davies, *Paul and Rabbinic Judaism: Some Rabbinic Elements in Pauline Theology* (2nd ed.; London: SPCK, 1955), 151–52.

8. June W. Allison, "Homeric Allusions at the Close of Thucydides' Sicilian Narrative," *American Journal of Philology* 118 (1997): 510–11.

9. See Francis Watson's treatment of Paul's use of quotations in *Paul and the Hermeneutics of Faith* (New York: T&T Clark, 2004).

10. See the range of uses of allusions in Christopher Stanley, "Paul and Homer: Greco-Roman Citation Practice in the First Century CE," *NovT* 32 (1990): 76. Further, see Stanley's discussion of the uses of quotations taken from Stefan Morawski (*Arguing with Scripture: The Rhetoric of Quotations in the Letters of Paul* [New York: T&T Clark, 2004], 174 n. 4). Morawski identifies four uses of quotations: to provide authority, to show erudition, to stimulate or amplify, and to ornament speech. If direct quotations serve these multiple purposes, we should expect no fewer kinds of uses of allusions.

11. For example, Richard Hays comments on the importance of the use of the

concern to connect the New Testament usage of the Hebrew Bible with its historical-critical meaning often seems motivated by a desire to say that the New Testament author's usage is legitimate (by our standards).[12] This concern may in fact keep us from understanding an allusion's function in a New Testament text.

This does not mean that the use of a passage in the tradition has nothing to do with the original context of the cited material. Allusive uses of texts often derive their significance from some attachment to the meaning found in the originating context. This is true for allusions to Homer (e.g., what characteristics a figure is known for in the *Iliad*)[13] even as it is of Israel's Scriptures in Second Temple Judaism. Such connections to the originating texts, however, may be only thematic or general and lack the precision of critical exegesis.

Drawing on the work of Porter, Stanley, and Beetham, this study will identify as an allusion a passage that (1) is an intentional indirect reference (2) to an identifiable source within Israel's Scriptures (whether a specific text or a person, event, etc.) that (3) is designed to be recognized by the reader—though this may only be true for those whom Stanley calls "informed readers" and "competent readers."[14] Less direct allusive material we will call echoes. Even though these are less direct references to texts, events, persons, or the like, recognition of them may enrich the meaning for the reader. Our author may live in the language of the text to such an extent that echoes are a part of his speech. In such cases, the echo may tell us more about the author than it does about the argument that he is making at the moment.[15] At the same time, these less direct references will probably be less important to the point the author is making. For example,

---

originating passage in the first century but then spends more time on the original context of the Hebrew Bible than on a passage's first-century usage (*Echoes of Scripture in the Letters of Paul* [New Haven: Yale University Press, 1989]). Once Beetham moves from discussion of criteria for identifying allusions, however, he actually spends more time than most interpreters on locating an identified allusion in its first-century environment.

12. Similarly, James W. Aageson, *Written Also for Our Sake: Paul and the Art of Biblical Interpretation* (Louisville: Westminster John Knox, 1993), 155.

13. See Stanley, "Paul and Homer," 48–78; and Capra, "Protagoras' Achilles," 275–76. See also Garner (*From Homer to Tragedy*, 47), who asserts that Aeschylus borrows images and similes from Homer without alluding to their original context.

14. See Stanley, *Arguing with Scripture*, 68–69.

15. See the example by Jeffrey S. Rogers, "Scripture is as Scripturalists Do: Scrip-

Stintson's study of Greek tragedy finds that less explicit allusions in that literature are less important for the point an author is making. When an allusion is important to the plot, the author makes it more explicit and provides the necessary information so that those who would not recognize the allusion do not miss the point.[16] Careful writers in other genres will probably take similar precautions.[17]

Allusions and Echoes in Colossians

No explicit quotations of Scripture appear in Colossians. Still, the writer does make several references to Scripture that help to support his argument. We will attend to these references in the order in which they appear in the text to explore what role Scripture plays in this letter. Before drawing some conclusions, we will give some attention to the presence of themes in Colossians that have parallels in the text of Scripture.

Colossians 1:6, 10: "Bearing Fruit and Growing"

The phrase "bearing fruit and growing" appears twice in the opening paragraphs of Colossians's thanksgiving. A number of interpreters hear in this expression echoes of Gen 1:22 and 1:28,[18] where the sea creatures and birds (v. 22) and humans (v. 28) are commanded to "grow [or 'multiply'] and fill" the earth. The same expression appears in Gen 9:1 and 9:7 after the flood, and it also appears in the singular in Gen 35:11, where God changes Jacob's name to Israel. In the LXX, the verbs αὐξάνω and πληθύνω also appear together in Gen 47:27, Jer 3:16, and Jer 23:3.[19] The Jeremiah texts promise

---

ture as a Human Activity in the Qumran Scrolls," in Evans and Sanders, *Early Christian Interpretation*, 32.

16. Stintson, "Scope and Limits," 67–74.

17. David Hay comments, "The less essential to its context an allusion is, the more we must be ready to regard it as a stereotyped truism, quite possibly inserted by the writer without much thought just because it was so familiar to himself and his readers" (*Glory at the Right Hand: Psalm 110 in Early Christianity* [SBLMS 18; Nashville: Abingdon, 1973], 40).

18. E.g., Eduard Lohse, *Colossians and Philemon* (Hermeneia; Philadelphia: Fortress, 1971), 20 n. 60; Peter T. O'Brien, *Colossians, Philemon* (WBC 44; Waco, Tex.: Word, 1982), 13; Beetham, *Echoes of Scripture*, 41–42.

19. The phrase in Gen 1:22, 28 and 9:1 has an additional verb. Thus those texts have αὐξάνω, πληθύνω, and πληρόω.

that after the exile the people will "grow [or 'multiply'] and fill" the land. The combination of multiplying and filling does seem to have some currency in Genesis and Jeremiah, and it does not appear in other writings within the LXX. It is never, however, used metaphorically in these books, but only for the literal increase of animals or humans. Although there are later texts that use these verbs within the same sentence (e.g., 1 En. 5:10, cited by Beetham as an example of a metaphoric use), the exact phrase does not appear (though perhaps the vocabulary in some cases echoes the earlier expression).

Neither does the exact LXX phrase appear in Colossians, which speaks of "bearing fruit and growing." Indeed, these two verses in Colossians are the only places in biblical Greek where the verbs καρποφορέω and αὐξάνω appear together. However, there is a close parallel in Mark 4:8 where the good seed "brings up fruit and grows" (the same order as in Colossians).[20] In Col 1:6 it is the gospel that is bearing fruit and growing, just as it is the word that is growing in Mark's parable. Further, Acts 6:7 and 12:24 contain the words "grew and filled," a phrase that repeats the language of Genesis and Jeremiah. Acts 19:20 similarly says that the "word" "grows and strengthens," and Stephen alludes to Gen 47:27 ("grow and fill") in his speech in Acts 7:17.

The combination of these metaphorical uses of growing in connection with the gospel message and the language of bearing fruit in Mark (and elsewhere in the Gospel traditions)[21] suggests that if the author of Colossians is alluding to Scripture with the phrase "bearing fruit and growing,"[22] it is Scripture that has been mediated to him through the church's tradition.[23] The citation does not further the argument significantly. Recognizing an allusion to a tradition about the word growing and filling would

---

20. Mark 4:8 continues with καὶ ἔφερεν and so uses the root of the compound verb of the Colossians texts.

21. Fruit bearing is a part of the Q traditions that Matthew and Luke use (Matt 7:16-20; 12:33/Luke 6:43-44). The image appears fairly often in Matthew and John.

22. Markus Barth and Helmut Blanke comment that this language is "reminiscent of imagery" in the Hebrew Bible and later Jewish texts. They seem to think that the author is aware of this connection and intentionally includes Gentiles in imagery that is usually used for Israel (*Colossians: A New Translation with Introduction and Commentary* [AB; New York: Doubleday, 1994], 158-59 and 158 n. 30).

23. James D. G. Dunn, following Hauck and Meeks, asserts that fruit-bearing was a familiar metaphor in Greek and Jewish thought of the era (*The Epistles to the Colossians and to Philemon* [NIGTC; Grand Rapids: Eerdmans, 1996], 61-62).

strengthen the author's claim about the growth of the gospel in 1:6. In 1:10, where attention has turned to the growth of the Colossians themselves, there is more resonance with the imperatival nature of the similar statement in most Genesis passages and with the demands in the evangelists' traditions that Jesus' followers bear fruit.[24]

This passage, then, tells us little about the way the author of Colossians uses Scripture. If he is echoing the Genesis passage(s) or Jeremiah (which itself seems to be alluding to Gen 1), his oblique reference functions as we suggested earlier for distant echoes. Since the reader[25] is able to understand the point without knowing the originating text or, perhaps here, the tradition, the author does not need to devise ways to be certain the readers catch the resonance. Nonetheless, if the readers were able to hear an echo of the church's tradition, their understanding would have been enriched by the metaphor's prior association with the growth and spread of the gospel, thus reinforcing the point the author is making about the way God is acting through the gospel in 1:6. Alternately, they might hear an echo of the image's imperative uses when they read 1:10, which calls them to grow in response to the gospel.[26]

Colossians 1:9: "Spiritual Wisdom and Understanding"

The author of Colossians opens the second paragraph of his thanksgiving/prayer for the recipients with a request that they be filled with knowledge

---

24. Matt 7:16–20; Matt 12:33/Luke 6:43–44; Luke 3:8–9; John 15:2–16. Such imagery also appears in the undisputed Paulines; see Gal 5:22; Phil 1:11.

25. Although I will refer to the audience of Colossians as readers, I recognize that the original audience would have been composed of more hearers than readers. At the same time, if Colossians was meant to be included among the letters of Paul, its author probably envisioned it being read multiple times in various settings, as his exhortation to have it read in Laodicea (4:15–16) indicates. Paul seems to expect his letters to be read multiple times, even as early as his writing of 1 Thessalonians (see 5:27).

26. For this understanding of 1:6 and 1:9, see Jerry L. Sumney, *Colossians: A Commentary* (NTL; Louisville: Westminster John Knox, 2008), 38–39, 48–49. Beetham has gone far beyond the evidence when he asserts that the echo "implies that the word of the gospel is creating a people who will fulfill the purpose of the original creation mandate" (*Echoes of Scripture*, 55). Such an understanding of the function of this echo requires too much of the readers. Not only do they need to know the originating text—they also need to know its uses in Jeremiah and read it with an explicit and specific eschatological lens that the author has not provided.

of God's will "with all spiritual wisdom and understanding." This appeal alludes to Isa 11:2 and echoes Isa 11:9. Colossians uses the same terms for wisdom and knowledge as Isa 11:2, and Colossians's use of "spiritual" draws on the same Isaiah verse which speaks of the future Davidic ruler having a spirit of wisdom and knowledge. Given this connection with Isa 11, it seems probable that the verse also echoes Isa 11:9, which speaks of this figure being "filled" with knowledge of God. While a number of passages speak of "wisdom and understanding,"[27] no others have as large a cluster of words and ideas as this Isaiah passage.

The promise of a ruler with knowledge and wisdom that is present in Isaiah 11 appears in a variety of Second Temple texts that bear the expectation that God's Messiah will have those characteristics (1 En. 49:3–4; Pss. Sol. 17:35–43; T. Levi 18:5, 7; 1QS28b).[28] The church's understanding of Christ would certainly have inclined it to identify this figure from Isaiah with Jesus.[29] Thus, the writer and perhaps the broader church would have read certain aspects of Isa 11 as descriptions of Christ.

The request of Col 1:9, however, asks God to give these things to the readers. This may be a new use of the language of Isaiah, intended to jar the readers because it is not simply a statement about Christ. Allusions often function to "build a shock of recognition at the transformation" in meaning that the new use conveys.[30] Here the disjuncture involves attributing to all members of the church the characteristics expected in the eschatologi-

---

27. Deuteronomy 4:6 and 1 Chr 22:12 speak of showing wisdom and understanding through observance of Torah. Broad meanings appear in 2 Chr 1:10–12 and 2:13; the former refers to what Solomon needs to possess to rule well, while the latter refers to the skills a builder needs to construct the temple. Similarly, in Exod 31:3, God tells Moses that "a divine spirit of wisdom and understanding" is on Bezalel so that he can build the tent of meeting according to God's specifications. Finally, in Theodotion's Dan 2:20, Daniel speaks of the wisdom and understanding of God.

28. These references appear in Beetham, *Echoes of Scripture*, 67–72. Such messianic interpretations are not the only places where this language comes together; the Spirit of God gives Enoch wisdom and understanding in 1 En. 37:3–4. Still, the prophetic nature of the originating text would have inclined later readers, particularly believers in Christ, to look for a messianic fulfillment of this Isaianic prophecy.

29. In fact, Matt 12:21 includes a fairly direct citation of Isa 11:10. NA[27] lists nineteen citations of Isa 11 in the New Testament. Many of these, however, are quite oblique and would perhaps not qualify as allusions or echoes under the criteria that we are using here.

30. Garner says this in connection with Sophocles's use of Homer (*From Homer to Tragedy*, 182).

cal messianic figure. Such a request could serve to reassure the readers of their status among the blessed without taking up the observances advocated by the teachers Colossians opposes.

As we saw with the previous echo, readers do not need to recognize the citation in order to get the primary point—namely, that they have access to "all spiritual wisdom and understanding" without adopting the other teaching. If the readers do recognize the allusion, however, it deepens their understanding of the point by clearly placing them in the eschatological, messianic time and perhaps identifying them with the Messiah and the blessings he possesses.

Since the author does not make an effort to help the readers identify an allusion here, he probably thinks they do not need to recognize it to understand his point. Furthermore, he does not use the allusion to establish a directly disputed point but only to open a way for readers to understand themselves and the gifts available to them. The vocabulary of Scripture may add weight to the request and to their vision of themselves, but it does not function directly as an authority here. Again, it is difficult to know whether the author knows this passage primarily from reading Isaiah or whether it comes to him principally through the church's use of the passage. Since the author is Jewish and alludes to language from Isa 11 that no other New Testament author cites, he probably knows the text directly. We cannot tell whether he knows this chapter from a collection of texts (e.g., a testimonium) or from the full text of Isaiah.

Colossians 1:12–14: Exodus Motif ("Inheritance," "Rescued," "Redemption")

As 1:12–14 introduces the liturgical material of 1:15–20, it draws on a number of themes associated with the exodus in biblical texts and later tradition. In addition, it employs some preformed confessional material.[31]

---

31. Among the reasons for identifying at least significant parts of vv. 13–14 as preformed material, note that v. 13 begins with ὅς, speaks of sins in the plural (which happens in the undisputed Paulines only in confessional material), refers to the kingdom of the son (rather than of God), and uses the expression "beloved son," which does not appear elsewhere in the Pauline corpus. Elements of v. 12 indicating that it, too, draws on preformed material include its reference to God as father (which is very uncommon in the Pauline corpus) and its use of the terms μερίς and κλῆρος, both of which are uncommon in the Pauline corpus. Additional confirmation of the pres-

Among the elements of these verses that echo exodus motifs are the metaphors for salvation: "share of the inheritance," "rescued," and "redemption." The combination of these images seems to allude primarily to Exod 6:6–8, but it also echoes other texts that speak of God's acts in the exodus narrative and of the establishment of David's house. The echo of 2 Sam 7:12–14, 18, where God promises to be a father to David's descendants and David declares that his house is not worthy of this honor, is particularly strong.

In Col 1:12 the author assures the recipients that they have been qualified to receive "the share of the inheritance of the saints in light." The terms used in this phrase echo language used to describe the portion of the land that the Israelites would receive in Canaan. Μερίς and κλῆρος, along with κληρονόμος, are used in Israel's Scriptures to describe their possession of the land. Both μερίς and κλῆρος are rare in the New Testament: κλῆρος appears ten times—four times in quotations or clear allusions to Ps 22:19 and two times in verses that speak of casting lots (none in the Pauline corpus), while μερίς appears only four other times, with only one of those occurrences in the Pauline corpus (1 Cor 6:15). The rarity of both terms increases the likelihood that they are drawn from earlier texts or traditions. The only places these two terms appear together in the LXX are in passages that speak of the Levites not receiving a "share and inheritance" in the land (Num 18:20–21; Deut 10:9, 12:12, 14:27, 18:1; Josh 14:2–4; 18:6–7). Thus, this formulation of what God has done for believers in Christ draws its language from this tradition but makes a very different claim—namely,

---

ence of traditional formulations comes from the parallels between the language here and that used to describe conversion in Acts 26:18. Among the interpreters who find elements of a preformed, probably baptismal, confession in vv. 13–14 are Eduard Schweizer, *The Letter to the Colossians: A Commentary* (Minneapolis: Augsburg, 1976), 53; Hans Hübner, *An Philemon, An die Kolosser, An die Epheser* (HNT 12; Tübingen: Mohr, 1997), 52; Andreas Lindemann, *Der Kolosserbrief* (ZBK.NT 10; Zürich: Theologischer Verlag, 1983), 22; and David Hay, *Colossians* (ANTC; Nashville: Abingdon, 2000), 48–49. Ernst Käsemann ("A Primitive Christian Baptismal Liturgy," in *Essays on New Testament Themes* [Philadelphia: Fortress, 1982], 149–68), Schweizer (*Letter to the Colossians*, 53), Lohse (*Colossians and Philemon*, 32–33), and Hay (*Colossians*, 48) are among those who consider v. 12 as a part of a baptismal tradition. Reinhard Deichgräber, however, finds too little evidence to identify v. 12 as a preformed piece. Still, he acknowledges that it and vv. 13–14 may come from a baptismal context (*Gotteshymnus und Christushymnus in der frühen Christenheit: Untersuchungen zu Form, Sprache und Stil der frühchristlichen Hymnen* [SUNT 5; Göttingen: Vandenhoeck und Ruprecht, 1967], 78, 145–46, 154).

that believers *do* receive the inheritance.³² This association with taking possession of the land ties this expression to the exodus motif.

Various Jewish texts draw on the metaphor of inheritance to speak of the blessings of the eschatological time, indicating that this metaphor was in current usage for the church or this author to adapt.³³ Colossians does not seem to draw this expression directly from the biblical text; rather, it has been mediated to the author through the church's tradition. The uncommon reference to God as father in the Pauline texts combined with these unusual terms suggests that the author is relying on traditional formulations here.³⁴ This sense is strengthened by the many parallels between this passage and Acts 26:18, a passage in which Luke has Paul describe his own "conversion." Among those parallels is use of the metaphor of inheritance (κλῆρος) for salvation. This increases the possibility that the readers would recognize that the writer has incorporated material from the tradition, thus adding weight to his assertion.

Colossians 1:13–14 more certainly incorporates confessional material.³⁵ This tradition alludes to Exod 6:6–8, which was also echoed in the inheritance language used in Col 1:12.³⁶ In Exod 6, God tells the Israelites that he is rescuing them, ransoming them, and giving them a new land. The exodus is clearly one of the strains of Israel's story that Paul expected his churches to know (see e.g., 1 Cor 10:1–13). Thus, we can expect readers in a Pauline church to recognize that elements of these images of salvation are derived from that narrative. Exodus 6:6–8, with its concentration of metaphors, may be one of the texts with which Pauline churches would be familiar.

The echo of Exod 6, however, is a part of the traditional formulation that Colossians cites more directly. While the audience hears resonances

---

32. Acts 8:21 is the only other place in the New Testament where these terms appear together. There the meaning coheres well with a remembrance that the formula referred to the Levites not receiving an inheritance because Peter is telling Simon Magus that he has no "part or inheritance" in possessing the power of the Spirit.

33. E.g., Dan 12:13; Wis 5:5; 1 En. 48:7; 1QS 11:7–8, 10–12.

34. Lindemann, however, finds this verse to be a reformulation of Phil 3:20 (*Der Kolosserbrief*, 22).

35. See the argument in note 25 above. Among the interpreters who find preformed material here are Lindemann, *Der Kolosserbrief*, 22; Hay, *Colossians*, 48; Hübner, *An die Kolosser*, 52; Lohse, *Colossians and Philemon*, 32–33.

36. Exodus 6:6–8 speaks of God bringing the people into the land and giving it to them as an inheritance.

of God's acts in the exodus, the same language also counters claims that the Roman Empire was making for itself. Thus they probably would have heard multiple layers of reverberation in this allusion to the tradition. The origin of these metaphors is the exodus narrative—perhaps Exod 6:6–8—but the meanings have expanded in Colossians to include both earthly and heavenly beings and cosmic rescue and transfer into an eschatological realm. The connections are clear; so are the expansions.

There may also be an echo of 2 Sam 7:12–14, 18, here in the reference to God's "beloved son." In the Samuel passage, God promises to be the father of David's descendants and says that they will be his sons. David's response is to ask why God has loved him so much. The expression "beloved son" appears nowhere else in the Pauline corpus, but this formulation in Colossians follows closely the use of the title in the announcements at Jesus' baptism as recorded in the Synoptics. So this expression within the confessional material probably draws on a widely known church tradition about Jesus' identity, perhaps already associated with his baptism. Either the church or the author of Colossians would find such interpretations ready to hand because this promise to David's descendants had already been given a messianic meaning in Second Temple Judaism. Perhaps this begins with Neh 13:26, which recalls the Samuel text. The same interpretation appears in Ps. Sol. 17 and at Qumran in 4QFlor 1.1–12 and 4Q252 5.1–4.[37] Even without those assurances from prior texts, we would expect the church to draw on 2 Sam 7 once it had interpreted Jesus as a reigning messianic figure.[38] For Gentile readers who did not have a developed sense of messianic expectation, it would probably be more meaningful to hear resonances with a traditional ecclesial formulation than to hear it as a fulfillment of the hope for a Davidic messianic figure. If most of the imagery and vocabulary of Col 1:12–14 appear as citations of pre-formed confessional material, we learn nothing about the way the author of Colossians reads or uses Scripture in his argument. We do see that he values and expects his audience to value the traditions of the church. He expects these citations to bolster his argument as he reminds the audience members of things they have confessed about Christ and the blessings they have received through him.

---

37. See these references in Beetham, *Echoes of Scripture*, 104–6.
38. See below on the use of Ps 110 in the church's tradition as evidence that Jesus was assigned this identity at an early time.

Colossians 1:15–20

The pre-formed liturgical material that the author of Colossians inserts at 1:15–20 contains a number of allusions to and echoes of Israel's Scriptures. These include the references to the "image of God" (Gen 1:26, 28), the firstborn (Ps 89:27 [88:28 LXX]; Exod 4:22–23), Christ as the beginning and a participant in creation (Prov 8:22–31), and God's indwelling in Christ (Ps 68:16 [67:17 LXX]). These references function in different ways within the passage.

The allusions to Prov 8 and the development of the wisdom tradition adopted in this liturgy represent a common use of scripture as a foundation on which believers constructed new understandings of Jesus.[39] Proverbs has Wisdom say that God created her at the beginning (ἀρχή, v. 22) before anything else was created, after which she participates with God in the work of creation (vv. 27–28). As Wisdom of Solomon develops this idea, she is the image (εἰκών) of God's goodness (7:26). Dunn argues that the development of the idea of Wisdom as the image of God bridges the gap between God and the visible world.[40] The person or community who composed the liturgy that Colossians incorporates shifts such ideas to Christ and expands the role of Christ beyond what the wisdom tradition said about hypostasized Wisdom. Most notably, "all things" were not only made through and exist in Christ, but also exist "for him" (vv. 16–17). Thus, the author of this liturgical tradition uses Scripture, as interpreted in a community with which he was conversant, as a starting point for reflection about the nature and work of Christ.[41] The second strophe adds an eschatological dimension to this reflection.

---

39. Gordon Fee has recently argued that Col 1:15–20 does not draw on wisdom traditions ("Old Testament Intertextuality in Colossians: Reflections on Pauline Christology and Gentile Inclusion in God's Story," in *History and Exegesis: New Testament Essays in Honor of Dr. E. Earle Ellis on His 80th Birthday* [ed. Sang-Wan Son; New York: T&T Clark, 2006], 212–20). The number of verbal and conceptual parallels between Proverbs 8 (along with other developments in the wisdom tradition) and this Colossians text, however, make his case unconvincing.

40. Dunn, *Epistles*, 88. He cites Wis 7:26; Philo, *Leg.* 1.43; and Philo's comments about the Logos in *Conf.* 97, 147; *Fug.* 101; and *Somn.* 1.239.

41. James M. Robinson argues that the concepts that connect the various parts of this poetic material come from "the λόγος, σοφία, ἄνθρωπος speculation of Hellenistic Judaism" and that this liturgy has applied this cluster of ideas to Jesus "*en bloc*" ("A Formal Analysis of Colossians 1 15–20," *JBL* 76 [1957]: 278). Lohse argues that the

This liturgy draws on multiple passages of Scripture. The reference to Christ as the "image of God" in verse 15 also alludes, perhaps second-handedly (i.e., as an echo), to the language of Gen 1:26–28,[42] even as it also adapts such terminology from what the wisdom tradition claimed for Wisdom.[43] This language probably does not reflect a "new Adam" Christology, since we find no clear references to such a theology in the liturgy. Following Burney, N. T. Wright argues that this poetic material evokes a tradition in which Gen 1:1 and Prov 8:22 are mutually explanatory. Whether or not Burney's more detailed explication of the passage is correct, the liturgy's author intends to apply to Jesus all that might be said about Wisdom while glancing at interpretations of the Genesis creation narratives.[44] The context of creation and the similarity of language (including the repetitions of "all" which are also found in Gen 1:28–31) support this reading. While the text draws on the language of the Genesis creation narrative (perhaps as used in the Wisdom tradition), there is no clear theological development from Genesis in this text. At the same time, the liturgy does seem to depend on the wisdom tradition's prior interpretation of "image" to add significance to its initial assertion.

Calling Christ "firstborn" draws on both broad cultural understandings of this status and Jewish understandings of the place of Israel and Israel's king. As noted in connection with Col 1:12–14, the church's tradition interpreted Christ through the Davidic promises found in 2 Sam 7:12–14, 18, in which God promises to be a father to David's descendants. The beginning of each strophe of Colossian's liturgy presses the image fur-

---

language of "image of God," "firstborn of all creation," and "beginning" are all designations of Wisdom in Hellenistic synagogues and that churches that arose from circles of Hellenistic Judaism adopted and adapted those designations to Christ (*Colossians and Philemon*, 46). See also 1 En. 49:1–4, where the spirit of wisdom dwells in the eschatological Elect One.

42. So e.g., Fee, "Old Testament Intertextuality," 212–15; Petr Pokorný, *Colossians: A Commentary* (Peabody, Mass.: Hendrickson, 1991), 74–76; Lohse, *Colossians and Philemon*, 46. Beetham, with appropriate caution, sees this "image" language as "a secondary echo" of Gen 1:28 (*Echoes of Scripture*, 131–32).

43. Beetham (*Echoes of Scripture*, 132) also notes that the echo of Gen 1 is an allusion to the tradition rather than directly to the text.

44. N. T. Wright, "Poetry and Theology in Colossians 1.15–20," *NTS* 36 (1990): 456–58. Lohse, while finding an allusion to Gen 1, rejects Burney's view that the Colossians liturgy is an interpretation of the Genesis passage (*Colossians and Philemon*, 46–47 n. 101).

ther by identifying Christ as God's "firstborn,"[45] the firstborn of creation in verse 15, and the firstborn of the church (the new creation) in verse 18.[46]

"Firstborn" conveys both priority and status, which were combined in general cultural use. Both ideas are also important in the two strophes of the Colossian liturgy. Verses 15–16 assert Christ's superior status in relation to all of creation by asserting his priority—he was in existence before all other beings who might offer something to or make threats against church members. If this passage draws, in part, from Exod 4:22–23, where Israel is named as God's firstborn, the emphasis is on status, not priority, though the status of Christ depends on his prior existence that permits him to participate in the creation of all other beings. There is no reason to suspect that the author of the liturgy has in view questions about whether Christ was a created or eternal being—his point requires only temporal priority.

Colossians 1:18 clearly relates chronological priority to superior status, as the ἵνα clause indicates: Christ is the "firstborn from the dead *so that* he might have preeminence in all things." This statement (whether inserted by the author of Colossians or not) assigns Christ the highest position in the church by identifying him as the one through whom God initiated the eschatological time by raising him from the dead. As the first to experience resurrection, Christ has superior status in relation to everyone within the church (that is, those who will experience resurrection), just as priority in (or to) creation positioned him above all created beings.

It seems probable that the liturgy's identification of Christ as firstborn alludes to Ps 89:27 (88:28 LXX), a psalm that celebrates the covenant with David and his descendants. This psalm has God calling David's descendant God's "firstborn" to assign him the rank of highest king on earth. The liturgist of Colossians accepted the church's interpretation of Christ as the awaited descendant of David who now has a cosmic role (see e.g.,

---

45. The presence of "firstborn" at the beginning of each strophe seems to increase the probability that this term is an allusion to a prior text. Garner's study of Greek poetry concludes that it is a very common convention to place allusions at the beginning of a strophe (*From Homer to Tragedy*, 181). If the Colossian liturgy follows this convention, even by nonintentional copying of a form, it makes it more likely that "firstborn" is an allusion.

46. The title "firstborn" also reflects language used for Wisdom in Philo, *Conf.* 62. Thus the influence of reflections on wisdom also informs the use of this title. For a fuller listing of the ways the Wisdom figure was developed in this era, see Beetham, *Echoes of Scripture*, 135–37.

Acts 2:25–36, esp. v. 30, combined with the many texts that cite Ps 110:1 to assert Christ's exaltation) and as the firstborn from the dead (e.g., Rom 8:29). Only the cosmic aspect of this status, not the Davidic or national meaning, plays a role here. Such interpretations of Christ depend on Ps 89 (and 110), but it is difficult for us to determine whether the writer of this liturgy knows those passages directly from Scripture or primarily through their uses within the church. In either case, this seems to be a place where Scripture has served as a basis for developing the church's understanding of Christ.

A final echo of Scripture appears in verse 19, where the liturgist asserts that "all the fullness was pleased to dwell in him." Psalm 68:16 (67:17 LXX) speaks of God being pleased to live in Mount Zion.[47] The Pauline school knows this psalm, as we see by its use in Eph 4:8.[48] The liturgy in Colossians transfers the psalm's declaration about a place to a person. Beyond this psalm, there are a number of passages that speak of God dwelling in Jerusalem or the temple, enough that we may see it as a recognizable theme.[49] The combination of the presence of εὐδοκέω with κατοικέω makes Ps 68 the more likely immediate source of the theme.

The liturgy adds "all the fullness"[50] to the psalm's declaration about Jerusalem as it shifts its reference to Christ. This is the earliest extant instance of the church using this language to claim that all of God's fullness was present in Christ.[51] It is not surprising to see such affirmations arising

---

47. Similar expressions of God choosing to dwell in Zion appear in Ps 132:13–14 (131:13–14 LXX) and Isa 8:18; cf. 49:20. See Lohse, *Colossians and Philemon*, 58. Barth and Blanke cite a number of other passages that speak of God's presence dwelling in particular locations and associated with εὐδοκέω (*Colossians*, 212 nn. 76, 78).

48. Although few commentators note an allusion to Ps 68 in Eph 4:8, the availability of the text and the parallels in wording suggest that this formulation may have developed in conjunction with this psalm.

49. Among those passages are 2 Sam 7:6; 1 Kgs 8:27 (cf. 2 Chr 6:18, where in the context of the dedication of the temple Solomon speaks of God dwelling on the earth); Pss 132:13–14 (131:13–14, LXX), 135:21 (134:21, LXX); Isa 8:18. Barth and Blanke cite these LXX uses of κατοικέω and further uses of κατασκηνόω to express this idea (*Colossians*, 212).

50. On the use of "fullness" in the wisdom tradition and other Second Temple texts, see Dunn, *Epistles*, 99–102.

51. It may be that John 1:16's reference to the fullness of Christ precedes this statement, but its implication that this fullness is the fullness of God is less clear than the Colossians statement. Moreover, Col 2:9 makes it clear that the letter's author understands the fullness to be the fullness of God's nature. At the same time, Col 2:10 says

in liturgical contexts rather than in theological argumentation. The early church's experience of God through Christ in worship contexts seems to be the origin of some of its exalted claims about Christ. If this is the case here, the Colossians liturgy is an example of the ways the church developed their ideas about Christ by combining their reading of Scripture and their corporate experience of the presence of God in worship. In this case, their worship experience seems to have shaped their reading of Scripture more than the "original context" of the passage.

If it is correct that Col 1:15–20 is a preformed piece (even with some editorial insertions), its use of Scripture tells us nothing about how the author of Colossians uses Israel's Scripture. It does indicate that the church drew on Scripture through interpretive traditions present within Judaism; that is, it did less consultation of the context of the originating texts and relied more on the ways those texts were mediated through prior and contemporaneous readings. We see this particularly in the liturgy's use of the wisdom tradition. The other reading matrix that seems prominent here is that of the church's worship experience. The use of Ps 68 and the wider theme present there suggests that the words of Scripture found new meanings in such settings and that the newly assigned meaning became more important than the meanings evoked from the text's original context.[52] The function of these references in the persuasiveness of the liturgy before its incorporation into Colossians remains unclear. The church's prior use of these texts seems more significant than the power that these citations might wield as proofs from Scripture. Still, the allusive use of the language of Scripture probably added weight to the assertions as they were first recited. It may be, however, that once the liturgy became known, the use of its language carried more persuasive weight than the perhaps more distant echo of Scripture.

Colossians 2:11: "Circumcision Not Done with Hands"

In Col 2:11–12, the writer asserts that at baptism believers receive a "circumcision not done with hands." In some ways this is a difficult interpretation of baptism because Gentiles generally did not see circumcision as a

---

that believers participate in the divine fullness through Christ, just as John says that believers receive grace through Christ's fullness.

52. This should make us even more hesitant to read a "second Adam" theology into the reference to the "image" wording of 1:15.

good thing.⁵³ Use of this metaphor and the shift in pronouns in the middle of verse 13 (from second-person plural to first-person plural) suggests that the author of Colossians was Jewish, while the recipients of the letter were not.

This metaphor derives from figurative uses of circumcision in two prophets and Deuteronomy. Jeremiah 4:4 and Deut 10:16 call on the people to circumcise their hearts so they can serve God properly. Colossians 2:11 parallels Ezek 44:7, 9, in speaking of those who are uncircumcised of flesh and heart. Deuteronomy 30:6 is the only passage in the Hebrew Bible that speaks of God circumcising the hearts of the people, something God will do after the exile.⁵⁴ Because only this text has God as the one acting, Beetham identifies Deut 30:6 as the specific text to which Col 2:11 alludes.⁵⁵ However, to make this argument he must assume that the author of Colossians (whom he identifies as Paul) knows the Hebrew text of this passage and makes his own translation because the LXX changes the terminology so that it says God will "purify" rather than circumcise their hearts. The figurative use of circumcision to speak of purifying one's life was current in the first century among at least some Jews, as its use at Qumran indicates (1QS 5:5). Furthermore, Phil 3:3, along with Rom 2:28–29 and 2 Cor 3:3,⁵⁶ suggests that using circumcision in a metaphorical sense was known within the Pauline communities.⁵⁷

Given the few precise wording parallels (which have in common only their use of a form of περιτέμνω or περιτομή) with a specific text, it seems best to see Col 2:11 as an allusion to the tradition of using circumcision as a metaphor rather than to a specific text. Beyond the small number of vocabulary parallels, none of the earlier texts (or indeed any other text in the whole LXX) uses ἀχειροποίητος.⁵⁸

---

53. See Sumney, *Colossians*, 135–36.
54. Beetham, *Echoes of Scripture*, 157.
55. Ibid., 157–58.
56. Dunn (*Epistles*, 156–57) sees these Pauline uses as an adaptation of the metaphorical use of circumcision (circumcision of the heart) found in Jewish tradition. In addition to the examples cited above, he lists 1QpHab 11:13; Jub. 1:23; and Philo, *Spec.* 1.305.
57. George E. Cannon (*The Use of Traditional Materials in Colossians* [Macon, Ga.: Mercer University Press, 1983], 40) argues that Col 2:11-13 is composed of fragments of baptismal confessions because of the accumulation of relative pronouns, prepositional phrases, and participial constructions.
58. Garner notes that Aeschylus sometimes draws imagery or similes from

Knowledge of the meaning of circumcision indicates that the readers possessed at least some broad understanding of Jewish religious practices and knew that these practices have their roots in scriptural stories, possibly including the stories of Abraham and the exodus. They may also have known of the metaphorical interpretation of the ritual in the biblical text. Even if they did not know the specifics of the textual uses of the image, however, they would miss little of the meaning conveyed in Colossians. All they need to know is that circumcision is an initiatory rite and that it is related to covenant membership. Also worth noting is the fact that the metaphoric use of circumcision in Deuteronomy, Qumran, and Philippians speaks of an eschatological reality. Since the circumcision of the Colossians is performed by God, it is an eschatological act that signals their admission into the covenant community.

Colossians 2:13: "In the Uncircumcision of Your Flesh"

Colossians 2:13 continues the metaphorical use of circumcision that began in 2:11. Now the writer comments that the Gentile readers were "dead in trespasses and the uncircumcision [or 'foreskin'] of your flesh." This expression parallels the reference to those uncircumcised in flesh and heart in Ezek 44:7, 9. Close verbal parallels can be seen in the expression "flesh of foreskin" in the LXX in Gen 17:11, 14, 24, 25; Lev 12:3; and Jdt 14:10. The expression seems to have the narrative of Abraham's circumcision in mind since the phrase appears most often in that text, which recounts the initiation of the rite as a symbol of covenant membership, and so of a special relationship with God. Similarly, Colossians uses the phrase in connection with the transition of the readers from the status of outsiders to being forgiven and granted a relationship with God.

Homer without alluding to the particular context in which the image appears (*From Homer to Tragedy*, 47). A number of interpreters see the use of "not made with hands" as an echo of the accusation made in various biblical texts that the gods of other peoples are merely "made by hands" (e.g., Lev 26:1; Isa 2:18). So e.g., Lohse, *Colossians and Philemon*, 102; Dunn, *Epistles*, 156. The allusive nature of this expression raises serious problems for the use of mirror-reading on this passage (and 2:11) to assert that the opponents require circumcision (as, e.g., Ernst Percy, *Die Probleme der Kolosser- und Epheserbriefe* [Lund: Gleerup: 1946], 140; Andrew T. Lincoln, *Paradise Now and Not Yet: Studies in the Role of the Heavenly Dimension in Paul's Thought with Special Reference to His Eschatology* [SNTSMS 43; New York: Cambridge University Press, 1981], 113).

Colossians, however, reverses the order of the wording so that it speaks of the "foreskin of the flesh" rather than the "flesh of the foreskin" as in the LXX passages.[59]

Cannon identifies Col 2:13 as a part of a section composed of a collection of baptismal confessions.[60] I noted in connection with Col 2:11 that the metaphor of circumcision of the heart was used in some circles within Judaism and was already a part of the Pauline tradition. Other Christian writers as early as Irenaeus (*Haer.* 4.16.1) and Tertullian (*Adv. Jud.* 3) connect Gen 17 and spiritual circumcision, so the link could well have been a part of the church's confessional traditions at a very early stage.[61] If this statement does derive from traditional material (whether Christian or Jewish), Colossians's use of the expression may rely on those traditions rather than on a direct appropriation of the Genesis text.

The readers do not need to recognize an allusion to Gen 17 to understand fully the point of the statement in Colossians. They were certainly aware of the distinction between Jews and Gentiles that circumcision marks, and they would have known that this difference was theologically important. The central point of the opening clause of verse 13 is to identify the status of the non-Jewish readers prior to their incorporation into Christ; they were dead in sin and this was manifested in their uncircumcision, the sign that they were outside of God's covenant.

---

59. Beetham notes that 1Q21 3.18-23 also reverses the wording. He asserts that this reversal is unintentional, but that the reversal in Colossians is intentional and laden with theological import (*Echoes of Scripture*, 186–89).

60. See note 57 above. Cannon argues further that while these verses do not quote a single confession or hymn, their grammatical substructure and the presence of baptismal motifs point to the use of available material (*Use of Traditional Materials*, 41). Bruce Vawter also sees vv. 12–14 as a part of a block of material that Colossians incorporates ("The Colossians Hymn and the Principle of Reduction" *CBQ* 33 [1971]: 74). Cf. F. O. Francis, "The Christological Argument of Colossians," in *God's Christ and His People* (ed. J. Jervell and Wayne A. Meeks; Oslo: Universitetsforlaget, 1977), 199; Herold Weiss, "The Law in the Epistle to the Colossians," *CBQ* 34 (1972): 309 n. 63. Dunn recognizes the hymnic nature of 2:9–12 and 13c–15, noting that it seems to draw on several prior and disparate traditions that the author brings into uncomfortable juxtaposition (*Epistles*, 145–46). This arrangement may seem to leave the reference to "foreskin of flesh" outside the traditional material, but Dunn's treatment of the phrase sees it drawing at least on Jewish traditional formulations (*Epistles*, 163).

61. Beetham cites these texts from Irenaeus and Tertullian (*Echoes of Scripture*, 190).

Again, this use of Scripture by the author shows us little about his method of appropriating the biblical text. If he is drawing on the Genesis text directly, he alludes to a memorable phrase in a well-known story. Since the originating text told of the initiation of the symbol of the covenant, it is well suited to his comparison with baptism as the rite that brings believers forgiveness and relationship with God. But only this general significance of the story functions within the argument of Colossians. Its point is clear without recognizing the allusion; the metaphor points to a crucial change.

If this reference to Gen 17 is mediated to the author of Colossians through the church's traditions, as seems somewhat probable, it tells us nothing about the way he interprets Scripture because this usage was determined before he adapted the tradition for his argument. In this case, the reference is more of an echo of the originating text than an intentional allusion. Still, when combined with the reference to circumcision in Col 2:11, it seems that the writer is intentionally citing baptismal traditions and assuming that his readers will recognize and accept them as good evidence for the points that he is making. The incorporation of this symbol into baptismal traditions indicates that the framers of those traditions thought the metaphor conveyed important ideas. The persistence of the tradition and its presence in Colossians suggest that early Gentile Christ-confessors were taught the meaning of circumcision and at least the broadest outline of the Abraham narrative. This is the case whether or not the audience of Colossians could have recognized a citation of Scripture here.

Colossians 2:16: "Festivals, New Moons, and Sabbaths"

The author of Colossians characterizes the demands of the teachers he opposes with a list that seems to allude to Scripture; he says they require observance of "festivals, new moons, and Sabbaths." This summary of Jewish calendrical celebrations appears in Hos 2:13 (LXX) and Ezek 45:17. The same three festal occasions serve as a summary, though in reversed order, in 1 Chr 23:31 and 2 Chr 2:3 (LXX), 31:3.[62] In their original contexts, these lists serve very different purposes. In Hosea the summary lists

---

62. The commentators who acknowledge this echo include J. B. Lightfoot, *St. Paul's Epistles to the Colossians and to Philemon* (rev. ed.; New York: Macmillan, 1879; repr., Grand Rapids: Zondervan, 1959), 193; Schweizer, *Letter to the Colossians*, 155; Barth and Blanke, *Colossians*, 339.

the things God will not accept because of the people's worship of Baal, while in Ezekiel it sets out the things expected when the temple is restored after the exile. The uses of the summary in Chronicles simply list expectations about celebrations at the temple.[63] Still, in all these places, the three types of observances serve as an inclusive summary for holy days within Judaism. The same list appears in 1QM 2:4 (in the order of Hosea, Ezekiel, and Colossians), where it summarizes observances at which the community's leaders will preside. At a later time, Justin Martyr (*Dial* 8.4) has the same three elements as a summary of Jewish observances. Thus, this is a known way to refer to Jewish festal observances as a set.

Colossians also employs this list as a summary of Jewish observances but makes no further use of it. It seems unlikely that the author is unaware that the list functions as a summary elsewhere. Given that he wants his audience to reject observance of these festivals, he does not have the Ezekiel passage in mind. Though Hosea has God reject these observances, the prophet issues no call for the people to discontinue them. Thus, Colossians does not have the context of a particular text in view, even as he alludes to a scriptural summary of Jewish observances.[64] If he is citing Scripture, we see nothing of his interpretive method beyond the fact that he draws on its language, perhaps to give a more authoritative tone to his assertion. Given this phrase's general usage, however, it remains unclear whether the author knows the summary from a broader tradition of usage or from the biblical texts. The former seems more likely, though this need not imply that he does not know that it has a biblical formulation.

If the audience members recognized this allusion, it would probably be because they knew it as a summary of observances rather than knowing that it came from a particular biblical text.[65] Even if they knew it from

---

63. Isaiah 1:13–14 also contains all three terms, though not consecutively or as a succinct list.

64. This is a fairly clear case where Beetham's requirement that a writer have a particular text in view seems to fail. This summary certainly draws on the lists in these multiple biblical texts, but probably not one particular passage.

65. It is not impossible that the visionary teachers at Colossae cite this formula from the Ezekiel text as a way to claim that believers in the eschatological time need to keep these festivals. If they did use it in this way, the readers would have recognized the citation. But then the author would need to find clear ways to connect it to the polemical uses of the phrase rather than Ezekiel's usage, which he does not do. There is no evidence that the opponents of Colossians used the Ezekiel text in this way. Further, if this is a citation of a prophetic text, we must avoid drawing conclusions

the biblical text, this knowledge would have added little to its meaning as a summary, perhaps only adding a sense of authority to the assertion which simply repeats the phrase without giving it any interpretation.

COLOSSIANS 2:22: "HUMAN COMMANDS AND TEACHINGS"

The second evaluation of the opponents' regulations in Col 2:22 alludes to Isa 29:13 in charging that they have their origin in "human commands and teachings" rather than in divine commands. The terms ἔνταλμα and διδασκαλία each appear only four times in the LXX,[66] and they appear together only in Isa 29:13. Thus the reference to this Isaiah passage seems certain and intentional. Beyond this similar wording, the Jesus tradition explicitly and more extensively quotes this Isaiah passage to accuse the Pharisees of hypocrisy in a dispute about ritual practices (Matt 15:8–9; Mark 8:6–7). Its use in the Jesus tradition is more significant because no other Jewish source of the period cites Isa 29:13.[67] Furthermore, ἔνταλμα appears only three times in the New Testament: these two Gospel texts and Col 2:22. Thus, the recipients of Colossians would probably have recognized this allusion to Isaiah through its presence in the Jesus tradition.[68] Its absence in other sources suggests that the author of Colossians also knew its presence in the Jesus tradition and thought of utilizing it in Colossians because of that usage.[69]

---

about the opponents' teaching from its wording, as do some who say that the reference to "commands" shows that their teaching has an ethical component. E.g., Werner Bieder, *Die Kolossische Irrlehre und die Kirche von heute* (ThSt 33; Zürich: Evangelischer Verlag, 1952), 28.

66. The term ἔνταλμα occurs in Job 23:11, 12; Isa 29:13; 55:11, and διδασκαλία is found in Prov 2:17; Sir 24:33; 39:8; Isa 29:13.

67. Beetham, *Echoes of Scripture*, 196.

68. Dunn, *Epistles*, 193. Pokorný also asserts that the similarity between the citations shows that the author of Colossians knows Mark (*Colossians*, 154). The prominence of Isaiah in Paul and the broader church tradition means that in Pauline churches this book would be better known than most other prophetic works.

69. Charles Nielsen seems to go too far when he asserts that the author of Colossians may not know that this is a quotation from Isaiah because he knows it through the church's tradition ("The Status of Paul and His Letters in Colossians," *Perspectives* 12 [1985]: 119). Given the explicit mention of Isaiah in that tradition, it is more likely that the writer of Colossians does know it is a quotation—even if he knows the text only because it appears in the Jesus tradition.

Both the originating text and the Jesus tradition use this formula to condemn other teachings.[70] Colossians uses it for the same purpose.[71] The author does not develop any theological points from this citation; he simply brings its words forward and applies them to the other teachings to bolster his argument. This shows that he expected such a reference to the words of Scripture to wield authority among his readers. He seems to have believed that his readers held that the words of Scripture as quoted by Jesus, even when placed in a new setting with no explicit interpretive justification, provided an authoritative message about the new setting.

The writer of Colossians expected the audience to understand this phrase as a condemnation because it comes between two other condemning evaluations. Thus, even if they could not recognize the allusion, they could still understand the accusation correctly. This is particularly so in a context in which the other teachers claimed to have received instruction from heavenly beings. If the readers did recognize the allusion, knowing that it came from Scripture would have given the assertion more authority. The probability that the audience would have recognized this allusion is increased because its use in the Jesus tradition identified these words as a quotation of Isaiah. If the audience knew of the citation's presence among the words of Jesus, this would add yet more authority to the author's words. Indeed, the appearance of the phrase in both Isaiah and the mouth of Jesus would have made it a devastating critique of the other teaching.

Colossians 3:1: "Seated at the Right Hand of God"

The theme-setting paragraph of 3:1–5 begins with an exhortation ("seek the things above") and supporting affirmations that draw on the exaltation of Christ (he is "above" and "seated at God's right hand"). The claim

---

70. Neither the Gospels nor Colossians quote this phrase precisely as it appears in the LXX. The Gospels change the wording in the same way (probably because Matthew is dependent on Mark at this point) and Colossians in a different way.

71. Troy Martin notes that the expression "human tradition" was used by Cynics to assert that their teaching was within a valuable tradition. Based on this he argues that the opponents of Colossians also use the phrase in this way (*By Philosophy and Empty Deceit: Colossians as a Response to a Cynic Critique* [JSNTSup 118; Sheffield: Sheffield Academic Press, 1996], 30). The form of Col 2:22, however, indicates that the author uses this as an accusation rather than as a less polemical description of the other teaching. O'Brien is among those who recognize this allusion as an accusation (*Colossians*, 151).

that Christ is seated at the right hand of God alludes to Ps 110 (109 LXX), a Davidic exaltation psalm. New Testament writers cite this psalm more often than any other.[72] Thus, it was well known in the church. It served as an early interpretation of the resurrection of Christ, helping believers rethink their eschatology and contributing significantly to the development of early Christology. O'Brien asserts that it "was an essential and regular element in the early apostolic preaching," as evidenced by its presence in the Gospels, Acts, Paul, Hebrews, 1 Peter, and Revelation.[73] Similarly, Hengel identifies this exaltation motif as "an extremely old Christological formula" that goes back to Ps 110.[74] Beyond the existence of this well-attested tradition of using Ps 110 to interpret the death and resurrection, or exaltation, of Christ, a number of interpreters find a quotation of a preformed tradition in Col 3:1. Its phraseology has a sort of "creedal character."[75] So it may well be a fairly direct quotation of a set formulation of that tradition.[76] Leppä argues more specifically that Col 3:1 draws on Rom 8:34 rather than directly on the psalm because there are more consecutive words from Romans than from the psalm.[77]

The author of Colossians seems to expect recognition and acceptance of this assertion about Christ, since he offers no substantiation for it. The citation provides support for the exhortation to "seek the things above," but the author does not use the psalm to ground any more extensive christological claims.[78] His use of the psalm assumes the appropriateness of

---

72. So Schweizer, *Letter to the Colossians*, 174. Hay identifies thirty-three citations of this psalm in the New Testament (*Glory at the Right Hand*, 15).

73. O'Brien lists these uses of Ps 110: Matt 26:64; Mark 12:36; Luke 20:41–44; Acts 2:33–35; 5:31; 7:55, 56; Rom 8:34; Heb 1:3, 13; 8:1; 10:12; 12:2; 1 Pet 3:22; Rev 3:21 (*Colossians*, 162).

74. Martin Hengel, "Hymn & Christology," in *Papers on Paul and Other New Testament Authors* (vol. 3 of *Studia Biblica 1978*; ed. E. A. Livingstone; JSNTSup 3; Sheffield: JSOT Press, 1980), 182.

75. Lohse, *Colossians and Philemon*, 133.

76. So Hay, *Colossians*, 115. Similarly, Francis, "The Christological Argument of Colossians," 197; Nielsen, "The Status of Paul and His Letters in Colossians," 118.

77. Outi Leppä, *The Making of Colossians: A Study on the Formation and Purpose of a Deutero-Pauline Letter* (Publication of the Finnish Exegetical Society 86; Göttingen: Vandenhoeck & Ruprecht, 2003), 158–59. Indeed, Rom 8:34 and Col 3:1 share ἐν δεξιᾷ τοῦ θεοῦ, while only the terms "sitting" and being at the "right hand" are the same in the psalm.

78. Hay claims this allusion to Ps 110 as one of those that adds "little or nothing"

applying its Davidic acclamation to Christ and expanding its claim to cosmic proportions. Since this interpretation of the psalm was so pervasive in the church's tradition, it may be that the author is simply accepting the church's interpretation without exercising his own hermeneutic.[79]

Given that the tradition's use of Ps 110 includes and in places even mentions explicitly (Mark 12:36; Luke 20:41–44; Acts 2:33–35; Heb 1:13) that it is a biblical citation, the readers would probably have recognized both that it was a foundational confession of the church and that it was built on Scripture. The church's extensive use of this psalm testifies to its usefulness as believers explored ways to understand the death and resurrection of Christ. We see nothing here about the interpretive methods of the author of Colossians because he does not develop the implications of the application of the psalm to Christ beyond what already existed in the tradition.

Colossians 3:10: "According to the Image of the One Who Created It"

In Col 3:8–11, the author asserts that believers must rid themselves of vices because they have been granted a new life; they have put on a "new self" that is constantly being renewed "according to the image of the one who created it." The mention of a person (ἄνθρωπος) being made in the image (εἰκών) of the one who creates it clearly alludes to Gen 1:26–27, where God creates the ἄνθρωπος in God's own image. In Colossians, the person created is an eschatological person who is still in the process of being created as the person conforms his or her life to the ethical expectations that Colossians sets out for believers.[80]

---

to the context, but is used because it is so familiar to the author and readers (*Glory at the Right Hand*, 40).

79. Hay thinks it is unclear whether the author of Colossians knows this psalm independently of the church's formulaic usage of it or even whether he knows that it refers to the psalm (*Glory at the Right Hand*, 44). Hay comments further that the absence of a reference to Christ subduing his foes, which appears in Ps 110:1c, suggests that Colossians is drawing the quotation from the tradition rather than from reading the psalm (*Colossians*, 116–17).

80. Given such differences, Margaret Y. MacDonald only goes as far as saying that this verse in Colossians "appears to be influenced by Gen 1:26–27" (*Colossians and Ephesians* [SP; Collegeville, Minn.: Liturgical Press, 2000], 146–47).

As always in the Pauline corpus, the creator is God. Even where Christ is the agent of creation, as in Col 1:15–17, God remains the creator. Thus in 3:10 God creates the new, eschatological person in God's own image. It is probably correct to identify this image of God with Christ,[81] so that the believer is both created and renewed on an ongoing basis in the image of Christ. Thus this act of creation is not a single moment but a continuing act of God that helps believers live as Colossians prescribes. This assertion infuses the Genesis creation narrative with new meaning. First, it sees the eschatological moment as a new act of creation that has important parallels with the original creation. (Perhaps we could call this a typological relationship.) Second, the new creative act has a new "image" of God according to whose likeness the new person is made.[82] Third, the ethical significance of being created in the image of God dominates Colossians's comments about the created person, while reigning over creation is dominant in the LXX's Genesis account.[83]

This use of Gen 1:26 draws on the general theme of creation and uses the vocabulary of the originating text to make new theological assertions. The apocalyptic tradition often saw the eschaton as a new act of creation, as the moment when the world would be as God intended it. The early church, as an apocalyptic movement, accepted new creation as a way to articulate what God was doing in Christ and in their communities (e.g., 2 Cor 5:16–21; Gal 6:15). Thus drawing on a creation text to give expression to that theology seems natural. Further, since Christ was already seen as the pattern for eschatological existence in the Pauline tradition (see 1 Cor

---

81. So most commentators, e.g., Lohse, *Colossians and Philemon*, 142–43; Murray J. Harris, *Colossians and Philemon* (Exegetical Guide to the Greek New Testament; Grand Rapids: Eerdmans, 1991), 153; Schweizer, *Letter to the Colossians*, 198; Hay, *Colossians*, 126. However, Lightfoot rejects this view, arguing that it is not Christ because Christ is not in the Eph 4:24 parallel and is not in Genesis (*Epistles to the Colossians and to Philemon*, 216). But it is not unusual for Ephesians to shift the meanings of what it adopts from Colossians, and the absence of Christ from the Genesis text would certainly not mean that these later authors would not use the passage to speak of Christ, as other examples from Colossians demonstrate (e.g., Ps 110:1).

82. This need not imply an Adam/Christ Christology, though many find that view here. See the problems this text presents for a "new Adam" schema in Barth and Blanke, *Colossians*, 141.

83. MacDonald suggests that the "in knowledge" phrase in v. 10 may also allude to the way knowledge figured into humanity's failure at the Fall (*Colossians and Ephesians*, 138).

15:20–49), it was a small step to adopt the language of "image" in the process of drawing on the creation narrative (especially since 1:15 has already called Christ the "image of God"). The baptismal liturgy in Gal 3:26–28 shows that the Genesis creation narrative had already been associated with the eschatological creation and that the church saw the beginning of that new creation breaking into the world in the baptism of its members.

The innovative move of Colossians is to use this creation language to ground exhortation.[84] The author creates a tension in this use of Gen 1:26, which points to a single act of creation, by talking about a continual renewal of this newly created person. This makes the phrase express a partially realized eschatology—the new is here, yet it is still being formed. By mentioning this tension, the author grants the recipients a new identity but can still exhort them to strive to live more ethical lives as they are empowered by God's continuing renewal of their new selves.

The use of Gen 1:26–27 in Col 3:10 is more fully integrated into the argument than any other passage of Scripture we have seen the author of the letter employ. His interpretation of Gen 1:26–27 draws on contemporaneous eschatological thought so that the experience of the church is a new enactment of the original creation narrative. Thus, again, the primary matrix for interpretation is usage in the first century rather than the originating historical or literary context. Put more carefully, the meaning of the originating text for Colossians develops as a result of the interplay among originating context, contemporaneous usage in Judaism and the early church, and the situation the author addresses.

Once again, however, we may not be able to fully attribute these exegetical methods to the author of Colossians. Colossians 3:11 clearly cites (and probably augments) the same baptismal tradition that Paul cites in Gal 3:26–28 and 1 Cor 12:13. The language beginning in Col 3:9b derives from a baptismal context (put on/put off; old person/new person). A number of interpreters have argued that the whole of verses 9b–11 relies on a new creation baptismal tradition.[85] If this is the case, the author of

---

84. Similarly Jacob Jervell, *Imago Dei: Gen 1,26f. im Spätjudentum, in der Gnosis und in den paulinischen Briefen* (FRLANT 58; Göttingen: Vandenhoeck & Ruprecht, 1960), 232–33. When 2 Cor 5:16–21 uses new-creation language to urge its readers to adopt a new way of viewing life, the relationship to ethical exhortation is less immediate than what we find in Col 3:10.

85. Jervell, *Imago Dei*, 232–33; Lohse, *Colossians and Philemon*, 142; MacDonald, *Colossians and Ephesians*, 145–46. Dunn, however, thinks these various passages

Colossians has probably inserted "being renewed in knowledge" into the formulation since it stands in some tension with the already accomplished creation of the "new person" in the surrounding material and the phrase better integrates the citation into the argument of 3:5–11.

If the citation of the confessional tradition does not begin until verse 11, Colossian's treatment of Gen 1:26–27 is still dependent on Paul's earlier use of the new creation motif. Thus we learn little of this writer's exegetical techniques or hermeneutical methods; he is accepting and adapting previous Pauline exegesis, probably more because it is from Paul than because he thinks it reflects proper exegetical method. We do get some indication of the way Colossians deals with Scripture here because he applies the tradition and its use of Scripture in a new way. In a more specific manner than what we find in earlier Pauline materials, this use of Gen 1:26–27 in connection with the new creation motif serves as the grounds for ethical exhortation. Thus he either takes the interpretation of the text current in the church and puts it to this new use or uses the new creation theme to develop an interpretation of Gen 1:26–27 that serves his rhetorical purpose. He draws out the newly found meaning and uses it to ground his exhortation. It may be important that the author does not simply allude to Scripture but supports the allusion with a citation of a well-known confession (v. 11). He seems, then, to think that the combination of Scripture and tradition is more persuasive than relying on the authority of Scripture alone.

If Colossians is citing a baptismal confession here, the author probably expected the audience to recognize it. Application of that confession would lend weight to his exhortation. If verse 10 is not part of such a confession, it still seems likely that many readers would have caught his allusion to the creation narrative and its understanding of humanity as being created in God's image. At a minimum, they would probably have recognized the Pauline theme of new creation. The support of Scripture or the Pauline tradition (or both) serves to make the exhortation more authoritative. At the same time, the allusion provides a basis for the writer's interpretation of the eschatological situation in which believers live.

---

reflect a "cherished theme" more than a set formula (*Epistles*, 223). Even if this is the case, the method of interpretation of Scripture that arrives at the theme is a part of the tradition. Barth and Blanke reject the idea that v. 9 adopts baptismal language at all, arguing that the old person / new person language is simply a creation of Paul that Colossians adopts (*Colossians*, 410–12).

Colossians 3:12: "As Elect of God, Holy"

Following his citation of the baptismal confession in Col 3:(10–)11, the author prepares to resume his explication of proper moral behavior by setting out the identity that believers receive in their baptism: they are the "elect of God, holy and beloved." Some interpreters hear an echo of Deut 7:6–8 in these titles.[86] The Deuteronomy text says that God elected Israel (though Colossians uses ἐκλεκτός, a nominal form that does not appear in the Deuteronomy passage or anywhere else in the Torah with this meaning) and calls Israel "holy." In addition, it calls Israel to obey God's commands. These parallels suggest that the way Colossians identifies believers in 3:12 echoes this particular passage. The language and theme of election are also uncommon in Paul; this noun appears in the undisputed Paulines only in Rom 8:33 and 16:13.[87]

Rather than being an echo of Deut 7:6–8, however, it seems more probable that Col 3:12 echoes the theme of election, not a specific passage. There are no occurrences of ἐκλεκτός and ἅγιος together in the LXX, though the idea that God requires holiness of the chosen people is common. This is at least the fourth time Colossians has referred to believers as "holy" or "saints" (1:2, 4, 26, and perhaps 1:12 ["saints of light"]; see also 1:22 ["to present you holy]"). So the holiness of believers is a theme of Colossians, and a reference to their possession of holiness is particularly apt here as a sanction for ethical living. Calling these Gentile believers "chosen" or "elect" may identify them with the heritage and promises of God to Israel,[88] though we may wonder what that would mean to them or how important identification with Israel would have been.[89] After all, the theme of election appears rather infrequently in the New Testament.[90] Still, asserting that these readers were chosen by God is important because

---

86. Dunn, *Epistles*, 228; Fee, "Old Testament Intertextuality," 210.
87. As Schweizer notes, however, the theme does appear more prominently in Rom 9–11 (*Letter to the Colossians*, 205).
88. So Dunn, *Epistles*, 227–28.
89. Even during Paul's lifetime the question of the value of attachment to Israel may have arisen. The issues that Paul addresses in Rom 14–15 may point to this. Questioning the value of connection to Israel may have been a concern of Ephesians and it was a central thesis of Marcion just a few decades later.
90. O'Brien comments that this theme is much more prominent in the LXX than it is in the New Testament (*Colossians*, 197–98).

it emphasizes that "the status of believers stems from a divine decision."[91] Connecting this divine action with the demand for holiness fits the model of election that we know from Israel's Scriptures.[92]

Any member of the audience who could relate "elect of God" and "holy" to a specific passage would have to have been thoroughly immersed in the study of Scripture. Many might, however, have recognized the theme of the relationship between election and holiness that is implicit in much of the biblical text. The audience would have gained little in this case by recognizing an echo of a particular passage or even knowing that the theme draws on Scripture. The connection between being one of God's people and proper living is already well established in Colossians.[93] Even if this were not the case, 3:12 makes the connection clear. Thus, while the point is important for Colossians, this phrase's possible echo of Scripture does little to undergird the argument.

Colossians 3:20: "Children, Obey Your Parents"

Given the prominence of the Ten Commandments within the narrative of the exodus story, it seems unlikely that the audience of Colossians would have failed to recognize that the command for children to obey their parents is one of the Sinai commands. This probability is strengthened by the place this command holds in Josephus's apology for Judaism (*C. Ap.* 2.28, 31). When the author of Colossians says that obeying one's parents is "pleasing in the Lord," he may be echoing the sanction given this command in both Exod 20:12 and Deut 5:16. In both, observing this command brings the promise of a long life in the promise land. The author of Ephesians quotes the command and makes this connection to the promise explicit (6:2–3). Citation of the promise may indicate that the tradition in

---

91. Hay, *Colossians*, 130.

92. MacDonald notes that "the notion of election is similar to that found in the Hebrew Bible (e.g., 1 Chr 16:13; Isa 43:20) and the Q[umran] L[iterature] (e.g., 1 QM 12.1)" (*Colossians and Ephesians*, 139). This assertion that the author understands election to function with church members as it functioned in Israel is a different claim from that of Dunn, who says that election language signals that believers have been brought into the heritage of Israel (*Epistles*, 227–28).

93. Barth and Blanke comment that the point of v. 12 is that as God's chosen they are to reflect the character of God seen in the messiah (*Colossians*, 418). Readers could have been prepared to understand this call to holiness in this way by the preceding reference to the "image" to which they are being conformed.

which both Colossians and Ephesians stand had already begun to emulate the prominence that this command receives in the Decalogue by having a promise attached to it.

If the author of Colossians expected his reference to remind the readers of the promise found in the Decalogue, his purpose seems to skew the expected promise. Instead of saying that such conduct is pleasing *to* the Lord, he says it is pleasing *in* the Lord. This changes the frame of reference in ways that may be significant—indeed, necessary—for the readers to understand his instructions properly.[94] Classical authors sometimes used allusions to make unexpected points, which made the point more emphatic.[95] Here in Colossians, the shift to saying that this obedience is "in the Lord" may point to obedience within the sphere of Christ's reign— an assertion that may allow (adult) children to disobey nonbelieving parents who might order them to discontinue contact with the church.[96] The allusion to the promise in Exodus and Deuteronomy helps the readers to recognize the precise point of the command in Colossians. Even without recognizing a reference to the promise in the Decalogue, however, readers would find the phrasing of verse 20 jarring. Thus, they could understand the point correctly, even without recognizing that it may play off the promise associated with the command in Scripture.

This use of Scripture differs from any that we have seen to this point in Colossians. Here the biblical text serves as a foil for the writer to make a rather different point by a simple change in the expected wording. Colossians does not seem to assert that the Decalogue's promise is wrong; it simply redefines the commandment by the way it restates the sanction.

Parallels and Recognizable Broader Themes

In addition to allusions and echoes, there are a number of passages in Colossians that seem to play off of various themes in Scripture and in the developing tradition of Judaism and the early church. Incorporating such recognizable themes could lend weight to an assertion or serve simply as ornamentation that demonstrates the author's familiarity with traditions that are important to the community. These qualify not as echoes of

---

94. See the reading of this verse as a "hidden transcript" in Sumney, *Colossians*, 244–46.

95. See Garner, *From Homer to Tragedy*, 8.

96. See Sumney, *Colossians*, 244–46.

particular texts but only as expressions that may expect some resonance in the audience, even if they were not meant to draw a particular set of meanings into the context. A modern parallel of such a use of Scripture might be some people's ability to sprinkle expressions from (their tradition's accepted translation of) Scripture throughout a conversation or a sermon. The argumentative value of such citations comes from the recognition that they reference an authority. Even if the hearer does not know where in that authority the citation is located (indeed, even the speaker may not know the precise origin of the expression), such references may be recognized by a change in cadence (perhaps an "-(e)th" on the end of a verb) or vocabulary. Perhaps the most significant argumentative force such recollections exert is that they enhance the ethos of the speaker; they demonstrate that the speaker has such advanced knowledge of the authoritative text that its words permeate her speech. Thus they lead the hearer to acknowledge that the speaker is an expert or an authority. Some examples of this kind of peppering of the text of Colossians with resonant vocabulary are discussed below.

1:5: "Word of Truth"

When Colossians describes the gospel as "the word of truth," it may be an intentional reminiscence of the description of Scripture found in Ps 119:43 and 119:160. Elsewhere, the LXX speaks of the word of God being true (e.g., Neh 9:16, Ps 119:142 [S has "word of truth"], and Mal 2:6 speak of the "law of truth"; cf. 2 Sam 7:28; 1 Kgs 17:24). This expression is taken up by Ephesians (1:13) and then by 2 Timothy (2:15). Similar expressions appear in John 17:17 and Jas 1:18. So it may have been a known way to refer to the gospel in some groups in the early church.

Colossians may have used the phrase to set the previously received teaching over against the teaching that the letter opposes. If the audience heard a reminiscence of Scripture here, it would have lent a bit of support to this passing jab at the other teaching. If they heard it as a citation of a phrase in the tradition, it would have packed yet more sting for the opponents.

3:17: "Name of the Lord"

Colossians exhorts its readers to do "everything in the name of the Lord Jesus." This may be a distant echo of the phrase "in the name of the Lord" that appears at least eighteen times in the LXX. The phrase is used in very different contexts; sometimes it means that a person speaks with God's authority (2 Sam 6:18), other times it is part of an oath formula (1 Sam 20:42), and still other times it is used for prayer (1 Kgs 8:44).[97] Thus it brings forward no specific context. Still, it may have a tone of remembrance that would add substance to the exhortation.

3:22: "People-Pleasers"

In its instructions to slaves, the household code of Colossians tells slaves to work not only when being watched or as "people-pleasers" but with sincerity because of their respect for their true lord, Christ (3:22). The unusual term ἀνθρωπάρεσκος[98] may be drawn from Ps 52:6 (53:6 LXX), where it is used to contrast those who try to please God with those who want to please people. This is its only occurrence in the LXX. Its only other appearance in the New Testament is Eph 6:6, which is probably dependent upon its presence here in Colossians. The rarity of the term makes it more likely that the author of Colossians is echoing the Psalm. It seems unlikely, however, that most readers would have heard a specific resonance with this text. The theme is not uncommon, and readers would not have missed the point if they did not hear a connection with Psalm 52. Still, the unusual vocabulary that the audience might associate with their sacred text might lend weight to the exhortation.

Finally, there are places where Colossians seems to parallel ideas that were derived from Scripture and developed in Second Temple Judaism. The author may have hoped that these expressions would arouse some recognition of themes or images, but their familiarity is the only thing they contribute to the argument. Such parallels may include the reference to "treasures of knowledge and wisdom" in 2:3. This expression may have some relationship to Isa 45:3 and other passages in contemporaneous literature that mention wisdom and knowledge together (e.g., Sir 21:18; Wis 1:6-7; 1QS 4:3, 22; 1QH 1:18-19; CD 2.3). Within the apocalyptic tradition, those taken on heavenly journeys sometimes saw the "hidden trea-

---

97. "In the name of the Lord" appears most often in the Deuteronomistic Histories and in Chronicles, but it also occurs outside that literature (e.g., Ps 20:7; Mic 4:5; Sir 47:18).

98. It is rare enough that the Liddell-Scott *Intermediate Lexicon* lists it simply as a New Testament word.

sures" in the heavens (e.g., 1 En. 18:1; 46:3). The author of Colossians may be echoing both the apocalyptic tradition (which would be particularly appropriate given the problems this church is having with visionaries) and the broader idiom of speaking of knowledge and wisdom together.

Conclusions

As is often noted, Colossians has no direct, multiple-word quotations of Scripture. We have seen, however, that its author does cite Scripture in various ways and that these citations play a number of different roles in the letter's argument. We can now see what conclusions we may draw from his allusions to and echoes of Scripture.

The first thing to note concerns the absence of citations in 1:24–2:5 (with the possible exception of a faint echo in 2:3), the section devoted to establishing Paul's ethos as the one who suffers for the audience and who is the bearer of the true gospel. We might have expected the author to connect Paul's suffering for the community with the biblical tradition of the prophets who suffer for proclaiming God's word or for the people. Other passages dedicated to establishing Paul's ethos cite Scripture to support his ministerial practices (e.g., 1 Cor 9:9; 2 Cor 4:6, 13), but Colossians takes another tack. This letter relates Paul's willingness to suffer for the audience to the way Christ was willing to suffer for all. Thus it is only Paul's correlation to Christ, not his connection to the servants of God in Israel's past, that Colossians chooses to mention as the way to identify Paul as the teacher to whom the audience should give their allegiance. This may suggest that the author of Colossians did not think connections with Israel's leaders or prophets would provide a substantive commendation of Paul to this audience.

A second (and surprising) observation concerns the nature of Colossians's allusions and echoes of Scripture: most involve citations of preformed and confessional material. Indeed, few if any depend on direct knowledge of Scripture. Citations of Scripture that appear to rely on church traditions of various sorts include 1:6, 10 (bearing fruit and growing); 1:12–14 (rescue, redeem, inheritance); 1:15–20 (image of God, agent of creation, firstborn); 2:22 (human commands and teachings); 3:1 (seated at the right hand); and 3:11 (image of the one who created). Passages that refer to phrases or themes drawn from Scripture but are cited as they were developed in Jewish and church traditions include 2:11, 13 (nonphysical circumcision); 2:16 (festivals, new moons, Sabbaths); 3:12 (election and holiness); and 3:20 (obey parents). The allusion to Isa 11 in Col 1:9 provides the most likely example of direct reliance on the biblical text. But even here the claim is problematic because Isa 11 was so widely used in both Jewish and church tradition that the author may well have known the text (and the fact that it came from Scripture) through these usages.

The references to nonphysical circumcision in 2:11 and 13 provide the next-best evidence for direct use of the biblical text, but there is no precise textual parallel for 2:11. Furthermore, 2:13 not only draws on a central episode in the Abraham narrative, it may also be a citation of a pre-existent tradition. Other allusions and echoes are even less likely to require independent knowledge of the biblical text. The Jewish author of Colossians probably needed no immediate access to the biblical text to know the Ten Commandments well enough to cite the form of the command to children alluded to in Col 3:20. Moreover, the author's association of election with a demand for holiness in 3:12 also draws on a theme that is prominent enough that the author need not have had Deut 7 in mind when composing his exhortation. Finally, the summary of Jewish practice found in 2:16 was probably known well enough that the writer of Colossians used it because of its general currency rather than because he knew it from a particular text.

This does not mean that Scripture was unimportant or unrecognized by either the author or the audience of Colossians. It does suggest that their primary contact with and understanding of Scripture was mediated through the church's formalized traditions. The author continues to speak the language of Scripture, and perhaps the audience could have recognized that some of the language came from Scripture, even if the exposure of both the author and audience to that wording came largely from recitation of confessions, repeated hearing of interpretations of texts, or episodes from the Jesus tradition. This observation may also suggest that extensive reading and interpretation of Scripture played a minor role in the communal activities of the churches addressed by Colossians.

It may help us to think about the place of Scripture in these churches if we identify what the Scripture citations in Colossians assume about the audience's knowledge of those texts. The author expected them to recognize allusions to the creation narrative of Gen 1, as he refers to the "image" of God twice with differing meanings (1:15; 3:11). It is possible that a further echo of this narrative sounds in the phrase "bearing fruit and growing" (1:6–7). The author assumes familiarity with the Abraham narrative, particularly the covenant-sealing ceremony of Gen 17. Indeed, the Gentile audience would have needed clear instruction about the meaning of circumcision within Judaism for this important metaphor of Colossians to make sense to them. Knowing the narrative of circumcision's inauguration as a covenant sign would likely comprise a part of that instruction. The exodus narrative and the metaphors associated with it also constitute an important part of the assumed knowledge of these readers. This narrative includes the giving of the Law and at least some knowledge of the Ten Commandments.

The citations from these narratives, however, come from a very limited range of texts. Only the creation account and a central feature of the Abraham saga (and perhaps the promise to Jacob) appear from Genesis. A reader need know only the first four chapters of Exodus and the giving of the law in chapter 20 to recognize all the allusions and echoes in Colossians from this book. Moreover, with the possible exception of references to nonphysical circumcision (from Deut 10 and 30), readers need to know only the first seven chapters of Deuteronomy to hear the connections that Colossians makes with that book. Thus, within the parameters of the Torah's central narratives, Colossians demands knowledge of a very narrow range of texts.

Colossians's citation of biblical texts outside the Torah includes some that point to the restoration of Israel and the Davidic ruler, which assume that the audience knows something of the fall of the Israelite kingdoms. The promises of restoration and the exaltation of a Davidic descendant stand out as texts these believers know through eschatological and christological interpretations. The interpretations of these texts consistently expand their national claims so that they become cosmic claims. This inserts new meanings into these texts, but meanings their interpreters within the church found legitimate.

The interpretation of Jesus as the promised Davidic descendant also draws on material in the Psalms. The affirmations about Christ in 1:15–20 and 3:1 build on this tradition as it appears in the Psalms. The extremely wide use of Ps 110 shows that the audience of Colossians would have known it as Scripture and knew its christological interpretation.

The citations of prophetic texts that we find in Colossians assume that readers have some familiarity with select portions of Isaiah and perhaps parts of Jeremiah, Ezekiel, and Hosea. That a Pauline church might have known these prophets, especially Isaiah, is not surprising given how prominent Isaiah is in the undisputed Pauline letters.

The lengthy poetic liturgy of Col 1:15–20 adopts and adapts elements from the Wisdom tradition, especially Prov 8, and later developments of those wisdom themes. The author *of the liturgy* certainly knows this stream of thought within Judaism and uses it to develop ideas about Christ. In this passage, we see the church using Scripture and its contemporaneous interpretation to give expression to its experiences of the presence of God in Christ. Scripture becomes the means through which the church's experiences and beliefs are formulated; it becomes the lens through which they find the meanings of the death and resurrection of Christ and the meanings of Christ's mediation of the presence of God. The appropriation of this text and its interpretive tradition assume a level of engagement with scriptural texts that we cannot assume for most members of the Pauline churches. Yet those who did breathe in this rarified atmosphere would have found connections with Scripture important, persuasive, and enriching. The development that we see in Col 1:15–20 seems to be an early example of the ways the church expounded and expanded its claims about Christ through its reading of Scripture. Such expanded claims found resonance with the wider church as they made sense of the community's experience of God in Christ.

Finding authors in the early church who knew and drew on Scripture and interpretive traditions may tell us little about how others in these congregations knew and appropriated Scripture. Those who recited the liturgy might have had little understanding of its origins in Scripture or the Wisdom tradition. Perhaps early uses of the liturgy were accompanied by explanations of the scriptural basis of its claims, though the parallels in other philosophic and religious contexts might have obviated the need for such explanations. If such explanations were initially given, they would probably not have continued after its use was established (and they are not given in the letter of Colossians). Those who used the tradition might well remember that it was rooted in Scripture, but this simple fact might be all that they passed on to those who adopted the material as time passed. Thus, even if the authors of the liturgy knew this part of Scripture well, those who used the liturgy in their worship might not have—they probably did not.[99]

On the other hand, the author of Colossians seems to assume that the letter's recipients would have recognized the major stories of Israel's past and known that these narratives appear in an authoritative text. Because

---

99. This is borne out in part by the scarcity of citations of the wisdom tradition in the New Testament.

these narratives appear in Scripture, the readers of Colossians would have seen them as legitimate paradigms through which to interpret present experience. Various interpretive techniques may have been used, but all would have recognized the authority of the texts.

While we see almost nothing of the exegetical techniques of the author of Colossians, we do see multiple ways in which the tradition appropriated Scripture. In the liturgy of Col 1:15–20 we see the church identifying Christ with the highest claims Scripture makes for any being other than God. Its claim that Christ was God's agent in creation seems to assume the claims to exaltation that developed in connection with Psalm 110. Thus, the claims of the first strophe are natural correlates of the eschatological element of the second strophe. The interpreters of texts that speak of the restoration of Israel and the Davidic promises shift the meanings of those texts so that they are no longer national promises; they now include Gentiles and, indeed, the whole cosmos. Again, such meanings assume Christ's exaltation. Other passages simply apply to the church the hopes that the texts originally expressed for Israel. For example, using nonphysical circumcision to interpret baptism takes a hoped-for change in Israelites and asserts that it has happened among believers in Christ—Jews and Gentiles. In still other places, the author expected that merely citing recognizable words of Scripture would have had persuasive value.

While the originating context of these scriptural texts may not have been completely disregarded, it is not the central matrix from which the traditions that Colossians cites work in their applications of Scripture. The readers' beliefs about Christ and the inauguration of the eschatological age evoked new meanings from Scripture texts. These meanings assumed a continuity with the story of God's prior acts, particularly among Israelites, but also that God had acted in unexpected ways which are nonetheless best understood through Scripture. Finding such expanded meanings of Scripture seems to cohere well with the interpretive techniques we see in later Christian authors such as Origen (or earlier with the Jewish interpreters at Qumran) and in many of the uses of Homer found outside the church.

The multiple meanings that Origen finds in biblical texts and the explanations he gives about them indicate that he sees arriving at the literal meaning that critical exegesis seeks from the original context the least important kind of interpretation. Of course, this view is radically different from that taken by historical-critical scholarship with its valuing of "original meaning." The traditions cited in Colossians seem to find multiple levels of meanings, sometimes with the eschatological or christological meaning overriding the original. In this respect, the interpretive technique is closer to Origen's than to that of critical exegetes. The traditions that Colossians uses usually maintain thematic connections to the originating text (and so do not stray as far from their earlier meanings as Philo's allegories),[100] but they give these themes new meanings that cannot be derived from the texts without the presuppositions of the beliefs and experiences of the church.

Uses of Homer have significant parallels with the ways we have seen Scripture used in Colossians. Like the church's uses of Scripture, the citations of Homer retain some continuity with the character, event, or saying in the originating text. But the citations also insert meaning from the new context so that the old and new contexts both contribute to the point being made with the citation. Also similar to Homer, the traditions that Colossians inserts draw on select portions of the originating text. Garner finds that most citations of Homer in Greek tragedies come from books 6 and 22 of the *Iliad*. He surmises from this that there is a discrete selection of material from within Homer that authors expected their audience to know. Hock notes that the earliest stages of Greek education used names drawn from Homer to teach the most elementary elements of writing.[101] Thus authors could assume that many of the characters from the Homeric epics, and their distinctive characteristics, were known to nearly everyone. This means that even people without the skills of "functional literacy," possessing little more than a basic recognition of the alphabet, knew central characters from Homer. A person did not need to be able to read Homer to recognize allusions to the plot and features of important figures in those texts.

The author of Colossians was Jewish (or at least purported to be) and so probably knew some Scripture because of his early synagogue education. Yet no detailed firsthand knowledge of an extensive segment of Scripture is evident in this letter. This may be due to his evaluation of his audience or to his lack of such knowledge. Given the limited range of materials the author expected this audience to recognize, perhaps we should envi-

---

100. Stanley notes this same sort of coherence with the originating context in the ways other authors cite Homer ("Homer," 54–55, 75–76).

101. Ronald F. Hock, "Homer in Greco-Roman Education," in *Mimesis and Intertextuality in Antiquity and Christianity* (ed. Dennis R. MacDonald; Studies in Antiquity and Christianity; Harrisburg, Pa.: Trinity Press, 2001), 59–63.

sion a relatively small body of material that early-church authors expected their audiences to recognize from Scripture, just as other authors usually presupposed knowledge of only discrete sections of Homer. This would consist of well-known characters (Abraham, David, etc.), basic plot lines (creation, exodus, etc.), and even the wording of important texts (Ps 110; Gen 1). These may have been gathered in testimonia for those who could read and held in memory by those who could not.

An author in the church would have been able to assume that the audience recognized these characters and plot lines from Israel's sacred texts. Some collection of texts must have begun to accumulate from the earliest days in Jerusalem, because some texts were so ubiquitous throughout different groups within the church that they must have been present near the beginning of the movement (e.g., Ps 110). The appearance of some of these texts in the preformed traditions that Colossians cites also supports this hypothesis. This view does not require that members of the church, especially those outside Judaism, actually learned or studied major portions of Israel's Scriptures. Just as most people could not recall the less famous parts of Homer but only certain well-known plot lines, themes, and sections, so the use of Scripture in Colossians suggests that its Gentile recipients probably had a similarly narrow exposure to and recall of material in Scripture.

Despite the absence of direct quotations of Scripture, the author of Colossians clearly saw it as an authority and expected his readers to view it similarly. Not only do the traditions he cites depend on its authority but the text also assumes that recitation of its wording carries persuasive force. Finding most of the citations of Scripture in traditional material suggests that the audience of Colossians knew these texts primarily through the meanings they were given in the church. While these meanings were not completely separate from the originating contexts, adherence to the meaning in the original (literary or historical) setting was not a goal of their interpretation. Instead, as we have noted, these texts were the means that church members used to interpret their present experience of God and the place of Christ in that experience.

While our reading suggests that Scripture had a basic authority for the author of Colossians and his readers and that their reading of Scripture derived from the church's tradition, it seems that the citation of tradition had a more immediate impact on the argument of this letter than its citation of Scripture. The church's tradition seems to have possessed a recognizable and direct authority. Tradition grounds many, probably most, of the letter's central assertions. Scripture in turn forms the basis for the tradition. Thus Scripture is the ultimate authority on which the tradition was built, but it became the tradition that constituted the most readily accessible authority. Some, perhaps most, may have known that the tradition incorporated and interpreted significant elements of Scripture, but Colossians's use of the tradition suggests that, even for these people, it was the church's interpretation of Scripture and not its originating/original context that bore authority. Indeed, it seems unlikely that most of the audience of Colossians would have been able to make such a distinction for most uses of the biblical text, since they knew it almost entirely through the church's usage. Still, as we observe the author's handling of Scripture from this distance, Scripture in this letter seems to exercise its authority through the way it is interpreted in the tradition more than as an independent authority.

Bibliography

Aageson, James W. *Written Also for Our Sake: Paul and the Art of Biblical Interpretation*. Louisville: Westminster John Knox, 1993.
Allison, June W. "Homeric Allusions at the Close of Thucydides' Sicilian Narrative." *American Journal of Philology* 118 (1997): 499–516.
Barth, Markus, and Helmut Blanke. *Colossians: A New Translation with Introduction and Commentary*. AB 34B. New York: Doubleday, 1994.
Beetham, Christopher A. *Echoes of Scripture in the Letter of Paul to the Colossians*. BIS 96. Leiden: Brill, 2008.
Bieder, Werner. *Die Kolossische Irrlehre und die Kirche von heute*. ThSt 33. Zürich: Evangelischer Verlag, 1952.
Cannon, George E. *The Use of Traditional Materials in Colossians*. Macon, Ga.: Mercer University Press, 1983.
Capra, Andrea. "Protagoras' Achilles: Homeric Allusions as a Satirical Weapon (Pl. Prt. 340A)." *Classical Philology* 100 (2005): 274–77.
Davies, W. D. *Paul and Rabbinic Judaism: Some Rabbinic Elements in Pauline Theology*. 2nd ed. London: SPCK, 1955.
Deichgräber, Reinhard. *Gotteshymnus und Christushymnus in der frühen Christenheit: Untersuchungen zu Form, Sprache und Stil der frühchristlichen Hymnen*. SUNT 5. Göttingen: Vandenhoeck & Ruprecht, 1967.
Dunn, James D. G. *The Epistles to the Colossians and to Philemon*. NIGTC. Grand Rapids: Eerdmans, 1996.
Fee, Gordon D. "Old Testament Intertextuality in Colossians: Reflections on Pauline Christology and Gentile Inclusion in God's Story." Pages

201–21 in *History and Exegesis: New Testament Essays in Honor of Dr. E. Earle Ellis on His 80th Birthday*. Edited by Sang-Wan Son. New York: T&T Clark, 2006.

Francis, Fred O. "The Christological Argument of Colossians." Pages 192–208 in *God's Christ and His People*. Edited by J. Jervell and Wayne A. Meeks. Oslo: Universitetsforlaget, 1977.

Garner, Richard. *From Homer to Tragedy: The Art of Allusion in Greek Poetry*. New York: Routledge, 1990.

Harris, Murray J. *Colossians and Philemon*. Exegetical Guide to the Greek New Testament. Grand Rapids: Eerdmans, 1991.

Hay, David M. *Colossians*. ANTC. Nashville: Abingdon, 2000.

———. *Glory at the Right Hand: Psalm 110 in Early Christianity*. SBLMS 18. Nashville: Abingdon, 1973.

Hays, Richard B. *Echoes of Scripture in the Letters of Paul*. New Haven: Yale, 1989.

Hengel, Martin. "Hymn & Christology." Pages 173–97 in *Papers on Paul and Other New Testament Authors*. Vol. 3 of *Studia Biblica 1978*. JSNTSup 3. Sheffield: JSOT Press, 1980.

Hock, Ronald F. "Homer in Greco-Roman Education." Pages 56–77 in *Mimesis and Intertextuality in Antiquity and Christianity*. Edited by Dennis R. MacDonald. Studies in Antiquity and Christianity. Harrisburg, Pa.: Trinity Press, 2001.

Hübner, Hans. *An Philemon, An die Kolosser, An die Epheser*. HNT 12. Tübingen: Mohr, 1997.

Jervell, Jacob. *Imago Dei: Gen 1,26f. im Spätjudentum, in der Gnosis und in den paulinischen Briefen*. FRLANT 58. Göttingen: Vandenhoeck & Ruprecht, 1960.

Kaiser, Walter C., Jr. *The Uses of the Old Testament in the New*. Chicago: Moody Press, 1985.

Käsemann, Ernst. "A Primitive Christian Baptismal Liturgy." Pages 149–68 in *Essays on New Testament Themes*. Philadelphia: Fortress, 1982.

Leppä, Outi. *The Making of Colossians: A Study on the Formation and Purpose of a Deutero-Pauline Letter*. Publication of the Finnish Exegetical Society 86. Göttingen: Vandenhoeck & Ruprecht, 2003.

Lightfoot, Joseph B. *St. Paul's Epistles to the Colossians and to Philemon*. Rev. ed. New York: Macmillan, 1879. Repr., Grand Rapids: Zondervan, 1959.

Lincoln, Andrew T. *Paradise Now and Not Yet: Studies in the Role of the Heavenly Dimension in Paul's Thought with Special Reference to His*

Eschatology. SNTSMS 43. New York: Cambridge University Press, 1981.

Lindemann, Andreas. *Der Kolosserbrief.* ZBK.NT 10. Zürich: Theologischer Verlag, 1983.

Lohse, Eduard. *Colossians and Philemon.* Hermeneia. Philadelphia: Fortress, 1971.

MacDonald, Margaret Y. *Colossians and Ephesians.* SP. Collegeville, Minn.: Liturgical Press, 2000.

Martin, Troy. *By Philosophy and Empty Deceit: Colossians as a Response to a Cynic Critique.* JSNTSup 118. Sheffield: Sheffield Academic Press, 1996.

Nielsen, Charles. "The Status of Paul and His Letters in Colossians." *Perspectives* 12 (1985): 103–22.

O'Brien, Peter T. *Colossians, Philemon.* WBC 44. Waco, Tex.: Word, 1982.

Percy, Ernst. *Die Probleme der Kolosser- und Epheserbriefe.* Lund: Gleerup, 1946.

Pokorný, Petr. *Colossians: A Commentary.* Peabody, Mass.: Hendrickson, 1991.

Porter, Stanley E. "Allusions and Echoes." Pages 29–40 in *As It Is Written: Studying Paul's Use of Scripture.* Edited by Stanley E. Porter and Christopher D. Stanley. SBLSymS 50. Atlanta: Society of Biblical Literature, 2008.

———. "The Use of the Old Testament in the New Testament: A Brief Comment on Method and Terminology." Pages 79–96 in *Early Christian Interpretation of the Scriptures of Israel: Investigations and Proposals.* Edited by C. A. Evans and J. A. Sanders. JSNTSup 148. Sheffield: Sheffield Academic Press, 1997.

Robinson, James M. "A Formal Analysis of Colossians 1:15–20." *JBL* 76 (1957): 270–87.

Rogers, Jeffrey S. "Scripture is as Scripturalists Do: Scripture as a Human Activity in the Qumran Scrolls." Pages 28–43 in *Early Christian Interpretation of the Scriptures of Israel: Investigations and Proposals.* Edited by Craig A. Evans and James A. Sanders. JSNTSup 148. Sheffield: Sheffield Academic Press, 1997.

Schweizer, Eduard. *The Letter to the Colossians: A Commentary.* Minneapolis: Augsburg, 1976.

Stanley, Christopher D. *Arguing with Scripture: The Rhetoric of Quotations in the Letters of Paul.* New York: T&T Clark, 2004.

———. "Paul and Homer: Greco-Roman Citation Practice in the First Century CE." *NovT* 32 (1990): 48–78.
Stintson, T. C. W. "The Scope and Limits of Allusion in Greek Tragedy." Pages 67–102 in *Greek Tragedy and Its Legacy: Essays Presented to D. J. Conacher*. Edited by M. Cropp, E. Fantham, and S. E. Scully. Calgary, Alberta: University of Calgary Press, 1986.
Sumney, Jerry L. *Colossians: A Commentary*. NTL. Louisville: Westminster John Knox, 2008.
Vawter, Bruce. "The Colossians Hymn and the Principle of Reduction." *CBQ* 33 (1971): 62–81.
Watson, Francis. *Paul and the Hermeneutics of Faith*. New York: T&T Clark, 2004.
Weiss, Herold. "The Law in the Epistle to the Colossians." *CBQ* 34 (1972): 294–314.
Wright, N. T. "Poetry and Theology in Colossians 1.15–20." *NTS* 36 (1990): 444–68.

Part 4
Scripture in Paul's Theology

Scripture and Other Voices in Paul's Theology

Linda L. Belleville

A common approach to analyzing Scripture in Paul is to identify explicit quotations and implicit allusions, or "echoes," and to consider what they have to say about Paul's theology. The underlying assumption is that Paul's theological *Sitz im Leben* was exclusively that of the Jewish Scriptures. Yet this can all too easily result in a leap-frog hermeneutical approach that overlooks the rich tradition of "other voices" reflected in Paul's theologizing.

This essay will explore "other voices" that shed light on Pauline texts that have commonly been labeled as theologically abstruse or the products of an overactive imagination.[1] Specifically, the voice of proverbial wisdom in 1 Cor 9:9 and 2 Cor 6:14, the voice of lyric poetry in 2 Cor 4:13, the voice of tradition history and Jewish folklore in Gal 3:19–20, and the voice of reread Scripture in 1 Cor 10:4 will be considered.

The Voice of Proverbial Wisdom: 1 Cor 9:9 and 2 Cor 6:14

One case where "other voices" help to explain what is otherwise an inexplicable use of Scripture is 1 Cor 9:9. Paul's overall argument in 1 Cor 9 is clear: those who are engaged in the work of the ministry deserve to be compensated for their labor. In support, Paul draws on such contemporary analogies as the pay received by those in military service, the produce that the farmer enjoys, and the milk that the shepherd obtains (v. 7). His citation of Deut 25:4 is contextually appropriate: "For it is written in the law of Moses, 'You shall not muzzle an ox while it is treading out the grain'" (οὐ

---

1. All quotations are from the NRSV unless otherwise indicated.

κημώσεις βοῦν ἀλοῶντα, 1 Cor 9:9).[2] Yet while it fits the overall argument of 1 Cor 9, the theological point that Paul draws from this Scripture does not:

> Do I say this on human authority? Does not the law also say the same? For it is written in the law of Moses, "You shall not muzzle an ox while it is treading out the grain." Is it for oxen that God is concerned? Or does he not speak entirely for our sake? It was indeed written for our sake, for whoever plows should plow in hope and whoever threshes should thresh in hope of a share in the crop. (1 Cor 9:8–10)

Richard Hays refers to Paul's use of Deut 25:4 here as "arbitrary prooftexting."[3] Christopher Stanley wonders if Paul might have chuckled as he applied Deut 25:4 to himself.[4] Francis Watson speaks of Paul's "relatively casual use" of Scripture.[5]

What then are we to make of Paul's use of Scripture? Richard Longenecker thinks that Paul is employing a rabbinic *qal wahomer* form of argumentation.[6] Yet the "by how much more" (πολλῷ μᾶλλον) language

---

2. Κημώσεις (B* D* F G 1739) is to be preferred to φιμώσεις (despite the strong external support of P[46] ℵ A B[3] C D[b,c] K L P), since the latter can be explained as a copyist's attempt to harmonize with the more familiar verb of LXX Deut 25:4. See Bruce Metzger, *A Textual Commentary on the Greek New Testament* (2nd ed.; Deutsche Bibelgesellschaft: Stuttgart, 1994), 492. Although Paul is thought to be explicitly citing Deut 25:4, the LXX has φιμώσεις, while Paul has κημώσεις—a word found nowhere else in the Greek Scriptures. Nor is anything comparable found in the Hebrew Scriptures. The MT has תחסם ("to block the mouth with a wood bar"). The Targumim have תיחוד תחיד ("to tie up the mouth"). A φιμός (as well as a κημός) was a leather nose-band commonly used on a horse's bridle; see both entries in LSJ.

3. Richard B. Hays, *Echoes of Scripture in the Letters of Paul* (New Haven: Yale University Press, 1989), 179. Hays seems to have modified his opinion in his commentary, calling 1 Cor 9:9 an elegant metaphor which Paul uses a fortiori in oracular fashion (*First Corinthians* [Louisville: Westminster John Knox, 1997], 151). See also Raymond Collins, *First Corinthians* (SP 7; Collegeville, Minn.: Liturgical Press, 1999), 339.

4. Christopher D. Stanley, *Arguing with Scripture: The Rhetoric of Quotations in the Letters of Paul* (New York: T&T Clark, 2004), 183.

5. Francis Watson, *Paul and the Hermeneutics of Faith* (New York: T&T Clark, 2004), 276.

6. Richard N. Longenecker, *Biblical Exegesis in the Apostolic Period* (Grand Rapids: Eerdmans, 1975), 126–127; also Dietrich-Alex Koch, *Die Schrift als Zeuge des Evangeliums: Untersuchungen zur Verwendung und zum Verständnis der Schrift bie Paulus* (BHT 69; Tübingen: Mohr Siebeck, 1986), 202–4. Cf. Matt 6:30: "If that is how

that characterizes Paul's a fortiori line of argument elsewhere is missing. For example, in 2 Cor 3:9, he argues, "If the ministry that condemns is glorious, *by how much more* [πολλῷ μᾶλλον] glorious is the ministry that brings righteousness." Indeed, Paul employs this very form of argument in 1 Cor 9:12: "If others share this rightful claim on you, do not we *still more* [οὐ μᾶλλον]?" But Paul does not do this with the laboring oxen. He does not say, "If God cared about laboring animals, *by how much more* does he care about laboring humans, especially those who labor among God's people."

Hans Conzelmann argues that Paul's exegesis is in accordance with the Hellenistic Jewish (versus rabbinic) allegorical principle that God's concern is with higher things.[7] We do find such a principle at work in Philo, who treats regulations concerning sacrificial animals in allegorical fashion. For example, Philo states, "You will find that this exceeding accuracy of investigation into the animals figuratively signifies the amelioration of your own disposition and conduct; for the law was not established for the sake of irrational animals, but for those who have intellect and reason" (*Spec.* 1.260).[8] Paul does engage in allegorical exegesis in such texts as Gal 4:21–31. But the pattern is not found here. The muzzle, the ox, treading, and grain are not treated as figures for a higher spiritual reality. Instead, Paul states that God is not concerned for the oxen's physical well being but for ours. A play on words is possible. Βοῦς ("ox") and βίος ("livelihood, property") are quite close. Paul would then be saying that God's concern is not for the βοῦς but for the βίος of human beings, particularly those who harvest spiritually in God's fields. Yet such a play on words is not the best contextual fit.

Paul does employ farming metaphors elsewhere. In 2 Cor 6:14–7:1, he takes a Mosaic law prohibiting the unequal yoking of an ox and a donkey ("You shall not plow with an ox and a donkey yoked together," Deut 22:10) and applies it to unequal spiritual yoking: "Do not be unequally yoked with unbelievers; for what partnership has righteousness with lawlessness? Or

---

God clothes the grass of the field, which is here today and tomorrow is thrown into the fire, will not he *much more* [πολλῷ μᾶλλον] clothe you?"

7. Hans Conzelmann, *1 Corinthians: A Commentary on the First Epistle to the Corinthians* (trans. J. Leitch; Hermeneia; Philadelphia: Fortress, 1975), 154–55.

8. All quotations from Philo are taken from *The Works of Philo: Complete and Unabridged* (trans. Charles D. Yonge; Peabody, Mass.: Hendrickson, 1993).

what fellowship has light with darkness?"⁹ What is to be noted in this text is the uniqueness of the Greek term ἑτεροζυγοῦντες ("yoked with a different kind"). The MT has יחדי ("together"), while the LXX has ἐπὶ τὸ αὐτό ("in the same place," "together"). In fact, ἑτεροζυγοῦντες is not found elsewhere in the New Testament, and in the LXX it only appears in a statute having to do with crossbreeding and not unequal yoking: "You shall not let your cattle breed with a different kind" (κατοχεύσεις ἑτεροζύγῳ, Lev 19:19).

Deuteronomy 22:10 does surface in extrabiblical Jewish writings. Josephus simply reiterates the command: "You are to plough your land with oxen and not to oblige other animals to come under the same yoke with them [ὑπὸ ζεύγλην ἄγοντας)], but to till your land with those beasts that are of the same kind with each other" (*Ant.* 4.228).¹⁰ Philo does the same: "Sacred law takes such exceeding care to provide for the maintenance of justice, that it will not permit even the ploughing of the land to be carried on by animals of unequal strength [μόσχον ἀροτριᾷ], and forbids a husbandman to plough with a donkey and a heifer yoked to the same plough [καταζεύξαντας]" (*Spec.* 4.205).

There is, however, an "other voice" to be considered here. Philo treats Deut 22:10 elsewhere as an aphorism that applies to the human realm: "[This] I imagine is to teach the judges most forcibly that they are never in their decisions to give the worse fate to the humbly born, in matters that depend not on birth but on virtue and vice" (*Spec.* 4.205). The same is true in Ps.-Phoc. 15, where ἑτερόζυγον is found in a series of exhortations about fair trade practices that are aphoristic in form: "Always dispense justice and let not your judgment be influenced by favor.... Do not make a balance unequal but weigh honestly [μὴ κρούειν ἑτερόζυγον ἀλλ᾽ ἴσον ἕλκειν]."

The texts in Philo and Pseudo-Phocylides raise the possibility that Paul is drawing similarly on a current aphorism. Maxims that draw on everyday life experiences such as μὴ γίνεσθε ἑτεροζυγοῦντες can be found elsewhere in the New Testament. Yeast maxims are particularly common. "A little yeast leavens the whole lump" appears twice in Paul (1 Cor 5:6; Gal 5:9). Jesus warns his disciples to "Be on your guard against the yeast of the Pharisees and Sadducees" (Matt 16:6; Luke 12:1; cf. Mark 8:15). While

---

9. Cf. 2 Cor 6:14: Μὴ γίνεσθε ἑτεροζυγοῦντες ἀπίστοις; and LXX Deut 22:10: οὐκ ἀροτριάσεις ἐν μόσχῳ καὶ ὄνῳ ἐπὶ τὸ αὐτο.

10. All quotations from Josephus are taken from *The Works of Josephus: Complete and Unabridged* (trans. William Whiston; Peabody, Mass.: Hendrickson, 1996).

the disciples did not initially understand the point of comparison, their response concerning bread indicates that the cultural understanding was there. Leaven maxims also appear in the Hebrew Scriptures. For example, Hos 7:4 states, "They are all adulterers, burning like an oven whose fire the baker need not stir from the kneading of the dough till it rises."

The same is true of 1 Cor 9:9. Much confusion regarding Paul's use of Scripture disappears when "You shall not muzzle an ox while it is treading out the grain" is understood as a common saying of the day. The unfamiliar vocabulary supports a cultural aphorism (οὐ κημώσεις βοῦν ἀλοῶντα). The verb κημόω ("to muzzle") appears only here and in 1 Tim 5:18 in the Greek Bible, while the verbal adjective ἀλοῶντα is found only in 1 Tim 5:18 in the New Testament and only in Isa 47:2 in the LXX.[11] Βοῦς for "ox" occurs elsewhere in the New Testament solely in 1 Tim 5:18, where the same maxim is invoked, and in Luke 13:15, where Jesus uses the law's care for oxen on the Sabbath as a warrant for the physical well-being of humans (Exod 23:4–5, 12).[12]

Deuteronomy 25:4 is itself confusing if not understood as a maxim. It has no parallels in the legal materials of the Pentateuch or elsewhere in the Old Testament, nor does it fit the broader context of the chapter. It appears as an offhanded comment in the middle of a casuistic legal passage that treats such matters as the number of lashes a judge can impose as punishment and the protocols for levirate marriage.[13] There is nothing remotely close in proximity that commands the humane treatment of one's livestock.[14] Nor does it work as a cultural command. Since Near Eastern

---

11. The LXX has the more familiar φιμάω. Cf. Matt 22:12, 34; Mark 1:25, 4:39; Luke 4:35; 1 Pet 2:15.

12. Exod 20:10: "But the seventh day is a Sabbath to the LORD your God; in it you shall not do any work, you, or your son, or your daughter, your manservant, or your maidservant, or your cattle, or the sojourner who is within your gates."

13. Hays states that it is not surprising Paul would have read Deut 25:4 as suggesting justice in human economic affairs, given that the rest of the chapter deals with such matters (*First Corinthians*, 151). Yet in *Echoes of Scripture* he states that there is no indication that Paul has wrestled seriously with Scripture; he "has simply appropriated [its] language to lend rhetorical force to his own discourse with minimal attention to the integrity of the semiotic universe of the precursor" (175). But this overlooks the fact that Deut 25:4 does not fit the broader context and that the Greek of this verse lacks a Septuagintal semiotic universe.

14. The closest injunctions are found in Exod 23:4–5 ("If you meet your enemy's ox or his donkey going astray, you shall bring it back to him. If you see the donkey of

cultures were primarily agrarian, any self-respecting farmer knew that he would get more out of his oxen if they were free to eat while treading. However, as an aphorism, it works; the wise farmer learns from experience how to get the most productivity from livestock. The aphoristic character of the verse has been duly noted by a number of commentators.[15]

Husbandry proverbs can be found elsewhere in Scripture. Proverbs 12:10–11 states, "The righteous know the needs of their animals, but the mercy of the wicked is cruel. Those who till their land will have plenty of food, but those who follow worthless pursuits have no sense."[16]

The proposal here is that Paul is drawing on Scripture and "other voices" to develop his theological argument. In this case, the "other voice" is the conventional wisdom of his day. Conventional wisdom is not unique to Scripture. Proverbial sayings have had an integral role in all cultures that value the wisdom of age and experience. Maxims such as "a stitch in time saves nine," "look before you leap," and "the early bird catches the worm" are still current today. Such maxims continue to be passed from one generation to the next. "You reap what you sow" (Gal 6:7) and "a little leaven leavens the whole lump" (1 Cor 5:6; Gal 5:9) are certainly not original to Paul. They are cultural maxims that Paul cites because they not only illustrate his point but also reflect shared communal values.

Paul's theological commentary also suits a proverbial application. As commentary on a Mosaic law, it makes little sense; as commentary on a proverb, it makes much sense: μὴ τῶν βοῶν μέλει τῷ θεῷ ἢ δι' ἡμᾶς πάντως λέγει δι' ἡμᾶς. The tenses are important. Paul does not comment on God's past intention ("In saying this God *did* not care about oxen"), but rather on God's present inclination ("God *does* not care.... he *is speaking* for our sake"). Δι' ἡμᾶς is placed first in its clause for empha-

---

one who hates you lying under its burden, you shall refrain from leaving him with it, you shall help him to lift it up") and Exod 23:12 ("Six days you shall do your work, but on the seventh day you shall rest, that your ox and your donkey may have rest, and the son of your bondmaid, and the alien, may be refreshed").

15. See, for example, Peter C. Craigie, *The Book of Deuteronomy* (Grand Rapids: Eerdmans, 1976), 313; G. Lisowsky, "Dtn. 25:4," in *Das ferme und nahe Wort* (ed. F. Maass; BZAW 105; Berlin: de Gruyter, 1967), 144–52.

16. LXX Prov 12:10: δίκαιος οἰκτίρει ψυχὰς κτηνῶν αὐτοῦ τὰ δὲ σπλάγχνα τῶν ἀσεβῶν ἀνελεήμονα. Cf. Let. Aris. 148–149 (second century B.C.E.): "By means of creatures like this Scripture has handed down (the lesson) to be noted by men of wisdom that they should be righteous."

sis: "On *our* behalf surely it says."¹⁷ To focus on the oxen is to miss the truism of the aphorism.¹⁸ Paul is not saying that God was not concerned about humane treatment of laboring livestock. There are other Mosaic laws mandating such treatment, including Sabbath rest for one's oxen, donkeys, and cattle (Exod 20:10; Deut 5:14); the equal yoking of farming animals (Deut 22:10); and relieving an animal of its burden (Deut 22:4), even if it belongs to one's enemy (Exod 23:5). Nor is Paul saying that God is concerned about fair labor laws. He merely states a truism: just as the farmer expects to share in the fruits of his labor, so also the laboring minister has a right to expect compensation.

Proverbial parallels are not lacking. For instance, Sir 6:19 states, "Come to her like one who plows and sows, and wait for her good harvest, for in her service you will toil a little while, and soon you will eat of her produce." A proverb similar to 1 Cor 6:10 appears in the teaching of Jesus: "A worker deserves his food" (ἄξιος γὰρ ὁ ἐργάτης τῆς τροφῆς αὐτοῦ, Matt 10:10) or "his wage" (ἄξιος γὰρ ὁ ἐργάτης τοῦ μισθοῦ αὐτοῦ, Luke 10:7). Matthew's context is the sending out of the Twelve, where Jesus says, "Take no bag for your journey, or two tunics, or sandals, or a staff; for the laborer is worthy of his food." Luke's context is the sending out of the seventy-two (or seventy): "Remain in that house, eating and drinking whatever they provide, for 'the laborer is worthy of his wage.'"¹⁹

Lest the Corinthians miss the point of comparison, Paul goes on to spell it out in 1 Cor 9:9b-10: "For it was written, 'The plowman plows

---

17. Hays argues that "on our behalf" has the church in view, making Deut 25:4 a prefigurement of Paul and his Gentile congregations (*Echoes of Scripture*, 165–66). His rationale is a perceived parallel with Rom 4:23–24: "Now the words, 'it was reckoned to him [Abraham],' were written not for his sake alone, but for ours also." Yet Rom 4:23 has "not for [Abraham's] sake *alone*" (Οὐκ ... δι' αὐτὸν μόνον), while 1 Cor 9:10 is absolute: "not for the oxen" (μὴ τῶν βοῶν).

18. The negative μὴ can introduce a question expecting the answer "no," so that ἢ would continue the question: "Surely God cares not about oxen but rather πάντως for our sake he says this?" Alternately, the negative μὴ could introduce a statement of fact and ἢ a point of contrast: "God does not care about oxen; rather, he speaks πάντως for our sake." The force of πάντως is also at issue. "Does God not on our behalf say *everywhere*?" is lexically possible, but "actually" is the better fit in the context: "Is it not on our behalf that God *actually* says this?"

19. Hays thinks Paul had the Lukan tradition in mind, even though it is not quoted explicitly (*First Corinthians*, 152). For the Luke 10:1 textual variations "seventy" and "seventy-two," see Metzger, *Textual Commentary*, 126–27.

in hope and the thresher threshes in hope of sharing in the crop'" (γὰρ ἐγράφη ὅτι ὀφείλει ἐπ' ἐλπίδι ὁ ἀροτριῶν ἀροτριᾶν καὶ ὁ ἀλοῶν ἐπ' ἐλπίδι τοῦ μετέχειν). In other words, workers deserve to share in the fruits of their labor. It is not clear whether Paul is pointing backward or forward here. Some take ἐγράφη ὅτι as "it [Deut 25:4] was written for our sake because the plowman should plow in hope and the thresher thresh in hope of sharing in the crop." But ἐγράφη ὅτι could also be introducing a second quote, "For on our behalf it was written, 'Whoever plows should plow in hope and whoever threshes should thresh in hope of a share in the crop.'"[20] Watson rightly points to the parallel in Rom 4:23: Οὐκ ἐγράφη δὲ δι' αὐτὸν μόνον ὅτι ἐλογίσθη αὐτῷ.[21] Johannes Weiss refers to verse 10 as a quotation from an apocryphon.[22] Collins thinks that Paul joined Deut 25:4 to a saying of unknown origin from oral *halakah* or traditional lore.[23]

Several points support the presence of a second quote here. First, there is a change of tense. Paul employs his typical perfect passive formula γέγραπται to introduce Deut 25:4 in v. 9, but then he switches to the aorist passive ἐγράφη "it was written" in verse 10. This is difficult to explain unless a second quote is in view. There is also a change of number. "Do not muzzle an ox" (singular) becomes "God does not care about oxen" (plural). Also, a formulaic usage of γράφω followed by ὅτι is typically recitative.[24]

As Collins and Watson observe, construing this verse as an adage fits the cadence of the text. The structure is chiastic: "{A} He ought [ὀφείλει] {B} in hope [ἐπ' ἐλπίδι] {C} the plower to plow [ὁ ἀροτριῶν ἀροτριᾶν] and

---

20. Cf. Conzelmann, *1 Corinthians*, 155 n. 41.

21. Although noting the aphoristic character of the verse, Watson attributes the maxim to Paul himself. He reads it as an interpretive paraphrase of Deut 25:4, functioning as an intermediate step between a legal injunction about animals and its application to the human sphere (*Paul and the Hermeneutics of Faith*, 424).

22. Johannes Weiss, *Der erste Korintherbrief* (Gottingen: Vandenhoeck & Ruprecht, 1925), 153-54.

23. Collins argues that 1 Cor 9:9-10 is a "pastiche of two texts linked with one another by means of the verb 'thresh' in accordance with the *gezera shawah* principle of biblical interpretation" (*First Corinthians*, 332, 340-41).

24. See γέγραπται ὅτι (Mark 7:6, 11:17; Luke 4:4; John 8:17); ὁ λόγος ὁ ἐν τῷ νόμῳ αὐτῶν γεγραμμένος ὅτι (John 15:25); καθὼς γέγραπται ὅτι (Rom 3:10, 4:17, 8:36); ἐν τῷ νόμῳ γέγραπται ὅτι (1 Cor 14:21); διότι γέγραπται [ὅτι] (1 Pet 1:16).

{C'} the harvester [καὶ ὁ ἀλοῶν] {B'} in hope [ἐπ' ἐλπίδι] {A'} to partake [τοῦ μετέχειν]."[25]

The same proverb with a similar interpretive maxim appears in 1 Tim 5:18. Unlike 1 Cor 6:9–10, the point of the proverbial saying, "Do not muzzle an ox when it is treading grain," is explicitly interpreted by the phrase, "a laborer deserves his wages." Although the interpretation is introduced by the common citation formula, λέγει ἡ γραφή,[26] there is no Scriptural parallel for these words. Some suppose that the author is applying ἡ γραφή to the words of Jesus.[27] But καί can just as well introduce an elaborative or clarifying statement. "A laborer deserves his wages" could just as well be an "other voice"—a wise saying of the day that both Jesus and the Pastorals used as a way of connecting with their respective audiences. Marshall wonders if the Lukan tradition and 1 Tim 5:18 reflect a basic principle that would have been accepted in the secular world and thus able to be applied with "authority" to the work of the ministry.[28] Based on extrabiblical evidence, Porter rightly suggests that this was an aphorism that children learned in a school setting.[29] It was already present in the Greek tragedies, as when Euripides depicts Dolon saying, "So must I toil, but for my pains I should receive fitting wages [δι' ἄξιον μισθὸν φέρεσθαι], for set a reward on any deed, and it breeds a double favor" (*Rhes.* 161). It can also be seen the in the first century text of Pseudo-Phocylides: "Give to him who labors hard his [deserved] wage" (μισθὸν μοχθήσαντι δίδου, *Sententiae* 19). This suggests that "a laborer deserves his wages" was a well-known maxim on which Jesus, Paul, and others drew, much like our modern proverb, "the early bird catches the worm."

The Voice of Lyric Poetry: 2 Cor 4:13

In some instances Paul's citation of Scripture does not appear to add any-

---

25. Collins, *First Corinthians*, 332, 340–41; Watson, *Paul and the Hermeneutics of Faith*, 424 n. 21.

26. See also Rom 4:3; 9:17; 10:11; 11:2; Gal 4:30; Jas 4:5; cf. John 7:38, 42.

27. H. Preisker speculates that the source is some book now lost that was received as Scripture and was on a par with the canonical OT ("μισθός," *TDNT* 4:698 n. 5).

28. I. Howard Marshall, *The Pastoral Epistles* (ICC; Edinburgh: T&T Clark, 1999), 616–17.

29. Stanley Porter, "Paul and Ancient Letter Writing," in *As It Is Written: Studying Paul's Use of Scripture* (ed. Stanley E. Porter and Christopher D. Stanley; SBLSymS 50; Atlanta: Society of Biblical Literature, 2008), 105 n. 24.

thing of theological significance to the argument. Second Corinthians 4:13 is often thought to be one such text. Indeed, Christopher Stanley identifies it as "one of the more obscure quotations in the Pauline corpus."[30]

> But just as we have the same spirit of faith that is in accordance with scripture, "I believed, and so I spoke" [κατὰ τὸ γεγραμμένον· ἐπίστευσα, διὸ ἐλάλησα], we also believe, and so we speak, because we know that the one who raised the Lord Jesus will raise us also with Jesus, and will bring us with you into his presence.

Despite the scant three-word citation, LXX Ps 115:1 is commonly credited as the source. The text of 2 Cor 4:13 matches the LXX exactly, and the Greek ἐπίστευσα διὸ ἐλάλησα is found only in Paul and Ps 115. Also, Paul's line of argument fits that of Ps 115. In both, it is the speaker's faith that prompts him to speak despite consequent persecution. The MT is profoundly different, excluding it as a possible source. In the Septuagint, the words "I believed, therefore I spoke" begin the psalm, while in the MT they occur midway (Ps 116:10). The import, too, is different. The LXX has "I believed, *therefore* I spoke, but I was greatly afflicted," while the MT has "I kept my faith, *even when I said*, 'I am greatly afflicted'" (האמנתי כי אדבר אני עניתי מאד). In the Septuagint, it is the psalmist's faith that prompts him to speak out despite the consequences; in the MT, it is the psalmist's faith that gets him through his current distress.

Why, however, should Paul cite a mere three words? It is not as if these words provide any kind of vital support for his argument.[31] There is no typological connection, no formulaic "in accordance with the scripture" or "as the scripture says." There is no pesher involved and no allegorical meaning that Paul proceeds to unpack. Nor does he go on to exegete the psalmist's words. He simply goes on to state, "Just as we have the same spirit of faith ... we also believe, and so we speak."

In short, a three-word citation is inexplicable unless one considers other hermeneutical possibilities. One such possibility is that Paul is quoting the psalmist's *lyrical* voice—the psalmist's sung story of an outspoken faith despite persecution. What appears to prompt the quote is Paul's rec-

---

30. Stanley, *Arguing with Scripture*, 98.
31. See, however, Stanley, who argues that the Ps 115:1 quote serves to justify Paul's ministry ("Paul's 'Use' of Scripture: Why the Audience Matters," in Porter and Stanley, *As It Is Written*, 147).

ognition that he and the psalmist have τὸ αὐτὸ πνεῦμα τῆς πίστεως. The psalmist's perspective on his circumstances parallels that of Paul; they have a similar faith. The psalmist states, "For you have delivered my soul from death, my eyes from tears, my feet from stumbling. I walk before the Lord in the land of the living" (LXX Ps 114:8–9). Paul says, "We know that the one who raised the Lord Jesus will raise us also with Jesus" (2 Cor 4:14). Both also have the same outspokenness despite the consequences. The Psalmist states, "I believed, therefore I spoke, but I was greatly afflicted" (LXX Ps 115:1). Paul says, "We are afflicted in every way, but not crushed; perplexed, but not driven to despair" (2 Cor 4:8). Finally, they have similar opponents. The psalmist states, "I said in my astonishment, 'Every person is a liar'" (LXX Ps 115:2). Paul says, "[We are] persecuted, but not forsaken; struck down, but not destroyed" (2 Cor 4:9).

There are differences as well. The psalmist speaks in first-person singular, while Paul speaks in the plural "we." Paul's perspective is a corporate one, the perspective of apostolic suffering found throughout 2 Corinthians. Moreover, though both authors have a common theology of divine deliverance, Paul's reason for preaching the gospel is not because he knows that there is life beyond the grave. He does it so that others can be the beneficiaries: "Everything we do and say is *for your benefit*" (τὰ γὰρ πάντα δι' ὑμᾶς, v. 15). The God who raised Jesus will not merely raise the gospel preacher but also the Corinthians (καὶ ἡμᾶς σὺν Ἰησοῦ ἐγερεῖ) and "present us together with you" (καὶ παραστήσει σὺν ὑμῖν, v. 14). Speech-act theory is helpful here. As Anna Wierzbicka points out, "At the moment of quotation, the quoting author takes on the *persona* of the original speaker, dramatically reenacting the original speech-event so that the two voices merge into one."[32] This fits with both the means of delivery—Paul dictated his letters—and with the mode of receipt—the letter carrier read the letter aloud to the recipients.[33] Some have dismissed this use of Scripture based on the fact that Paul's predominately Greek lower-class audience would not have been literate enough (let alone biblically literate) to grasp what Paul was doing.[34] Yet biblical literacy need not be in written form. A culture with a strong tradition of oral communication and memorization should not be dis-

---

32. Stanley, *Arguing with Scripture*, 25, summarizing Anna Wierzbicka, "The Semantics of Direct and Indirect Discourse," *Papers in Linguistics* 7 (1973): 273.

33. See John White's chapter on "Greek Letter Writing" in *Light from Ancient Letters* (Philadelphia: Fortress, 1986), 189–220.

34. Stanley, *Arguing with* Scripture, 57–58.

counted. The Corinthian church would have heard the Scriptures preached each week. According to 1 Tim 4:13, it was the role of the pastor to attend "to the public reading of Scripture, to exhortation, and to teaching" (τῇ ἀναγνώσει, τῇ παρακλήσει, τῇ διδασκαλίᾳ). Likewise, 2 Pet 3:15–16, which speaks of "some things in [Paul's letters]" being "hard to understand" and of "the ignorant and unstable" who "twist" Paul words "as they do the other scriptures" (τὰς λοιπὰς γραφὰς), assumes a certain amount of familiarity that had to be gained by some means of communication.

It is important to note that lyric poetry as a genre is intended to cause the listener to enter into the world of the author. Lyrical poetry as a genre evokes images, involves the senses, and stirs the listener's emotions. The memorable character of lyric poetry is crucial. Not only would the psalmist's words, "I believed, therefore I spoke," evoke the entire lyrical poem, but the same could be expected from the hearer of Paul's "spoken" words.

Hymnody was a vital part of the first-century worship experience. Like the first line of a hymn, 2 Cor 4:13, when spoken out loud, could bring to mind not only all the lyrics of LXX Ps 115 but the music as well. The Passover liturgy is a reminder of how often Psalms 113–118 were sung and, hence, familiar. Jesus sang the Hallel with his disciples before crossing the Kidron Valley and ascending the Mount of Olives: "After they sang the Hallel [ὑμνήσαντες], they went out to the Mount of Olives" (Mark 14:26). Paul instructs the Corinthian congregation, "When you come together, each one has a psalm [ψαλμὸν], a lesson, a revelation, a tongue, or an interpretation" (1 Cor 14:26). Earlier in 1 Corinthians he states, "Christ our Passover lamb has been sacrificed" (5:7), and at the end of the letter he informs them that he will stay in Ephesus "until Pentecost" (16:8). While this could simply be Paul's Jewish heritage surfacing, his exhortation to celebrate the Passover feast with sincere and true unleavened bread indicates something more substantial and intentional (ὥστε ἑορτάζωμεν ... ἐν ἀζύμοις εἰλικρινείας καὶ ἀληθείας, 5:8). In a similar way, references to the singing of psalms (ψαλμοῖς), hymns, and spiritual songs to God (Eph 5:19; Col 3:16), together with the exhortation, "Are any cheerful? Let them sing psalms" (ψαλλέτω, Jas 5:13), indicate that the Psalter was an integral part of worship and daily life. It is reasonable to suppose that LXX Psalm 115, as one of the Hallel songs, continued to play a liturgical role in the early church.[35]

---

35. See Craig A. Evans, *Mark 8:27–16:20* (WBC 34B; Nashville: Thomas Nelson, 2001), 399–400.

Lyric poetry can shape a person's self-understanding. LXX Psalm 115 shaped Paul's theological understanding of himself as a suffering servant. As N. T. Wright rightly observes, LXX Psalm 115 is a prayer of one who is suffering terribly but trusts in God and is delivered.[36] That makes it a prayer common to all human experience, and thus one that would also resonate cross-culturally. As the Psalmist recounts how his faith gave him the courage to speak out despite the crippling opposition that he faced, the community of faith hears an "other voice" that leads them to enter into the life experience of the psalmist.

The Voice of Tradition History/Jewish Folklore: Gal 3:19

The presence of details in Paul's engagement with the biblical narratives that go beyond what is explicitly stated in the Hebrew Scriptures has long been noted. Some have attributed these details to Paul's creativity. Yet these same details can be found in extrabiblical Jewish materials.[37] In some cases what is implicit in a biblical narrative is made explicit in their retelling. One example is διαταγεὶς δι' ἀγγέλων in Gal 3:19.

In answer to his own question, Τί οὖν ὁ νόμος; Paul responds, "it was added χάριν transgressions" and "administered through angels [διαταγεὶς δι' ἀγγέλων, NET] by the hand of the mediator [ἐν χειρὶ μεσίτου, AT]." The aorist διαταγεὶς is likely a divine passive. God is the agent; angels are his instrument. The NRSV's "by a mediator" is literally "by the hand of the mediator [ἐν χειρὶ μεσίτου]."[38] Apollonius's Canon, which states that two nouns in regimen should be taken as definite, applies here.[39] There are, of course, exceptions to this rule, but in these cases, it is typically the article with the *nomen rectum* that is dropped. That is not so here. The Greek ὁ δὲ μεσίτης ἑνὸς οὐκ ἔστιν of v. 20, which includes the articles, supports a defi-

---

36. N. T. Wright, *Justification* (Downers Grove, Ill.: InterVarsity Press, 2009), 33.

37. The midrashim show the need that was felt to fill in the gaps left in the biblical narratives regarding events and personalities.

38. Watson thinks "by the hand of the mediator" is an echo of the phrase "by the hand of Moses" in Lev 26:46 (*Paul and the Hermeneutics of Faith*, 317).

39. This is particularly the case with the kind of fixed prepositional phrase found in Gal 3:19. See Friedrich Blass and Albert Debrunner, *A Greek Grammar of the New Testament and Other Early Christian Literature* (trans. and rev. Robert W. Funk; Chicago: University of Chicago Press, 1961), §259; Edwin Mayser, *Grammatik der Griechischen Papyri aus der Ptolemäerzeit* (Berlin: de Gruyter, 1933–1936), 2.2:118.

nite μεσίτου. Thus the possessive genitive, "by the mediator's hand," takes on the character of a title.

There is a scholarly consensus that τί οὖν ὁ νόμος points to the Sinai tradition of law giving. Yet no angels appear in the Hebrew narrative. Exodus 19:18 has Yahweh descending on Mount Sinai באש ("in fire"), accompanied by smoke and the quaking of the mountain. Deuteronomy 33:2 adds that Yahweh came "from [the midst of] holy myriads" (מרבבת קדש). The rest of the verse is textually uncertain. As bracketed, it translates "from his right hand a fiery law for them" (מימינו [אש] [דת] למו; see also Symmachus, Aquila, and the Vulgate).[40] The Targumim have "from his right hand there was flashing lightning" (ימיניה מגו אישתא אוריתא), which may reflect another Hebrew text that was in circulation at the time.

Some suppose that Paul added διαταγεὶς δι' ἀγγέλων to show the inferiority of the Mosaic law to the Abrahamic promise.[41] If these words were in fact produced by Paul's creative hand, a case for theological inferiority could definitely be made. But references to the presence of angels at Mount Sinai predate Paul. The LXX of Deut 33:2 has Yahweh descending on Mount Sinai "with myriads of *Kadēs* [σὺν μυριάσιν Καδης] and angels with him on his right hand [ἐκ δεξιῶν αὐτοῦ ἄγγελοι μετ' αὐτου]."[42] Similarly, LXX Ps 68:17 translates the Hebrew אדני בם as ὁ κύριος ἐν αὐτοῖς. The Göttingen critical edition has "with his angels per Deut 33:2."[43] Indeed, the very fact that Paul offers no explanation for or elaboration concerning angelic mediators indicates that the tradition was well established.

The law διαταγεὶς δι' ἀγγέλων is a tradition that also appears in a wide range of extrabiblical materials. *Jubilees* 1:27-28 has "[God] said to the angel of the presence, 'Write for Moses from the first creation until

---

40. The Göttingen critical edition surmises that the Greek translator had אשור אליהם instead of אש דת למו in his text. See John W. Wevers, *Notes on the Greek Text of Deuteronomy* (SBLSCS 39; Atlanta: Society of Biblical Literature, 1995), 540 n. 3.

41. F. F. Bruce, *The Epistle to the Galatians: A Commentary on the Greek Text* (NIGTC; Grand Rapids: Eerdmans, 1982), 177; Hans Dieter Betz, *Galatians: A Commentary on Paul's Letter to the Churches in Galatia* (Hermeneia; Philadelphia: Fortress, 1979), 171-72; Walter Hansen, *Galatians* (IVPNTC 9; Downers Grove, Ill.: InterVarsity Press, 1994), 103; Longenecker, *Biblical Exegesis*, 120.

42. Some retain Καδης as a transliterated proper noun. But the Jewish association of Καδης with holiness (as in Aquila's translation ἀπὸ μυριάδων ἁγιασμοῦ) makes "holy ones" a probable rendering.

43. See Wevers, *Notes*, 540 n. 3.

my sanctuary is built in their midst forever and ever."[44] Philo states, "The sacred scripture calls them angels, for indeed they do administer [διαγγέλουσι] the injunctions of the father [God] to his children [Israel], and the necessities of the children to the father (*Somn.* 1.141–142). Some suppose that τῷ πατρὶ διαγγέλλουσι is a reference to human messengers rather than to angels. But the broader context makes is clear that Philo is speaking of angels. Indeed, he states that ὁ δὲ ἱερὸς λόγος ἀγγέλους εἴωθε καλεῖν. Josephus asserts, "The most excellent of our doctrines and our most holy things in the laws we learned from God through angels" (δι᾽ ἀγγέλων παρὰ τοῦ θεοῦ, *Ant.* 15.136).[45] There is no inferiority of the Mosaic law in any of these texts.

The presence of angels and their role as Sinai mediators were understood even by the early church to signify the great glory of the law. Sinai angelic traditions appear three times in the New Testament. Acts 7:53 reads, "You are the ones that received the law as instituted by angels, and yet you have not kept it" (οἵτινες ἐλάβετε τὸν νόμον εἰς διαταγὰς ἀγγέλων καὶ οὐκ ἐφυλάξατε). The two nouns in regimen, διαταγὰς ἀγγέλων, leave little room for ambiguity; the law is "the ordinance of the angels."[46] A Sinai angelic tradition is also found in Heb 2:2, where the law is identified as "the word spoken through angels" (ὁ δι᾽ ἀγγέλων λαληθεὶς λόγος). The aorist λαληθεὶς is likely a divine passive similar to Gal 3:19. God is the agent; the angels are his instruments (δι᾽ ἀγγέλων). Εἰ with the indicative ἐγένετο βέβαιος assumes the factual character of what is being reported: "*Since* the word spoken through the ordinance of the angels was firm and every transgression or disobedience received a just penalty...."[47] The line of argumentation is an a fortiori one: "How will we escape if we turn our backs on a salvation so much greater" (τηλικαύτης). The law is "good," but salvation through Christ is "so much greater."[48]

---

44. Cf. T. Dan 6:2, "Draw near to God and to the angel [τῷ ἀγγέλῳ] who intercedes for you because he is the mediator between God and humans [μεσίτης θεοῦ καὶ ἀνθρώπων] for the peace of Israel."

45. Watson supposes that δι᾽ ἀγγέλων is a reference to Scripture writers rather than to angels (*Paul and the Hermeneutics of Faith*, 280 n. 17). But such a usage is unprecedented.

46. See note 39 and the discussion surrounding it.

47. Εἰ with the indicative of all tenses denotes a simple conditional assumption with emphasis on the reality of the assumption (BDF, 371).

48. Watson thinks that the evidence for an angelic presence at Sinai is less clear than is often thought (*Paul and the Hermeneutics of Faith*, 280 n. 17). But given the

The same is true in Gal 3:19. The contrast is between the mediator Moses who represents "the many" of Israel and the "one" God who represents himself. Although Gal 3:20 is terse and hence difficult, Paul's basic point is clear. While Moses is Israel's mediator, the angels are not Yahweh's mediator. God may choose to use them, but he is "one," perhaps as opposed to Greco-Roman polytheistic culture. Ὁ δὲ θεὸς εἷς ἐστιν likely echoes the Shema of LXX Deut 6:4: κύριος ὁ θεὸς ἡμῶν κύριος εἷς ἐστιν. Hence, Yahweh needs no mediator.[49]

Israel, however, did. They sent Moses up Mount Sinai because their fear was too great. "Go near and listen to all that the LORD our God says; then tell us whatever the LORD our God tells you. We will listen and obey" (Deut 5:27). The LXX of Deut 5:5 identifies Moses as μέσον ("mediator"), and his role is defined as εἱστήκειν ἀνὰ μέσον κυρίου καὶ ὑμῶν ("to stand between the Lord and you"). The need for mediating angels because of human frailty is found in other Jewish materials. In *T. Dan* 6:2, Israel is instructed to "draw near to God and to the angel [τῷ ἀγγέλῳ] who intercedes for you because he is the mediator [μεσίτης] between God and humans beings [οὗτός ἐστι μεσίτης θεοῦ καὶ ἀνθρώπων]." Philo notes similarly that it was Israel, not God, who was in need of mediators. For God himself,

> who knows everything, has no need of interpreters. But because it is the lot of us miserable mortals to use speech as a mediator and intercessor, because of our standing in awe of and fearing the Ruler of the universe, and the all-powerful might of his authority, we are in need of mediators [τῶν μεσιτῶν, Exod 20:19] to speak for us. God, however, proffers us of his own accord, without employing the ministrations of any other beings. (*Somn.* 1.143–145).

Hence, angelic mediators reflect not the inferiority of the law but rather the frailty of humans. God with his "myriads of angels" is at once a picture of the *Shekinah* glory and the inability of humans to bear that glory. Paul's statement in Gal 3:19 is therefore in theological accord with his Jewish contemporaries.[50]

---

witness of the LXX, the Psalter, Acts, Paul, Hebrews, and a range of other Jewish authors, the evidence is quite substantial.

49. For further discussion, see Linda Belleville, "'Under Law': Structural Analysis and the Pauline Concept of Law in Galatians 3:21–4:11," *JSNT* 26 (1986): 53–78.

50. For other examples of Jewish traditions in the New Testament, see Peter Enns,

The Voice of Jewish Folklore: 1 Cor 10:4

Israelite exodus-wilderness history is either explicitly or implicitly invoked throughout 1 Cor 10:1–11. The single explicit citation is found in verse 7: "Do not become idolaters as some of them did; as it is written, 'The people sat down to eat and drink, and they rose up to play'" (LXX Exod 32:6).[51] However, implicit references abound. As Watson notes, portions of Exodus and the breadth of Num 11–25 are in evidence here.[52] Paul makes mention of Israel under the cloud, passing through the sea, being baptized into Moses in the cloud and in the sea, and eating divinely provided food and drink. His thrice-repeated ταῦτα ... ἐγενήθησαν ("these things occurred," v. 6), ταῦτα ... συνέβαινεν ("these things happened," v. 11) and [ταῦτα] ... ἐγράφη ("these things were written," v. 11) also support his dependence on the wilderness narrative.

The paraenetic focus of this text is to be noted. Paul references the poor choices made by the exodus-wilderness generation as a warning about continuing involvement in idolatrous practices and sexually immoral associations. His moral exhortation begins at verse 6: "Now these things occurred as examples for us, so that we might not desire evil as they did. Do not become idolaters as some of them did.... We must not indulge in sexual immorality as some of them did" (vv. 6–8). The consequences for Israel were the death of twenty-three thousand in a single day (v. 8), destruction by serpents on another occasion (v. 10), and death at the hands of "the Destroyer" on still another (v. 11). What happened to the exodus-wilderness generation is invoked by Paul because the Israelites, like the Corinthians, had enjoyed unprecedented spiritual privileges and blessings: "In every way you have been enriched in him, in speech and knowledge of every kind ... so that you are not lacking in any spiritual gift (1 Cor 1:5–7).[53] But the receipt of such divine blessings did not assure a

---

"'The Moveable Well' in 1 Cor 10:4: An Extrabiblical Tradition in an Apostolic Text," *BBR* 6 (1996): 23–38.

51. Wayne Meeks argues that 1 Cor 10 is a midrash on Exod 32:6. Verses 1–4 elaborate on "the people sat down to eat and drink"; vv. 6–10 elaborate on "and they rose up to play" ("'And Rose Up to Play': Midrash and Paraenesis in 1 Corinthians 10:1–22," *JSNT* 16 [1982]: 64–78). Cf. E. Earle Ellis, *Paul's Use of the Old Testament* (Grand Rapids: Eerdmans, 1957), 126–35 and 156 n. 36.

52. See Watson, *Paul and the Hermeneutics of Faith*, 354–411.

53. Stanley et al. identify the Corinthian spiritual blessings as the bread and wine of the Eucharist. Just as Israel was nourished by divinely provided manna and water, so

positive end for the Israelites, and neither will the Corinthians' spiritual blessings do so for them.[54]

One might ask what Gentile Corinth has to do with Jewish Jerusalem. Why does Paul even bother to invoke Israelite history? A rationale can be found in Paul's inclusive opening statement, "for our [common] ancestors" (ὅτι οἱ πατέρες ἡμῶν, v. 1). Although "our ancestors" could include only Paul and his Jewish kinsmen, the hortatory subjunctives that follow show Jew–Gentile inclusion: "Let us not engage in sexual immorality (μηδὲ πορνεύωμεν) as some of [our ancestors] did" (vv. 8–11). Paul assumes thereby that the story of Israel is the Corinthians' story as well.[55] The matter-of-fact character of Paul's statements supports Corinthian knowledge of this common heritage and of the biblical narratives as their shared tradition.

The basis for the Corinthians' inclusion is found in Paul's second hortatory subjunctive, "Let us not test Christ as some of them did." There is some textual variation here. Τὸν Χριστόν has the weighty and diverse support of P[46] D F G Byz as well as the Old Latin, Vulgate, Syriac, and Coptic versions, while τὸν κύριον finds support in ℵ B C P and θεὸν in A and 81. Τὸν Χριστόν is to be preferred not simply on the basis of external evidence

---

the Corinthians were nourished by the bread and wine of the Eucharist (*Arguing with Scripture*, 87). Yet this assumes a sacramental understanding of the Lord's Supper that is not explicitly in evidence, and it does not take into account the other Exodus blessings named here: the divine cloud, passage through the sea, and baptism into Moses. Some go even further and argue that Paul is responding to a Corinthian belief that baptism and the Eucharist ensured their salvation. See C. K. Barrett, *A Commentary on The First Epistle to the Corinthians* (2nd ed.; London: Black, 1971; repr., Peabody, Mass.: Hendrickson, 1993), 224; and Gordon Fee, *The First Epistle to the Corinthians* (NICNT; Grand Rapids: Eerdmans, 1987), 443. See also Meeks, who identifies the point of comparison as the Israelites' eating and drinking to Baal and the Corinthians eating and drinking to idols ("And Rose Up to Play," 64–78).

54. Some go further and posit Paul's use of a preexisting midrash on Numbers. There is some justification for this; there are a number of words that only occur here and in Numbers. See Collins, *First Corinthians*, 364.

55. Stanley understands "our ancestors" to be a rhetorical rather than a theological move on Paul's part (*Arguing with Scripture*, 75–76, 86). Paul does not really see himself and his Gentile converts as having a common ancestry; he includes the Corinthians merely as a means to gain a hearing. On the other hand, the idea of Abraham and his descendants as the common ancestors of both Jewish and Greek believers is a core Pauline conviction in Rom 4 and Gal 3. For further discussion, see Hays, *Echoes of Scripture*, 95–96.

but also as the more difficult reading. The difficulty of explaining how the ancient Israelites in the wilderness could have tempted Christ probably prompted some copyists to substitute either the ambiguous κύριον or the unobjectionable θεόν.[56] If τὸν Χριστόν is original, then, as Hays notes, "We must not put Christ to the test, as some of them did" has profound ecclesial significance.[57]

Some have raised doubts about the Corinthians' theological self-understanding, given the opening line, οὐ θέλω γὰρ ὑμᾶς ἀγνοεῖν (v. 1). To be sure, Paul typically uses the epistolary formula to disclose new information.[58] Yet their common ancestry is not what is presented as new. Paul's new information only begins at verse 6, "Now these things occurred as examples for us [ταῦτα δὲ τύποι ἡμῶν], so that we might not desire evil as they did," and again at verse 11, "Now [δὲ] these things happened as an example [τυπικῶς] and were written down for our instruction [ἐγράφη δὲ πρὸς νουθεσίαν ἡμῶν]." This new information elicits the command three verses later, "Therefore, my dear friends, flee from the worship of idols" (v. 14).

Central to understanding Paul's use of the exodus-wilderness narratives are the terms τύποι (v. 6) and τυπικῶς (v. 11). Some take τύποι as a prefigurement of something yet to come—an Old Testament shadow that finds its substance in the New Testament.[59] When the "substance" becomes a reality, the "shadow" no longer has a purpose and fades into the sunset. While this certainly is what Paul says elsewhere about the Mosaic covenant (e.g., Gal 3:19, "until the seed comes," and 3:24, "until Christ"; cf. 2 Cor 3:7–11, 13), this is not what τύποι means here. Israel's golden calf incident is not a foreshadowing of Gentile idolatry and sexual immorality.

Others argue that God's provision of manna, quail, and water is a *type* or foreshadowing of the bread and wine of the Eucharist.[60] Yet no explicit typology is drawn between the two in these verses. Instead, Paul's fourfold

---

56. Bruce Metzger, *Textual Commentary*, 494.
57. Hays, *Echoes of Scripture*, 91–104.
58. See Rom 1:13; 11:25; 1 Cor 12:1; 2 Cor 1:8; and the positive formulation, "I want you to know" in 1 Cor 11:3; Col 2:1.
59. For instance, Andrew Bandstra, "Interpretation in 1 Corinthians 10:1–11," *CTJ* 6 (1971): 6–14.
60. See, for example, Hays, who argues that Israel's story is a prefigurement of the church with its sacraments (*Echoes of Scripture*, 95). See also W. F. Orr and J. A. Walther, *I Corinthians* (AB 32; New York: Doubleday, 1976), 245; Fee, *First Epistle to the Corinthians*, 446–47.

prohibition ("Do not ... let us not ... let us not ... Do not ..."), leading up to the command at v. 14 to "flee idolatry," makes 1 Cor 10 paraenetic in form and function.[61] This accords with the semantic range for τύπος, which includes "the impression made by a blow."[62] What happened to Israel left an ethical impression and provides a set of moral footprints not to be followed. Paul's statement, "it was written down for us," indicates as much. The act of writing assured a story's value as a lesson for subsequent generations. One can, therefore, speak of certain Scripture passages as τύποι texts—texts that leave a "moral impression."[63]

Paul recalls key exodus-wilderness narrative events in 1 Cor 10:1-13. "Our ancestors were all under the cloud, and all passed through the sea and all were baptized into Moses in the cloud and in the sea" (vv. 1-2) is a highly condensed summary of Israel's deliverance from Pharoah's army via passage through the Red Sea and of God's provision as Israel made its way to Mount Sinai (Exod 13:12-22, 14:21-22). "All ate the same spiritual food and all drank the same spiritual drink" (vv. 3-4) recalls how God provided for Israel's physical needs in the wilderness through manna from the sky, quail from the land, and water from a rock (Exod 16:1-36, 17:1-7; Num 20:2-13, 21:16-17).[64] Paul then goes on to state matter-of-factly that the source of Israel's water supply was "the spiritual rock that followed [them] through the wilderness," and that "the rock was Christ" (v. 4).

Did Paul's creative thinking get out of hand and lead him to impulsively fill in the blanks here? After all, Moses strikes a rock at the beginning of their wilderness journey (Exod 17:6), then forty years later he strikes another rock (Num 20:8-11). How did Israel get its water in between? Perhaps Paul surmised that there must have been a rock that traveled with Israel and provided their water in the wilderness—a "traveling rock." Some think that Paul got his inspiration from Deut 32, where God five times is said to be Israel's "Rock."[65] Yet when Paul does cite Scripture, it is the Greek

---

61. For instance, Raymond Collins, *First Corinthians*, 367. See also Conzelmann, *1 Corinthians*, 168.

62. τύπος, LSJ.

63. Conzelman, *1 Corinthians*, 157.

64. Πνευματικὸς can mean that the food and water have typological significance, foreshadowing the bread and blood of the Eucharist. See, for example, Koch, *Die Schrift als Zeuge*, 215-16. But there is no explicit connection drawn between the two, so it seems more likely that they refer to food and water that were supernaturally provided by an act of God.

65. Deut 32:4, "The Rock, his work is perfect"; 32:15, "[Jacob] scoffed at the

and not the Hebrew, since the Septuagint (or a similar Greek text) was the Bible of his Greek-speaking converts. And while the MT has צוּר ("rock"), the LXX has θεός instead: "He [Jacob] scoffed at the Rock (צוּר) of his salvation" (MT Deut 32:15; contrast LXX, ἐγκατέλιπεν θεὸν τὸν ποιήσαντα αὐτόν).

God's provision of water by means of a traveling rock can actually be found in a wide range of Jewish materials, beginning with the Psalter and continuing through rabbinic literature. It is this "other voice" of tradition history—Jewish folklore—that accounts for Paul's mobile rock in 1 Cor 10:4.[66] Tradition history filled in the narrative blanks between the first rock striking and the second one forty years later. The start of this tradition can be found in MT Ps 78:15–16. Verse 15 recalls both rock strikings: "He split rocks [plural] open in the wilderness, and gave them drink abundantly as from the deep." But what was Israel's ongoing source of water? Verse 16 goes on to say, "[The Lord] made streams come out of the rock, and caused waters to flow down like rivers" (cf. LXX Ps 77:16, ἐξήγαγεν ὕδωρ ἐκ πέτρας καὶ κατήγαγεν ὡς ποταμοὺς ὕδατα)—a detail not found in the exodus-wilderness tradition. The Septuagint has a singular rock (unlike the MT), which may well be the basis for further embellishments: Moses "split open a rock in the wilderness" (διέρρηξεν πέτραν ἐν ἐρήμῳ, v. 15).[67] By the Hellenistic period, *a* rock had become *the* rock that quenched Israel's thirst: "On you they called when they were thirsty, and from the rocky cliff [ἐκ πέτρας ἀκροτόμου] water was given them, from hard stone a remedy for their thirst" (Wis 11:4, NJB).[68] The picture is that of a specific rock standing in wait to provide water for Israel, whenever it called upon God.

Rock of his salvation"; 32:18, "You were unmindful of the Rock that bore you"; 32:30, "unless their Rock had sold them"; 32:31, "For their rock is not as our Rock." Cf. Deut 32:13, "he suckled him with honey out of the rock and oil out of the flinty rock"; 32:37, "Where are their gods, the rock in which they took refuge?"

66. Cf. A. McEwen, "Paul's Use of the Old Testament in 1 Corinthians 10:1–4," *Vox Reformato* 47 (1986): 7–8; W. L. Willis, *Idol Meat in Corinth: The Pauline Argument in 1 Corinthians 8 and 10* (SBLDS 68; Chico, Calif.: Scholars Press, 1985), 133–42; Enns, "Moveable Well," 241–44. Commentators who see Paul utilizing a well-established piece of Jewish lore include C. Wolff, *Der erste Brief des Paulus an die Korinther* (THKNT 7/2; Berlin: Evangelische Verlagsanstalt, 1982), 42–43; P. Bachmann, *Der erste Brief an die Korinther* (KNT 7; Leipzig: Deichert, 1921), 330; Barrett, *First Epistle to the Corinthians*, 86–88; and Fee, *First Corinthians*, 448.

67. Enns, "Moveable Well," 30.

68. πέτρας ἀκροτόμου is a steep rock cliff, not "flinty rock," as translated by the RSV and NRSV. See πέτρα (ἀκροτόμου), LSJ.

By Paul's day, the tradition was fully formed. Philo speaks of "Moses who smote the precipitous rock which poured forth water in a stream, so that it not only then furnished a relief from thirst, but also supplied for a long time an abundance of drink for so many myriads of people" (*Mos.* 210–211). Pseudo-Philo goes further: "It [the water] followed them in the wilderness forty years and went up to the mountain with them and went down into the plains" (*L.A.B.* 11.15). The presence of a moving source of water in Pseudo-Philo shows that such a tradition was roughly contemporaneous with Paul.[69]

Further embellishments can be found in post-Pauline rabbinic materials. The rock becomes a well that traveled up hill and down dale with Israel: "The well which was with the Israelites in the wilderness was a rock, the size of a large round vessel, surging and gurgling upward, as from the mouth of its little flask, *rising with them up onto the mountains, and going down with them into the valleys*" (t. Sukkah 3.11 [196]).[70] It is found in the Targumim as well: "The well which the leaders of the people dug ... *went down with them to the valleys*, and from the valleys it went up with them to the high country. And from the high country to the descents of the Moabite fields, at the summit of the height" (Tg. Onq. Num 21:16–20). The change from "rock" to "well" is probably due to the influence of Num 21:16–17, "From there they continued to Beer; that is the well of which the LORD said to Moses, 'Gather the people together, and I will give them water.' Then Israel sang this song: 'Spring up, O well!—Sing to it!'" Pseudo-Philo includes both rock and well traditions: "Now he led his people out into the wilderness; for forty years he rained down for them bread from heaven and brought quail to them from the sea and brought forth *a well of water to follow them*" (*L.A.B.* 10:7; see above).

Why, though, does Paul reference this piece of Jewish lore? What does this "other voice" contribute theologically? The fact that Paul supplies no source or explanation suggests that the Corinthians were aware of this part of the story. Paul may have included it in his preaching and teaching prior to the writing of 1 Corinthians. Is it possible that Paul was not conscious of what he was doing? Some see in Paul's seemingly offhanded reference a use of "interpreted Bible." Paul was not consciously adducing an existing exegetical tradition but, rather, simply telling the biblical story in the form

---

69. A first-century date for Pseudo-Philo is the scholarly consensus.
70. Cf. b. Ta'an. 9a; Num. Rab. 1.2; b. Šabb. 35a.

he had learned it as a child.[71] Yet his interpretive comment, "and Christ was the rock," indicates intentionality on Paul's part. It could well be, as Willis proposes, that the tradition was simply "in the air" during Paul's day.[72] Or it could have been one of the Bible stories that Jewish children learned and that Paul, in turn, passed along to his Gentile converts. The telling of stories was very much a part of Jewish culture. According to m. Pesaḥ. 10.4, the father is to answer his son's four questions at the Passover Seder by starting with "my father was a wandering Aramean" and continuing until the story is complete.[73]

Every story has a point, and the traveling rock story makes an important theological contribution. It attests to God's constant care and provision for his people. God's greatness and faithfulness are highlighted by Paul in the opening verses of chapter 10. No one is excluded from God's care. The word "all" is repeated four times. *All* passed through the Red Sea on dry ground. God didn't lose one Israelite in the process. *All* were led by means of a divine cloud. None fell by the wayside. *All* ate the miraculously provided food. *All* drank the miraculously provided water. Israel's God was so committed to his people that he gave them a watering hole—a rock that followed them throughout the wilderness years. Yet, despite God's show of greatness and faithfulness, Israel turned away and worshipped other so-called gods. "Do not become idolaters as some of them did; as it is written," Paul states, "'The people sat down to eat and drink, and they rose up to play.'" In other words, the tradition of the "traveling rock" highlights the enormity of Israel's sin. The enormity of the offense is underlined by Paul's final statement in 1 Cor 10:4: "This rock was Christ."

---

71. For Paul as the heir of "interpreted Bible," see David Garland, *1 Corinthians* (Baker Exegetical Commentary Series; Grand Rapids: Baker, 1987), 456; Enns, "Moveable Well," 23–38.

72. See Willis, *Idol Meat in Corinth*, 137–38.

73. Cf. the familiar hymn, "Tell Me the Old, Old Story." Martin McNamara thinks in terms of an extrabiblical tradition that Paul takes so much for granted that he has forgotten that his Gentile converts might not be as well informed in such Jewish lore as he himself was (*Palestinian Judaism and the New Testament* [Wilmington, Del.: Glazier, 1983], 241). Enns pushes it one step further and posits that such Jewish lore actually represented Paul's his own understanding of the event ("Movable Well," 33 n. 18).

The Voice of Reread Scripture: 1 Cor 10:4

While Paul's use of traveling-rock folklore is intriguing, his further identification of "the rock that followed [Israel]" with "Christ" is without parallel: ἡ πέτρα δὲ ἦν ὁ Χριστός. In these words, Paul moves from a theology of God's faithfulness (πνευματικῆς ἀκολουθούσης πέτρας) to Christology. While a traveling rock can be deduced from the exodus-wilderness narrative, Christ as that rock cannot. Is this, then, where we see Paul's creative genius at work? Or is there a valid Scriptural basis for Paul's rock Christology?

Allegorical interpretations of the wilderness "rock" and "well" are well-represented among the Jewish writers of Paul's day.[74] Philo's allegorical interpretation of the wilderness rock as the Wisdom of God is perhaps the closest parallel to 1 Cor 10:4: "For the cliff rock is the Wisdom of God, which, being both sublime and the first of things, he quarried out of his own powers, and of it he gives drink to the souls that love God" (*Leg.* 2.86). But the precedent is already there in Wis 11:1-5: "Wisdom prospered their works by the hand of a holy prophet. They journeyed through an uninhabited wilderness.... When they thirsted they called upon you [Wisdom] and water was given them out of flinty rock and slaking of thirst from hard stone."

Some see in Paul's rock Christology an example of Jewish pesher, which was certainly a well-established Jewish exegetical methodology in Paul's day.[75] Inanimate objects in the Scripture are interpreted as animate: for example, "the stone [λίθον] that the builders rejected" (LXX Ps 117:22) is identified in the New Testament as Jesus (Rom 9:32-33, 1 Pet 2:6). Similarly, in Acts 4:11, "'The stone' is this one, Jesus" (οὗτός ἐστιν ὁ λίθος). Paul does this himself. Yahweh in the "old covenant" becomes the Spirit in the new covenant. Moses unveiled his face when he entered the tabernacle to come before the Lord (πρὸς κύριον, 2 Cor 3:16). "Now *this* Lord today," Paul states, "is the Spirit" (ὁ δὲ κύριος τὸ πνεῦμά ἐστιν, v. 17).[76] However, in the case of 1 Cor 10:4, Paul does not say that the wilderness rock back then *is now* to be understood as Christ. He says that the rock back then *was* Christ.

---

74. See, for example, CD 6.4: "The 'well' is the Law [Num 21:16-17]."
75. See Longenecker, *Biblical Exegesis*, 38-45.
76. Linda Belleville, *Reflections of Glory: Paul's Polemical Use of the Moses-Doxa Tradition in 2 Corinthians 3.1-18* (JSNTSup 52; Sheffield: JSOT, 1991), 248-73.

Richard Hays is probably close to the mark in seeing 1 Cor 10:4 as a "re-reading of the Exodus narrative in light of Christology"—Jewish folklore interpreted through the lens of salvation history.[77] It is fairly easy to see how Paul got here. First, there is the Exodus tradition of God caring for Israel in the wilderness through a rock which Moses struck once at the beginning of their journey and then again at the end. Second, there is the Psalter tradition of God providing for Israel's ongoing water needs by means of a river that gushed forth from the rock. Third, there is the logical conclusion that in order for Israel's God to provide a steady water source, the rock must have followed them during their journey. After all, God provided direction for Israel by means of a traveling cloud by day and a traveling pillar of fire by night. Why not a traveling rock? Moreover, if God was a traveling cloud, who was the traveling rock? In such a context, ἡ πέτρα δὲ ἦν ὁ Χριστός would have been a natural christological way to reread Scripture. Such a reading might seem to reflect uncommon logic for moderns, but it would not be so for a Jewish rabbi, who was trained in the rabbinic "pearl-stringing" method of associating words, phrases, and concepts found throughout Scripture.[78]

There is also contextual support for a christological rock. Paul exhorts the Corinthians not to "put Christ to the test, as some of [the Israelites] did, and were destroyed by serpents" (1 Cor 10:9, using the accepted variant).[79] He also warns, "You cannot drink the cup of the Lord and the cup of demons. You cannot partake of the table of the Lord and the table of demons. Or are we provoking the Lord to jealousy? Are we stronger than he?" (v. 22). Theologically, "the cup of blessing that we bless" is "a sharing in the blood of Christ" and "the bread that we break" is "a sharing in the body of Christ" (v. 16).

Christological "rock" interpretations can be found elsewhere in the New Testament. The Fourth Gospel recounts, "On the last day of the festival, the great day, while Jesus was standing there, he cried out, 'Let anyone who is thirsty come to me, and he who believes in me, as the scripture has said, "Out of its [or "his"] belly [ἐκ τῆς κοιλίας αὐτοῦ] shall flow rivers of living water"'" (John 7:38). While this text has its own exegetical challenges, it is clear that the exodus-wilderness narrative is in view. A case has been made by Johannine scholars that Exod 17:6 and Num 20:11 were

---

77. Hays, *First Corinthians*, 151; contrast *Echoes of Scripture*, 95–102.
78. See Longenecker, *Biblical Exegesis*, 114–17.
79. See Metzger, *Textual Commentary*, 494.

among the Scriptures read during the Feast of Tabernacles. The MT of Exod 17:6 has מִמֶּנּוּ ("from within") and the LXX has ἐξ αὐτῆς [τὴν πέτραν], the interior cavity of the rock from which the wilderness water sprung forth. The Johannine ἐκ τῆς κοιλίας αὐτοῦ ῥεύσουσιν ὕδατος ζῶντος can thus be translated as "out of its [the rock's] cavity will flow rivers of running water." It could be that the tradition history reflected in John 7:38 was current in Paul's day. Oscar Cullmann, in fact, proposes this very thing, arguing that Paul and the Fourth Gospel were drawing on the same (or a similar) source.[80]

Conclusions

This study has attempted to demonstrate that Pauline texts typically labeled as the product of an overactive imagination can be accounted for on the basis of "other voices." First, we saw the "other voice" of proverbial wisdom in 2 Cor 6:14 and 1 Cor 9:9. Both Philo and Pseudo-Phocylides show that "do not be unequally yoked" (2 Cor 6:14) was a current aphorism in Paul's day. Confusion regarding Paul's use of the statement, "Do not muzzle an ox when it is treading grain" (1 Cor 9:9) disappears if it is understood not as a command but as a proverbial saying. As a proverb, the point would be straightforward: A laborer in the gospel ministry deserves financial support.

Next, there is the "other voice" of lyric poetry in 2 Cor 4:13. When understood as a commonly sung Hallel psalm, Paul's three-word citation of LXX Psalm 115:1 becomes understandable. As the psalmist recounts how his faith gave him the courage to speak out despite strong opposition, Paul and the community of faith hear "another voice"—the voice of liturgical prayer that captures feelings and emotions common to all human experience.

Then there is the "other voice" of tradition history. Here we find the source of Paul's statement that the Mosaic law was given through angels by the hand of the mediator (Gal 3:19). The "other voice" of Jewish folklore is likewise audible as the wilderness rock becomes a traveling stone that attests to God's constant care and provision for his people (1 Cor 10:4).

Finally, there is the "other voice" of reread Bible. Ἡ πέτρα δὲ ἦν ὁ Χριστός in 1 Cor 10:4 can be seen as a rereading of the exodus-wilderness

---

80. Oscar Cullmann, "πέτρα," TDNT 6:97.

narrative and salvation history through a christological lens. Salvation history by its very nature is personal. Yahweh relates to his people in very tangible ways—a cloud, a voice, a pillar of fire—all visible manifestations of his care-giving nature. Early Christian hymns such as "[Christ] who, though he was in the form of God, did not regard equality with God as something to be exploited, but emptied himself, taking the form of a slave, being born in human likeness" (Phil 2:6) prepare the way for rereading certain exodus-wilderness events in light of a tangible Christology.

Studies of Paul's use of Scripture need to go beyond the standard labels of *peshat* (literal), *pesher* (typology, prefigurement), *midrash* (commentary), and *allegory* (metaphor) to consider the rich tradition history in which he stands and to explore where it surfaces and how it informs (or does not inform) his theology. The all-too-common leap-frog hermeneutical approach that sees Paul engaging only with the text of Scripture overlooks these "other voices" and the way they shaped Paul's theological understanding.

Bibliography

Bachmann, P. *Der erste Brief an die Korinther.* KNT 7. Leipzig: Deichert, 1921.
Bandstra, Andrew. "Interpretation in 1 Corinthians 10:1–11." *Calvin Theological Journal* 6 (1971): 6–14.
Barrett, C. K. *A Commentary on The First Epistle to the Corinthians.* 2d ed. London: Adam & Charles Black, 1971. Repr., Peabody, Mass.: Hendrickson, 1993.
Belleville, Linda L. *Reflections of Glory: Paul's Polemical Use of the Moses-Doxa Tradition in 2 Corinthians 3.1–18.* JSNTSup 52. Sheffield: JSOT Press, 1991.
———. " 'Under Law': Structural Analysis and the Pauline Concept of Law in Galatians 3:21–4:11." *JSNT* 26 (1986): 53–78.
Betz, Hans Dieter. *Galatians: A Commentary on Paul's Letter to the Churches in Galatia.* Hermeneia. Philadelphia: Fortress, 1979.
Bruce, F. F. *The Epistle to the Galatians: A Commentary on the Greek Text.* NIGTC. Grand Rapids: Eerdmans, 1982.
Büchsel, Friedrich. "Εἰδωλολάτρης." *TDNT* 2:379–80.
Collins, Raymond F. *First Corinthians.* SP 7. Collegeville, Minn.: Liturgical Press, 1999.

Conzelmann, Hans. *1 Corinthians: A Commentary on the First Epistle to the Corinthians*. Translated by James W. Leitch. Hermeneia. Philadelphia: Fortress, 1975.

Craigie, Peter. *The Book of Deuteronomy*. 2nd ed. NICOT. Grand Rapids: Eerdmans, 1976.

Cullmann, Oscar. "πέτρα." *TDNT* 6:95–99.

Ellis, E. Earle. *Paul's Use of the Old Testament*. Grand Rapids: Eerdmans, 1957.

Enns, Peter. "'The Moveable Well' in 1 Cor 10:4: An Extrabiblical Tradition in an Apostolic Text." *BBR* 6 (1996): 23–38.

Evans, Craig A. *Mark 8:27–16:20*. WBC 34B. Nashville: Thomas Nelson, 2001.

Fee, Gordon D. *The First Epistle to the Corinthians*. NICNT. Grand Rapids: Eerdmans, 1987.

Fung, Ronald. *The Epistle to the Galatians*. NICNT. Grand Rapids: Eerdmans, 1988.

Garland, David. *1 Corinthians*. Baker Exegetical Commentary Series. Grand Rapids: Baker Academic, 1987.

Hansen, Walter. *Galatians*. InterVarsity Press New Testament Commentary 9. Downers Grove, Ill.: InterVarsity Press, 1994.

Hays, Richard B. *Echoes of Scripture in the Letters of Paul*. New Haven: Yale University Press, 1989.

———. *First Corinthians*. Louisville: Westminster John Knox, 1997.

Josephus. *The Works of Josephus*. Translated by William Whiston. Rev. ed. Peabody, Mass.: Hendrickson, 1987.

Koch, Dietrich-Alex. *Die Schrift als Zeuge des Evangeliums: Untersuchungen zur Verwendung und zum Verständnis der Schrift bei Paulus*. BHT 69. Tübingen: Mohr Siebeck, 1986.

Lisowsky, G. "Dtn. 25:4." Pages 144–52 in *Das ferne und nahe Wort*. Edited by F. Maass. BZAW 105. Berlin: Töpelmann, 1967.

Longenecker, Richard N. *Biblical Exegesis in the Apostolic Period*. Grand Rapids: Eerdmans, 1975.

———. *Galatians*. WBC 41. Dallas: Word Books, 1991.

Marshall, I. Howard. *The Pastoral Epistles*. ICC. Edinburgh: T&T Clark, 1999.

Mayser, Edwin. *Grammatik der Griechischen Papyri aus der Ptolemäerzeit*. 3 vols. Berlin: de Gruyter, 1933–1936.

McEwen, A. "Paul's Use of the Old Testament in 1 Corinthians 10:1–4." *Vox Reformato* 47 (1986): 3–10.

McNamara, Martin. *Palestinian Judaism and the New Testament*. Good News Studies 4. Collegeville, Minn.: Liturgical Press, 1983.
Meeks, Wayne A. "'And Rose Up To Play': Midrash and Paraenesis in 1 Corinthians 10:1–22." *JSNT* 16 (1982): 64–78.
Metzger, Bruce M. *A Textual Commentary on the Greek New Testament*. 2nd ed. Stuttgart: Deutsche Bibelgesellschaft, 1994.
Orr, W. F., and J. A. Walther. *I Corinthians*. AB 32. New York: Doubleday, 1976.
Philo. *The Works of Philo*. Translated by Charles D. Yonge. Rev. ed. Peabody, Mass.: Hendrickson, 1993.
Porter, Stanley E. "Paul and Ancient Letter Writing." Pages 97–124 in *As It Is Written: Studying Paul's Use of Scripture*. Edited by Stanley E. Porter and Christopher D. Stanley. SBLSymS 50. Atlanta: Society of Biblical Literature, 2008.
Preisker, H., and E. Wurthwein. "μισθός." *TDNT* 4:695–728.
Stanley, Christopher D. *Arguing with Scripture: The Rhetoric of Quotations in the Letters of Paul*. New York: T&T Clark, 2004.
———. "Paul's 'Use' of Scripture: Why the Audience Matters." Pages 125–55 in *As It Is Written: Studying Paul's Use of Scripture*. Edited by Stanley E. Porter and Christopher D. Stanley. SBLSymS 50. Atlanta: Society of Biblical Literature, 2008.
Watson, Francis. *Paul and the Hermeneutics of Faith*. New York: T&T Clark, 2004.
Weiss, Johannes. *Der erste Korintherbrief*. KEKNT 5. Göttingen: Vandenhoeck & Ruprecht, 1910.
Wevers, John W. *Notes on the Greek Text of Deuteronomy*. SBLSCS 39. Atlanta: Society of Biblical Literature, 1995.
White, John L. *Light from Ancient Letters*. Philadelphia: Fortress, 1986.
Wierzbicka, Anna. "The Semantics of Direct and Indirect Discourse." *Papers in Linguistics* 7 (1974): 267–307.
Willis, W. L. *Idol Meat in Corinth: The Pauline Argument in 1 Corinthians 8 and 10*. SBLDS 68. Chico, Calif.: Scholars Press, 1985.
Wolff, C. *Der erste Brief des Paulus an die Korinther*. THNT 7/2. Berlin: Evangelische Verlagsanstalt, 1982.
Wright, N. T. *Justification*. Downers Grove, Ill.: InterVarsity Press, 2009.

Beyond Hays's *Echoes of Scripture in the Letters of Paul*: A Proposed Diachronic Intertextuality with Romans 10:16 as a Test Case*

Matthew W. Bates

The vocabulary and cadences of Scripture—particularly of the LXX—are imprinted deeply on Paul's mind, and the great stories of Israel continue to serve for him as a fund of symbols and metaphors that condition his perception of the world, of God's promised deliverance of his people, and of his own identity and calling. His faith, in short, is one whose articulation is inevitably intertextual in character, and Israel's Scripture is the "determinate subtext that plays a constitutive role" in shaping his literary production.[1]

I suspect that one would be hard pressed to find a contemporary Pauline scholar who would fundamentally disagree with the above quotation taken from Hays's *Echoes of Scripture*. While some scholars from past generations could forcefully argue that the Septuagint played little or no role in arranging Paul's mental furniture,[2] recent scholarship is more prone to

---

* For a fuller and more definitive treatment of some of the seminal ideas contained herein, the reader is invited to consult Matthew W. Bates, *The Hermeneutics of the Apostolic Proclamation: The Center of Paul's Method of Scriptural Interpretation* (Waco, Tex.: Baylor University Press, 2012).

1. Richard B. Hays, *Echoes of Scripture in the Letters of Paul* (New Haven: Yale University Press, 1989), 16.

2. See Adolf von Harnack, "The Old Testament in the Pauline Letters and in the Pauline Churches," in *Understanding Paul's Ethics: Twentieth Century Approaches* (ed. Brian S. Rosner; trans. George S. Rosner and Brian S. Rosner; Grand Rapids: Eerdmans, 1995), 27–49; Albert Schweitzer, *The Mysticism of the Apostle Paul* (trans. William Montgomery; New York: Henry Holt, 1931), esp. his remarks on 208; Rudolf Bultmann, "The Significance of the Old Testament for the Christian Faith," in *The Old*

view the Septuagint not as merely responsible for situating the furniture but as the very wood, nails, staples, fabric, and stuffing from which the furniture is constructed in the first place.³ This turning of the scholarly weathervane should not be attributed to fickle breezes. On the contrary, the irresistible blast of a veritable Northeaster of scholarship has caused this shift, giving every appearance of steadily, indeed irreversibly, pushing the arrow of the weathervane in this new direction.⁴ I have no intention of calling into question the centrality of the Septuagint to Paul's thought—in fact, I reaffirm this fact without reservation. What I would like to argue is that Pauline scholarship as a whole, in its nearly single-minded focus on Paul's relationship to the Scriptures of Israel, has neglected vital data that could substantially enrich our understanding of Paul's scriptural exegesis. In fact, this narrow focus on how various New Testament authors use the Septuagint to the exclusion of other crucial data is a problem that transcends Pauline scholarship and is endemic to the discipline of New Testament studies as a whole. By revisiting the theoretical foundations of intertextuality as it was developed in literary studies, a more robust intertextual method can be crafted that is more suitable for biblical scholarship. In short, I shall argue that when trying to understand any given

---

Testament and the Christian Faith: A Theological Discussion (ed. and trans. Bernhard W. Anderson; New York: Harper & Row, 1963), 8–35.

3. The most forceful presentation of this position is Francis Watson, *Paul and the Hermeneutics of Faith* (London: T&T Clark, 2004).

4. Some of the most important full-scale studies affirming the centrality of the Scriptures to Paul's thought include Otto Michel, *Paulus und seine Bibel* (BFCT 2/18; Gütersloh: Bertelsmann, 1929; repr., Darmstadt: Wissenschaftliche Buchgesellschaft, 1972); E. Earle Ellis, *Paul's Use of the Old Testament* (Grand Rapids: Eerdmans, 1957); Richard B. Hays, *The Faith of Jesus Christ: The Narrative Substructure of Galatians 3:1–4:11* (2nd ed.; Grand Rapids: Eerdmans, 2002), 63; Dietrich-Alex Koch, *Die Schrift als Zeuge des Evangeliums: Untersuchungen zur Verwendung und zum Verständnis der Schrift bei Paulus* (BHT 69; Tübingen: Mohr Siebeck, 1986); Hays, *Echoes of Scripture*; Christopher D. Stanley, *Paul and the Language of Scripture: Citation Technique in the Pauline Epistles and Contemporary Literature* (SNTSMS 74; Cambridge: Cambridge University Press, 1992); Daniel Boyarin, *A Radical Jew: Paul and the Politics of Identity* (Berkley: University of California Press, 1994); Florian Wilk, *Die Bedeutung des Jesajabuches für Paulus* (FRLANT 179; Göttingen: Vandenhoeck & Ruprecht, 1998); Christopher D. Stanley, *Arguing with Scripture: The Rhetoric of Quotations in the Letters of Paul* (London: T&T Clark, 2004); J. Ross Wagner, *Heralds of the Good News: Paul and Isaiah "in Concert" in the Letter to the Romans* (NovTSup 101; Leiden: Brill, 2002); Watson, *Paul and the Hermeneutics of Faith*.

moment of scriptural exegesis by a New Testament author such as Paul, it is vital to examine not just the *pre-text* (the Septuagint), but also *co-texts* and *post-texts*. After developing my methodological proposal more fully, I will attempt to illustrate its usefulness by showing an example of how the inclusion of co-texts and post-texts in addition to the Septuagintal pre-text can tip the scales of probability in new and unexpected directions when examining Paul's scriptural exegesis.

Reappraising Intertextuality

Richard Hays deserves the lion's share of the credit for bringing the modern literary study of intertextuality to the attention of New Testament scholarship with his *Echoes of Scripture in the Letters of Paul*. This is not to say that the intertextual model that he employed was without flaws.[5] Hays begins with the simple observation that "certain approaches to intertextuality that have developed within literary criticism prove illuminating when applied to Paul's letters."[6] Hays acknowledges that the concept of intertextuality as "cultural codes" in literary theory is usually traced back to Julia Kristeva (who was herself influenced by Saussure and Bakhtin),[7] but he adopts a different use of the term, focusing on citation and allusion, in order to keep his project concrete.[8] Drawing on John Hollander's *The Figure of Echo*,[9] Hays settles on an aural metaphor to explain the intertextual method that he seeks to employ. Just as an echo distorts the originating sound in order to reproduce it, so also an author who cites or alludes to a source text inevitably alters the meaning of the source text by importing it into a new literary context. In the process, a new trope is gen-

---

5. In biblical scholarship, an important predecessor to Hays's *Echoes of Scripture* is Michael Fishbane, *Biblical Interpretation in Ancient Israel* (Oxford: Oxford University Press, 1985), although Fishbane's intertextual theory, which is built on the interplay of *traditum* with *traditio*, is not as conversant with recent literary approaches.

6. Hays, *Echoes of Scripture*, 15.

7. See Graham Allen, *Intertextuality* (The New Critical Idiom; London: Routledge, 2000), 9–60. For a succinct overview, see Stephen Heath, "Intertextuality," in *A Dictionary of Cultural and Critical Theory* (ed. Michael Payne; Oxford: Blackwell, 1996), 258–59.

8. Hays, *Echoes of Scripture*, 15.

9. John Hollander, *The Figure of Echo: A Mode of Allusion in Milton and After* (Berkeley: University of California Press, 1981). Discussion of Hollander can be found in Hays, *Echoes of Scripture*, 18–21.

erated. Thus the point of intertextual literary criticism is to identify and explain the alterations and the new trope.[10] Hays elaborates this method by explaining how unstated associations bound up with the source text can be tapped by the second text (i.e., the text that cites the source text), allowing these unstated associations to be recovered and reutilized by the second text. Hays (following Hollander) calls the suppression of these unstated aspects of the source text "transumption" and their recovery within the new trope "metalepsis."[11] The important point for Pauline exegesis is that the source text which Paul echoes (the LXX) can have transumed material as part of its baggage that can then be reconstituted by the citation, resulting in a series of correspondences between the two texts which the interpreter can then tease out.

As Hays freely acknowledges, however, his own intertextual method is not in sync with the way modern literary theorists use it.[12] For example, Julia Kristeva, who is generally credited with the introduction of this term to modern literary studies, uses "intertextuality" to refer to the way in which every text is "a mosaic of quotations," by which she means that every text is created by, subsumes, and reacts to other texts.[13] Kristeva explicitly draws on the dialogism of the Russian formalist M. M. Bakhtin, whose dialogism stresses the *relational* function of words—the manner in which they bridge the gap between the speaker and the addressee. As such, the words that a speaker utters are inevitably borrowing from or responding to previous discourse, which is itself inescapably part of a sociohistorical worldview complex. As Bakhtin states, "The utterance is addressed not only to its object [the addressee], but also to others' speech about it."[14] According to Bakhtin, all utterances are double-voiced, responding to the discourse of the cultural milieu that generated them as well as to the addressee. Kristeva extends Bakhtin's notion of double-voiced utterances, seeing not just utterances but *all texts* as exhibiting this dialogism. Every text is created by its surrounding sociohistorical environment and

---

10. Hays, *Echoes of Scripture*, 15.
11. Ibid., 20. "Metalepsis" can be glossed as "participation" (LSJ).
12. Ibid., 15.
13. Julia Kristeva, *Desire in Language: A Semiotic Approach to Literature and Art* (ed. Leon S. Roudiez; trans. Thomas Gora, Alice Jardin, and Leon S. Roudiez; New York: Columbia University Press, 1980), 66.
14. M. M. Bakhtin, *Speech Genres and Other Late Essays* (ed. C. Emerson and M. Holquist; trans. V. W. McGee; Austin: University of Texas Press, 1986), 94.

responds to it, regardless of any explicit purposes that the text might otherwise serve.

As an example, consider a mundane text such as a new phonebook. A phonebook's explicit purpose is to guide the addressee in dialing the telephone. It is obvious that any new phonebook is a response to previous attempts to create a phonebook. A new model responds to the old by (at the very least) updating obsolete information. Yet it is perhaps less obvious that a phonebook is the product of a prior sociohistorical discourse in which the use of telephones for various business and pleasure purposes makes sense in our social world. Hence the phonebook is in a very real way created by the discourse of our social setting, which is reflected in the more prominent display of certain well-to-do business numbers over against the more subdued typesetting of home telephone numbers, as well as a myriad of other features. The phonebook is double-voiced, speaking to the addressee by giving dialing information while also speaking in an indirect way to its social matrix, saying, "You need money and a business address in order to have an *important* phone number."

Perhaps even more crucially, the phonebook, which is itself the product of prior discourse, is an agent of transformation with respect to current and future discourse. Current discourse will never be quite the same once the new phonebook is introduced, and subsequent phonebooks will respond in some way to this new edition. New features in the phonebook are institutionalized, perhaps by the addition of new sections like "state government" or "coupons."[15] For Kristeva and others such as Roland Barthes, the result of this double voice, or *heteroglossia*, is that the "subject" who speaks in any given text is radically destabilized. The result is that "signification" or "meaning" can no longer be equated with authorial intention, since multiple "meanings" or "significations" (polysemy) are invariably produced by the play of intertextual forces.[16]

Hays shows no interest in the sort of intertextuality championed by the founders of modern literary intertextuality, which valorizes dialogism, heteroglossia, and polysemy. I believe that Hays is prudent to steer clear of some of the excesses that have characterized the poststructural context of Kristeva and Barthes, such as the "death of the author," and indeed a number of more recent intertextual theorists concur with Hays's senti-

---

15. The phonebook example does not derive from Kristeva; rather, it is my attempt to ground her leading ideas in a practical example.
16. Allen, *Intertextuality*, 52–56, 66–67.

ment.¹⁷ Literary-critical rumors of the "death of the author" can be met with the same dry wit that was used by Mark Twain—"the report of my death was an exaggeration."¹⁸ The attempt to unshackle authorial intention from textual meaning has proven to be a rather messy divorce, to say the least.¹⁹ Hays also wisely avoids the inordinate disdain among some intertextual theorists for tracing historically oriented genetic "influences" between texts.²⁰ Having passed through the gauntlet of deconstruction and reader-response criticism run wild, scholarship today is in better position to recognize the manner in which meaning is a negotiation between authorial intention, unintended meanings, and reader appropriation. My own feeling is that Hays is well aware of these matters and that he negotiates this balancing act fairly well.²¹ In the revised intertextual model which I will present below, I follow Hays in insisting that properly tracing the genetic influence between texts is not marginal to the assessment of any given moment of Pauline exegesis, but critical.

Nonetheless, reflection on the fundamental disjuncture between Hays's intertextuality, which focuses only on prior-occurring texts, and that of modern literary critics such as Kristeva, which also includes coeval and subsequent texts, results in a fresh method for analyzing Paul's use of the scriptures and the discovery of a relatively untapped data base. The essential point I would like to make is that Hays's introduction of intertextuality into biblical studies generally, and Pauline studies more specifically, was narrowly conceived in terms of method. Others have followed Hays's methodological lead, resulting in the exclusion of important data.

In terms of both method and content, Hays chose to focus single-mindedly on Israel's Scriptures, since they are the "single great textual pre-

---

17. E.g., see the discussion in Susan S. Friedman, "Weavings: Intertextuality and the (Re)Birth of the Author," in *Influence and Intertextuality in Literary History* (ed. Jay Clayton and Eric Rothstein; Madison: University of Wisconsin Press, 1991), 146–56.

18. As cited in Gregg Camfield, ed., *The Oxford Companion to Mark Twain* (New York: Oxford University Press, 2003), 217. Intriguingly, at least according to Camfield, this famous maxim of Twain is often misquoted as "The reports of my death have been greatly exaggerated," which ironically but fittingly exaggerates the original!

19. For a critical analysis, see Ben F. Meyer, *Critical Realism and the New Testament* (Allison Park, Penn.: Pickwick, 1989), 15–55.

20. Cf. the approach taken by Roy Ciampa, "Scriptural Language and Ideas," in *As It Is Written: Studying Paul's Use of Scripture* (ed. Stanley E. Porter and Christopher D. Stanley; SBLSymS 50; Atlanta: Society of Biblical Literature, 2008), 42 n. 3.

21. See Hays, *Echoes of Scripture*, 25–29.

cursor" to Paul's citations.[22] Thus Hays devoted himself almost exclusively to Paul's engagement with the Septuagint. My concern is that in deviating from the theoretical formulations of intertextuality in literary-critical studies, Hays inadvertently placed a methodological limitation upon intertextual approaches among his legions of followers in the biblical studies guild.[23] Indeed, one might go so far as to say that he is a victim of his own tremendous success. *Hays's intertextual model obscures the need to look beyond the source text to coeval and subsequent texts within a fully healthy intertextual model.* This is not to say that Hays's work in *Echoes* is methodologically faulty, nor is it to blame him for not doing the study which he might have done, one that incorporated not only source texts but also coeval and subsequent texts. This would be a petty criticism, since all studies must have reasonable boundaries. My point is simply that Hays's initial methodological description of intertextuality and his subsequent application of this approach was limited and incomplete inasmuch as it did not encourage the exploration of coeval texts and reception history as a tool for illuminating the use of the Septuagint by the New Testament authors. The enormous (and well-deserved) success of Hays's intertextual model has produced a methodological blind spot in contemporary scholarship that results in the exclusion of interesting data. This methodological weakness pervades not only Pauline studies but also the entire scholarly

---

22. Ibid., 15.

23. Hays is undoubtedly guilty of perpetuating semantic confusion by using intertextuality in an idiosyncratic manner. But since Hays is by no means alone in this matter, it is perhaps a bit unfair to single him out—especially since Hays was aware of the deviation he had introduced in the first place and has subsequently signaled a desire to take a broader view of intertextuality (see, e.g., his comments regarding Eco's concept of an intertextual encyclopedia in "Paul and the Hermeneutics of Truth," *Pro Ecclesia* 16 [2007]: 126–40, esp. 131). As Graham Allen notes (*Intertextuality*, 2), "[Intertextuality] is in danger of meaning nothing more than whatever each particular critic wishes it to mean." The fact of the matter is that idiosyncratic definitions and deployments of intertextuality abound. My observation here is anticipated by Hans Hübner, "Intertextualität—Die hermeneutische Strategie des Paulus," *TLZ* 116 (1991): 881–98. Hübner faults Hays for defining "intertextuality" in an idiosyncratic way, for relying on intuition rather than rigorous method, for seeing intertextuality merely in terms of content without considering form, and for failing to identify more distant pre-texts. Apart from his general rebuke to Hays for introducing terminological confusion, I am not fully sympathetic to Hübner's critique, especially in light of the practical impossibility of tracing out an infinite chain of prior occurring texts (on which see also the comments by Roy Ciampa, "Scriptural Language and Ideas," 42).

enterprise that is frequently but anachronistically termed "the study of the use of the Old Testament in the New Testament."

The recent group effort headed up by G. K. Beale and D. A. Carson, *Commentary on the New Testament Use of the Old Testament*, well illustrates this problem. The *Commentary* surveys all occurrences of the use of the Old Testament in the New Testament using an explicitly formulated six-part approach. This approach includes a detailed analysis of New Testament context, Old Testament context, use of citations in Second Temple and early Judaism, the textual foundations of citations, the nature of the connections between texts, and the theological import of references.[24] Unfortunately, the method laid out in the *Commentary* does not even hint at two other crucially important questions: (1) how was each New Testament text that cites the Old Testament *subsequently* understood in the early church? and (2) how was that Old Testament quotation received in early Christianity *apart from* its instantiation in the New Testament text at issue?[25] Following the recent corrective trend emphasizing the Jewish matrix in which the New Testament was birthed,[26] coeval and subsequent interpretations of the Old Testament text in Judaism are helpfully explored, but early Christian sources, especially those beyond the horizons of the New Testament, are systematically neglected.[27] This methodological over-

---

24. G. K. Beale and D. A. Carson, eds., *Commentary on the New Testament Use of the Old Testament* (Baker: Grand Rapids, 2007), xxiii–xxvi.

25. Sometimes this second question is tacitly asked when the commentator looks at how the Old Testament text was used elsewhere in the New Testament, but the arbitrary exclusion of early Christian material which falls outside of the New Testament shows that this is not a methodological priority.

26. It should be stressed that this corrective trend emphasizing the Jewish origins of Christianity is necessary, commendable, and praiseworthy. For an example of this trend in the study of Paul's interpretation of the Jewish scriptures, see Watson, *Paul and the Hermeneutics of Faith*, 1. Watson seeks to foreground the fact that "Paul was a Jew" to such a high degree that this bald assertion is the opening sentence of his book on Pauline hermeneutics. In fact, the entirety of Watson's *Paul and the Hermeneutics of Faith* is outstanding among its peers in its intertextual awareness of Jewish co-texts with respect to Paul's *texts*. Nonetheless, Watson does not avail himself (except in rare cases) of the more intertextually prominent early Christian post-texts and co-texts. For like-minded emphases on the Jewish matrix, see Boyarin, *A Radical Jew*, 1–4; Stephen DiMattei, "Biblical Narratives," in Porter and Stanley, *As It Is Written*, 59–93, esp. 75 and 93; Stanley, *Arguing with Scripture*, 1; Richard N. Longenecker, *Biblical Exegesis in the Apostolic Period* (2nd ed.; Grand Rapids: Eerdmans, 1999), 88–116.

27. Some of the individual commentators do consult coeval and subsequent

sight is not unique to the Beale and Carson volume; it is endemic to the entire cottage industry that has grown up around "the use of the Old Testament in the New Testament."[28] It is this widespread neglect of the early Christian sources as an essential historical-critical and literary matrix for understanding Paul that I believe is in need of correction.[29]

A Proposed Model: Diachronic Intertextuality

The model that I propose can be termed *diachronic intertextuality*. Diachronic intertextuality seeks to recapture Kristeva's fundamental insight that a text is informed by all of the sociohistorical discourse that precedes, surrounds, and follows it, while simultaneously dispensing with Kristeva's problematic disregard for the role of genetic influence between texts in providing meaning.

Within this diachronic intertextual model, I offer some proposed technical definitions to facilitate ongoing discussion with respect to the New Testament in general and Paul in particular.

(1) A *text* shall be defined as any specific instance in which a New Testament author such as Paul directly cites the Scriptures.[30] A *text* is the New Testament author's citation of the scriptures, not the *Vorlage* itself (e.g., Paul's citation of Hab 2:4b LXX in Rom 1:17 is a *text*).

Christian interpretations on an ad hoc basis. My point is simply that on the level of basic *method*, this consultation has been deemed extraneous by the editors.

28. As one example among many, consider the method utilized in Steve Moyise, *The Old Testament in the New Testament: An Introduction* (London: Continuum, 2001).

29. I stress the neglect of Christian sources not because Jewish ones are less valuable but because intertextually informed biblical scholarship is not, generally speaking, neglecting the latter.

30. Of course, this delimitation prompts a further question: what counts as a citation? This has been a surprisingly difficult question to answer. I have no interest in advancing my own theory in this regard but rather refer the interested reader to the discussion of this matter as it pertains to Paul in Koch, *Schrift als Zeuge*, 11–24; and Stanley, *Paul and the Language of Scripture*, 33–37. For a more general discussion, see Stanley E. Porter, "The Use of the Old Testament in the New Testament: A Brief Comment on Method and Terminology," in *Early Christian Interpretation of the Scriptures of Israel: Investigations and Proposals* (ed. C. A. Evans and J. A. Sanders; JSNTSup 148; Sheffield: Sheffield Academic Press, 1997), 79–96; and idem, "Further Comments on the Use of the Old Testament in the New Testament," in *The Intertextuality of the Epistles: Explorations of Theory and Practice* (ed. Thomas L. Brodie, Dennis R. MacDonald, and Stanley E. Porter; NTM 16; Sheffield: Sheffield Phoenix, 2007), 98–110.

(2) An *antecedent text* is any specific instantiation of sociohistorical discourse which occurred in the past before the particular New Testament author penned the quotation. This is not to say, of course, that every discourse which occurred prior to the creation of a *text* was equally prominent or present to the New Testament author.[31]

(3) A *pre-text* shall be a specific textual source that the New Testament author utilized (e.g., Hab 2:4b LXX).

(4) A *vehicle for the pre-text* is an interpretative tradition that indirectly mediated the scriptures to the New Testament author (e.g., any pre-Pauline messianic tradition associated with Hab 2:4b that might have affected Paul's exegesis).[32]

(5) A *relevant coeval text* shall be defined as any work contemporaneous with the *text* which shows awareness of the *pre-text* but not the *text*.

(6) A *co-text* is a specific subset of coeval texts: a direct citation by a different early Jewish or Christian author of the same *pre-text* that the *text* cites, independently of the *text* (e.g., Heb 10:38a citing Hab 2:4b independently of Rom 1:17 or Gal 3:11).[33]

(7) A *subsequent text* will be defined as any sociohistorical discourse that emerges in the wake of the *text*.

(8) A *post-text* is a subset of *subsequent texts*: a subsequent direct citation of the *text* or a direct citation of the *pre-text* as otherwise mediated through the *text* (e.g., Irenaeus, *Epid.* 35, citing Hab 2:4b via Rom 1:17).

(9) Finally, *inter-text* will be a catchall term for any *relevant coeval text* or *subsequent text* that is not specifically a *co-text* or *post-text* but nonetheless has special relevance to a *text* because it uses a closely related *pre-text* or a pertinent passage in the near context of the *pre-text* (e.g., Heb 10:37 and 10:38b citing Hab 2:3b–2:4a would be categorized as an *inter-text*

---

31. See Roy E. Ciampa, "Scriptural Language and Ideas," 42 n. 3.

32. Hays is criticized for neglecting this dimension by Craig A. Evans, "Listening for Echoes of Interpreted Scripture," in *Paul and the Scriptures of Israel* (ed. Craig A. Evans and James A. Sanders; JSNTSup 83; Sheffield: JSOT Press, 1993), 47–51, and Christopher D. Stanley, "'The Redeemer Will Come ἐκ Σιών': Romans 11:26–27 Revisited," in Evans and Sanders, *Paul and the Scriptures of Israel*, 120.

33. Of course, it is possible that Hab 2:4b in Hebrews is actually dependent on Paul, i.e., it is not absolutely certain that Heb 10:38a is really a co-text and not a post-text. Most scholars agree, however, that this is quite unlikely, since the citation in Hebrews is much longer, has a slightly different textual form (Hebrews includes μου, which Paul omits), is not rhetorically foregrounded in a comparable fashion, and lacks a contrast with the performance of the law.

because this material is a *relevant coeval text* but not specifically a *co-text*, since only Heb 10:38a overlaps with Paul's citation of Hab 2:4b).

My methodological rationale can be stated succinctly in light of this new vocabulary: if a particular passage in the New Testament that utilizes the Jewish Scriptures is dubbed a "text," then why has there been an almost exclusive focus among scholars on Jewish pre-texts, vehicles for the pre-texts, co-texts, and relevant coeval texts at the expense of the more inter-textually proximate Christian co-texts, post-texts, and inter-texts?[34] For example, certain early Christian authors, such as Justin Martyr and Irenaeus, have read Paul and show evidence of having borrowed his specific scriptural arguments (post-texts). When they depend on a Pauline scriptural argument, they are in fact providing valuable insight into how they understood that particular example of Pauline exegesis.[35] Of course, when such authors make use of a Pauline scriptural argument, they inevitably transform it in some way due to their differing sociohistorical locations. As a result, it is not always a simple matter to unravel how they understood

---

34. In using the labels "Jewish," "Christian," and the like, I do not mean to suggest that there was no fluidity between Judaism and emerging Christianity, nor that the specific nomenclature that delineated and reinforced the boundary markers between these two groups was already in full bloom—points stressed by a number of recent studies, e.g., Daniel Boyarin, *Border Lines: The Partition of Judeo-Christianity* (Philadelphia: University of Pennsylvania Press, 2004); Pamela Eisenbaum, *Paul Was Not a Christian: The Original Message of a Misunderstood Apostle* (New York: HarperCollins, 2009). Regardless of the fluidity, however, one sees already in the earliest New Testament literature, beginning with Paul, a distinction in some basic worldview constituents between the two groups, such as symbol, story, praxis, and the answers to certain key questions, as has been demonstrated by N. T. Wright, *The New Testament and the People of God* (Minneapolis: Fortress, 1992; see esp. his summary on 444–64). Although the terms "Christian" and "non-Christian" are anachronistic for Paul's situation, there is no widely accepted nonanachronistic alternative system of nomenclature that can be employed. Thus, these labels are to be understood as a convenient and imperfect shorthand pointing to individuals and social groups that were offering some divergent answers to basic worldview questions, while also acknowledging that the boundaries between these groups was sometimes porous.

35. The most careful examination of the reception of Paul's scriptural exegesis in the early fathers is actually found not in the *Wirkungsgeschichte* genre but in source-critical studies such as Robert A. Kraft, "The Epistle of Barnabas, Its Quotations and Their Sources" (Ph.D. diss., Harvard, 1961); Donald A. Hagner, *The Use of the Old and New Testaments in Clement of Rome* (NovTSup 34; Leiden: Brill, 1973); Oskar Skarsaune, *The Proof from Prophecy: A Study in Justin Martyr's Proof Text Tradition: Text-Type, Provenance, Theological Profile* (NovTSup 56; Leiden: Brill, 1987).

Paul. Still, they supply crucial data regarding how they understood Paul, data that must be taken seriously due to their linguistic, cultural, intertextual, and hermeneutical proximity to Paul. In a like manner co-texts can illuminate a text, even though they are less intertextually proximate than post-texts.

Although it is helpful to have all of these terms at our disposal for heuristic purposes in articulating the model, in actual practice the example which follows will primarily examine how a certain text in the Pauline corpus can be better understood when a more robust diachronic intertextuality replaces the standard intertextual model. The specific text I would like to examine is Rom 10:16, citing Isa 53:1. I would like to show that when early Christian co-texts, post-texts, and inter-texts are employed as part of a methodological strategy, surprising dimensions of meaning that have not been previously observed are unveiled.

Deploying Diachronic Intertextuality: Rom 10:16 as a Test Case

In the midst of his protracted defense of God's fidelity to Israel as part of his covenant promises, Paul speaks about how the "utterance of faith" (ὁ ῥῆμα τῆς πίστεως, Rom 10:8), that is, the gospel message of Christ's lordship (Rom 10:9), can in fact be brought near (Rom 10:14–18):

> Therefore, how shall they call upon whom they have not believed? And how shall they believe upon him of whom they have not heard? And how shall they hear apart from preaching? And how will they preach unless they are sent? As it is written, "How beautiful are the feet of those who proclaim glad tidings" [Isa 52:7]. But not all have obeyed the gospel. For Isaiah says, "O Lord, who has believed our audible message?" [Isa 53:1a] Consequently, faith comes from the audible message, and the audible message through the spoken word about Christ. But surely they have not "not heard," have they? They certainly have heard, for "their voice has gone out to all the earth, their words to the boundaries of the known world [Ps 18:5 LXX]."[36]

---

36. Πῶς οὖν ἐπικαλέσωνται εἰς ὃν οὐκ ἐπίστευσαν; πῶς δὲ πιστεύσωσιν οὗ οὐκ ἤκουσαν; πῶς δὲ ἀκούσωσιν χωρὶς κηρύσσοντος; πῶς δὲ κηρύξωσιν ἐὰν μὴ ἀποσταλῶσιν; καθὼς γέγραπται· ὡς ὡραῖοι οἱ πόδες τῶν εὐαγγελιζομένων [τὰ] ἀγαθά. Ἀλλ᾽ οὐ πάντες ὑπήκουσαν τῷ εὐαγγελίῳ. Ἡσαΐας γὰρ λέγει· κύριε, τίς ἐπίστευσεν τῇ ἀκοῇ ἡμῶν; ἄρα ἡ πίστις ἐξ ἀκοῆς, ἡ δὲ ἀκοὴ διὰ ῥήματος Χριστοῦ. ἀλλὰ λέγω, μὴ οὐκ ἤκουσαν; μενοῦνγε·

On the basis of contextual considerations and the diachronic intertextual model proposed above, I shall argue that Paul did *not* regard Isaiah as the ultimate speaker of Isa 53:1 ("O Lord, who has believed *our* audible message"), the citation which appears in the middle of the chain in Rom 10:16. Rather, Paul has made a surprising interpretative move: instead of taking Isaiah as speaking *qua* Isaiah alone[37] or construing Isaiah and Paul as joining together in concert[38] or reading the text as the words of confessing Israel,[39] Paul understands Isaiah to be speaking *in the character of the apostles of Christ* in Rom 10:16.[40] Such an identification of the speaker has not been posited by any commentators of whom I am aware. The exegetical technique employed by Paul here, which involves assigning dramatic characters (πρόσωπα) to explain a scriptural text, was widely practiced in antiquity, though it has not hitherto come to the general attention of biblical scholarship. I have discussed this passage and the interpretative technique employed in it—best termed "prosopological exegesis"—in detail elsewhere, both on the theoretical level as practiced in ancient Jewish, pagan,

---

εἰς πᾶσαν τὴν γῆν ἐξῆλθεν ὁ φθόγγος αὐτῶν καὶ εἰς τὰ πέρατα τῆς οἰκουμένης τὰ ῥήματα αὐτῶν. See note 42 below regarding the complex text-critical issues pertaining to 10:15.

37. The precise identity of the "our" (ἡμῶν) in the citation is not often discussed in the secondary literature, presumably because Isaiah alone is assumed to be the speaker for Paul by most commentators. As a result, there is little secondary literature to engage on this point. No discussion can be found in C. K. Barrett, *A Commentary on the Epistle to the Romans* (BNTC; New York: Harper & Row, 1957), 205; C. E. B. Cranfield, *A Critical and Exegetical Commentary on The Epistle of Paul to the Romans* (2 vols.; ICC; Edinburgh: T&T Clark, 1975–1979), 2:535–36; Ulrich Wilckens, *Der Brief an die Römer* (3 vols.; EKKNT; Neukirchen-Vluyn: Neukirchener, 1978–1982), 2:229; Ernst Käsemann, *Commentary on Romans* (trans. Geoffrey W. Bromiley; Grand Rapids: Eerdmans, 1980), 294–95; or Joseph A. Fitzmyer, *Romans: A New Translation with Introduction and Commentary* (AB 33; New York: Doubleday, 1993), 598.

38. Wagner, *Heralds of the Good News*, 179, thinks that Paul sees Isaiah as the speaker, but that Paul deliberately joins Isaiah as a cospeaker of sorts (see further below). Robert Jewett, *Romans: A Commentary* (Hermeneia; Minneapolis: Fortress, 2007), 641, follows Wagner's conclusions.

39. The safest supposition on the basis of Isa 53:1 itself (in the MT) for the identity of the "we" might be that the "you" addressed in the oracle is now responding to God. Accordingly, modern commentators generally identify the "our" as confessing Israel throughout this oracle—so Brevard S. Childs, *Isaiah* (OTL; Louisville: Westminster John Knox, 2001), 413.

40. Direct address is signaled in the LXX by the vocative form κύριε rather than the nominative κύριος. In this regard, the LXX is a plus over against the MT.

and Christian sources and also for Paul more specifically.[41] Here I offer a brief summary for the reader who wishes to see an example of prosopological exegesis before becoming fully acquainted with the method and terminology and how it relates to the proposed diachronic intertextual model. First, however, a few words are necessary about the context of Rom 10:16, since Paul's interpretation of Isa 52:7 in Rom 10:15 lends vital support to my thesis that in Rom 10:16 Paul views Isa 53:1 as having been spoken from the πρόσωπα *of the apostles of Christ*.

Contextual Considerations: Isa 52:7 in Rom 10:15

The citation of Isa 52:7 in Rom 10:15 ("How beautiful are the feet of those who proclaim glad tidings") immediately prior to the citation of Isa 53:1a in Rom 10:16 lends plausibility to the notion that Paul has assigned the apostles as the collective dramatic character who is the ultimate speaker of Isa 53:1a. For in his drastically modified citation of Isa 52:7 LXX in Rom 10:15,[42] Paul has read himself and the Christian mission into the Isaianic discourse. For example, Paul has modified the singular "herald" to the plural "heralds," seemingly in order to include himself and other ἀπόστολοι within the purview of the Isaianic citation. Moreover, Koch spots a second

---

41. See Bates, *The Hermeneutics of the Apostolic Proclamation*. Chapter 4 contains a general discussion of prosopological exegesis as defined and practiced in antiquity. Chapter 5 examines numerous instances (including Rom 10:16) in which Paul uses prosopological exegesis to interpret the Jewish Scriptures (Septuagint).

42. Paul's text usually approximates to our modern critical LXX, so it is surprising to see here the degree to which Paul deviates from it. In fact, the *Vorlage* of his text would appear to be closer to our modern MT. I count seven ways in which Paul deviates from the critical LXX edition of Ziegler, relying on my previous analysis in Matthew W. Bates, "Beyond *Stichwort*: A Narrative Approach to Isa 52,7 in Romans 10,15 and 11Q Melchizedek (11Q13)," *RB* 116 (2009): 408–9. (1) Isa 52:7a is regarded as an independent clause as in the MT. (2) ὡραῖοι ("lovely") is used in place of ὥρα ("season") as in the MT; (3) ἐπὶ τῶν ὀρέων ("upon the mountains") is omitted, contrary to the MT; (4) "heralds" appears rather than "herald," against the MT; (5) ὡς is omitted before "feet," as in the MT; (6) the definite article is lacking before "feet," which is ambiguous in the MT; (7) εὐαγγελιζομένου ἀκοὴν εἰρήνης ("of one proclaiming an audible message of peace") is lacking, contrary to the MT and many important LXX manuscripts, which instead read εὐαγγελιζομένου εἰρήνην (e.g., ℵ² D F G Ψ and Iren.—see below on Irenaeus). For additional discussion, see Stanley, *Paul and the Language of Scripture*, 134–41. Stanley notes (135) Paul's proximity to the so-called "Lucianic" recension of the LXX here.

deliberate change. Paul's omission of ἐπὶ τῶν ὀρέων ("on the mountains") seems to be an attempt to remove reference to the mountains surrounding Jerusalem and thus to universalize the text toward Gentile inclusion.[43] In effect, Paul has identified himself and his coworkers as "those who bring glad tidings" in Isa 52:7 and has deliberately universalized the location in which this message is being heard in light of the Gentile mission.

This interpretation, namely, that Paul has identified the apostles (himself included) as the subject of the action mentioned in Isa 52:7, is reinforced by an early Christian post-text to Isa 52:7 found in Irenaeus's *Adversus haereses*. Irenaeus polemicizes against the Marcionite elevation of Paul as the teacher of truth par excellence, asserting that Paul himself acknowledges that other apostles were equally involved in the promulgation of the early Christian kerygma (*Haer.* 3.13.1).

> For our Lord never came to save Paul alone, nor is God so limited in means, that he should have only one apostle who knew the dispensation of his Son. And again, when Paul says, "How beautiful are the feet of those bringing glad tidings of good things, and preaching the gospel of peace," he shows clearly that it was not merely one, but there were many who used to preach the truth.[44]

---

43. Koch, *Schrift als Zeuge*, 122. Koch is followed in this observation by Stanley, *Paul and the Language of Scripture*, 137; Wagner, *Heralds of the Good News*, 173; and Bates, "Beyond *Stichwort*," 409. Stanley notes that the omission of ἐπὶ τῶν ὀρέων is supported by only one extant and relatively minor LXX manuscript—MS 88—lending plausibility to an intentional Pauline modification. I do not, however, side with Wagner in seeing the omission of "of one proclaiming an audible message of peace" as a deliberate assimilation to the "word of Christ" in Rom 10:16–17.

44. Text (Irenaeus, *Haer.* 3.13.1): "Neque enim Paulum solum uenit saluare Dominus noster; nec sic pauper Deus ut unum solum haberet apostolum qui dispositionem Filii sui cognosceret. Et Paulus autem dicens: *Quam speciosi pedes euangelizantium bona, euangelizantium pacem*, manifestum fecit quoniam non unus, sed plures erant qui ueritatem euangelizabant" (Rousseau and Doutreleau, SC 211; trans. ANF [slightly modified]). Rousseau and Doutreleau reconstruct Irenaeus's text of Paul's citation of Isa 52:7 to read ὡς ὡραῖοι οἱ πόδες τῶν εὐαγγελιζομένων ἀγαθά, τῶν εὐαγγελιζομένων εἰρήνην ("How lovely are the feet of those proclaiming glad tidings, of those proclaiming peace"). Thus Irenaeus's original Greek text of Rom 10:15, as well as it can be reconstructed, follows Paul's probable original text in the main, but adds a clause (τῶν εὐαγγελιζομένων εἰρήνην) that is found in many other manuscripts of Romans but is probably not original to Paul (perhaps omitted due to haplography in Paul's *Vorlage*, as Koch suggests). The additional clause is present in most LXX manuscripts, which suggests (among other possibilities) that Irenaeus was citing Paul

In this manner it becomes clear that Irenaeus has understood Paul's citation of Isa 52:7 as a deliberate attempt by Paul to include himself and his fellow apostles under the prophetic auspices of the Isaianic text.[45] Thus when we come to Paul's citation of Isa 53:1a LXX in Rom 10:16 ("O Lord, who has believed our audible message"), we already have plausible grounds in the preceding citation for suspecting that Paul has identified himself and his fellow apostles as the referents implied in the "our" of the quotation.[46] Though the prophet Isaiah is nominally speaking, for Paul the characters who are really voicing the words are the apostles themselves. In other words, Paul is practicing prosopological exegesis. Further evidence can be elicited by examining Isa 53:1 by way of the diachronic intertextual model outlined above.

Isa 53:1a in Light of Early Christian Sources

The supposition that the apostles are speaking in Rom 10:16 is elevated from merely plausible to probable in light of certain post-texts—namely, the prosopological interpretation of Isa 53:1 by Justin Martyr, which is seconded by Origen. In addition to the explicit prosopological exegesis of Isa 53:1 by Justin, the text is also cited by Clement of Rome and the Gospel of John, but these latter quotations as co-texts are not as decisive in fixing the identity of the speaker that Paul has assigned to Isa 53:1a in Rom 10:16.

A reading of Isa 53:1 that identifies the apostles as the collective speaker akin to what has been suggested for Paul in Rom 10:16 is clearly evidenced in Justin Martyr, *Dial.* 42.2:

---

via Isaiah, or that the scribal corruption of Rom 10:15 reflected in Irenaeus's exemplar had already occurred before Irenaeus wrote, or that the extant manuscript tradition for Irenaeus represents an assimilation to the LXX even though it originally stood closer to Paul's text, or possibly that Irenaeus might indeed accurately represent Paul's original, even though the evidence in favor of this is less than probable. One might also posit that the "corrected" text of Paul evidenced in Irenaeus followed Symmachus and Theodotion in reducing ἀκοὴν εἰρήνης to εἰρήνην, perhaps under the influence of Nah 1:15 LXX (2:1 MT). See Koch, *Schrift als Zeuge*, 81–82; and Stanley, *Paul and the Language of Scripture*, 138–39, for judicious discussions of Paul's text with respect to the complex Septuagintal literary remains.

45. Cf. Irenaeus, *Epid.* 86, which is discussed further below.

46. Paul's citation of Isa 53:1a shows no deviation from the almost completely uniform LXX tradition regarding Isa 53:1a; cf. Stanley, *Paul and the Language of Scripture*, 141.

And Isaiah, while speaking as if from the person of the apostles [ὡς ἀπὸ προσώπου τῶν ἀποστόλων], has the apostles saying that certain men did not believe their audible message, but only [believed] by means of the display of power of the one having sent them. Therefore he [Isaiah] speaks thus: "O Lord, who has believed our audible message? And to whom has the arm of the Lord been revealed? And we proclaimed before him as if a child, as if a root in thirsty ground" [Isa 53:1–2], and the rest of the prophecy as it has already been articulated above.[47]

Thus we see that Justin, using the introductory formula ὡς ἀπὸ προσώπου (a common way of marking prosopological exegesis), explicitly identifies the apostles as the ultimate speakers of Isa 53:1, the ones who stand behind the prophetically mediated word.[48] Justin goes on to identify several shifts in speaker and addressee in Isa 53 while, of course, identifying Christ himself as the suffering subject in Isa 53. Nowhere else in Justin's corpus is there an explicit identification of the apostles as the speakers of Isa 53:1, but Justin's other references to Isa 53:1 either lean heavily in this direction (*1 Apol.* 50.5) or are otherwise amenable to this interpretation (*Dial.* 13.3, 114.2, 118.4).

It is striking that Origen makes this same assessment, determining that the apostles are the true speakers of the oracle.

But Isaiah seems to prophesy this under the *persona* of the Apostles, to whom the task of preaching had been entrusted. And when they saw how "few" believers there would be, especially from the people of Israel, they say to the Lord, "Lord who has believed our message?" just as that also is said under their *persona*, "We have announced as a child before him, as a root in the thirsty ground."[49]

---

47. Καὶ ὁ Ἡσαΐας, ὡς ἀπὸ προσώπου τῶν ἀποστόλων <λέγων>, λεγόντων τῷ Χριστῷ ὅτι οὐχὶ τῇ ἀκοῇ αὐτῶν πιστεύουσιν <ἄνθρωποι,> ἀλλὰ τῇ αὐτοῦ τοῦ πέμψαντος αὐτοὺς δυνάμει· διὸ λέγει οὕτως· Κύριε, τίς ἐπίστευσε τῇ ἀκοῇ ἡμῶν; Καὶ ὁ βραχίων κυρίου τίνι ἀπεκαλύφθη; Ἀνηγγείλαμεν ἐνώπιον αὐτοῦ ὡς παιδίον, ὡς ῥίζα ἐν γῇ διψώσῃ, καὶ τὰ ἑξῆς τῆς προφητείας προλελεγμένα (cf. *Dial.* 13.2–9, citing Isa 52:10–54:6, and *Dial.* 114.2).

48. See Bates, *The Hermeneutics of the Apostolic Proclamation*, ch. 4, on signals and criteria for detecting prosopological exegesis. Hanson, *Jesus Christ and the Old Testament*, 41, has totally misconstrued the evidence—as the subsequent discussion will show—when he claims that "Justin interprets this sentence [Isa 53:1] as uttered by the Son to the Father."

49. *Comm. Rom.* 8.6.2; trans. Thomas P. Scheck, FC 103.

Thus we find corroborating evidence from the early church that suggests that Paul regarded the apostles as the collective speaker of the oracle uttered by Isaiah (who is thus seen as mediating the apostolic speech) in Isa 53:1a.

There is a further connection between Justin, Irenaeus, and Paul that lends additional credibility to the notion that the apostles are the speakers of Isa 53:1 in Rom 10:16. Paul follows up his exegesis of Isa 53:1a ("O Lord, who has believed *our* audible message") with a citation of Ps 18:5 LXX, which serves as a confirmation that the "audible message" preached by the apostles did in fact issue forth to its intended audience: "their voice has gone out to all the earth, their words to the boundaries of the known world" (Rom 10:18).[50] Justin, instead of following up his citation of Isa 53:1 with that of Ps 18:5 as in Romans, *prefaces* Isa 53:1 with a citation of Ps 18:5, claiming that the sound of the apostles' voices had rung forth throughout the earth (*Dial.* 42.1; cf. *1 Apol.* 40.1-4). In fact, according to Justin, the high priest wore twelve bells on his robe to symbolize the twelve apostles and their ringing voices (*Dial.* 42.1; cf. Tertullian, *Marc.* 4.13.3-4). Strikingly, Irenaeus makes a similar move in *Epid.* 86, where he interprets Isa 52:7 (cf. Rom 10:15) and Ps 18:5 (cf. Rom 10:18) in light of the worldwide mission of the apostles (cf. *Epid.* 68 on Isa 52:13-53:5, and *Epid.* 21 on Ps 18:5).

The collocation of the same basic texts by Justin (*Dial.* 42.1-2), Irenaeus (*Epid.* 86), and Paul (Rom 10:14-18) is probably not coincidental. Oskar Skarsaune believes, correctly in my opinion, that Justin is directly dependent on Romans 10:16 for Isa 53:1a in *Dial.* 114.2, making this a highly proximate post-text (a direct interpretation). Moreover, Justin also depends on Paul as his ultimate source in *Dial.* 42.2 and 118.4, though he has already looked up the pre-text in a full Isaiah scroll in order to expand the citation (making these indirectly mediated post-texts),[51] a practice characteristic of Justin in his use of other sources in the *Dialogue*. Meanwhile, Rolf Noormann declares that the influence of Paul on Irenaeus *Epid.* 86 is certain, though he leaves open the possibility

---

50. Paul's citation of Ps 18:5 LXX shows no deviation from the primary LXX manuscript traditions, which are unified here.

51. Oskar Skarsaune, *The Proof from Prophecy*, 116. As evidence that Justin had access to the full text surrounding Isa 53:1 in addition to whatever extracts were at his disposal, consider the lengthy citation of Isa 52:10-54:6 in *Dial.* 13.2-9.

that Paul was mediated to Irenaeus via Justin or a *testimonia* collection.[52] Since Justin and Irenaeus received their respective scriptural exegeses of these passages from Paul, they are likewise the earliest interpreters of Paul's exegesis of Isa 53:1a in Rom 10:16. As highly intertextually proximate post-texts, the exegesis which is displayed explicitly in Justin and seemingly assumed by Irenaeus weighs strongly in favor of Paul's identification of the apostles as the ultimate collective speaker of Isa 53:1a in Rom 10:16.

Clement of Rome (1 Clem. 16.3) also cites Isa 53:1. In context, Clement's quotation of Isa 53:1–12 is an exhortation to leaders of the flock to imitate Christ's humility (1 Clem. 16.1–14). It is unlikely that Clement depends in any way on Paul for his citation since it is so much longer (twelve verses of the LXX) than what we see in Rom 10:16 (half a verse). Furthermore, there is nothing in the context that would indicate that Clement is making use of Romans, so the citation is a somewhat less intertextually proximate co-text rather than a post-text.[53] Since Clement does not provide a detailed exegesis of Isa 53:1, we are not able to determine whether Clement makes the same identification as was explicitly made by Justin.

The quotation of Isa 53:1 in John 12:37–41 has been reserved for last. It neither decisively supports nor undermines the possibility that the apostles were understood to be the collective speaker of Isa 53:1 in Rom 10:16, but its mention of the "arm of the Lord" is suggestive.

> Although Jesus had performed so many signs in their presence, they still were not believing in him, in order that the word of Isaiah the prophet

---

52. Rolf Noormann, *Irenäus als Paulusinterpret: Zur Rezeption und Wirkung der paulinischen und deuteropaulinischen Briefe im Werk der Irenäus von Lyon* (WUNT 66; Tübingen: Mohr Siebeck, 1994), 111–12.

53. The possibility that 1 Clement might be dependent on Romans here is not suggested in any of the source-critical studies which I consulted: A. J. Carlyle, "Clement of Rome," in *The New Testament in the Apostolic Fathers* (ed. Oxford Society of Historical Theology; Oxford: Clarendon, 1905), 37–40; Albert E. Barnett, *Paul Becomes a Literary Influence* (Chicago: University of Chicago Press, 1941), 88–104; Donald A. Hagner, *The Use of the Old and New Testaments in Clement of Rome* (NovTSup 34; Leiden: Brill, 1973), 214–20; Andrew F. Gregory, "1 Clement and the Writings That Later Formed the New Testament," in *The Reception of the New Testament in the Apostolic Fathers* (ed. Andrew F. Gregory and Christopher M. Tuckett; Oxford: Oxford University Press, 2005), 148–51.

might be fulfilled: "O Lord, who has believed our audible message, and to whom has the arm of the Lord been revealed?" [Isa 53:1] And so they were not able to believe, and this also because Isaiah said further: "He has blinded their eyes and hardened their heart, lest they see with their eyes, and lest they understand with their heart and lest they turn—and I would heal them" [Isa 6:10]. Isaiah said these things because he saw his glory and spoke concerning him.[54]

John makes two moves with the cited text. First, he correlates the "signs" performed by Jesus with the displays of power exhibited by the "arm of the Lord." The "arm of the Lord" is often associated with miraculous divine action;[55] in fact, numerous strands of early Christian exegesis designate Jesus himself as the "Arm of the Lord,"[56] and Tertullian expressly reads this very passage in such a fashion (*Prax*. 13.3). It may well be that John aligns himself with this latter tradition and thus directly identifies Jesus as the "Arm of the Lord." This possibility merits serious consideration for Paul as well, even though Paul cites not this portion of Isa 53:1 but only the first half of the verse (see further below). Second, John employs the Isaianic texts to highlight the response of unbelief, which puzzlingly persists in spite of the very signs that are calculated to inspire belief (John 2:11, 4:48, 7:31, 20:30–31), while noting that this hardening was prophesied in advance by Isaiah (Isa 6:10, 53:1). Ross Wagner has correctly pointed out the numerous affinities between the exegeses of John and of Paul at this juncture, affinities that increase the likelihood of a shared exegetical tradition regarding Isa 53:1.[57]

---

54. Τοσαῦτα δὲ αὐτοῦ σημεῖα πεποιηκότος ἔμπροσθεν αὐτῶν οὐκ ἐπίστευον εἰς αὐτόν, ἵνα ὁ λόγος Ἠσαΐου τοῦ προφήτου πληρωθῇ ὃν εἶπεν· κύριε, τίς ἐπίστευσεν τῇ ἀκοῇ ἡμῶν; καὶ ὁ βραχίων κυρίου τίνι ἀπεκαλύφθη; διὰ τοῦτο οὐκ ἠδύναντο πιστεύειν, ὅτι πάλιν εἶπεν Ἠσαΐας· τετύφλωκεν αὐτῶν τοὺς ὀφθαλμοὺς καὶ ἐπώρωσεν αὐτῶν τὴν καρδίαν, ἵνα μὴ ἴδωσιν τοῖς ὀφθαλμοῖς καὶ νοήσωσιν τῇ καρδίᾳ καὶ στραφῶσιν, καὶ ἰάσομαι αὐτούς. ταῦτα εἶπεν Ἠσαΐας ὅτι εἶδεν τὴν δόξαν αὐτοῦ, καὶ ἐλάλησεν περὶ αὐτοῦ.

55. E.g., Exod 6:1, 6; 15:16; 32:11; Deut 3:24, 4:34; 2 Macc 15:24; Ps 97:1 LXX; Isa 30:30, 52:10; Luke 1:51; John 3:2; Acts 13:17.

56. E.g., Justin, *Dial*. 11.3; 13.3; *1 Apol*. 32.12; Cyprian, *Test*. 2.4; Ps-Gregory, *Test*. 1.8.3 (PG 46:200). I owe the reference to Cyprian, *Test*. 2.4, to Martin C. Albl, *Pseudo-Gregory of Nyssa: Testimonies against the Jews* (SBLWGRW 8; Atlanta: Society of Biblical Literature, 2004), 96. Also, the reference to Ps.-Gregory is drawn from the numeration in his edition.

57. Wagner, *Heralds of the Good News*, 247–51, esp. 251 n. 103.

John does not identify the speaking character, or characters, that he has assigned to the "our" of the quotation, "O Lord, who has believed *our* audible message"—that is, if he has assigned any speaking character at all. It is slightly less likely that John has the apostles in mind as the primary referent of the word "our," since the prophecy is correlated with the rejection of Jesus himself during his earthly ministry (John 12:34–36, 42–43), not with the subsequent period of apostolic proclamation. Of course, one must be a bit cautious in this assessment, since John is more than capable of using the narrative about Jesus' life as a vehicle for addressing pressing issues in his own setting.[58] Moreover, John's Gospel is seemingly preoccupied with the continued rejection of Jesus by the Jewish community in the face of Christian proclamation, which leaves open the possibility of a double entendre in the "our" of the citation.[59] In the end, it is simply unclear whether the author of John made the same assignment of the speaker using prosopological exegesis that was made by Justin and Origen, and I argue, by Paul as well.

Summary of Paul's Exegesis of Isa 53:1a

The case for identifying the apostles (Paul included) as the collective speaker of Isa 53:1a ("O Lord, who has believed our audible message") in Rom 10:16 is two-pronged. First, Paul's intentional modification of the words of Isa 52:7 in Rom 10:15 strongly favors the identification of the apostles as the

---

58. As is the case in all likelihood with John's repeated references to expulsion from the synagogue in 9:22, 12:42, and 16:2—see Raymond E. Brown, *The Gospel according to John* (2 vols.; AB 29, 29A; New York: Doubleday, 1966–1970), 1:lxvii–lxxix.

59. Brown, *Gospel of John*, 1:lxxii, believes that the evangelistic mission to the Jews had essentially ceased by the time the Gospel of John took on its final form, since invitation has now hardened into polemic. I think, however, that Brown has imposed a modern assumption here. Although polemic and invitation may be mutually exclusive in our hyper-polite twenty-first-century Western civilizations, such was not the case in antiquity, as a tract such as Justin's *Dialogue* makes readily apparent; see, e.g., *Dial.* 141.2 for evidence of an evangelistic invitation to the Jews (despite the fierce polemic throughout the *Dialogue*) and *Dial.* 39.2, which shows that the invitation was still being accepted by Jews in Justin's day. On the abundant evidence for Christian and Jewish missionary contact and relations in the second century, see Reidar Hvalvik, *The Struggle for Scripture and Covenant: The Purpose of the Epistle of Barnabas and Jewish-Christian Competition in the Second Century* (WUNT 82; Tübingen: Mohr Siebeck, 1996), 216–322.

"our" in Rom 10:16 on independent grounds. The citation of Ps 18:5 LXX in Rom 10:18 points in the same direction. In fact, both Isa 52:7 and Ps 18:5 LXX are collocated elsewhere in early Christian exegesis, along with Isa 53:1, showing that these texts were considered mutually interpretative in some strands of early Christian literature. Second, and most vitally, the most proximate post-text, the first interpretation of Rom 10:16 that is found in Justin Martyr and subsequently echoed in Origen, explicitly identifies the "apostles" as the *prosopa* represented by the "our" of Isa 53:1. Other related early Christian post-texts in Justin Martyr and Irenaeus also support or are congenial to this reading, while two co-texts in 1 Clement and the Gospel of John neither confirm nor deny this identification.

I have avoided until now one additional question that should be answered: If the apostles are the speakers, then who is the addressee? The vocative κύριε ("O Lord") makes it clear that this is a first-person address to the "Lord," but should this be identified as the Lord Christ or as God? Part of the reason I have avoided answering this question is that the identity of the speakers can be fixed with greater certainty using the proposed diachronic intertextual method than that of the addressee, and I wanted to show, without the more speculative search for the addressee impinging as a distraction, that the speakers are probably the apostles.

The "O Lord" in the united LXX manuscript tradition is not present in the MT, so no hint can be gained by a comparison with the probable *Vorlage* of the Septuagint to see if יהוה or אדני is represented—a hint that would be of questionable value for Paul regardless since there is no clear evidence that Paul was in the habit of using the MT. Although the raw lexical data from Paul substantially favors the identification of the "Lord" as Christ by Paul, it also permits the identification of the "Lord" as God,[60] and this latter option is preferable here. Assuming that Paul had access to the entire verse, the phraseology of 53:1 taken as a whole suggests that the addressee would be God rather than Christ: "O Lord, who has believed our audible message? And to whom has the arm of the Lord been revealed?" The "Lord" in 53:1a is probably the same as the "Lord" in the expression "arm of the Lord" in 53:1b, and since the "Lord" in the phrase

---

60. According to Gordon D. Fee, *Pauline Christology* (Peabody, Mass.: Hendrickson, 2007), 25–27, 631–38, there are 12 instances in the Pauline corpus in which God is clearly identified as κύριος, all of which are in LXX citations. By contrast, there are 152 references to Jesus or the Christ as κύριος, and these are found both inside and outside of LXX citations.

"arm of the Lord" would almost certainly be understood by Paul as God, with the "arm" itself perhaps representing Christ,[61] we can fix God as the most likely addressee. Thus, although certainty is not possible, it is probably best to see the apostles (including Paul himself) as addressing God with their words, "O Lord, who has believed our report?" in Paul's exegesis of Rom 10:16.

THE SIGNIFICANCE OF ISAIAH THE PROPHET FOR PAUL: AN ASSESSMENT OF J. ROSS WAGNER'S PROPOSAL

While in general I strongly endorse the magisterial work of Ross Wagner in his *Heralds of the Good News*, with respect to Rom 10:16 I would like to offer a modest critique of the model put forward by Wagner, who suggests that Paul and Isaiah speak "in concert" in Rom 10:16 as fellow evangelists proclaiming the good news. Wagner states:

> Paul allows Isaiah to speak in his own voice about the rejection of "*our* message." It is of tremendous significance for understanding Paul's appropriation of the Book of Isaiah to recognize that this quotation assumes a fundamental correspondence between Paul's apostolic proclamation and Isaiah's message. It is not simply that Isaiah long ago predicted something that is now fulfilled in Paul's ministry. Rather, Isaiah remains a living voice for Paul, one who speaks alongside the apostle as an authoritative witness to the gospel.[62]

But does Paul mean for the "our" in the Isaianic citation to refer collectively to himself, Isaiah, and his fellow apostles, as Wagner has argued? I would assert, on the contrary, that the supposition that Isaiah is to be included in the "our" as understood by Paul is not probable in light of the results obtained above, especially the manner in which the pre-text (Isa 53:1a) and the text (Rom 10:16) are interpreted in early Christian co-texts, post-texts, and inter-texts. Isaiah and Paul may indeed speak "in concert" in a nominal sense, but Isaiah qua Isaiah the human prophet would seem to be a relatively trivial figure for Paul. The dramatic characters utilized

---

61. In the MT of Isa 53:1b the "arm of the Lord" is the "arm of יהוה," but even apart from this, the identification of κύριου with God is obvious in the LXX without any reference to the Hebrew *Vorlage* on the strength of the occurrence of this phrase or related terminology elsewhere—e.g., Exod 6:6; 15:6; Num 11:23; Isa 51:9; 59:1.

62. Wagner, *Heralds of the Good News*, 179–80, emphasis original.

by the divine author (here the apostles) in speaking through Isaiah are of much greater import, and in this case those characters are identified by Paul as himself and his fellow apostles.[63]

Concluding Thoughts

It has been my intention to articulate the need for a fuller diachronic intertextual model in New Testament scholarship that takes into account the relationship between not only the pre-text and the text but also relevant co-texts and post-texts. I have also attempted to demonstrate the utility of this diachronic intertextual model by a close examination of how Paul's exegesis of Isa 53:1a in Rom 10:16 was paralleled and received in the early church. My hope is that the diachronic intertextual model articulated and exemplified in this essay will encourage others to explore the numerous ways in which co-texts and post-texts can illuminate not only Paul's letters but all instances of intertextuality in the New Testament and other early Christian literature.

Bibliography

Allen, Graham. *Intertextuality*. The New Critical Idiom. London: Routledge, 2000.
Attridge, Harold W. *The Epistle to the Hebrews*. Hermeneia. Minneapolis: Fortress, 1989.
Bakhtin, M. M. *Speech Genres and Other Late Essays*. Edited by C. Emerson and M. Holquist. Translated by V. W. McGee. Austin: University of Texas Press, 1986.
Barnett, Albert E. *Paul Becomes a Literary Influence*. Chicago: University of Chicago Press, 1941.
Barrett, C. K. *A Commentary on the Epistle to the Romans*. BNTC. New York: Harper & Row, 1957.
Bates, Matthew W. "Beyond Stichwort: A Narrative Approach to Isa 52,7 in Romans 10,15 and 11Q Melchizedek (11Q13)." *RB* 116 (2009): 387–414.
———. *The Hermeneutics of the Apostolic Proclamation: The Center of*

---

63. For a more complete engagement with Wagner and a discussion of the broader implications for Pauline hermeneutics, see Bates, *The Hermeneutics of the Apostolic Proclamation*, ch. 6.

Paul's Method of Scriptural Interpretation. Waco, Tex.: Baylor University Press, 2012.
Beale, G. K., and D. A. Carson, eds. *Commentary on the New Testament Use of the Old Testament.* Grand Rapids: Baker, 2007.
Boyarin, Daniel. *Border Lines: The Partition of Judeo-Christianity.* Philadelphia: University of Pennsylvania Press, 2004.
———. *A Radical Jew: Paul and the Politics of Identity.* Berkeley: University of California Press, 1994.
Brown, Raymond E. *The Gospel according to John.* 2 vols. AB 29, 29A. New York: Doubleday, 1966–1970.
Bultmann, Rudolf. "The Significance of the Old Testament for the Christian Faith." Pages 8–35 in *The Old Testament and the Christian Faith: A Theological Discussion.* Edited and translated by Bernhard W. Anderson. New York: Harper & Row, 1963. Translation of "Das Bedeutung des Alten Testament für den christlichen Glauben." Pages 126–50 in *Glauben und Verstehen I.* Tübingen: Mohr Siebeck, 1933.
Camfield, Gregg, ed. *The Oxford Companion to Mark Twain.* New York: Oxford University Press, 2003.
Carlyle, A. J. "Clement of Rome." Pages 37–62 in *The New Testament in the Apostolic Fathers.* Edited by Oxford Society of Historical Theology. Oxford: Clarendon, 1905.
Childs, Brevard S. *Isaiah.* OTL. Louisville: Westminster John Knox, 2001.
Ciampa, Roy. "Scriptural Language and Ideas." Pages 41–57 in *As It Is Written: Studying Paul's Use of Scripture.* Edited by Stanley E. Porter and Christopher D. Stanley. SBLSymS 50. Atlanta: Society of Biblical Literature, 2008.
Cranfield, C. E. B. *A Critical and Exegetical Commentary on The Epistle of Paul to the Romans.* 2 vols. ICC. Edinburgh: T&T Clark, 1975–1979.
DiMattei, Steven. "Biblical Narratives." Pages 59–93 in *As It Is Written: Studying Paul's Use of Scripture.* Edited by Stanley E. Porter and Christopher D. Stanley. SBLSymS 50. Atlanta: Society of Biblical Literature, 2008.
Eisenbaum, Pamela. *Paul Was Not a Christian: The Original Message of a Misunderstood Apostle.* New York: HarperCollins, 2009.
Ellis, E. Earle. *Paul's Use of the Old Testament.* Grand Rapids: Eerdmans, 1957.
Evans, Craig A. "Listening for Echoes of Interpreted Scripture." Pages 47–51 in *Paul and the Scriptures of Israel.* Edited by Craig A. Evans and James A. Sanders. JSNTSup 83. Sheffield: JSOT Press, 1993.

Fee, Gordon D. *New Testament Exegesis*. Rev. ed. Louisville: Westminster John Knox, 1993.

———. *Pauline Christology: An Exegetical-Theological Study*. Peabody, Mass.: Hendrickson, 2007.

Fishbane, Michael A. *Biblical Interpretation in Ancient Israel*. Oxford: Oxford University Press, 1985.

Fitzmyer, Joseph A. *Romans: A New Translation with Introduction and Commentary*. AB 33. New York: Doubleday, 1993.

Friedman, Susan S. "Weavings: Intertextuality and the (Re)Birth of the Author." Pages 146–80 in *Influence and Intertextuality in Literary History*. Edited by Jay Clayton and Eric Rothstein. Madison: University of Wisconsin Press, 1991.

Gregory, Andrew F. "*1 Clement* and the Writings That Later Formed the New Testament." Pages 129–57 in *The Reception of the New Testament in the Apostolic Fathers*. Edited by Andrew F. Gregory and Christopher M. Tuckett. Oxford: Oxford University Press, 2005.

Hagner, Donald A. *The Use of the Old and New Testaments in Clement of Rome*. NovTSup 34. Leiden: Brill, 1973.

Hanson, Anthony T. *Jesus Christ in the Old Testament*. London: SPCK, 1965.

Harnack, Adolf von. "The Old Testament in the Pauline Letters and in the Pauline Churches." Pages 27–49 in *Understanding Paul's Ethics: Twentieth Century Approaches*. Edited by Brian S. Rosner. Translated by George S. Rosner and Brian S. Rosner. Grand Rapids: Eerdmans, 1995. Translation of "Das Alte Testament in den paulinischen Briefen und in den paulinischen Gemeinden." Pages 124–41 in *Sitzungsberichte der preussischen Akademie der Wissenschaften*. Berlin: de Gruyter, 1928.

Hays, Richard B. *Echoes of Scripture in the Letters of Paul*. New Haven: Yale University Press, 1989.

———. *The Faith of Jesus Christ: The Narrative Substructure of Galatians 3:1–4:11*. 2nd ed. Grand Rapids: Eerdmans, 2000.

———. "Paul and the Hermeneutics of Truth." *Pro Ecclesia* 16 (2007): 126–40.

Hoffmann-Aleith, Eva. *Paulusverständnis in der Alten Kirche*. BZNW 18. Berlin: Töpelmann, 1937.

Hollander, John. *The Figure of Echo: A Mode of Allusion in Milton and After*. Berkeley: University of California Press, 1981.

Hübner, Hans. "Intertextualität—Die hermeneutische Strategie des Paulus." *TLZ* 116 (1991): 881–98.

Hvalvik, Reidar. *The Struggle for Scripture and Covenant: The Purpose of the Epistle of Barnabas and Jewish-Christian Competition in the Second Century*. WUNT 82. Tübingen: Mohr Siebeck, 1996.
Irenaeus. *Contre les hérésies*. Edited and translated by Adelin Rousseau et al. 10 vols. SC. Paris: Cerf:, 1965–1979.
———. *Proof of the Apostolic Preaching*. Translated by Joseph P. Smith. ACW 16. New York: Newman, 1952.
Jewett, Robert. *Romans: A Commentary*. Hermeneia. Minneapolis: Fortress, 2007.
Käsemann, Ernst. *Commentary on Romans*. Translated by Geoffrey W. Bromiley. Grand Rapids: Eerdmans, 1980. Translation of *An die Römer*. 4th ed. Tübingen: Mohr Siebeck, 1980.
Koch, Dietrich-Alex. *Die Schrift als Zeuge des Evangeliums: Untersuchungen zur Verwendung und zum Verständnis der Schrift bei Paulus*. BHT 69. Tübingen: Mohr Siebeck, 1986.
Kraft, Robert A. "The Epistle of Barnabas, Its Quotations and Their Sources." Ph.D. diss., Harvard University, 1961.
Kristeva, Julia. *Desire in Language: A Semiotic Approach to Literature and Art*. Edited by Leon S. Roudiez. Translated by Thomas Gora, Alice Jardin, and Leon S. Roudiez. New York: Columbia University Press, 1980.
Lake, Kirsopp. *Paul: His Heritage and His Legacy*. New York: Oxford University Press, 1934.
Lightfoot, J. B., and J. R. Harmer, eds. *The Apostolic Fathers*. 2nd ed. Edited by Michael W. Holmes. Grand Rapids: Baker, 1992.
Lindemann, Andreas. *Paulus im ältesten Christentum*. BHT 58. Tübingen: Mohr Siebeck, 1979.
Longenecker, Richard N. *Biblical Exegesis in the Apostolic Period*. 2nd ed. Grand Rapids: Eerdmans, 1999.
Marcovich, Miroslav, ed. *Iustini Martyris Apologiae pro Christianis*. Patristische Texte und Studien 38. Berlin: de Gruyter, 1994.
———. *Iustini Martyris Dialogus cum Tryphone*. Patristische Texte und Studien 47. Berlin: de Gruyter, 1997.
Massaux, Édouard. *The Influence of the Gospel of Saint Matthew on Christian Literature before Saint Irenaeus*. 3 vols. Edited by Arthur J. Bellinzoni. Translated by Norman J. Belval and Suzanne Hecht. New Gospel Studies 5. Macon, Ga.: Mercer University Press, 1990–1993.
Meyer, Ben F. *Critical Realism and the New Testament*. Allison Park, Pa.: Pickwick, 1989.

Michel, Otto. *Paulus und seine Bibel*. BFCT 2/18. Gütersloh: Bertelsmann, 1929. Repr., Darmstadt: Wissenschaftliche Buchgesellschaft, 1972.

Moyise, Steve. *The Old Testament in the New Testament: An Introduction*. London: Continuum, 2001.

Noormann, Rolf. *Irenäus als Paulusinterpret: Zur Rezeption und Wirkung der paulinischen und deuteropaulinische Briefe im Werk der Irenäus von Lyon*. WUNT 66. Tübingen: Mohr Siebeck, 1994.

Origen. *Commentary on the Epistle to the Romans*. Translated by Thomas P. Scheck. FC 103–104. Washington, D.C.: Catholic University of America Press, 2001–2002.

Porter, Stanley E. "Further Comments on the Use of the Old Testament in the New Testament." Pages 98–110 in *The Intertextuality of the Epistles: Explorations of Theory and Practice*. Edited by Thomas L. Brodie, Dennis R. MacDonald, and Stanley E. Porter. NTM 16. Sheffield: Sheffield Phoenix, 2007.

———. "The Use of the Old Testament in the New Testament: A Brief Comment on Method and Terminology." Pages 79–96 in *Early Christian Interpretation of the Scriptures of Israel: Investigations and Proposals*. Edited by C. A. Evans and J. A. Sanders. JSNTSup 148. Sheffield: Sheffield Academic, 1997.

Pseudo-Gregory of Nyssa: Testimonies against the Jews. Translated by Martin C. Albl. SBLWGRW 8. Atlanta: Society of Biblical Literature, 2004.

Rothschild, Clare K. "Hebrews as a Guide to Reading Romans." Pages 537–73 in *Pseudepigraphie und Verfasserfiktion in frühchristlichen Briefen*. Edited by Jörg Frey, Jens Herzer, Martina Janßen, and Clare K. Rothschild. Tübingen: Mohr Siebeck, 2009.

Schelkle, K. H. *Paulus Lehrer der Väter: Die Altkirchliche Auslegung von Römer 1–11*. Düsseldorf: Patmos, 1956.

Schweitzer, Albert. *The Mysticism of the Apostle Paul*. Translated by William Montgomery. New York: Henry Holt, 1931. Translation of *Die Mystik des Apostels Paulus*. Tübingen: Mohr Siebeck, 1930.

Skarsaune, Oskar. *The Proof from Prophecy: A Study in Justin Martyr's Proof Text Tradition: Text-Type, Provenance, Theological Profile*. NovTSup 56. Leiden: Brill, 1987.

Stanley, Christopher D. *Arguing with Scripture: The Rhetoric of Quotations in the Letters of Paul*. London: T&T Clark, 2004.

———. *Paul and the Language of Scripture: Citation Technique in the Pauline Epistles and Contemporary Literature*. SNTSMS 74. Cambridge: Cambridge University Press, 1992.

———. "'The Redeemer Will Come ἐκ Σιων': Romans 11:26-27 Revisited." Pages 118-42 in *Paul and the Scriptures of Israel*. Edited by Craig A. Evans and James A. Sanders. JSNTSup 83. Sheffield: JSOT Press, 1993.

Wagner, J. Ross. *Heralds of the Good News: Paul and Isaiah "in Concert" in the Letter to the Romans*. NovTSup 101. Leiden: Brill, 2002.

Watson, Francis. *Paul and the Hermeneutics of Faith*. London: T&T Clark, 2004.

Wilckens, Ulrich. *Der Brief an die Römer*. 3 vols. EKKNT. Neukirchen-Vluyn: Neukirchener, 1978-1982.

Wilk, Florian. *Die Bedeutung des Jesajabuches für Paulus*. FRLANT 179. Göttingen: Vandenhoeck & Ruprecht, 1998.

Wimsatt, W. K., and Monroe D. Beardsley. "The Intentional Fallacy." Pages 3-18 in *The Verbal Icon: Studies in the Meaning of Poetry*. Edited by William K. Wimsatt. Lexington: University of Kentucky Press, 1954.

Wright, N. T. *The New Testament and the People of God*. Minneapolis: Fortress, 1992.

Approaching Paul's Use of Scripture in Light of Translation Studies

Roy E. Ciampa

Translation studies is a young and energetic field of study that applies a broad range of disciplinary approaches to issues in translation and interpretation services. Numerous graduate programs offer masters and doctoral degrees in the field, often as part of literature or linguistics departments. The field also has several professional organizations, such as the American Translation and Interpreting Studies Association (ATISA), the European Society for Translation Studies (ESTS), and others. Dozens of academic journals are dedicated to the field, including *Translation Studies*, *Translation: A Translation Studies Journal*, the *International Journal of Translation Studies*, *New Voices in Translation Studies*, and many more.[1] Routledge, Benjamins, and St. Jerome have published numerous academic studies on the subject.[2] The interdisciplinary field draws on insights and research done in comparative literature, linguistics, cultural studies, communication studies, critical theory, and other fields to shed light on the process of translation, the work of translators (including interpreters mediating between people[s] of different languages), and the practical and theoretical implications of their work.

While translation studies normally focuses on actual translations of texts or spoken discourse, the field has also looked more widely at trans-

---

1. See the links provided at http://www.monabaker.com/tsresources/links.htm (cited 21 December 2011).

2. For an easy entry into the field, I recommend Anthony Pym, *Exploring Translation Theories* (London: Routledge, 2010); or Jeremy Munday, *Introducing Translation Studies: Theories and Applications* (3rd ed.; London: Routledge, 2012). Another option would be Lawrence Venuti, ed., *The Translation Studies Reader* (London: Routledge, 2000).

lation as a very common phenomenon, including translation from one medium to another ("translating" a book into a film or Broadway production). It also considers other ways in which humans "translate" cultural realities and ways in which translation may serve as a metaphor for much of what people communicate intentionally or unintentionally.

This essay will explore some of the potential of the growing field of translation studies for the study of Paul's use of Scripture, including points from descriptive translation studies (e.g., polysystem theory), functionalist approaches (*Skopostheorie*), postcolonial approaches to translation, and the understanding of translation as cultural mediation. Particular approaches and perspectives will be considered that have the potential to broaden the scope of issues that inform our understanding of Paul's use of Scripture, including seeing that usage as part of his role as one of the key translators of the message of early Christianity for the Gentile communities to which he ministered. In the latter half of the essay I will focus on the ways in which looking at Paul's use of Scripture in light of translation studies might help us as we think about his use of Scripture in light of his theology and vice versa.

Most studies of Paul's use of Scripture to date have given primary attention to comparing his quotations to their *Vorlage*. That is, they do much the same thing as when researchers study translations by making close comparisons between the resulting translation and the original text that was translated. Differences are carefully registered and catalogued and classified in terms of their faithfulness or lack of faithfulness to the original. In the modern period, such comparisons have usually been carried out under the assumption that the work should reflect the type of disinterested objectivity that is valued in post-Enlightenment academic settings and from a prescriptive framework that assumed that a strictly scientific analysis could discern and judge between proper and improper or between appropriate and inappropriate citation or translation.

Before the development of the field of translation studies, people teaching translation tended to follow prescriptive approaches that dictated what translators should or should not do based primarily on traditional translation practices and what practitioners believed were the best practices. Within the field of biblical studies, scholars of every stripe tended to assume that our modern, scientifically informed historical methods should serve as the proper point of departure for judging the appropriateness or inappropriateness of any ancient use of Scripture. Scholars of a more conservative stripe tended to argue that what Paul (and other New

Testament authors) had done was consistent with their own (unassailable) approach to interpretation. Scholars reacting to such claims were tempted to suggest that it must have been Paul's opponents who were interpreting the text in the way that they would, since Paul's own interpretations were clearly not consistent with modern practices. Either way, the study of Paul's use of Scripture was caught in the midst of a fight rooted in prescriptive approaches in which modern practices served as the beginning and ending points of the analysis.

From Prescription to Description, and on to Polysystem Theory

In the field of translation studies (henceforth TS), scholars have generally moved beyond such prescriptive stances to various positions that agree in recognizing that there are various translation strategies and approaches that a translator might adopt (though now we also find different kinds of prescriptive approaches, as we shall see). The field has also developed an amazingly broad range of approaches to analyzing translations that might be helpful to us as we consider how we might more creatively assess Paul's use of Scripture in his writings. Within TS, scholars have turned from telling students how to translate properly toward developing more theoretical and analytical approaches to describing what it is that people actually do when they translate. These latter approaches analyze why translators do not all translate in the same way, examining what might cause them to intentionally or unintentionally handle the same phenomena in different ways and what this might reveal about what people are doing when they translate.

In the study of Paul's use of Scripture, we might make some productive steps forward if we were to declare a (temporary) moratorium on judging whether Paul or his opponents interpreted Scripture in ways that we consider appropriate or acceptable today and spend more time seeking to gain a better understanding of how their interpretive practices fit within their own context. Francis Watson's *Paul and the Hermeneutics of Faith* was a valuable start in this direction inasmuch as he compared Paul's interpretations of Scripture with other ancient Jewish interpretations of the same texts or themes. One of the things that stands out in such an analysis is that no one was interpreting Scripture at that time in the way that we would interpret it today. This is of course what we should have expected if we had had a little more historical self-awareness. Modern scholarly discussions of the subject have been tainted by the shadow of the twentieth-century fundamentalist–modernist debates and various apologetic interests that all tended to assume modern presuppositions as the starting point for defending or critiquing Paul's work.[3] This is not to suggest that critical judgments should be avoided but rather that more subtle work should first be carried out in which Paul's interpretations are more fully and broadly analyzed in light of his own context and competing interpretations from his own time rather than ours. I will return to other types of evaluative approaches later in this essay.

One of the ways in which TS theorists expanded their approach to analyzing translations was by moving from the simple comparison of a translation with the original text to finding a broader range of relationships within which translations could be compared. In the 1970s, Itamar Even-Zohar introduced polysystem theory, using the term "polysystem" to describe "the aggregate of literary systems, including everything from 'high' or 'canonized' forms (e.g., innovative verse) such as poetry to 'low' or 'non-canonized' forms (e.g., children's literature and popular fiction, in a given culture." According to Edwin Gentzler, "Even-Zohar recognized both the 'primary' (creating new items and models) as well as 'secondary' (reinforcing existing items and models) importance of translated literature in literary history."[4] Gideon Toury appropriated the polysystem idea and used it to establish "the larger framework of a comprehensive theory of translation" in his *In Search of a Theory of Translation*.[5] As Gentzler

---

3. The same could be said of the debate regarding whether modern interpreters should follow the example set by Paul and other New Testament authors; see G. K. Beale, ed., *The Right Doctrine from the Wrong Text?* (Grand Rapids: Baker, 1994), 387–404; Richard B. Hays, *Echoes of Scripture in the Letters of Paul* (New Haven: Yale University Press, 1989), 178–92; Richard N. Longenecker, *Biblical Exegesis in the Apostolic Period* (Grand Rapids: Eerdmans, 1999), xxxiv–xxxix, 193–98. Since interpreters are not agreed on exactly how New Testament authors like Paul interpret Scripture, it would be premature (and possibly close the door on further analysis of the subject) to give a definitive affirmation or negation of the proposal. While both Beale and Hays affirm that contemporary Christians should follow the interpretive example of the authors of the New Testament, they do not think the same thing is going on and thus find themselves giving different kinds of permission to their readers.

4. Edwin Gentzler, *Contemporary Translation Theories* (Topics in Translation; Clevedon: Multilingual Matters, 2001), 106, referencing Itamar Even-Zohar, *Papers in Historical Poetics* (Tel Aviv: Porter Institute for Poetics and Semiotics, 1978), 7–8.

5. Gideon Toury, *In Search of a Theory of Translation* (Tel Aviv: Porter Institute for Poetics and Semiotics, 1980).

points out, both men built on foundations laid by the Russian Formalists, including their "correlations between central and peripheral literature as well as between 'high' and 'low' types" as "one of their major hypotheses in explaining the mechanism of change in literary history."[6]

This approach was adopted and adapted by José Lambert and Hendrik van Gorp in their essay, "On Describing Translations,"[7] where they present the following diagram and explanation of some of the questions and issues that polysystem theory raises for the analysis of translations.[8]

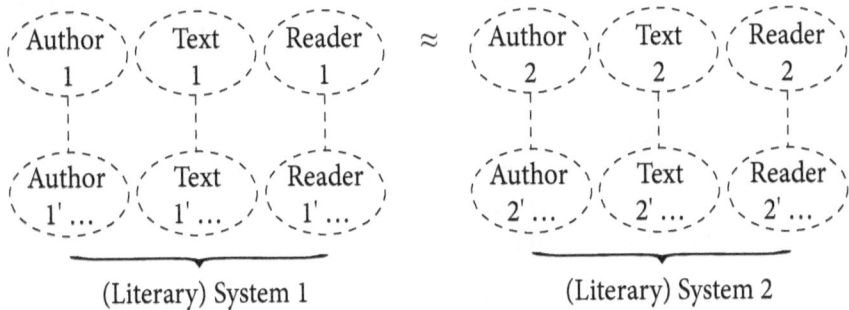

Explanation

- Text 1 = source text; Text 2 = target text.
- Author 1 and Reader 1 belong to the system of the source text.
- Author 1 is to be situated among the authors of the source system.
- Text 1' and Reader 1' are to be situated within the source system.
- System 1 refers to the system of source text, source author and source reader; this system is not necessarily a strictly literary one, since literary systems cannot be isolated from social, religious, or other systems.
- Author 2, Text 2, Reader 2, etc., are to be situated within the target system.

---

6. Even-Zohar, *Papers in Historical Poetics*, 11, cited in Gentzler, *Contemporary Translation Theories*, 109.

7. José Lambert and Hendrik van Gorp, "On Describing Translations," in *The Manipulation of Literature: Studies in Literary Translation* (ed. Theo Hermans; London: Croom Helm, 1985), 42–53.

8. Lambert and van Gorp, "On Describing Translations," 43.

- The dashed oval signifies that all elements of this communication scheme are complex and dynamic.
- The symbol ≈ indicates that the link between source and target communication cannot really be predicted; it stands for an open relation, the exact nature of which will depend on the priorities of the translator's behavior, which in turn has to be seen as a function of the dominant norms of the target system.

The point is that translations need to be analyzed not only in terms of their relationship with the source text but also in terms of (a) how the target text's place within its adoptive literary system (as well as the social, religious, and other systems of which it is a part) relates to the source text's place within its adoptive literary and other systems, and (b) how the place of the author of the source text within his culture and context relates to his place within the target text's culture and context, and so forth. Lambert and Gorp suggest that "all relations mentioned in the scheme deserve to be studied."[9]

- T1 — T2 (the relations between individual texts, i.e., between the original and its translation)
- A1 — A2 (the relations between authors)
- R1 — R2 (the relations between readers)
- A1 — T1 ≈ A2 — T2 (authorial intentions in the source and target systems, and their correlation)
- T1 — R1 ≈ T2 — R2 (pragmatics and reception in the source and target systems, and their correlation)
- A1 — A1', A2 — A2' (the situation of the author in respect to other authors, in both systems)
- T1 — T1', T2 — T2' (the situation of both the original and the translation as texts in respect to other texts)
- R1 — R1', R2 — R2' (the situation of the reader within the respective systems)
- Target System — Literary System (translations within a given literature)
- (Literary) System 1 — (Literary) System 2 (the relations, whether in terms of conflict or harmony, between both systems).

---

9. Lambert and van Gorp, "On Describing Translations," 44.

In other words, Lambert and Gorp are arguing that analysts should look not just at the relationship between the original text and the translation but at all of the relationships between the original text and its literary, linguistic, and sociocultural context, while also situating the translated text within its own literary, linguistic, and sociocultural context. In considering a translation of Shakespeare into Japanese, for example, one would look at the place and status of Shakespeare's work in the English literary, linguistic, and sociocultural context as well as the place of the translation within the Japanese literary, linguistic, and sociocultural context. One might also examine the differences between the impact of Shakespeare's work in English literature and culture and the impact of the translation in Japanese literature and culture, or the status of knowledge of Shakespeare in English versus the status of knowledge of Shakespeare in Japanese culture (to list only a few of the very numerous possibilities). One would also look at the status of translated works as a whole within the Japanese literary system, or world, and the place of this particular translation of Shakespeare within that literary system, and so on.

Applying an extension of this approach to Paul as one "translating" the early Christian message for the sake of his Gentile communities (and his use of Scripture as part of that work of translation), we would go beyond comparing his interpretations of Scripture with what we might take to be the original meaning of those texts to look at questions such as how the original texts fit within a larger literary system and how Paul's interpretations of them fit (or not) within the literary system(s) of his readers.[10] We could also compare the place of Paul's interpretations in his readers' contexts with the place held by alternative interpretations (Jewish or Christian) of the Jewish Scriptures (or of other works being translated or interpreted into those same contexts). We could think about the differences between the demographics of the various readers, consumers, and recipi-

---

10. Given the primarily oral/aural nature of the reading experience at Paul's time, it should be understood here and elsewhere that Paul's "readers" are composed of those who read the text publicly or privately as well as those who had the text read to them by such readers. It might be that the word "readers" should be replaced with "audiences" or "addressees," though these words also have special limiting denotations or connotations that are not completely appropriate. Some texts (e.g., Acts 15:31; 2 Cor 1:13; Eph 3:4; Col 4:16) seem to suggest that active forms of the verb ἀναγι(γ)-νώσκω could be used with subjects that are understood to include those who had a text read aloud to them. In this paper, references to "readers" of Paul's time should be similarly understood.

ents of the original texts, or compare the demographics of Palestinian Christian consumers of early Christian interpretations of those texts with Paul's own audiences. We could ask where the consumers of Paul's "translation" fit within their own sociocultural context and how that compares to the place of the consumers of the "original" Christian message within their own sociocultural context. We could explore how the consumers of other ancient Jewish or Jewish Christian interpretations of Scripture were similar to or different from the people to whom Paul was presenting his interpretations. We could investigate how Paul's authority in relation to his readers relates to the authority of the authors of other texts in relation to their readers and how this might affect the reception of Paul's interpretations and his need to engage in various types of interpretation.

The authors of the texts that Paul cites would be located within the systems (literary, religious, political, economic, etc.) of which they were a part (A1 – A1'), and Paul would be located within the systems (literary, religious, political, economic, etc.) of which he was a part (A2 – A2'). The texts that Paul cites would be located within the systems (literary, religious, political, economic, etc.) of which they were a part (T1 – T1'), and his use of them would be located within the systems (literary, religious, political, economic, etc.) of which his writings were a part (T2 – T2'). The original readers of the texts that Paul cites would be located within the systems (literary, religious, political, economic, etc.) of which they were a part (R1 – R1'), and Paul's own readers would be located within the systems (literary, religious, political, economic, etc.) of which they were a part (R2 – R2'). The relationships and differences among each of the elements within and between each system would also be taken into consideration.

Most studies of the use of the Old Testament in the New Testament have focused entirely on the perceived relationship between T1 and T2 (or between A2 and T1). Some notable exceptions include Christopher Stanley's *Paul and the Language of Scripture*, which compared Paul's quotation technique with other ancient approaches to quotations, and even more significantly Francis Watson's *Paul and the Hermeneutics of Faith*, which exemplified an approach that pays attention to the relationship between T2 and T2' (how Paul's interpretations relate to other interpretations of the same texts in his environment) with some attention to how these relate to T1 (the meaning of the texts in their Old Testament canonical context).

Some of our questions about why Paul interprets the Scriptures the way he does may never be answered if our focus is limited to shifting back and forth between those interpretations and the texts being interpreted.

In Paul's letters, the texts of Scripture are being "translated" into a completely different context, and interpretations that may have made perfectly good sense in the original context may not be relevant or even coherent in the new context into which they are being introduced. The better we understand the whole host of complex relationships entailed in a translation (or interpretation) process and their implications, the better we will be prepared to understand aspects of that translation that might have been overlooked or misunderstood. The cognitive environment into which the interpretation or translation is being launched differs in innumerable ways from the cognitive environment in which the original text or message was formulated. The challenges that this poses have been a primary concern of the application of relevance theory to the work of translation.

Translation and Relevance Theory

Relevance theory was proposed by Dan Sperber and Deirdre Wilson and applied to translation theory by Ernst-August Gutt.[11] The theory argues that human communication does not take place through a strict process of coding and decoding of meanings by use of language but is largely dependent upon the human "ability to draw inferences from people's behavior." Language is a form of human behavior that allows for relatively more explicit inferences to be drawn, but the general principle that communication takes place through inference remains the same.

According to relevance theory, an individual infers the meaning of a person's speech and other behavior based on information found in the "total cognitive environment," which is "the set of all the facts that he can perceive or infer: all the facts that are manifest to him. An individual's total cognitive environment is a function of his physical environment and his cognitive abilities."[12] Communication works on the basis of the "principle of relevance," namely, that "every act of ostensive communication communicates the presumption of its own optimal relevance."[13] That is, people

---

11. See Dan Sperber and Deirdre Wilson, *Relevance: Communication and Cognition* (2nd ed.; Oxford: Blackwell, 1995); idem, "Relevance Theory," in *The Handbook of Pragmatics* (ed. Laurence R. Horn and Gregory L. Ward; Malden, Mass.: Blackwell, 2004), 607–32. See Ernst-August Gutt, *Translation and Relevance: Cognition and Context* (Manchester: St. Jerome, 2000).
12. Sperber and Wilson, *Relevance*, 39.
13. Ibid., 158, cited in Gutt, *Translation and Relevance*, 32.

observe the speech and actions of those communicating with them and infer their meaning on the assumption that the message is relevant to them and their context.

For a person to interpret a statement or a text in the same way that the original listener or reader was expected to interpret it, the interpreter would have to share the same cognitive environment as the original listener or reader. Since readers of translations (especially readers of translations of ancient literature) naturally do not share the same cognitive environment as the original texts (approximation of which is a goal of the work of *Neutestamentlers*), it becomes quite difficult to see how they will interpret a translation in precisely the same way that the original text was expected to be interpreted without significant help.

One approach is to explicate in the translation information that is understood to be implicit in the original communication situation but that would not be implicit for the reader of the translation.[14] Gutt argues, however, that the multiplying of explications within the translation itself cannot be counted on to lead the readers to the same implicatures as suggested to the original readers. In fact, he suggests that one of the problems with the explications given in domesticating translations is that they often provide a meaning that is more determinate and closed than is actually appropriate given the "indeterminacy and open-endedness of implicature."[15] This solution may also overlook the fact that problems in interpretation come not only from a failure to recognize implicit information from the original communication situation but also from interference caused by inferences drawn by the readers of the translation from their own cognitive environment, which are not easily canceled out.[16] The translation may also end up being filled with what will amount to an unacceptably high level of information processing that does not seem relevant to the reader of the translation, resulting in its disuse.[17]

Gutt uses the analogy of direct and indirect quotation to suggest that we think in terms of two kinds of translation: direct translation and indirect translation. Just as a direct quotation attempts to preserve exactly what the other person said, direct translation seeks to attain complete

---

14. See the detailed discussion of this issue in Gutt, *Translation and Relevance*, 83–98.
15. Ibid., 92.
16. See ibid., 94–95.
17. Ibid., 96–97.

interpretive resemblance. With direct translation, the translator works on the assumption that the readers have access to the same cognitive environment as the original listeners or readers and will make the same inferences that they would, as long as the translation includes all of the same communicative clues found in the original text. In the case of a direct translation, the translator's task is to ensure that the translation conveys "all and only those explicatures and implicatures that the original text was intended to convey"[18] so that its readers may come to share the same cognitive environment as the original readers. Clearly such an approach has its advantages for the translator.

> For the translator, one of the important consequences of [carrying out a direct translation] is that it makes the explication of implicatures both unnecessary and undesirable. It makes it unnecessary because the reason for such explication was mismatches in contextual information in the cognitive environment of the receptors. Since in direct translation it is the audience's responsibility to make up for such differences, the translator need not be concerned with them. It also makes such explication undesirable because it would be likely to have a distorting influence on the intended interpretation.[19]

It seems obvious that interpretation is such an ubiquitous activity in part because so many of those wanting to engage certain texts or cultures do not share the cognitive environment that is required for direct access. Even the provision of extended commentaries, footnotes, or other paratextual materials cannot provide new readers with the complete cognitive environment of the original.

Gutt describes indirect translation on the analogy of indirect quotations, which are reworded (and typically marked as reworded) in such a way that they only partially resemble the original discourse. Indirect discourse and indirect quotations retain only those parts of the discourse or its meaning that are relevant to those to whom the indirect quotation is transmitted. In indirect discourse or quotations, the discourse is reworded to a greater or lesser extent to simplify its assimilation to the new context, to focus on the relevance of the original discourse for the reporter's point or argument, or both. In the same way, indirect translation is translation

---

18. Ibid., 99.
19. Ibid., 175.

that aspires not to complete interpretive resemblance to the original but only to partial resemblance, with alterations made in order to adapt the text in ways that optimize its relevance for the receptors.

Just as indirect quotations may either modify the original statement only slightly or transform it significantly, so also indirect translation may make only slight accommodations for the sake of the intended receptors or more significant accommodations for the sake of relevant communication with the receptors. In any case, it is expected that indirect translation, like indirect quotation, will resemble the original "closely enough in relevant respects."[20]

In Gutt's view, "The importance of ensuring that the intended resemblance be known to both parties, and the danger of relying on tacit assumptions in this matter, can hardly be overemphasized," since "insufficient awareness in this area has contributed greatly to the misunderstandings, unjustified criticism, confusion, and frustration that tend to accompany translation. Mismatches in these expectations do matter, sometimes only a little, but sometimes very much so."[21]

Leaving the translation metaphor behind for a moment, Paul's letters may be understood as providing a combination of direct quotation and indirect quotation. He sometimes quotes directly from the LXX or other Greek versions and sometimes adapts the texts to a greater or lesser extent. Indirect quotations typically reflect (as in the common use of indirect discourse) modifications intended to simplify assimilation of the original text to the new context or to highlight the relevance that the reporter (here, Paul) sees in the cited text for the point or argument of the new text, or other motivations. The material surrounding his quotations may properly be understood as paratextual material, intended to guide and inform the interpretation of those direct and indirect quotes. Returning to translation as a metaphor again, we may consider Paul's overall engagement with Scripture (in direct and indirect quotes, allusions, echoes, use of concepts and ideas, etc.) to function as a type of indirect translation rather than direct translation.

If polysystem theory helps us recognize, among other things, the tremendous extent to which the cognitive environment of contemporary readers and hearers differs from that of the original recipients of the origi-

---

20. Sperber and Wilson, *Relevance*, 137, cited in Gutt, *Translation and Relevance*, 191.

21. Gutt, *Translation and Relevance*, 193.

nal texts, relevance theory reminds us that the interpretive equivalent of a direct translation would be unlikely to have been comprehensible to Paul's audience. Although we may debate the extent to which he expected his readers to be familiar with the contexts and original meanings of the texts he cites or alludes to, it would clearly be expecting too much of his audience to think that he could simply provide unadapted quotations of key texts and they would understand both their original meaning and how Paul thought the texts were relevant for them. Paul's interpretative method is closer to the idea of an indirect translation—one that that only partially resembles the original text and its meaning, retaining only those parts that are relevant to those to whom his interpretation is being transmitted. He may be aspiring not to complete interpretive resemblance with the original but only to partial resemblance, making alterations in order to adapt the text and its message in ways that optimize its relevance for his congregations.

In short, some of our judgments about Paul may have been based on misunderstandings of the type of resemblance intended by him, resulting in just the sort of misunderstandings, unjustified criticism, confusion, and frustration that tend to accompany translations where expectations are not met. As Gutt says, "Mismatches in these expectations do matter."[22]

SKOPOSTHEORIE AND THE QUESTION OF PURPOSE IN TRANSLATION (AND INTERPRETATION)

Among the more influential models in TS are the functionalist approaches, the most well known being *Skopostheorie*, or Skopos theory.[23] Skopos theory may be used as either a descriptive or a normative approach. It is one of several different movements that shift away from a narrow focus on the relationship between the translated text and the original text to one that places more emphasis on the relationship between the translated text and its intended readers or between the readers of the translation and the original text and its translation.

---

22. See note 21.
23. Drawing on the metaphorical extension of the Greek σκοπός with the meaning of "aim" or "end." For the theory, see Hans J. Vermeer and Katharina Reiß, *Grundlegung einer allgemeinen Translationstheorie* (Tübingen: Niemeyer, 1984); Christiane Nord, *Translating as Purposeful Activity: Functionalist Approaches Explained* (Manchester: St. Jerome, 1997); and idem, "Scopos, Loyalty, and Translational Conventions," *Target* 3 (1991): 91–109.

Skopos theory argues that the intended function of any translation will and should be a determining factor in the translation approach that is adopted. The register that is adopted, the vocabulary that is used, the rigidity or freedom in the translation of key terms, the preservation, omission, or transformation of idiomatic expressions in the original text (and the extent to which idiomatic expressions from the receptor language are introduced), the preservation or transformation of literary forms and genres, the modification of names of people or places, and much more will be decided in light of the intended audience and function of the translation. In fact, Skopos theory argues that a translation is to be evaluated primarily on the basis of whether it satisfies the purposes of the intended readers and allows them to do with the translation what they wished.

Within Skopos theory, the *Skopos* rule states that one should "translate/interpret/speak/write in a way that enables your text/translation to function in the situation in which it is used and with the people who want to use it and precisely in the way they want it to function."[24] Christiane Nord, one of the key advocates of Skopos theory, argues that "the *Skopos* of a particular translation task may require a 'free' *or* a 'faithful' translation, or anything between these two extremes, depending on the purpose for which the translation is needed. What it does *not* mean is that a good translation should *ipso facto* conform or adapt to target-culture behavior or expectations, although the concept is often misunderstood in this way."[25] She also recognizes that there is a type of negotiation that may need to take place between the translator, a client, and the receivers of the translation (since typically it is not those who will receive the translation who commission the translator to begin with).

Here is Nord's summary of the translator's role:

> In the case of a translation, the translator is a real receiver of the source text who then proceeds to inform another audience, located in a situation under target-culture conditions, about the offer of information made by the source text. The translator offers this new audience a target text whose composition is, of course, guided by the translator's assump-

---

24. Vermeer, cited in Nord, *Translating as Purposeful Activity*, 29. According to Nord, "loyalty" to the original text "means that the target text purpose should be compatible with the original author's intentions" (Nord, *Translating as Purposeful Activity*, 125).

25. Ibid., 29.

tions about their needs, expectations, previous knowledge, and so on. These assumptions will obviously be different from those made by the original author, because source-text addressees and target-text addressees belong to different cultures and language communities. This means the translator cannot offer the same amount and kind of information as the source-text producer. What the translator does is offer another kind of information in another form.[26]

Before translating Shakespeare into Japanese, a translator informed by Skopos theory would seek to find the answers to a long list of questions, including the following: What do the Japanese readers of this translation of Shakespeare want from it, or what will they do with it? Do they want to sense the flavor of his prose? Do they want to understand the ideology of the text? Are they interested in analyzing Shakespeare's historical imagination? Do they want a crib to help them read Shakespeare in English?

If we extend functionalist approaches to translation to Paul's use of Scripture, we begin to engage more directly with the issues related to the role of Scripture in Paul's theology. Too often, Paul's use of Scripture has been discussed as though he simply read Scripture to further or deepen his own understanding of what the texts meant and commented on them in order to deepen his readers' understandings of the original meanings and their applications of whatever texts he happened to use. In this view, Paul's primary commitment would or should have been to the plain and simple exposition of the meanings of biblical texts without being influenced by any other agenda. In thinking about an extension of Skopos theory to Paul as an interpreter of Scripture, we are reminded that Paul understood himself to be commissioned by God to proclaim the (biblical/Jewish) good news of Christ to non-Jewish people living in the Roman Empire. His approach to Scripture is qualified by the commission that he has received from God to proclaim the gospel to the Gentiles, and his reading of Scripture will be (and clearly is) guided by his understanding of the needs of his (mainly) Gentile Christian readers. His readers are not interested in his interpretations of Scripture as historical or literary feats or artifacts. In Paul's understanding, God expects him (and his readers need him) to "translate" the message of the gospel so that Gentiles can understand how they also fit into God's plans and how they can (literally and metaphorically) sit at the same table with Jewish believers as they follow Christ in

---

26. Ibid., 35.

their own cities and culture. There were doubtless many aspects of the meanings of scriptural texts that would not engage the needs and interests of Paul's readers. Paul's goal, aim, or end was not so much to show them how to carry out exegesis of the type that people today might recognize and endorse but to help them understand Scripture as a book which has them and their needs in mind and which addresses their particular challenges. Paul has often been described as a "task theologian," and the term applies well to his reading and interpretation of Scripture. In carrying out this task, he is loyal not merely to the texts of Scripture as objects of interpretive interest but also to "translating" (i.e., interpreting) them in such a way that the particular ways in which they might be helpful to his readers and their challenges are most fully exploited. In this he reflects his loyalty to the one who has commissioned him to do that work of translation and to those for whom his "translations" are being prepared. Such an extension of Skopos theory to Paul suggests that we need to pay more attention to the needs and interests of Paul's readers and how his use of Scripture was conditioned by their concerns and interests when he engaged with the Scriptures. Rather than giving specific examples at this point, however, it would be better to move on to the next development in recent approaches to TS, which relates directly to the points raised here, and then to discuss a few specific examples which relate to Skopos theory as well as to issues of power and activism in translation.

Power, Agency, Resistance, and Activism in Translation (and Interpretation)[27]

In the modern world, translation has traditionally been thought of as something that is undertaken with objectivity, even if one did need to decide how literally or freely to translate. Skopos theory likewise sees the translator's role as being fairly objective. Once the translator discovers the commissioner's purpose, the target group's needs, and the purpose for the translation, he or she should carry out the work in a way that conforms to those requirements.

---

27. On this subject, see especially Maria Tymoczko and Edwin Genzler, eds., *Translation and Power* (Amherst: University of Massachusetts Press, 2002); Maria Tymoczko, ed., *Translation, Resistance, Activism* (Amherst: University of Massachusetts Press, 2010); and Maria Tymoczko, *Enlarging Translation, Empowering Translators* (Manchester: St. Jerome, 2007).

In recent years, however, more attention has been given to the place of translators as interested and committed agents whose ideological commitments play a significant role in what they do. Translators have been understood to play significant roles as intercultural mediators. TS scholars have focused on the key role that translators and translations may play in promoting mutual understanding between peoples of diverse languages and cultures and on avoiding the problems that arise when people of different languages and cultures misunderstand each other.[28] Even where there is no significant conflict, translators are likely to think about how their translation of Shakespeare's works from English into Japanese or of Japanese works into English might help English- and Japanese-speaking people to understand each other more clearly and reduce unnecessary conflicts between them. We might ask to what extent Paul hoped that his "translation" of the gospel message through his scriptural interpretations would promote mutual understanding between the Jewish and Gentile members of the communities to which he wrote. If the collection for the church in Jerusalem was intended, among other things, to build trust and bonds of brotherhood between his churches and the Jerusalem community, might his biblical interpretations be intended to do the same? One could also ask whether Paul as a "translator" of the Christian messianic Jewish message to Gentile communities (and interpreter of Scripture as part of that translation role) effectively promotes or undermines mutual understanding between his readers and the Palestinian Christian communities, the Diaspora Jewish communities, or the wider Roman world and try to come up with effective ways of answering the question.

TS proponents have also given attention to postcolonial criticism in light of the perception that translators and translations have played key

---

28. See, e.g., David Katan, *Translating Cultures: An Introduction for Translators, Interpreters, and Mediators* (Manchester: St. Jerome, 2004); Humphrey Tonkin and Maria Esposito Frank, eds., *The Translator As Mediator of Cultures* (Amsterdam: Benjamins, 2010); Raymond Mopoho, "Interpreters and Translators as Political Mediators in Colonial Subsaharan Africa," UNESCO International Symposium on Translation and Cultural Mediation, 22–23 February 2009. Cited 8 February 2012. Online: http://www.unesco.org/fileadmin/MULTIMEDIA/HQ/CLT/languages/pdf/MOPOHO-Interpreters%20and%20translators%20as%20political%20mediators%20in%20colonial%20Subsaharan%20Africa-ENG.pdf. See also David Limon, "Translators as Cultural Mediators: Wish or Reality? A Question for Translation Studies," in *Why Translation Studies Matters* (ed. Daniel Gile, Gyde Hansen, and Nike K. Pokorn; Benjamins Translation Library; Amsterdam: Benjamins, 2010), 29–40.

roles in advancing the interests of modern colonizing empires. TS is thus interested in the place that translators and translation can play in either advancing or resisting colonial interests and in marginalizing or advancing the distinctive perspectives of colonized peoples. R. S. Sugirtharajah points out that "Bible translation has long been implicated in diverse imperialist projects in Africa, Asia, the Caribbean, and South America." Translators and translations are thus seen as tools of imperial ambitions. "Since the invader and invaded spoke different languages and practiced different religions, translation played a crucial role in conquering and converting the other."[29]

Contemporary approaches to translation also tend to be more fully aware of the problems caused by ideological or cultural bias or distortion in the past and more committed to translating in ways that do not promote injustice or alienation or serve cultural agendas, especially those of the powerful at the expense of the powerless. Translators, as contemporary writer-readers and speaker-listeners, have become more sensitive to ethnic, cultural, gender, and other types of bias or manipulation,[30] so that they now try to avoid perpetuating such biases in their translations or seek to use the power of translation to advance what they consider to be a more just agenda and social structure.

Activist translators promote social, religious, or other agendas in a variety of ways. Perhaps the most obvious is through the selection of materials to be translated. In Western culture, we recognize that the decision to "translate" (i.e., adapt) a book into the "language" of film often reflects a political and social agenda, for example, a commentary on the ethics of extraordinary rendition or the dangers of religious (or some other kind

---

29. R. S. Sugirtharajah, *Postcolonial Criticism and Biblical Interpretation* (Oxford: Oxford University Press, 2002), 156.

30. In the introduction to their book on *Translation and Power*, Edwin Gentzler and Maria Tymoczko suggest that, in the second part of the last century, translation became even more intentionally tied up with issues of ideology and manipulative power: "In the 1950s and 1960s, as Madison Avenue tightened its grip on the United States and the world and pioneered techniques for using mass communications for cultural control, practicing translators began consciously to calibrate their translation techniques to achieve effects they wished to produce in their audiences, whether those effects were religious faith, consumption of products, or literary success. In short, translators began to realize how translated texts could manipulate readers to achieve desired effects" (xi).

of) intolerance. A decision to translate *Peter Pan* or *Don Quixote* into the language of a nation under an oppressive dictatorship can be a subversive move, since the titular characters "can be seen as anarchic figures, failing to respect authority."[31]

TS scholars are in the midst of a debate over the ethics of domesticating a foreign text. Is it more ethical to recognize and respect the "otherness" of the voice of another or to assimilate it so that it sounds much like one's own voice? Laurence Venuti recognizes both advantages and problems with domesticating translations:

> The popular aesthetic requires fluent translations that produce the illusory effect of transparency, and this means adhering to the current standard dialect while avoiding any dialect, register, or style that calls attention to words as words and therefore preempts the reader's identification. As a result, fluent translation may enable a foreign text to engage a mass readership, even a text from an excluded foreign literature, and thereby initiate a significant canon reformation. But such a translation simultaneously reinforces the major language and its many other linguistic and cultural exclusions while masking the inscription of domestic values. Fluency is assimilationist, presenting to domestic readers a realistic representation inflected with their own codes and ideologies as if it were an immediate encounter with a foreign text and culture.[32]

Venuti clearly favors foreignizing versions, but he recognizes that all translations are domesticating to one extent or another. Translation "inevitably domesticates foreign texts, inscribing them with linguistic and cultural values that are intelligible to specific domestic constituencies." He judges translations by the attitude that they transmit towards the foreign culture.

> Bad translation shapes toward the foreign culture a domestic attitude that is ethnocentric: "generally under the guise of transmissability, [it] carries out a systematic negation of the strangeness of the foreign work" (Berman 1992:5). Good translation aims to limit this ethnocentric negation: it stages "an opening, a dialogue, a cross-breeding, a decentering"

---

31. John Milton, "The Resistant Political Translations of Monteiro Lobato," in Maria Tymoczko, *Translation, Resistance, Activism*, here 201.

32. Laurence Venuti, *The Scandals of Translation: Towards an Ethics of Difference* (London: Routledge, 1998), 12.

and thereby forces the domestic language and culture to register the foreignness of the foreign text (ibid.:4).[33]

In his view, a translator can and should limit the ethnocentric movement inherent in translation by taking into account "the interests of more than just those of a cultural constituency that occupies a dominant position in the domestic culture." In contrast to the "loyalty" that should govern translation according to *Skopostheorie*, a translator should be "prepared to be disloyal to the domestic cultural norms that govern the identity-forming process of translation by calling attention to what they enable and limit, admit and exclude, in the encounter with foreign texts."[34] His view is that such an approach may "create a readership that is more open to linguistic and cultural differences."[35]

Maria Tymoczko argues that Venuti's position is insufficiently nuanced.

> Although at times foreignization may be an appropriate resistance technique in dominant cultures such as the United States, it is not at all suited to subaltern cultures that are already flooded with foreign materials and foreign linguistic impositions (often from the United States or other Eurocentric cultures) and that are trying to establish or shore up their own discourses and cultural forms. Foreignization has also been rightly criticized as potentially an elitist strategy, more appropriate to a highly educated target audience than to a broad readership or a cultural situation in which the normal education level is more modest than it is in Europe or the United States.[36]

Tymoczko discusses resistant and assertive approaches to writing and translation. She points out that authors

> may choose to present cultural material with absolutely no explanation, taking the position that the audience should be able to understand the material on the basis of general knowledge, absent which it will fall to the readers to do the homework necessary to fill in the cultural background for themselves. Colonized populations are often in this position, needing

---

33. Venuti, *The Scandals of Translation*, 81, citing Antoine Berman, *The Experience of the Foreign: Culture and Translation in Romantic Germany* (trans. S. Heyvaert; Albany: State University of New York Press, 1992).
34. Venuti, *The Scandals of Translation*, 83.
35. Ibid., 87.
36. Maria Tymoczko, *Enlarging Translation*, 211–12.

to acquire enough education about the colonizers' culture to understand "metropolitan" texts whether in the original language or in translation.[37]

When a similar approach is taken by writers from colonized nations, it is seen as "resistant" writing. She gives James Joyce as an example. "In Ulysses all manner of cultural material about Ireland is presupposed, from the history of the country to the geography of Dublin, from religious contestations to cultural habits and demotic speech. The result is a steep learning curve for readers who are not Irish (and for many Irish readers as well)."[38] Such a strategy is seen "to position the reader within limits, thus decentering the power and privilege of readers from dominant cultures."[39]

What light might the issues raised by activist approaches to TS and the questions of power and agency in the work of translation shed on the topic that most interests us—Paul's use of Scripture? How does Paul's translation of the Christian message (and his use of Scripture as part of that translation process) relate to these kinds of interests and concerns? Paul is not a disinterested interpreter of Scripture. He believes that God has given him a particular mission, which in turn leads him to adopt the role of the key advocate for the full inclusion of Gentiles in the early Christian churches. His reading, pondering, and interpretation of Scripture are, more often than not it seems, guided by his activist role in explaining and defending the place of Gentiles alongside Jews in God's redeemed community. As he says in Rom 11:13, he magnifies, or glorifies ("makes much of"), his ministry as apostle to the Gentiles. Paul intentionally exerts power through his scriptural interpretations for the sake of his readers (and for the sake of the survival and advancement of his own ministry agenda).

This recognition leads us to look at a number of issues more carefully. For instance, Paul's choices of texts to quote and the scriptural themes that he brings into his letters reflect his particular agenda in each case. Apart from the precise wording of his scriptural citations and allusions, his choice of topics such as Abraham and his justification, his focus on texts accusing Jews/Israelites (as well as Gentiles) of being sinners, his interest in texts that speak of Gentiles or all nations worshipping God along with Jews, and so on reflect his activist commitment to defending the Gentiles' place in God's redemptive plan as being on an equal footing

---

37. Ibid., 229.
38. Ibid.
39. Ibid., 230.

with Jewish believers in Christ. In the case of a text like Hab 2:4, we might wonder about his omission of any pronoun (and about the relationship between the LXX version and the Hebrew), but the text is important to Paul because it establishes a basis for justification that applies to Gentiles as well as it does to Jews. Paul tends to choose texts that defend Gentiles and place Jews on an equal footing, that humble the arrogant (or those who think of themselves as wise [1 Cor 1:19]) and support the humble, or that express soteriology in terms that apply as easily to Gentile believers as Jewish believers (1 Cor 1:31).

When we think about issues of imperialism or colonization, it is interesting that Paul seems to use scriptural allusions or themes in ways that subtly subvert Roman ideology (e.g., Phil 2:9–11), while he is less subtle in representing Jewish-Christian impositions on Gentile believers as hostile military actions that could have imperialistic tendencies. He directs his comments about freedom versus bondage not only against the powers of sin and of the law but also against those who seek to impose the law upon his churches.[40]

The issue of resistant writing and translations raises questions about our tendency to assume that we can move easily from our perception of Paul's implied readers to conclusions about his actual readers. Some scholars have been too quick to assume that if Paul leaves some information unexplained or assumes certain knowledge about Scripture or Jewish background, his readers must have possessed that knowledge. Could Paul instead be demonstrating what TS would call an assertive or resistant strategy in which he positions his Gentile readers "within limits, thus decentering the power and privilege of readers from dominant cultures"[41] and leads them to recognize their need to educate themselves in order to fully understand the discourse of the Christian community? Could he be asserting cultural elements and concepts that might be foreign to them in the expectation that they would have to work and learn how to process his references in order to fully enter into the material?

When Paul quotes and argues from Scripture, to what extent does he domesticate his language, and to what extent does he foreignize it? Does he seek to enrich the vocabulary and linguistic repertoire of his readers, or

---

40. See, e.g., the discussion in Roy E. Ciampa, "Abraham and Empire in Galatians," in *Perspectives on Our Father Abraham: Essays in Honor of Marvin R. Wilson* (ed. Steven Hunt; Grand Rapids: Eerdmans, 2010), 153–68.

41. Tymoczko, *Enlarging Translation*, 230.

does he translate the terms and concepts so that they can be assimilated by people who are not familiar with the idioms and terminology found in the Jewish Scriptures? What might the answers to these questions tell us about his theology and the ways in which his use of Scripture might affect subtle issues of power in his churches?

Paul's (modified) quotation of Hab 2:4 is an interesting case in point. A search of Greek literature, inscriptions, and papyri[42] indicates that, despite the frequency of both the preposition and the noun, the expression ἐκ πίστεως does not show up in extant Greek until Hab 2:4 LXX and then in the New Testament, where it shows up twenty-one times in Romans and Galatians. It would not have been a familiar construction to Paul's readers, except that they may have known it from Hab 2:4. Paul does not hesitate to use the expression over and over again (at least in those two letters), more often than not keeping to that precise formulation. But he also rewords the phrase at times to provide clarification of how he thinks they should understand it, such as using διὰ πίστεως (Rom 3:22; Gal 2:16; Phil 3:9, etc.), ἐν πίστει (Gal. 2:20), or εἰς πάντας τοὺς πιστεύοντας (Rom 3:22, probably clarifying the meaning of εἰς πίστιν as another gloss on ἐκ πίστεώς in Rom 1:17).[43] Many other expressions that Paul frequently uses come from the Scriptures and would not have been familiar to Gentile readers who were unaware of its idioms. For example, a search of *Thesaurus linguae graecae* suggests that the expressions associated with being reckoned righteous (Rom 4:3, ἐλογίσθη αὐτῷ εἰς δικαιοσύνην; Rom 4:6, λογίζεται δικαιοσύνην, etc.) were only found in the LXX and the Letter of Aristeas before showing up repeatedly in Paul (Rom 2:26; 3:28; 4:3, 5–6, 9, 11, 22; Gal 3:6). Similarly, the expression "works of the law" has only recently been clearly identified as predating Paul, though still in a Jewish source (4QMMT). Yet he does not hesitate to use it repeatedly, and he apparently expects his Gentile readers to become familiar with it (see Rom 3:20, 28; Gal 2:16; 3:2, 5, 10).

In short, it seems that Paul wants to introduce new expressions and enrich the vocabulary of those not familiar with biblical idioms while also giving enough commentary that they can be assimilated and adopted by those who were previously outsiders to this language. He expects his

---

42. Using TLG, http://papyri.info/, and http://epigraphy.packhum.org/inscriptions (accessed 21 December 2011).

43. See Francis Watson, *Paul and the Hermeneutics of Faith* (London: T&T Clark, 2004), 54–71.

non-Jewish readers to learn to think of themselves as "Gentiles" (using the scriptural and Jewish lingo with its claims to ideological power) rather than as Romans or however they used to think of themselves, but also as "the circumcision," "sons of Abraham" and of God, and "brothers and sisters" with their Jewish co-religionists. Paul is teaching his Gentile readers to use Jewish and scriptural vocabulary, but he is simultaneously transforming that vocabulary by using it in ways that will be new and challenging to his Jewish brothers as well.

In a variety of ways Paul's use of Scripture seems to strike some sort of balance between privileging Jewish and scriptural ideas and frames of reference (and thus forcing his Gentile readers to master some of the lingo of this Jewish messianic faith) and emphasizing in other ways (such as his selection and exposition of texts and themes) the equal status of Gentile believers in Christ and the need to beware of the temptation that some Jewish Christians might have had to mimic the imperialistic approach of the Romans by imposing their own understanding of the Jewish law as colonizers within the colonizing empire. His translation of the Christian faith for the sake of his Gentile churches empowers Gentile believers even while it challenges and stretches them. In other places he empowers those perceived to be weak or foolish and humbles those seeming to be strong and wise.

Most of these aspects of Paul's use of Scripture reflect his theological understanding of his calling and mission—the commission that he received from God who appointed him as chief missionary to the Gentile world—while also advocating for a community in which Jews and Gentiles find their proper places side by side. As a result, his scriptural interpretation is sometimes resistant, sometimes assertive, and virtually always activist and concerned to undermine improper exertions of power at the expense of fellow believers.

In this essay I have neglected many of Paul's primary scriptural themes (including sin, cross/death, life/resurrection, etc.) and passed over many of the extremely diverse approaches and insights that are currently being developed within the field of translation studies. Hopefully, the few basic concepts and perspectives that I have introduced here are enough to give an idea of some of the ways in which TS might fruitfully inform future research into the use of Scripture by Paul and other ancient interpreters.

Bibliography

Beale, G. K., ed. *The Right Doctrine from the Wrong Text?* Grand Rapids: Baker, 1994.
Berman, Antoine. *The Experience of the Foreign: Culture and Translation in Romantic Germany.* Translated by S. Heyvaert. Albany: State University of New York Press, 1992.
Ciampa, Roy E. "Abraham and Empire in Galatians." Pages 153–68 in *Perspectives on Our Father Abraham: Essays in Honor of Marvin R. Wilson.* Edited by Steven Hunt. Grand Rapids: Eerdmans, 2010.
Even-Zohar, Itamar. *Papers in Historical Poetics.* Tel Aviv: Porter Institute for Poetics and Semiotics, 1978.
Gentzler, Edwin. *Contemporary Translation Theories.* Topics in Translation. Clevedon: Multilingual Matters, 2001.
Gentzler, Edwin, and Maria Tymoczko. Introduction to *Translation and Power.* Edited by Maria Tymoczko and Edwin Gentzler. Amherst: University of Massachusetts Press, 2002.
Gutt, Ernst-August. *Translation and Relevance: Cognition and Context.* Manchester: St. Jerome Press, 2000.
Hays, Richard B. *Echoes of Scripture in the Letters of Paul.* New Haven: Yale University Press, 1989.
Katan, David. *Translating Cultures: An Introduction for Translators, Interpreters, and Mediators.* Manchester: St. Jerome Press, 2004.
Lambert, José, and Hendrik van Gorp. "On Describing Translations." Pages 42–53 in *The Manipulation of Literature: Studies in Literary Translation.* Edited by Theo Hermans. London: Croom Helm, 1985.
Limon, David. "Translators As Cultural Mediators: Wish or Reality? A Question for Translation Studies." Pages 29–40 in *Why Translation Studies Matters.* Edited by Daniel Gile, Gyde Hansen, and Nike K. Pokorn. Benjamins Translation Library. Amsterdam: Benjamins, 2010.
Longenecker, Richard N. *Biblical Exegesis in the Apostolic Period.* Grand Rapids: Eerdmans, 1999.
Milton, John. "The Resistant Political Translations of Monteiro Lobato." Pages 190–210 in *Translation, Resistance, Activism.* Edited by Maria Tymoczko. Amherst: University of Massachusetts Press, 2010.
Mopoho, Raymond. "Interpreters and Translators as Political Mediators in Colonial Subsaharan Africa." UNESCO International Symposium on Translation and Cultural Mediation, 22–23 February 2009. Cited

21 December 2011. Online: http://www.unesco.org/fileadmin/MULTIMEDIA/HQ/CLT/languages/pdf/MOPOHO-NUOVO.pdf.

Munday, Jeremy. *Introducing Translation Studies: Theories and Applications*. 3rd ed. London: Routledge, 2012.

Nord, Christiane. "Scopos, Loyalty, and Translational Conventions." *Target* 3 (1991): 91–109.

———. *Translating as Purposeful Activity: Functionalist Approaches Explained*. Manchester: St. Jerome Press, 1997.

Pym, Anthony. *Exploring Translation Theories*. London: Routledge, 2010.

Sperber, Dan, and Deirdre Wilson. *Relevance: Communication and Cognition*. 2nd ed. Oxford: Blackwell, 1995.

Sperber, Dan, and Deirdre Wilson. "Relevance Theory." Pages 607–32 in *The Handbook of Pragmatics*. Edited by Laurence R. Horn and Gregory L. Ward. Malden, Mass.: Blackwell, 2004.

Sugirtharajah, R. S. *Postcolonial Criticism and Biblical Interpretation*. Oxford: Oxford University Press, 2002.

Tonkin, Humphrey, and Maria Esposito Frank, eds. *The Translator As Mediator of Cultures*. Amsterdam: Benjamins, 2010.

Toury, Gideon. *In Search of a Theory of Translation*. Tel Aviv: Porter Institute for Poetics and Semiotics, 1980.

Tymoczko, Maria. *Enlarging Translation, Empowering Translators*. Manchester: St. Jerome Press, 2007.

———, ed. *Translation, Resistance, Activism*. Amherst: University of Massachusetts Press, 2010.

Tymoczko, Maria, and Edwin Genzler, eds. *Translation and Power*. Amherst: University of Massachusetts Press, 2002.

Venuti, Laurence. *The Scandals of Translation: Towards an Ethics of Difference*. London: Routledge, 1998.

———, ed. *The Translation Studies Reader*. London: Routledge, 2000.

Vermeer, Hans J., and Katharina Reiß. *Grundlegung einer allgemeinen Translationstheorie*. Tübingen: Niemeyer, 1984.

Watson, Francis. *Paul and the Hermeneutics of Faith*. London: T&T Clark, 2004.

Part 5
Conclusions

What We Learned—And What We Didn't

Christopher D. Stanley

In the introduction to the first volume of essays from the "Paul and Scripture Seminar,"[1] I listed six broad questions that the seminar participants had decided should guide our discussions of the methodological problems associated with research in Paul's engagement with Scripture.

1. What do we mean by Paul's "use" of Scripture?
2. What kinds of data yield the best understanding of Paul's engagement with the text of Scripture?
3. How does one recognize references to Scripture in Paul's letters?
4. How do Paul's references to the Jewish Scriptures relate to their original context?
5. What can we presume about the biblical literacy of Paul's audiences?
6. What role does Scripture play in Paul's theology and rhetoric?

All of these questions were in fact addressed by the seminar during the course of its six-year term, along with many others that we had not anticipated. Along the way, the participants were able to reach a measure of consensus on some points while remaining divided over others. In this essay, I will highlight some of the key points of agreement and disagreement that resulted from the work of the seminar and identify some areas of further research that emerged from our conversations.

---

1. "Paul and Scripture: Charting the Course," in *As It Is Written: Studying Paul's Use of Scripture* (ed. Stanley E. Porter and Christopher D. Stanley; SBLSymS 50; Atlanta: Society of Biblical Literature, 2008), 3–12. Each of these questions is explained more fully on pp. 8–10 of the original essay.

The Six Questions

The simplest way to describe what the seminar did and did not accomplish is to review how the members engaged with each of the six guiding questions that were identified in the first session of the seminar.

1. What do we mean by Paul's "use" of Scripture? During the course of the seminar, it became clear that Paul's engagement with his ancestral Scriptures was more complex than many people who have worked in this area have supposed. Too often, investigations of Paul's "use" of Scripture have focused on explicating the way Paul read and interpreted the biblical text without regard to the historical, social, and rhetorical contexts in which he composed his letters. In these studies, Paul comes across like a modern scholar sitting alone at his desk trying to make sense of a difficult text rather than as a traveling missionary writing letters to ensure that congregations of Christ-followers understood and remained faithful to his "gospel" in the face of challenges from alternate viewpoints that were at times grounded in interpretations of the Jewish Scriptures

A careful study of Paul's letters reveals least three different ways in which he appears to have "used" the Scriptures of Judaism: (a) to explicate for himself the meaning and implications of the Christ-event and the rise of the Christian house-church movement; (b) to counter, correct, or agree with interpretations of Scripture that he or the people in his congregations might have heard from Jewish or Christian teachers other than Paul; and (c) to add persuasive force to his arguments by appealing to a source beyond himself that was respected by his audiences as a source of truth. Each of these "uses" of Scripture represents a valid area of research, and scholars should be careful not to exalt one above the others. In the end, they are complementary and not mutually exclusive, though there are certainly tensions both within and among the various approaches at certain points. A full-orbed understanding of what Paul was doing with the text of Scripture must include all of these perspectives, and possibly others as well.

2. What kinds of data yield the best understanding of Paul's engagement with the text of Scripture? Another broad point of agreement within the seminar concerns the importance of attending to the many and diverse ways in which Paul expresses his dependence on the Jewish Scriptures. Most obvious are the direct quotations, which have attracted the lion's share of scholarly attention over the years. But Paul's letters are also filled with explicit and implicit allusions and echoes of biblical texts, reappropriations of biblical stories, and a vast array of biblical ideas and language that reflect both his own deep roots in Judaism and his continuing studies as a Christ-follower. As a consequence, studies of Paul's engagement with Scripture cannot be limited to the explicit quotations but must take into account other modes of biblical presence as well. Investigation must also extend beyond the *Hauptbriefe* to include the other letters where the influence of Scripture is less visible

Individual researchers are of course free to restrict their studies to a particular aspect of Paul's interaction with the biblical text, but they must remain alert to the fact that they are only examining part of the evidence and thus avoid making unwarranted generalizations. This does not preclude scholars from arguing that one aspect of Paul's engagement with the biblical text might be more pertinent to a particular task than others; for example, one might argue that the quotations are a better guide to Paul's rhetorical use of Scripture than other modes, or that the echoes offer more insight into the deeper influence of Scripture on Paul's thinking. In fact, one of the chief points that the seminar failed to resolve was how much of Paul's biblical language he expected his audiences to recognize and how much was the unconscious product of his own deep roots in the Jewish Scriptures.[2]

3. *How does one recognize references to Scripture in Paul's letters?* Identifying direct quotations of Scripture in Paul's letters is not difficult, though interpreters sometimes disagree over whether it is proper to use the term "quotation" to refer to unmarked citations (those that lack an introductory formula). Many of Paul's allusions and appropriations of biblical narratives are also clearly marked, as when he refers to several episodes of the exodus story in 1 Cor 10. Scholars might argue over what sense Paul derived from the texts that he so marks, but there is no dispute over whether a reference was intended.

Problems arise, however, over some of the other types of biblical references in Paul's letters. In the case of unmarked allusions and echoes, the question is whether the link that a contemporary reader claims to see between a particular text in Paul's letters and a passage in the Jewish Scriptures reflects an implicit or unconscious reference on the part of Paul or simply the creative imagination of the modern interpreter. In general, the seminar participants appeared to accept the seven criteria for identifying echoes that Richard Hays laid out in *Echoes of Scripture in the Letters*

---

2. This point is discussed under question 5 below.

of Paul, though questions were raised about the validity or usefulness of some of the criteria.[3] In the end, however, all seemed to agree that the burden rested upon the interpreter to convince others that an unmarked allusion or echo was indeed present, and that scholars could legitimately disagree over the validity of such an argument. A similar point can be made about some of the unmarked references to biblical narratives that scholars claim to have identified in Paul's letters, such as the creation story in Rom 7 or Phil 2 or the Exodus traditions in Rom 8.

A different type of question that arose from time to time in the seminar concerned how to judge whether Paul was engaging directly with the text of Scripture or with Jewish interpretive traditions that he knew either from his own experience in the Jewish community or from other Christian interpreters, including those commonly labeled his "opponents." In the case of broad concepts like "covenant" or "law," which were clearly derived from the Jewish Scriptures but had gained independent currency within the Jewish community, there is generally little need to search for a specific text to which Paul might be referring, though evidence can always be cited to argue for a particular textual reference. In other cases an engagement with Jewish traditions seems reasonably assured, as when Paul identifies Jesus as the "spiritual rock" that followed the Israelites in the desert (1 Cor 10:4). In still other cases the evidence is unclear.[4] Judging from our discussions, the seminar participants seemed to be convinced of the importance of attending to the influence of Jewish interpretive traditions on Paul, including the possibility that in some cases he was interacting with those traditions rather than directly with the text of Scripture, but little progress was made on the methodological question of how one goes about identifying such cases, apart from the obvious task of looking for parallels in the extant Jewish literature of the time. More research is needed in this area.

4. *How do Paul's references to the Jewish Scriptures relate to their original context?* In view of the importance of this question to contemporary studies of Paul's use of Scripture, a full seminar session was devoted to

---

3. Richard B. Hays, *Echoes of Scripture in the Letters of Paul* (New Haven: Yale University Press, 1989); the criteria are described on pp. 29–33. For a critical review of Hays's criteria, see Stanley E. Porter, "Allusions and Echoes," in Porter and Stanley, *As It Is Written*, 36–39.

4. See the essays by Linda Belleville and Bruce Fisk in the present volume for discussions of possible engagements with Jewish interpretive traditions on the part of Paul.

its discussion,⁵ and the question also arose from time to time in debates over particular passages. Unfortunately, it would be hard to say that the seminar made much progress on this issue. Those who believe that Paul engages seriously with the literary and theological contexts of the passages to which he refers will probably continue to regard those who reject their readings as tone-deaf, while those who highlight the tensions and discrepancies between Paul's applications of texts and any natural meaning that they might have held in their original contexts will continue to believe that the proponents of "faithfulness to context" have overactive imaginations that produce readings so flexible that they can never be disproved. All would agree that Paul hews closer to the natural sense of the biblical text in some cases than in others; the question concerns the status of those places where discrepancies are apparent

The seminar did discuss the methodological question of whether it is anachronistic to use modern notions of "context" when analyzing the interpretive practices of ancient authors, but the issue was not resolved. The idea that some of Paul's more creative readings might reflect the use of a "testimony book" in which verses had been divorced from their original literary setting was broached but never seriously discussed. For now, the question of how far Paul follows or strays from the "original meaning" of the language of Scripture will remain open, and interpreters will continue to argue for competing notions of what Paul was doing in particular passages. At this point it is hard to imagine what kind of criteria might be developed to adjudicate such disputes.⁶

5. *What can we presume about the biblical literacy of Paul's audiences?* This question came up repeatedly in the seminar sessions and appeared to increase in significance as the years went on. At stake is the question of what Paul was attempting to do from a communicative and rhetorical standpoint when he inserted explicit and implicit references to the Jewish Scriptures

---

5. The session included a paper by Steve Moyise that centered on a critical analysis of the work of Francis Watson and Ross Wagner, followed by responses from Christopher Tuckett and Gregory Beale. Unfortunately, Moyise's paper had already been promised to another publisher, so he wrote another essay on the same question specifically for the present volume. The essay by Mitchell Kim and Moyise's response were written after the end of the seminar.

6. Whether the essays by Moyise and Kim in the present volume will prove helpful in this area remains to be seen, since they were not discussed by the seminar participants.

into his letters. On the one side are those who believe that (i) Paul expected his audiences to recognize the vast majority of his biblical references, including a significant percentage of his unmarked allusions and echoes; (ii) Paul believed that his audiences would supply the broader literary context of the texts to which he refers and engage thoughtfully (and favorably) with his interpretations; (iii) a significant number of individuals in Paul's churches possessed the literary competence (whether from prior experience in Jewish synagogues or instruction in the Christian community) to do what Paul expected and to explain the meaning of Paul's references to those who did not; and (iv) Paul's communicative purposes required that this last task be carried out—that his audiences should understand and approve his "Christian" readings of the Jewish Scriptures. At the heart of this model lies the presumption that Paul would not have made such extensive use of Scripture in his letters if he had known that his audiences were incapable of appreciating his interpretations of specific biblical texts.

Standing against this position are other scholars who believe that (i) Paul's audiences would have been largely illiterate and therefore incapable of either recognizing or engaging with the intricacies of Paul's interpretive practices; (ii) the few literate members of Paul's audiences would have found it difficult (though not impossible) to engage in reasoned reflection on Paul's interpretive moves due to the low availability of biblical texts, the lack of effective reading aids, and the opaqueness of much of Paul's biblical argumentation; (iii) anyone in Paul's churches who succeeded in retracing his arguments would have found many of his interpretations to be tendentious/or contrary to any natural reading of the biblical text, leading them to question rather than embrace his arguments; (iv) Paul supplies enough cues in his letters to indicate to his audiences how he meant for his identifiable biblical references to be understood; and (v) most of the unmarked biblical references in Paul's letters reflect his own deep immersion in the language and thought-world of the Jewish Scriptures and played little if any role in his communicative intentions. Behind this model lies the assumption that Paul was a reasonably competent rhetor who would have taken into account the literary capabilities of his audiences when dictating his letters and crafted them accordingly.

By the end of the seminar, there appeared to be broad agreement that the majority of people in Paul's audiences would have been illiterate and thus incapable of reading the text of Scripture for themselves, but deep differences remained over the implications of this piece of data. Eventually it became apparent that the two sides held different conceptions of what

Paul was trying to accomplish by including biblical references in his letters. Those who believed that Paul expected his audiences to follow and approve his interpretations of the biblical text tended to credit Paul with an active desire to shape his congregations through the content of his letters, including the expectation that they would continue to read and study his writings as a guide for Christian living under the direction of their more knowledgeable members. Those who argued that Paul framed his arguments so that the meaning of his biblical references could be understood with little or no resort to the original text tended to see Paul engaging in rhetorical fire-fights in which he appealed to the authority of Scripture to shore up his arguments and thus persuade his audiences to embrace or reject a particular course of action. The fact that his audiences might have continued to study his letters after they had (hopefully) achieved their rhetorical purpose played little or no role in Paul's communicative purposes under this model.

In the end, the seminar failed to resolve the differences between these competing views of Paul's reasons for including both marked and unmarked biblical references in his letters. At the same time, there seemed to be a growing move toward some kind of mediating position that would incorporate the best observations of both sides. This remains a task for future research.

6. *What role does Scripture play in Paul's theology and rhetoric?* The question of how vital a role Scripture played in Paul's theology and rhetoric arises from two competing lines of evidence that have been noted by many researchers in the field. On the one hand, Paul's letters are thoroughly steeped in biblical language and ideas, leading virtually everyone to conclude that the Jewish Scriptures played a formative role in Paul's thought. On the other hand, only four of his assured letters contain any explicit quotations from the text of Scripture, and there are many places where he carries on important arguments with no significant references to the sacred text.

Within the seminar, few questions were raised about the centrality of Scripture in Paul's thought. Debates did arise, however, over the role of Scripture in Paul's rhetoric, and to a lesser extent over the link between his biblical rhetoric and his theology. The main point of contention was whether the many unmarked biblical echoes and allusions in Paul's letters were intended to carry rhetorical weight, which would require that they be recognized by his audience, or whether they simply reflect Paul's own tendency to speak in biblical language even when the references might be invisible to his audiences. A related question that arose less often was whether Paul's explicit quotations are a reliable guide to the role and importance of Scripture in his theology or whether their rhetorical orientation renders them suspect for this purpose. To put it differently, does Paul cite biblical texts because they were central to his own thinking or because he was forced to do so by the nature of the issues that confronted him in his churches? Most of the seminar participants seemed to view Paul's quotations as helpful indicators of the place of Scripture in his theology, though there were dissenters who questioned the propriety of inferring underlying thought-patterns from rhetorical texts. By contrast, few questions were raised about the echoes and allusions, since it seems reasonably clear that they reflect Paul's ordinary patterns of thought and speech regardless of whether his audiences were able to recognize them

Extending the Discussion

During its six-year term, the seminar discussed many issues pertaining to "Paul's use of Scripture" that could not be subsumed under any of the six questions that were spelled out at the beginning of the program. Several of those points are worth noting due to their significance for ongoing research in the field

(a) One of the questions that came up repeatedly during conversations about the biblical literacy of Paul's audiences pertained to how the Jewish Scriptures were (or were not) used in the Pauline house-churches. On one side were those who believed that the people in Paul's churches had regular access to biblical scrolls and that the biblical text was read and taught regularly both when the community gathered for worship and in more individualized catechetical sessions. On the other side were scholars who highlighted the many practical difficulties associated with this model and questioned whether the reading and application of Scripture played any significant role in the life of Paul's churches. Evidence was laid out on both sides of this debate, but little effort was made to resolve it. Similar questions can be raised about the use of Paul's letters in his churches after they had served their immediate rhetorical purpose. What can we know or surmise about the use of written texts in Paul's churches, and in the early Christian community more generally? Were people actively taught to memorize biblical texts, or did this occur only as a byproduct of repeated exposure to the text of Scripture, or not at all? Are texts describing practices in later periods (e.g., the second century) relevant to the question, or do they reflect a fundamentally different social context from the early Pauline communities? A careful collation and evaluation of the pertinent evidence would be helpful for clarifying the debate in this area.

(b) Another question that came up from time to time concerned whether Paul's references to the Jewish Scriptures might have played a role in his broader program of resistance to Roman imperial propaganda. The question arose due to the observation that some of the "biblical" terms and ideas that Paul uses in his letters can also be found in Roman texts celebrating the character and accomplishments of the Emperor. This recognition opens up the possibility that Paul might have been engaged in a sort of double-edged intertextuality in which he presented not only Christ but also the Jewish Scriptures as an alternative channel of divine power and wisdom over against the claims of the Roman Empire. This in turn raises questions about the social and ideological functions of the Jewish Scriptures in the early Christian communities, including their possible political implications. The seminar did little more than broach these issues, but they are clearly worthy of further attention from scholars working in this area.

(c) A related question that came up briefly from time to time but never received any serious attention concerns Paul's intertextual relation to non-biblical Greek literature. A few scholars have recently begun to explore the influence of the works of Homer and other Greek authors on early Christian literature, but their work has been virtually ignored by scholars who study intertextuality in Paul's letters. The fact that Paul almost never quotes or refers explicitly to Greek authors only heightens the problem, since he appears to have been raised in a Greek cultural environment. Does Paul engage in the same kind of double-edged polemic with Greek literature that he seems to do with Roman imperial propaganda? Or did he have a more benign attitude toward Greek literature, or ignore it entirely? The question is important not only for its bearing on the question of Paul's education but also for recent efforts to read Paul in dialogue with the social and intellectual currents of his day. This is another area where more research could be helpful in advancing the discussion of Paul's use of Scripture.

(d) Finally, the seminar provided a venue for exploring the application of new methods and approaches to the study of Paul's engagement with the Jewish Scriptures. Deconstruction, postcolonial studies, feminist studies, and translation studies were all represented in papers that were presented to the seminar and included in the ensuing collections of essays. Insights from literary studies, the philosophy of language, and social identity theory also made their way into the discussion from time to time. Conversations took place about the theoretical and practical meanings of the term "intertextuality" as it applies to the study of Paul's interpretive practices, including the possible value of using texts from other times and cultures to shed light on Paul's engagement with the biblical text. These and other approaches will help to shape the future of research in this area as in other subfields of New Testament studies.

Conclusion

During the course of its six-year term, the Paul and Scripture Seminar of the Society of Biblical Literature represented the cutting edge of scholarship on the apostle Paul's interaction with his ancestral Scriptures. By grappling tenaciously with age-old methodological problems and opening the door to new methodological approaches, the seminar has helped to bring fresh air to a discussion that has at times grown stale due to the limited nature of the evidence upon which it is based. Time alone will tell whether the work of the seminar has a lasting impact on the nature and quality of research in this area. Those who were present for its conversations, however, have little doubt about its value.

Bibliography

Hays, Richard B. *Echoes of Scripture in the Letters of Paul*. New Haven: Yale University Press, 1989.

Porter, Stanley E. "Allusions and Echoes." Pages 29–40 in *As It Is Written: Studying Paul's Use of Scripture*. Edited by Stanley E. Porter and Christopher D. Stanley. SBLSymS 50. Atlanta: Society of Biblical Literature, 2008.

Stanley, Christopher D. "Paul and Scripture: Charting the Course." Pages 3–12 in *As It Is Written: Studying Paul's Use of Scripture*. Edited by Stanley E. Porter and Christopher D. Stanley. SBLSymS 50. Atlanta: Society of Biblical Literature, 2008.

Contributors

Matthew W. Bates is Assistant Professor of Theology at Quincy University, Quincy, Illinois. He is the author of a number of research articles as well as a book on St. Paul's approach to reading Scripture: *The Hermeneutics of the Apostolic Proclamation: The Center of Paul's Method of Scriptural Interpretation* (Baylor University Press, 2012).

Linda L. Belleville is Adjunct Professor of New Testament at Grand Rapids Theological Seminary, Grand Rapids, Michigan. She has authored six books, two monographs, and forty-five articles and essays. Her publications include *Reflections of Glory: Paul's Polemical Use of the Moses-Doxa Tradition in 2 Corinthians 3.1–18* (Sheffield Academic Press, 1991) and commentaries on 1 Corinthians, 2 Corinthians, and 1 Timothy.

Roy E. Ciampa is Professor of New Testament at Gordon-Conwell Theological Seminary, South Hamilton, Massachusetts. His publications include *The Presence and Function of Scripture in Galatians 1 and 2* (Mohr Siebeck, 1998) and *The First Letter to the Corinthians* in the Pillar New Testament Commentary series (Eerdmans, 2010), as well as numerous articles and essays.

Bruce N. Fisk is Professor of New Testament at Westmont College, Santa Barbara, California. He is the author of *Do You Not Remember? Scripture, Story, and Exegesis in the Rewritten Bible of Pseudo-Philo* (Sheffield Academic Press, 2001) and numerous articles on rewritten Bible. His latest book is *A Hitchhiker's Guide to Jesus: Reading the Gospels on the Ground* (Baker Academic, 2011).

Stephen E. Fowl is Professor of Theology at Loyola University Maryland, Baltimore, Maryland. He has written or edited ten books, including *Engaging Scripture: An Essay in Theological Interpretation* (Blackwell,

1998); *Theological Interpretation of Scripture* (Cascade, 2010); and a commentary on Ephesians in the New Testament Library series (Westminster John Knox, 2012).

Leonard Greenspoon holds the Klutznick Chair in Jewish Civilization at Creighton University, Omaha, Nebraska. He has written or edited numerous books and articles on translations of the Bible, especially Jewish translations from the oldest (the Septuagint) to the most current, as well as various topics in Jewish studies. He has also published and lectured extensively on religion (especially Judaism) and popular culture.

E. Elizabeth Johnson is J. Davison Philips Professor of New Testament at Columbia Theological Seminary, Decatur, Georgia. She is the author of *The Function of Apocalyptic and Wisdom Traditions in Romans 9–11* (Scholars Press, 1989) as well as dozens of articles on a variety of New Testament topics, including most recently the essays on Ephesians and Colossians for the revised and updated edition of the *Women's Bible Commentary* (Westminster John Knox, 2012).

Mitchell M. Kim is Lead Pastor at the Living Water Alliance Church in Warrenville, Illinois. He is the co-author of *Expanding Eden: The Mission of God from Creation to New Creation* (InterVarsity Press, forthcoming).

Steve Moyise is Professor of New Testament at the University of Chichester, United Kingdom. He has authored or edited a dozen books on early Christian interpretation of Scripture, including *The Old Testament in the New* (T&T Clark, 2001); *Evoking Scripture: Seeing the Old Testament in the New* (T&T Clark, 2008); and *Paul and Scripture* (SPCK/Baker, 2010). He also serves as chair of the "Seminar for the Study of the Old Testament in the New Testament" that is held annually at various sites in the United Kingdom.

Jeremy Punt is Professor of New Testament at Stellenbosch University, South Africa. He has published widely on various aspects of New Testament hermeneutics, past and present. His recent research has focused on critical theory in New Testament interpretation, including the relevance of postcolonial theory and queer theory to the letters of Paul.

Christopher D. Stanley is Professor of Theology at St. Bonaventure University, St. Bonaventure, New York. He has written or edited six books and numerous articles on New Testament themes, including *Paul and the Language of Scripture: Citation Technique in the Pauline Epistles and Contemporary Literature* (Cambridge University Press, 1992) and *Arguing with Scripture: The Rhetoric of Quotations in the Letters of Paul* (T&T Clark, 2004). He founded and chaired the Society of Biblical Literature's seminar on "Paul and Scripture."

Jerry L. Sumney is Professor of Biblical Studies at Lexington Theological Seminary in Lexington, Kentucky. He is the author of seven books and editor of three others on various aspects of New Testament studies. His publications include *Identifying Paul's Opponents: The Question of Method in 2 Corinthians* (Sheffield Academic Press, 1990); *Servants of Satan, False Brothers, and other Opponents of Paul* (Sheffield Academic Press, 1999); and commentaries on Philippians (Hendrickson, 2007) and Colossians (Westminster John Knox, 2008).

Index of Ancient Sources

Hebrew Bible/Old Testament

Genesis
Ref	Pages
1	220, 225
1:1	198
1:2	146
1:9	79
1:22	189
1:26	197, 211, 212
1:26–27	210, 212, 213
1:26–28	198
1:28	189, 197
1:28–31	198
4	79
4:1–16	81
9:1	189
9:7	189
12:7	71, 72
15	149
15:1	144
15:5	46
15:6	41, 42, 46, 80, 109
15:16	148, 152, 153
17	204, 205, 220
17:5	46
17:11	203
17:14	203
17:24	203
17:25	203
22	79
22:17	74
26:4	74
26:24	74
32	79
33	149
34	81
35:11	189
38:24	79
41:38	146
47:27	189, 190

Exodus
Ref	Pages
1	79
3:8	72
3:17	72
4:14	147
4:22–23	197, 199
6:1	282
6:6	282, 285
6:6–8	194, 195, 196
9:16	149
9:20	144
13:12–22	252
14:11–12	71
14:21–22	252
15:6	285
15:16	282
16:1–36	252
16:7–12	174
17:1–7	252
17:3	174
17:6	257, 258
19:18	246
20	221
20:10	237, 239
20:12	215
23:4–5	237
23:12	237, 238
24	79
31:3	192

Exodus (cont.)		4:34	282
32:6	249	5:5	248
32:10–11	147	5:14	239
32:11	282	5:16	215
		5:26	145
Leviticus		5:27	248
12:3	203	7	69, 220
18:5	99, 109	7:6	73
19:4	145	7:6–8	214
19:19	236	10	221
22:10	236	10:9	194
26:1	203	10:16	202
		11:28	145
Numbers		12:12	194
3:16	144	14:2	73
11–25	249	14:27	194
11:1	147	17:14	66
11:10	147	17:14–15	66
11:23	285	17:15	65
14	79	18:1	194
14:2–4	72	22:4	239
14:27–29	174	22:10	235, 236, 239
16	79	25:4	17, 97, 233, 234, 237, 239, 240
16:30	81	27:26	44, 99
16:32	81	30	221
16:34	81	30:6	202
16:41	174	30:10	145
17:5	174	32	69, 252
17:6	252	32:1–14	176
17:10	174	32:4	176, 252
18:20–21	194	32:5	177, 181
20:2–13	252	32:13	253
20:8–11	252	32:15	252, 253
20:11	257	32:16–17	88
21:16–17	252, 254, 256	32:18	252
22	79	32:21	88, 89
23:5	239	32:30	252
24:2	146	32:31	253
25	85, 86	32:37	253
25:11	86	33:2	246
25:13b	86		
		Joshua	
Deuteronomy		3:10	145
3:24	282	14:2–4	194
4:6	192	18:6–7	194

1 Samuel		1 Kingdoms (LXX)	
8–12	64	12:20–25	62
8:5	64		
8:5–6	62	1 Kings	
8:7–8	66	8:27	200
8:18	67	8:44	165, 218
8:19	62	17:24	217
8:20	64	18:4	85
9–11	63	18:13	85, 143
9:16	63, 68	18:40	85, 86
10:1	63	19:9–18	84
10:6	146	19:10	80, 85, 87, 143
10:10	146	19:10b-13	87
10:16	63	19:11–12	86
10:19	62	19:14	80, 86, 87, 143
10:24–25	63	19:15–17	82
11:15	63	19:15–18	86, 87
11:16	146	19:18	83, 84, 86
12:1	63		
12:3	63	2 Kings	
12:5	63	23:27	61
12:12	62, 66		
12:15	68	3 Kingdoms (LXX)	
12:17	66	19:10	78, 81–82, 86
12:17–20a	67	19:14	81, 82, 86
12:19	63	19:14ff.	18
12:20–25	62, 63, 68	19:18	78, 83
12:22	62, 63, 82		
12:25	68	4 Kingdoms (LXX)	
15:11	68	21:14	60
16:13	146		
17:26	145	1 Chronicles	
17:36	145	16:13	215
19:16	145	22:12	192
20:42	218	23:31	205
24:12	147		
		2 Chronicles	
2 Samuel		1:10–12	192
6:18	218	2:3	205
7:6	200	2:13	192
7:12–14	194, 196, 198	6:18	200
7:18	194, 196, 198	15:3	145
7:28	217	31:3	205
		35:19	61

Nehemiah
9:16	217
9:26	143
13:26	196

Esther
6:13	145
6:16	145

Job
13	181
13:16	171, 172, 173
13:17	172
13:18	172
18:21	145
23:11–12	207
24:13–14	148

Psalms
2	102
17:33 LXX	107
18:5 LXX	274, 280, 284
20:7	218
22:19	194
32:1–2	80
42:2	145
43:8	165
43:10 LXX	61
43:23 LXX	61
43:24 LXX	61
44:9	61
44:22	61
44:23	61
45:1	107
47:7 LXX	151
48:3–7	151
52:6	218
53:6 LXX	218
62:5	165
67:17 LXX	197, 200
67:36	107
68:16	197, 200
68:17 LXX	246
77:16 LXX	253
78:6	145
78:15–16	253
79:6 LXX	145
84:3	145
85:8	145
88:28 LXX	197, 199
89	200
89:27	197, 199
93:14 LXX	62, 68, 69
94:14	68
97:1 LXX	282
104:13	165
109 LXX	208
110	196, 208, 210, 221, 223, 225
110:1	200, 210, 211
113–18	244
113:13 LXX	108
114:8–9 LXX	243
115 LXX	244, 245
115:1 LXX	242, 243, 258
115:2 LXX	243
116:10	242
117:22 LXX	256
119:43	217
119:142	217
119:160	217
131:13–14 LXX	200
132:13–14	200
134:16 LXX	108
134:21 LXX	200
135:21	200

Proverbs
2:17	207
8:22	198
8:22–31	197
12:10	238
12:10–11	238
22:8	17

Isaiah
1:9	80
1:10	144
1:13–14	206
2:18	203
6:10	282

INDEX OF ANCIENT SOURCES

8	221	65:2	81
8:18	200	65:3	89
10:22	84		
10:22–23	80	Jeremiah	
11	220	1:2	144
11:2	192	2:37	61
11:9	192	3:16	189
11:10	192	4:4	202
13:6–8	151–52	4:30–31	152
28:11–12	117	6:24	152
28:16	98, 102	7:9–11	101
29:13	207	9:23–24	101
30:30	282	10:10	145
37:4	145	10:25	145
37:17	145	13:21	152
40–55	166	22:23	152
42:6	176, 177	23:3	189
45:3	218	23:36	145
43:20	215	30:5–6	152
45:20–25	170	31:31	46
45:21–25	170	48:40–41	152
45:22	145	49:24	152
45:23	165, 166, 168, 169, 170, 171	50:43	152
47:2	237		
49:6	176, 177	Ezekiel	
49:20	200	1:3	144
50:4–9	170	5:11	61
51:9	285	5:13	61
51–52	99	6:8	61
52:3–6	99	6:9	145
52:5	99, 101, 102, 103, 104	11:16	61
52:7	99–100, 105, 274, 276–78, 283–84	11:16b-17	61
		14:6	145
52:10	282	18:30	145
52:10–54:6	279, 280	33:11	145
52:13–53:5	280	36:16–27	101
53	102	36:22	101
53:1	274, 275, 276, 278–86	37:5	146
53:1–2	278	44:7	202, 203
53:1–12	281	44:9	202, 203
55:11	207	45:17	205
59:1	285		
59:7–8	149	Daniel	
59:17	149, 151, 152, 153	2:20	192
65:1–2	88	5:23	133

Daniel (cont.)
6:10	133
6:20	145
6:26	145
7	102
10–12	110
12:3	177
12:13	195

Hosea
1:10	67, 80, 123, 132, 133, 137, 138, 145
2:1 LXX	133
2:13 LXX	205
2:21–22	125, 131
2:23	67, 80, 116, 123, 124, 125, 127, 132, 137, 138
2:25 LXX	123–24
7:4	237
9:17	61
12:3	147
13:14	112

Joel
1:15	147
2:32	98, 112
3:5 LXX	98

Amos
5:18–20	147

Obadiah
15	147

Jonah
3:8	145

Micah
4:5	218
7:17	145

Nahum
1:2–8	110
1:15 LXX	105, 278
2:1	278

Habakkuk
1:2–3b	106
1:3b-4	106
1:4	106
1:5	110
1:12	106, 107
2:1–3	106
2:1–4	110
2:3	109
2:4	44, 98, 105, 106, 109, 110, 111, 112, 271, 272, 273, 314, 315
2:5–7	106
2:5–20	106, 107
2:18	107, 108
3:2	110
3:2–15	106
3:2–17	107
3:3–15	110
3:16–17	106
3:19	106, 107

Zephaniah
1:14–18	147

Malachi
2:6	217

New Testament

Matthew
1:1	45
2:12	78
2:18	117
2:22	78
6:30	234
7:16–20	190, 191
10:10	239
12:21	192
12:33	190, 191
15:8–9	207
16:6	236
21:41–44	76
22:12	237
22:34	237
24:8	151

INDEX OF ANCIENT SOURCES

24:43–44	148	12:42–43	283
26:64	209	15:2–16	191
		15:25	240
Mark		16:2	283
1:25	237	17:17	217
4:8	190	20:30–31	282
4:39	237		
7:6	240	Acts	
8:6–7	207	2:25–36	200
8:15	236	2:33–35	209, 210
11:17	240	4:11	256
12:36	209, 210	5:31	209
13:8	151	6:7	190
14:26	244	7:17	190
		7:53	247
Luke		7:55	209
1:51	282	7:56	209
2:29–32	176	8	169
2:26	78	8:21	195
3:8–9	191	10:22	78
3:34–38	45	12:24	190
4:4	240	13:17	282
4:35	237	13:47	177
6:43–44	190, 191	15:31	299
10:1	239	17:10–13	169
10:7	239	19:20	190
12:1	236	22:3	55
13:15	237	26:18	194, 195
20:41–44	209, 210		
21:20–24	76	Romans	
24:44–45	168	1:2	111
		1:13	251
John		1:16	106
1:16	200	1:16–17	106, 109
2:11	282	1:17	98, 105, 106, 109, 110, 271, 272, 315
3:2	282		
4:48	282	2–3	42
7:31	282	2:1–3:20	106, 107
7:38	241, 257, 258	2:9	106
7:42	241	2:11	111
8:17	240	2:17	102
9:22	283	2:17–23	104, 105, 106
12:34–36	283	2:17–29	101
12:37–41	281	2:24	99
12:42	283	2:26	315

Romans (cont.)

Reference	Page(s)
2:28–29	202
3:3–4	111
3:5	60
3:9–10	108
3:10	240
3:20	109
3:21–22	109
3:22	315
3:25–26	111
3:26	86
3:28	315
4	43, 44, 105
4:1	47
4:1–25	41, 47
4:2	47
4:3	42, 47, 80, 315
4:5–6	315
4:9	47, 315
4:11	315
4:12	47
4:13	47, 241
4:16	47
4:17	240
4:17–18	46
4:18–21	106
4:20	48
4:22	315
4:23	239, 240
4:23–24	42, 239
5:1–5	106
5:1–11	107
5:6–11	106
5:10	89
6:3	79
6:16	79
7	324
7:1	79
7:24	106
8	136, 324
8–11	61
8:18–27	106
8:18–39	107
8:28–39	106
8:29	200
8:33	214
8:34	209
8:36	61, 240
9–10	80
9–11	42, 60, 122, 124
9:3	87
9:4–6a	75
9:6	111, 122
9:7	47
9:11	84
9:14–18	149
9:17	241
9:22–24	123
9:24	124
9:24–26	67, 80
9:25–26	59, 123
9:25	123, 124
9:26	116, 125, 126, 132, 133, 136, 137
9:27	84
9:27–29	80, 84
9:32–33	256
9:33	98
10	59, 89
10:1	64
10:1–12	88
10:5–21	105
10:8	274
10:9	88, 274
10:11	98, 102, 241
10:13	98, 112
10:14–18	274, 280
10:15	59, 104, 275, 276, 280, 283
10:16	263, 274, 275, 276, 280, 281, 283–86
10:16–17	277
10:16–21	88
10:18	280
10:19	80, 88
10:20–21	59, 88
10:21	68, 80
11:1	47, 59, 63, 69, 86, 87
11:1–2	61, 62, 69
11:1–7	59
11:2	59, 68, 75, 87, 241
11:2ff.	17–18

11:2b–3	82	6:9	79
11:2b–5	78–84	6:9–10	241
11:2–6	60	6:10	239
11:3	80, 81	6:15	79, 194
11:4	80, 81, 82, 83, 84, 87	6:16	79
11:5	68, 80, 84, 86, 87	6:19	79
11:6	83	7:29	154
11:7	84	7:38	158
11:11	89	8:5	59
11:11–12	89	9:7	233
11:12	84	9:8	60
11:13	313	9:8–10	234
11:15	84, 89	9:9	17, 97, 159, 219, 233, 234, 237, 240, 258
11:19–21	75		
11:20	89	9:9–10	239, 240
11:23	84, 89	9:10	239, 240
11:24	89	9:12	235
11:25	251	9:13	79–40
11:25–26	124	9:24	79
11:25–32	84	10	323
11:28	69, 84, 89	10:1	250, 251
11:33–36	106	10:1–2	252
12:22	68	10:1–4	249
14–15	214	10:1–11	249, 251
14:11	165	10:1–13	195, 252
15:3	59	10:3–4	252
16:2	59	10:4	55, 57, 233, 249, 252, 253, 255, 256, 257, 258, 324
16:13	214		
16:25	107, 154	10:6	249, 251
16:25–27	106	10:6–8	249
		10:6–11	249
1 Corinthians		10:8–11	250
1:5–7	249	10:9	257
1:18	157	10:10	174, 175, 181, 249
1:19	314	10:11	42, 249, 251
1:21	158	10:14	251, 252
1:24	107	10:15	60, 253
1:31	101, 314	10:16	257
3:16	79	10:22	257
5:3	154	11:3	251
5:6	79, 236, 238	11:9	59
5:7	244	11:23–26	34, 39
5:8	244	11:25	46
6:2	79	12:1	251
6:3	79	12:2	107

1 Corinthians (cont.)

12:13	59
12:14	59
13:13	147
14:8	59
14:10	108
15:20–49	211–12
14:21	117, 240
14:26	244
15:23	154
15:52	155
15:55	112
16:8	244

2 Corinthians

1:8	251
1:13	299
2:10	59
3:1–18	256
3:3	202
3:7–11	251
3:13	251
3:16	256
3:17	256
3:9	235
3:10	59
4:6	219
4:8	243
4:9	243
4:13	219, 233, 241–42, 244, 258
4:14	243
4:15	243
5:2	59
5:4	59
5:16–21	211, 212
5:17	154
6:14	233, 236, 258
6:14–7:1	235
9:7	17
10:2	154
10:11	154
10:17	101
11:9	154
11:17	60
11:22	47
11:23	60
12:1–10	154
12:9	158
13:2	154
13:4	59
13:10	154

Galatians

1–2	43
1:12	135, 154
1:14	55
2:2	154
2:14	43, 176
2:16	176, 315
2:20	315
3	105
3–4	44, 49
3:1–4:11	42, 47
3:2	315
3:5	315
3:6	42, 47, 315
3:6–9	99
3:7	47
3:8	47
3:9	47
3:10	42, 315
3:10–12	99
3:10–14	44
3:11	98, 272
3:12	99
3:14	47
3:15	60
3:16	46, 47
3:18	47
3:19	245, 247, 248, 251, 258
3:19–20	99, 233
3:20	245–46, 248
3:24	251
3:26	133
3:26–28	212
3:29	45, 47
4:13	154
4:19	151
4:21–31	235
4:21–5:1	43, 45

INDEX OF ANCIENT SOURCES

4:22	47	3:20	195
4:30	241	4:1–3	174, 175
5:2	97		
5:9	236, 238	Colossians	
5:22	191	1:2	214
6:7	238	1:4	214
6:15	154, 211	1:5	216
		1:6	189, 190, 191, 219
Ephesians		1:6–7	220
1:13	217	1:9	191, 192, 220
3:4	299	1:10	189, 191, 219
4:8	200	1:12	193, 194, 195, 214
4:24	211	1:12–14	193, 196, 198, 219
5:19	244	1:13	193
6:2–3	215	1:13–14	193, 194, 195
6:6	218	1:15	198, 199, 201, 212, 220
6:13–17	150	1:15–16	199
		1:15–17	211
Philippians		1:15–20	193, 197, 201, 219, 221, 222, 223
1:6	175	1:15–23	34
1:6–10	175	1:16–17	197
1:11	191	1:18	199
1:18	171	1:19	200
1:19	171, 172, 173, 178, 179, 181	1:22	214
1:20	171	1:24–2:5	219
1:27–30	181	1:26	214
1:27–2:18	177	2:1	251
1:29–30	173	2:3	218, 219
2	324	2:9	200
2:1–11	170	2:9–12	204
2:5–11	170, 173	2:10	200–201
2:6	258	2:11	201, 202, 203, 204, 205, 219, 220
2:6–11	34, 166	2:11–12	201
2:9–11	166, 314	2:11–13	202
2:10–11	165, 168, 169, 170, 179, 181	2:13	201, 203, 204, 219, 220
2:11	165	2:13c–15	204
2:12–18	173, 174, 178, 179, 181	2:16	219, 220
2:13	175	2:22	207, 208, 219
2:14	174, 175, 181	3:1	208, 209, 219, 221
2:15	176, 177, 181	3:1–5	208
2:16	176, 177	3:5–11	213
2:19–30	173	3:9	212, 213
2:27	59	3:9–11	212
3:3	202	3:10	210, 211, 212
3:9	315		

Colossians (cont.)

Reference	Pages
3:10–11	214
3:11	212, 213, 219, 220
3:12	214, 215, 219, 220
3:16	244
3:17	217
3:20	215, 216, 220
3:22	218
4:15–16	191
4:16	299

1 Thessalonians

Reference	Pages
1:1	144
1:2–8	155
1:3	144, 147, 155
1:4	144, 145
1:5	144, 155, 156
1:6	144, 155, 156
1:6–10	34
1:7	156
1:8	144, 155, 156, 157
1:9	144, 145
1:9–10	155
1:10	144, 146, 155
2:1	156
2:2	144, 155, 156
2:3	155
2:4	144, 156
2:5	155, 156
2:7	144, 156, 158
2:7–12	157–58
2:8	144, 155, 156
2:9	144, 155, 156
2:10	144, 156
2:12	144, 146, 155
2:13	144, 145, 155, 156
2:13–16	147, 149
2:14	144, 156
2:14–16	143, 148, 149, 152, 157
2:15	144, 149
2:16	144, 148
2:17	157–58
2:19	144, 155
3:1–10	155
3:2	144, 155
3:3–4	157
3:3b–4	147
3:4	59, 157
3:5	156
3:6	155, 156
3:7	157
3:8	156
3:9	144
3:11	144
3:12	144, 155
3:12–13	155
3:13	144, 155
3:14	144
4:1	147, 155
4:2	144, 156
4:3	144
4:4	158
4:5	144, 145
4:6	144, 146, 159
4:8	144, 146, 155, 157
4:9	144, 147
4:10	59, 155
4:11	156
4:12	159
4:13–5:11	154
4:14	144
4:15	144, 155
4:16	144, 155
4:16–17	157, 159
4:17	144
4:18	155, 157
5:2	144, 146, 148
5:3	147, 148, 151, 152
5:8	147, 149, 152
5:9	144
5:11	156
5:14	157, 159
5:15	159
5:18	144
5:19	146
5:20	156
5:21	31
5:23	144, 146, 155
5:23–28	155
5:24	145

5:26	191	Revelation	
5:27	144, 159	3:21	209
5:28	144	12:2	151

EARLY CHRISTIAN LITERATURE

2 Thessalonians
3:10 — 59

1 Clement
16.3	281
16.1–14	281

1 Timothy
4:13	244
5:18	237, 241

Augustine, *De doctrina Christiana*
2.30–31 — 22

2 Timothy
2:15	169, 217
4:13	10

Cyprian, *Ad Quirinum testimonia adversus Judaeos*
2.4 — 282

Hebrews
1:3	209
1:13	209, 210
2:2	247
8:1	209
8:5	78
10:21	209
10:37	272
10:38	272, 273
11:7	78
11:8–19	45
12:2	209

Irenaeus, *Adversus haereses*
3.13.1	277
4.16.1	204

Irenaeus, *Epideixis tou apostolikou kērygmatos*
35	272
68	280
86	278, 280, 281

John Chrysostom, *Homily* 6 — 175

James
1:18	217
4:5	241
5:13	244

Justin, *Apologia i*
32.12	282
40.1–4	280
50.5	279

1 Peter
1:16	240
2:6	256
2:15	237
3:22	209

Justin, *Dialogus cum Tryphone*
8.4	206
11.3	282
13:2–9	279, 280
13.3	279
39.2	283

2 Peter
2:6	44
3:8	44
3:15–16	244

42.1	280
42.1–2	280
114.2	279
118.4	279
141.2	283

Origen, *Commentarii in Romanis*	
8.6.2	279
Origen, *De oratione*	
31.3	169
Pseudo-Gregory of Nyssa, *Testimonies against the Jews*	
1.8.3	282
Tertullian, *Adversus Judaeos*	
3	204
Tertullian, *Adversus Marcionem*	
4.13.3–4	280
Tertullian, *Adversus Praxean*	
13.3	282

Apocrypha and Pseudepigrapha

1 Enoch	
18:1	219
37:3–4	192
46:3	219
48:7	195
49:1–4	198
49:3–4	192
62:4	151
1 Maccabees	
2:24	85
2:26–27	85
2 Baruch	
3:1–9	76
82:1–9	76
85:1–9	76
2 Maccabees	
2:4	78
2:25	22
6:13b–14	149
6:14	148
15:24	282

3 Maccabees	
6:18	145
6:28	145
4 Ezra	
3:1–2	76
3:28–36	76
4:23–24	76
4:40–42	151
5:21–30	76
6:55–59	76
8:15–19	76
10:19–24	76
16:35–39	151
4 Maccabees	
5:24	145
17:4	147
Apocalypse of Abraham	
25:4–27:12	76
Bel	
1:5	145
1:6	145
1:24	145
1:25	145
Jubilees	
1:27–28	246
31:2	58
Judith	
14:10	203
Letter of Aristeas	
148–149	238
Liber antiquitatum biblicarum (Pseudo-Philo)	
1	79
1–2	79
2:1	58
4:5	71
9:3	58

7:4	71	56:2	67
8	79	56:3	67, 68
8:3	71		
8:7	81	Psalms of Solomon	
9:3	71	7:1–3	70
9:4	73, 74	7:5–10	70
9:5	79	9:8–11	71
10:2	71	17	196
10:7	254	17:35–43	192
11:1	71		
11:3	71	Pseudo-Phocylides	
11:5	71	15	236
11:15	79, 254	19	241
12:5	58		
12:9	75	Sibylline Oracles	
12:9–10	71	5.514	151
13:6	71		
13:10	73, 74	Sirach	
15:4	72	6:19	239
15:6	79	21:18	218
16.2	79	24:33	207
16:2–3	81	39:8	207
18:5	58	47:18	218
18:5–6	79	49:10	110
18:11	73		
19:2	73	Testament of Dan	
21:5	73	6:2	247, 248
22:7	71		
23:1–2	71	Testament of Levi	
23:11	71	6:1–11	149
23:13	73	6:11	148–49
28:2	71	18:5	192
28:5	71	18:7	192
30:4	71		
30:7	71	Wisdom	
32:8	71	1:6–7	218
32:12–14	71	5:5	195
35:2	73	5:17–20	150
35:3	73	7:26	197
39:6	74	11:1–5	256
39:7	75	11:4	253
49:3	73, 75	12:27	145
49:6	74		
56–57	64		
56:1	64, 66		

Dead Sea Scrolls		Other Jewish Literature	
1QapGen		b. Baba Batra	
21:5	58	9b	150
1QH		b. Šabbat	
1:18–19	218	35a	254
3:7–10	151		
6:7–8	88	b. Taʿanit	254
		9a	254
1QM			
2:4	206	Josephus, *Antiquitates judaicae*	
12:1	215	1.12.2–4	43
13:8–9	88	3.9.3	43
14:8–9	88	3.99–101	81
		4.228	236
1QpHab		5.42	78
11:13	202	6.38	66
		8.328–354	81
1QS		8.338	86
4:3	218	10.13	78
4:22	218	12.271	85–86
5:5	202	15.136	247
11:7–8	195		
11:10–12	195	Josephus, *Contra Apionem*	
		2.28	215
1Q21		2.31	215
3.18–23	204		
		m. Pesaḥim	255
1QS28b	192		
		Philo, *De confusione linguarum*	
4Q252		62	199
5.1–4	196	97	197
		147	197
4QpIsa^{a, c}	88		
		Philo, *De fuga et inventione*	
4QFlor		101	197
1.1–12	196		
		Philo, *De specialibus legibus*	
CD		1.260	235
1:4	88	4.205	236
2.3	218		
6:4	256	Philo, *De somniis*	
		1.239	197
		1.141–142	247

Philo, *De vita Mosis*
 210–211   254

Philo, *Legatio ad Gaium*
 1.43   197

Philo, *Legum allegoriae*
 2.86   256

Rabbah Numbers
 1.2   254

t. Sukkah
 3.11   254

Targum Onqelos
 Num 21:16–20   254

Greco-Roman Literature

Euripides, *Rhesus*
 161   241

Index of Modern Authors

Abasciano, Brian 183
Aageson, J. W. 84, 88, 89, 188, 226
Aichele, George 134, 139
Albl, Martin C. 282, 290
Allen, Graham 265, 267, 269, 286
Allison, Jr., D. C. 47, 50
Allison, June W. 187, 226
Amir, Y. 78, 90
Assmann, Jan 28, 29, 30, 31, 32, 35, 40, 43, 44–45, 46–49, 50
Attridge, Harold 70, 90, 286
Ayres, Lewis 169, 183
Baarda, Tjitze 149, 160
Bachmann, P. 253, 259
Bakhtin, M. M. 266–67, 286
Balla, Peter 17
Bandstra, Andrew 251, 259
Barclay, John M. G. 77, 90
Barnett, Albert E. 281, 286
Barrett, C. K. 250, 253, 259, 275, 286
Barth, K. 89
Barth, Markus 190, 200, 205, 211, 213, 215, 226
Barthes, Roland 267
Barton, Stephen C. 11, 23
Bassler, Jouette M. 158, 160
Bates, Matthew 5, 263, 276, 277, 279, 286
Bauckham, Richard 58, 90, 166, 170, 183
Beale, G. K. 23, 126, 128, 137–38, 270, 287, 296, 317
Beardsley, Monroe, D. 291
Beetham, Christopher A. 185, 189, 190, 192, 196, 198–99, 202, 204, 206–7, 226
Beker, J. C. 77, 90, 153, 160
Belleville, Linda 5, 247, 256, 259

Berkley, Timothy 101–3, 104, 105, 113
Berman, Antoine 312, 317
Betz, Hans Dieter 246, 259
Bieder, Werner 207, 226
Blanke, Helmut 190, 200, 205, 211, 213, 215
Blass, Friedrich 245
Bockmuehl, Marcus 165, 176, 177, 183
Bogaert, P.-M. 76, 90
Bonsirven, Joseph 55, 90
Boyarin, Daniel 264, 270, 273, 287
Braxton, Bradley R. 29, 50
Brett, Mark 166, 183
Brown, Jeannine 118, 121, 128
Brown, Raymond 283, 287
Bruce, F. F. 246, 259
Büchsel, Friedrich 259
Bultmann, Rudolf 263, 287
Burke, Peter 36, 37, 50
Burnette-Bletsch, Rhonda 76, 90
Byrne, Brendan 100, 113
Byrskog, S. 25, 31, 34, 38, 50
Calvert-Koyzis, Nancy 76, 90
Cameron, Averil 32, 41, 51
Camfield, Gregg 268, 287
Campbell, William S. 77, 90
Cannon, George E. 202, 204, 226
Capra, Andrea 185, 188, 226
Carlyle, A. J. 281, 287
Carruthers, Mary 10, 12, 19
Carson, D. A. 23, 270
Carusi, Annamaria 37, 51
Childs, Brevard S. 275, 287
Ciampa, Roy 5, 17, 144, 146, 160, 268, 269, 272, 287, 314, 317

Clements, Ronald E. 80, 90
Cohn, Leopold 71, 90
Collins, Raymond 234, 240–41, 250, 252, 259
Conzelmann, Hans 235, 240, 252, 260
Craigie, Peter C. 238, 260
Cranfield, C. E. B. 83, 84, 89, 90, 275, 287
Cullmann, Oscar 258, 260
Davies, W. D. 55, 91, 187, 226
Debrunner, Albert 245
Dehay, Terry 36, 51
Deichgräber, Reinhard 194, 226
DiMattie, Stephen 270, 287
Dinter, Paul 78, 80, 88, 91
Dodd, C. H. 122, 128
Duling, D. C. 29, 51
Dunn, James D. G. 60, 61, 83, 86, 88, 89, 91, 146, 160, 190, 197, 200, 202, 204, 207, 212–13, 214, 215, 226
Eisenbaum, Pamela 273, 287
Elliott, Neil 146, 160
Ellis, E. Earle 16, 23, 80, 91, 249, 260, 264, 287
Enns, Peter 247–48, 253, 255
Esler, P. F. 31, 51
Evans, Craig A. 57, 58, 80, 91, 163, 183, 244, 260, 272, 287
Even-Zohar, Itamar 296, 297, 317
Fee, Gordon D. 176, 177, 183, 197, 198, 214, 226, 250, 251, 253, 260, 284, 288
Fernández Marcos, Natalio 17
Fishbane, Michael 56, 58, 77, 83, 91, 265, 288
Fisk, Bruce N. 4, 19, 20, 23, 56, 57, 58, 60, 65, 71, 72, 76, 77, 79, 83, 91
Fitzmyer, Joseph A. 55, 92, 275, 288
Foer, Joshua 19, 23
Fowl, Stephen 4, 166, 183
France, R. T. 125, 128
Francis, F. O. 204, 209, 227
Frank, Maria Esposito 309
Friedman, S. 268, 288
Fung, Ronald 260
Funk, R. W. 154, 160

Gamble, Harry Y. 163, 168, 183
Gandhi, Leela 34, 35, 51
Garland, David 255, 260
Garner, Richard 185, 188, 192, 199, 202–3, 216, 227
Gaston, L. 89
Gaventa, Beverly Roberts 157, 160
Gentzler, Edwin 296, 308, 310, 317
Ginzburg, Louis 68, 92
Given, Mark 69, 92
Gnilka, Joachim 176, 183
Goodwin, Mark J. 133, 139
Gorp, Hendrik van 297–99
Greenspoon, Leonard 3, 21, 22, 23
Gregory, Andrew F. 281, 288
Guijarro, Santiago 28, 29, 30, 51
Gutt, Ernst-August 301–4, 317
Hagner, Donald A. 56, 57, 92, 149, 160, 273, 281, 288
Halbwachs, Maurice 28, 29, 51
Hansen, Walter 246, 260
Hanson, Anthony T. 78, 92, 279, 288
Harnack, Adolf von 263, 288
Harrington, Daniel 64, 92
Harris, Murray J. 211, 227
Harris, Willam V. 12, 23
Hay, David 189, 194, 195, 209, 210, 211, 215, 227
Hays, Richard B. 5, 42, 51, 56, 57, 58, 59, 60, 61, 62, 77, 78, 80, 88, 92, 99–100, 104, 105, 108, 110–11, 113, 124, 128, 132, 133, 136, 137, 163, 172, 183, 185, 187–88, 191, 227, 234, 237, 239, 250, 251, 257, 260, 263, 264, 265–70, 288, 296, 317, 323–4, 330
Headlam, A. C. 88
Heath, Stephen 265
Hendrix, Holland Lee 148, 161
Hengel, Martin 209, 227
Heszer, Catherine 13, 24
Hock, Ronald F. 224, 227
Hoffman-Aleith, Eva 288
Hogan, Robert E. 33
Hollander, John 265–66, 288
Holmberg, Bengt 25, 26, 51

INDEX OF MODERN AUTHORS

Horsley, Richard A. 36, 51
Hübner, Hans 128, 194, 195, 227, 269, 288
Hvalvik, Reidar 283, 289
Jacobson, Howard 58, 64, 65, 71, 73, 76, 92
Jaffee, Martin S. 12, 24
James, M. R. 64, 92
Jellicoe, Sidney 17, 24
Jervell, Jacob 212, 227
Jewett, Robert 275, 289
Johnson, E. Elizabeth 4, 60, 77, 92, 155, 158, 161
Käsemann, Ernst 83, 86, 92, 194, 227, 275, 289
Kaiser, Walter C., Jr. 187, 227
Katan, David 309, 317
Keesmaat, Sylvia 47, 51, 77, 92
Keightley, Georgia M. 35, 39, 51
Kelber, W. 32, 39, 52
Kim, Mitchell 4, 131–32, 134–38
Kleinknecht, Hermann 146
Koch, Dietrich-Alex 41, 52, 57, 93, 128, 234, 252, 260, 264, 271, 276–77, 278, 289
Kotre, John 117–18
Kraft, Robert A. 273, 289
Krentz, Edgar 143
Kristeva, Julia 5, 265–68
Kugel, James 55, 56, 65, 93
Lake, Kirsopp 289
Lambert, José 297–99, 317
Lamp, Jeffery S. 148–49, 161
Leppä, Outi 209, 227
Levison, Jon R. 146, 161
Lieu, Judith M. 25, 26, 27, 32, 33, 34, 37, 38, 39, 40, 41, 42, 43, 44, 45, 46, 47, 50, 52
Limon, David 309, 317
Lincoln, Andrew T. 203, 227
Lightfoot, J. B. 205, 211, 227, 289
Lindemann, Andreas 194, 195, 228, 289
Lisowsky, G. 238, 260
Lohse, Eduard 189, 195, 197–98, 200, 209, 211, 212, 228

Longenecker, Richard N. 234, 246, 256, 257, 260, 270, 289, 296
MacDonald, Margaret, Y. 210, 211, 212, 215, 228
Mackay, E. Anne 11, 24
Malherbe, Abraham 144, 145, 157, 161
Marchal, Joseph 37, 52
Marrou, Henri 10, 24
Marshall, I. Howard 241, 260
Martin, Troy 208, 228
Martyn, J. Louis 154, 161
Massaux, Éduoard 289
Mayser, Edwin 245, 260
McEwen, A. 253, 260
McNamara, Martin 255, 261
Mead, Richard 116–17
Meeks, Wayne 147, 161, 249, 250, 261
Mendels, Doron 32, 52
Metzger, Bruce 234, 239, 251, 257, 261
Meyer, Ben F. 268, 289
Michel, Otto 264, 290
Millar, Fergus 33, 52
Milton, John 311, 317
Mopoho, Raymond 309, 317
Moyise, Steve 4, 99, 108, 113, 115, 116, 117, 123, 124, 126, 127, 128, 132, 138, 139, 271, 290
Munday, Jeremy 293, 318
Murphy, Frederick J. 58, 71, 76, 93
Nickelsburg, George W. E. 76, 93
Nielsen, Charles 207, 209, 228
Noorman, Rolf 280–81, 289
Nora, Pierre 30, 35, 36, 52
Nord, Christiane 305, 306–7, 318
O'Brien, Peter 176, 183, 189, 208, 209, 214, 228
Oepke, Albrecht 154
Olick, J. K. 26, 28, 29, 31, 35, 52
Orr, W. F. 251, 261
Pao, David W. 128
Percy, Ernst 203, 228
Pokorný, Petr 198, 228
Polanyi, Michael 115, 116, 118–19, 121, 128

Porter, Stanley E.   1, 6, 11, 13–15, 24, 115, 121, 128, 145, 149, 161, 185, 228, 241, 261, 271, 290, 324, 330
Preisker, H.   241, 261
Prosch, Harry   119
Punt, Jeremy   3, 28, 41, 42, 43, 45, 48, 52
Pym, Anthony   293, 318
Reinmuth, Eckart   58, 71, 77, 93
Reiß, Katharina   305
Richard, Earl J.   151, 161
Ricoeur, Paul   26, 32, 35, 38, 40, 47, 52
Robinson, James, M.   197, 228
Rogers, Jeffrey S.   188–89, 228
Rosenfield, Israel   29, 52
Rothschild, Clare K.   290
Rosner, Brian S.   17
Runesson, Anders   25, 43, 53
Sanday, William   88, 93
Sanders, E. P.   11, 21, 24, 55, 69, 88, 93
Sanders, James A.   57, 163
Sayler, Gwendolyn B.   76, 93
Schelkle, K. H.   290
Schoeps, Hans J.   56, 93
Schubert, Paul   156, 161
Schweizer, Eduard   194, 205, 209, 211, 214, 228
Schweitzer, Albert   263, 290
Scott, James M.   143, 149, 161
Segal, Alan F.   40, 53
Seifrid, Mark   84, 93, 133, 139
Sharpe, Jim   35, 36, 37, 53
Shepherd, Michael   110, 111–12
Shostak, Debra   33, 48, 53
Singh, Amritjit   33, 53
Skarsaune, Oskar   273, 280, 290
Skerrett, Joseph, Jr.   33
Skinner, Quentin   166, 183
Small, Jocelyn Penny   11, 24
Smith, Abraham   148, 161
Sperber, Dan   301, 304, 318
Stanley, Christopher D.   1, 6, 15, 18, 20, 22, 24, 57, 78, 79, 93, 102, 103–4, 105, 113, 128, 145, 161, 163, 183, 187, 188, 224, 229, 234, 242, 243, 249–50, 261,
264, 270, 271, 272, 276, 277, 278, 290, 291, 300, 321, 330
Stintson, T. C. W.   185, 189, 229
Stone, Michael E.   76, 94
Stuckenbruck, Loren, T.   11
Sugirtharajah, R. S.   310, 318
Sumney, Jerrry   4, 191, 202, 216, 229
Swete, Henry Barclay   16, 18, 24
Telbe, Mikael   38, 53
Thiselton, Anthony C.   42, 53
Thrall, M. E.   17
Tonkin, Humphrey   309, 318
Toury, Gideon   296, 318
Tymoczko, Maria   308, 310, 312–13, 314, 318
Vanhoozer, Kevin J.   121, 128
Vawter, Bruce   204, 229
Venuti, Lawrence   293, 311–12, 318
Vermeer, Hans J.   305, 318
Wagner, J. Ross   13, 15, 20, 21, 22, 24, 57, 59, 60, 61, 62, 63, 67, 69, 79, 80, 81, 83, 87, 94, 101, 103, 113, 122, 124, 128, 133, 136, 163, 168, 183, 264, 275, 277, 282, 285–86, 291
Walther, J. A.   251
Watson, Francis   56, 60, 78, 94, 108–9, 110, 114, 128, 187, 229, 234, 240–41, 245, 247, 249, 261, 264, 270, 291, 295, 300, 315, 318
Watts, James W.   88, 94
Watts, Rikki E.   106–7, 110, 114, 122, 128
Wedderburn, A. J. M.   77, 94
Weiss, Herold   204, 229
Weiss, Johannes   240, 261
Wevers, John W.   246, 261
White, John   243, 261
Wierzbicka, Anna   243, 261
Wilckens, Ulrich   275, 291
Wilk, Florian   264, 291
Willis, W. L.   253, 255, 261
Wilson, Deirdre   301, 304
Wimsatt, W. K.   291
Wold, Benjamin G.   11
Woolf, C.   253, 261

Wright, N. T. 58, 77, 94, 128, 198, 229,
  245, 261, 273, 291
Xu, Ben 38, 49, 53
Young, Robert J. C. 34, 53